COMPUTER
DICTIONARY

COMPUTER DICTIONARY

FOURTH EDITION

Donald D. Spencer, Ph.D.

CAMELOT PUBLISHING COMPANY
Ormond Beach, Florida

Published by
Camelot Publishing Company
P.O. Box 1357
Ormond Beach, FL 32175

This book was laser typeset in Helvetica.
Printed on acid free paper.

TRADEMARKS

Trademarked names appear throughout this dictionary. Rather than list
the names and entities that own the trademarks or insert a trademark
symbol with each mention of the trademarked name, the publisher states
that it is using the names only for editorial purposes and to the benefit of
the trademark owner with no intention of infringing upon that trademark.

ISBN 0-89218-239-3

Library of Congress Cataloging-in-Publication Data

Spencer, Donald D.
   Computer dictionary / Donald D. Spencer. -- 4th ed.
     p.   cm.
   ISBN 0-89218-239-3 : $24.95
   1. Computers--Dictionaries. 2. Electronic data processing-
-Dictionaries.   I. Title.
QA76.15.S64 1993   92-34432
004'.03--dc20   CIP

CONTENTS

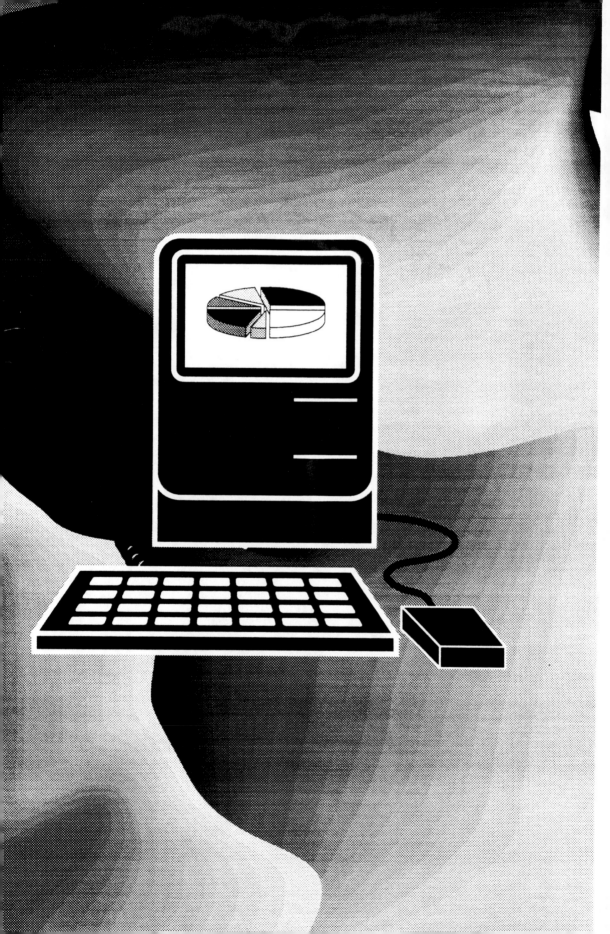

PREFACE

Computers are revolutionizing every aspect of our lives. The offices where we work, the stores in which we shop, the schools we attend, the banks that handle our money, even the devices we use in our homes are being radically altered by computers. Computer usage is growing by leaps and bounds in business, industry, government, colleges, schools, and utilities. The student, the businessman, the homeowner, the executive, the teacher, the artist, the doctor, all interact with the ubiquitous computer in one way or another. Consequently, almost everyone has been subjected to new ideas, new concepts, and a new dynamic language, with its own syntax and semantics. In the computer field, old words have taken on new connotations, and new terms have evolved; acronyms, abbreviations, and contractions abound. To understand and utilize the computer and to successfully cope with this new technology, a comprehensive, current, and easy-to-use dictionary of computer technology is essential.

The primary objective of the *Computer Dictionary* is to present concisely the most common terms currently used by computer scientists, information processing personnel, and other computer users. The book is for anyone who is using or who wants to learn more about computers. The Fourth Edition has been thoroughly updated and revised to reflect the dynamic changes and new developments in this rapidly growing field.

Familiarity with the vocabulary of any academic course, business, organization, or profession is absolutely essential to success. Lack of knowledge causes anger, failure, frustration, and loss of time and effort. This book will help students and other computer users overcome many of the problems associated with learning the terminology of an unfamiliar field. It may be used as a personal reference book or as a supplementary text. Managers, professionals, teachers, technical people, and others will find it a helpful resource.

The keynote of this book is clarity, with no sacrifice of authority or definitional precision. The definitions are simple and they stand as independent units of explanation. Most of the terms are explained in nontechnical language. In those few cases that require special terminology, the expressions are carefully defined, and cross-references indicate terms or concepts.

At the end of the book you will find a section that includes pictures of famous computer pioneers.

I would like to thank the many educators, scientists, engineers, researchers, and authors who have identified new terms and written about new computer devices and techniques. Only through these people's works can I keep up-to-date with the ever-growing vocabulary of computer terminology. I am particularly grateful to my wife, Rae, for typesetting the book.

I hope this dictionary becomes a handy reference work and succeeds in helping readers learn about computers or solving their problems.

Donald D. Spencer
Ormond Beach, Florida

HOW TO USE THIS DICTIONARY

The terms in this dictionary appear in alphabetical order of the complete term (spaces and hyphens don't count); for example, **computerization** comes between **computer graphics** and **computer literacy**. This order contrasts with some dictionaries in which the alphabetical order is based on a heavier weighing of the first word in a term; for example, all terms commencing with "computer" precede all terms commencing with "computerization." Most terms appear in alphabetical order rather than under a general heading. For example, the terms **floppy disk** and **hard disk** appear under **F** and **H**, although they are mentioned and cross-referenced under the general description of **magnetic disk**.

The terms normally appear in boldface lower case characters. Proper names and nouns are headed by an upper case letter, for example, **Pascal, Blaise**. Acronyms are presented in boldface caps and the proper letters are amplified in the text; for example, **BASIC** stands for Beginners All-purpose Symbolic Instruction Code. Cross-references that are important to an understanding of a term are included.

If you cannot find a word, it might be listed in a slightly different form. For example, you might try looking for "graphics output unit" and find the description under "graphic output device." I have included only one definition to keep from cluttering the book with the obvious.

The area from which the head word is derived, is usually indicated in the definition, for example: In desktop publishing, In computer graphics, In object-oriented programming, In artificial intelligence... If more than one definition is related to a head word, then the entry is itemized to reflect this and the relevant field indicated in each sub-entry.

A significant feature of this dicitonary is the inclusion of brief descriptions of important calculating machines and snapshot views of many important computer pioneers. Seventy-four important computer people are also illustrated in a section on pages 437-458.

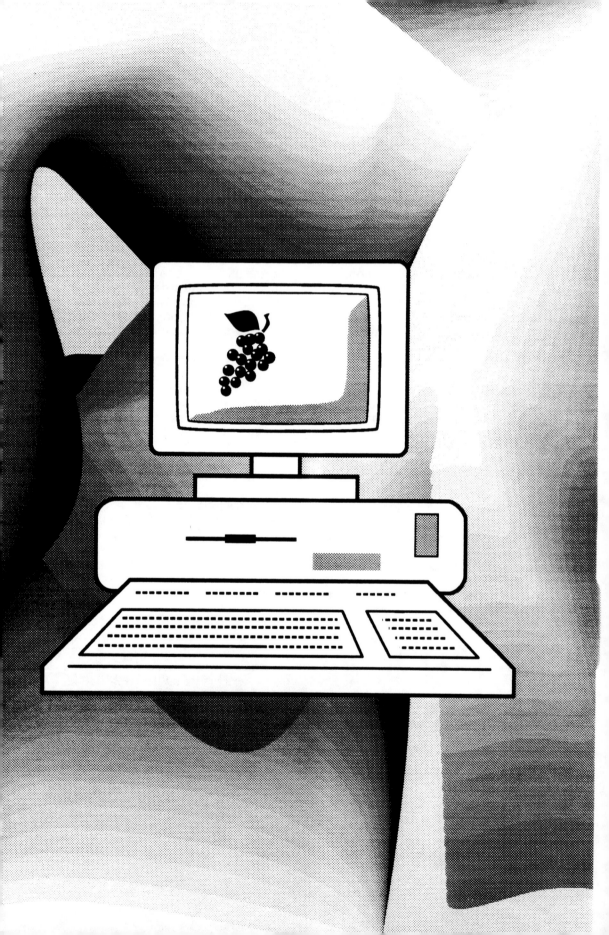

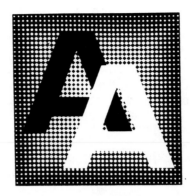

A:drive A designation for the first floppy disk drive in IBM-compatible microcomputers; B:drive is the second floppy disk drive; C:drive is the hard disk drive.

AAAI Acronym for American Association for Artificial Intelligence, professional organization concerned with advancing artificial intelligence.

abacus Ancient device for doing simple calculations that uses movable beads threaded on a grid of wires. First used in ancient Mediterranean cultures and ancient China. Still used in several oriental countries.

ABC computer An early digital computer, completed in 1942 by Iowa State Professor, John Atanasoff, and his assistant, Clifford Berry.

abend Acronym for ABnormal ENDing. Early termination of a program due to an error condition (erroneous software logic or hardware failure).

abnormal termination Stopping of a program before it has finished running because of some problem.

abort Procedure for terminating a program when a mistake, malfunction, or error occurs.

abscissa X axis of a graph or chart. Contrast with ordinate.

absolute address Address that is permanently assigned by the machine designer to a particular storage location. Addresses 0000, 0001, 0002, and 0003 might be assigned to the first four locations in a computer's storage. Also called machine address.

absolute coding Coding that uses machine instructions and absolute addresses. Can be directly executed by a computer without prior translation to a different form. Contrast with symbolic coding.

absolute value Magnitude of a number, regardless of its algebraic sign, equal to the positive value of a number. The absolute value of -82, for example, is 82.

absolute vector In computer graphics, a vector with end points designated in absolute coordinates.

abstract class In object-oriented programming, a class that has no instances.

abstraction In object oriented programming, the process of creating a superclass by extracting common qualities or general characteristics from more specific classes or objects.

accelerator A device to speed up either the computer or monitor. Typically a circuit card with an extra processing chip and/or additional RAM.

acceptance test Test used to demonstrate the capabilities and workability of a new computer system. Usually conducted by the manufacturer to show the customer that the system is in working order.

access Generally, the obtaining of data. To locate desired data.

access arm Mechanical device in a disk file storage unit that positions reading and writing mechanisms.

access code Group of characters or numbers that identifies a user to the computer system.

access control The process whereby use of a computer is constrained to individual authorized users.

access light The light on the front of your system unit, that tells you when the computer is reading from or writing to a disk.

access mechanism Mechanical device in the disk storage unit that positions the read/write heads on the proper tracks.

access method Any of the data management techniques available to users for transferring data between storage and an input/output device.

access monitoring A method of giving a system user only a certain number of attempts to give the correct password.

accessory card An additional circuit card that can be mounted inside a personal computer and connected to the system bus.

access time Time a computer takes to locate and transfer data to or from storage. Composed of seek time and transfer rate.

account number A unique number assigned to an individual or to a group that is used to gain access to the system. After entering the account number the operator enters a password which is checked by the operating system software.

accumulator Register or storage location that temporarily holds the result of an arithmetic or logic operation. Commonly used when a series of calculations are to be totaled.

accuracy Degree of exactness of an approximation or measurement. Accuracy normally denotes absolute quality of computed results; precision usually refers to the amount of detail used in representing those results. Four-place results are less precise than six-place results; yet a four-place table could be more accurate than an erroneously computed six-place table.

ACK Acronym for ACKnowledge, an international transmission control code that is returned by a receiving terminal to a transmitting terminal to acknowledge that a frame of information has been correctly received.

ACM See Association for Computing Machinery.

acoustical sound enclosure Device that fits over a printer or other machine to reduce noise. Most noticeable when absent.

acoustic coupler A type of modem. It translates computer signals into telephone tones and the reverse. This allows computers to communicate with each other by the telephone network. An acoustic coupler looks like a plastic box in which a telephone handset is placed.

acronym A word formed from the first letter (or letters) of each word in a phrase or name (e.g., VDT stands for Visual Display Terminal and IC stands for Integrated Circuit).

action Activity resulting from a given condition.

action entry One of the four sections of a decision table. Specifies what actions should be taken.

action-oriented management report Exception report used to alert management to abnormal situations that require special attention.

action statement Statement that tells the computer to perform some action.

action stub One of four sections of a decision table. Describes possible actions applicable to the problem to be solved.

active cell In an electronic spreadsheet, the cell on the matrix that is highlighted by the cursor. Information may be entered, altered, or deleted by the user when the cell is active. Also called the current cell.

active file File currently being used.

active object In object oriented programming, an object that monitors events occurring in an application and takes action autonomously. An object that encompasses its own thread of control.

active window   In a window environment, the window in which the user is currently working.

activity   One of the subunits of work that comprise a task.

activity ratio   When a file is processed, ratio of the number of records in the file that have activity to the total number of records in that file. Sometimes confused with volatility.

actor   In object-oriented programming, an object that can operate upon other objects but is never operated upon by other objects.

ACTOR   An object-oriented programming language with a Pascal-like syntax.

actuator   In a disk drive, mechanism that moves the read/write head to the desired position over the disk surface.

ACU   See Association of Computer Users.

Ada   An extremely powerful high-level structured programming language designed by the United States Department of Defense to ensure transportability of programs. Ada was derived from the Pascal language but has major semantic and syntactical extensions. Ada was named after the first programmer Augusta Ada Byron, Countess of Lovelace (1815-1852). It was she who suggested to Charles Babbage (1792-1871), an English mathematician who invented the machine which was the forerunner of the modern computer, several programming principles that remain valid to this day.

adapter   (1) Device that allows compatibility between different equipment. (2) Device that changes alternating current to direct current.

adapter boards   Printed circuit boards that connect a system board to peripheral I/O devices or add specialized functions to the system.

adaptive systems   System displaying the ability to learn, change its state, or otherwise react to a stimulus. Any system capable of adapting itself to changes in its environment.

adder   Device capable of forming the sum of two or more quantities.

add-in   Component that can be placed on a printed circuit board already installed in a computer, such as memory chips inserted in empty slots in a microcomputer.

add-on   Component or device added to a computer system to increase its storage capacity, to modify its architecture, or to upgrade its performance.

address   Identification—such as a label, number, or name—that designates a particular location in storage or any other data destination or source.

address bus   Bus that conveys address data from one system component to another.

addressing   (1) Locating a required piece of data by specific techniques (2) Data communications control method whereby the host computer specifies the particular terminal for which it has data.

address register   Register containing the address of the instruction currently being executed.

add time   Time required for a computer to perform an addition, exclusive of the time required to obtain the quantities from storage and put the sum back into storage.

administrative data processing   Field of data processing concerned with the management or direction of an organization.

Adobe Illustrator   See Illustrator.

Adobe Photoshop   See Photoshop.

Adobe Type Manager   A font generator and utility for the Apple Macintosh computer from Adobe Systems Inc.

advanced BASIC   A generic term used to describe versions of the BASIC programming language that include features and operators not found in standard BASIC.

AFIPS   Acronym for American Federation of Information Processing Societies. An organization having as members leading U.S.-based technical societies in the field of information technology.

aftermarket   The market for peripherals and software created by the sale of a large number of a specific brand of computer.

agent   In object-oriented programming, an object that can both operate upon other objects and be operated upon by other objects. An agent is usually created to do some work on behalf of an actor or another agent.

aggregate class   In object-oriented programming, a class that is constructed primarily by inheriting from other classes and rarely adds its own structure and behavior.

AI   An acronym for artificial intelligence, the study of how to make computer systems behave more as if they were bright and helpful humans.

Aiken, Howard Hathaway (1900-1973)   Headed the team of people who designed and built an early electromechanical computer, the Automatic Sequence Controlled Calculator, at Harvard University, between 1937 and 1944.

aiming symbol   A movable screen cursor on a display screen.

aircraft simulator A computer controlled device that is used to train pilots. All of the instruments of a modern jet cockpit are there to make the simulation as close to reality as possible. The simulator includes a large screen, like a windshield, on which a mind boggling array of graphics are generated. These sophisticated simulators are so realistic that the Federal Aviation Administration equates them to flying an actual aircraft.

Aldus PageMaker See PageMaker.

alert box A screen display, usually in a small window, which asks a question or warns the user of an impending doom if his or her next move is the wrong move. The user answers by clicking a mouse button on a choice or giving a key command.

alert messages Messages that inform you that the operation you are performing is improper or impossible.

algebra Form of mathematics in which letters representing numerical values can be operated upon according to basic rules of arithmetic.

algebra of logic System of logical relations expressed as algebraic formulas; first introduced by George Boole.

ALGOL Acronym for ALGOrithmic Language, an international high-level programming language used to code problem-solving algorithms. ALGOL was the first structured procedural programming language; developed 1957-1960 during conferences attended by computer scientists from the U.S. and several European countries. Although it never gained widespread use commercially, ALGOL had an important influence on several other languages: Pascal, C, and Ada.

algorithm Prescribed set of well-defined, unambiguous rules or processes for the solution of a problem in a finite number of steps. Commonly used as integral parts of computer programs. Thus the study of computers and the study of algorithms are closely related subjects.

algorithmic Based on algorithms.

aliasing Undesirable visual effects in computer-generated images caused by improper sampling techniques. Most common effect is a jagged edge along object boundaries.

aligning edge That edge of a form that, in conjunction with the leading edge, serves to position correctly a document to be scanned by an OCR device. Also called reference edge.

alignment Adjustment of tolerances within the mechanism of a device so it will operate properly.

Allen, Paul G Cofounder of Microsoft Corporation (with William Gates) in 1975. He and Gates wrote the first BASIC interpreter for the Intel 8080 microprocessor which was used in the Altair 8800 microcomputer. Versions of Microsoft BASIC were licensed to the IBM Corporation, Apple Computer, Tandy Corporation, and many other hardware vendors. Microsoft Corporation continued to develop a wide variety of software products. Allen left Microsoft and founded his own software company called Asymetyrix Corporation.

allocation   Process of reserving computer storage areas for instructions or data. Sometimes done by a programmer, or sometimes automatically by a program.

all points addressable   A graphics mode in which each pixel on the display screen can be accessed directly by a program.

alphabetic string   String in which the characters are letters or pertain to an agreed alphabet set.

alphanumeric   General term for alphabetic letters A-Z, numerical digits 0-9, and special characters—such as -, /, *, $, (,), +, and — that are machine processable.

alphanumeric sort   Process in which a computer system puts a list into alphabetical or numerical order or both.

alpha test   The product test stage during the research and development of a new product during which the first manufactured version of a system is tested with application software. The preliminary testing stage of software development.

Altair 8800   The first commercially successful personal computer. It was introduced in 1974 by Micro Instrumentation Telemetry Systems (MITS) of New Mexico. It was based on the Intel 8080 microprocessor, had 256 bytes of RAM, received input through a bank of panel switches, and displayed output via a row of light emitting diodes. In 1975 it was packaged with Microsoft Corporation's MBASIC interpreter written by William Gates and Paul Allen.

alternate track   A space track on a hard disk that is used if a regular track is determined to be damaged or unusable.

Alto   A personal computer designed by the Xerox Corporation in 1973. This computer pioneered the icon operating system environment and the use of a mouse. The Alto was the progenitor of the Xerox Star and the Apple Macintosh.

ALU   Acronym for Arithmetic-Logic Unit, the portion of the central processing unit where arithmetic and logical operations are performed.

ambient conditions   Environmental conditions that surround a computer system, such as light, temperature, and humidity.

ambient temperature   Temperature surrounding a piece of equipment.

Amdahl, Gene   Designer of several early IBM computers. Created an architectural revolution in designing the IBM System/360 computer series in 1964, the first computer to use integrated circuits. An early promoter of the concept of hardware compatibility, he later designed several computers for the Amdahl Corporation. In 1979, he formed Trilogy and now he heads up Andor Corporation, a manufacturer of smaller IBM compatible mainframes.

Amdahl Corporation   A computer manufacturer founded in 1970 by Gene Amdahl. Its purpose was to build IBM compatible mainframes with better performance; first mainframe was the 470/V6 computer released in 1975.

American Federation of Information Processing Societies (AFIPS) Organization representing computer science and data processing organizations. It was founded in 1961 and activities include committee work on education, research, government activities, standards and practices, and the history of computing. American representative of the International Federation for Information Processing (IFIP).

American National Standards Institute (ANSI)   Organization that acts as a national clearinghouse and coordinator for voluntary standards in the United States. It was founded in 1918 and is supported by more than a thousand professional societies, trade organizations and companies.

American Society for Information Science (ASIS)   Professional organization that provides a forum for librarians, information specialists, and scientists who seek to improve the communication of information. Members are highly educated, involved administrators, managers, coordinators, information technologists, and scientists who work in systems analysis and design; manage information programs and services; search, prepare, and analyze information; market information programs, services, and databases; consult; and program.

American Standard Code for Information Interchange   See ASCII.

ampere   Base SI unit of electric current. A current of 1 ampere means that 6.25×10^{18} electrons are flowing by a point each second; 1 ampere equals 1 coulomb per second.

Amiga   Brand name for a family of microcomputers manufactured by Commodore Business Machines, Inc. The Amiga computers have been used extensively in the areas of computer graphics and animation. The Amiga personal computers are based on the Motorola 68000 family of microprocessors.

amplifier   Electronic circuit that increases the voltage, current, or power of an input signal, or that isolates one part of a system from another.

amplitude   The height of the carrier wave in analog transmission; it indicates the strength of the signal.

analog computer   Computer that measures continuously changing conditions, such as temperature and pressure and converts them into quantities.

analog data Physical representation of information such that the representation bears an exact relationship to the original information. Electrical signals on a telephone channel are analog data representations of the original voice data.

analog model Model that relates physical similarity to the actual situation.

analog representation Representation that does not have discrete values but is continuously variable.

analog signal Signal that varies continuously in wave form, such as the human voice.

analog-to-digital converter (A-D converter) Mechanical or electrical device used to convert continuous analog signals to discrete digital numbers.

analog transmission Transmission of data as continuous wave patterns.

analyst Person skilled in the definition and development of techniques for solving a problem, especially those techniques for solutions on a computer.

analytical engine A mechanical calculating machine invented in 1833 by Charles Babbage, a British mathematician, to solve mathematical problems. A forerunner of the modern digital computer.

analytical graphics Traditional line graphs, pie charts, and bar charts used to illustrate and analyze data. A type of presentation graphics built into a spreadsheet, database, or word processing program.

AND Logical connector, as in the statement A AND B, which means that the statement is true if, and only if, both A and B are true simultaneously. Also called logical multiply.

AND gate (1) Binary circuit with two or more inputs and a single output, in which the output is logic one only when all inputs are logic one, and the output is logic 0 if any one of the inputs is logic 0. (2) In a computer, a gate circuit with more than one input terminal. No output signal will be produced unless a pulse is applied to all inputs simultaneously.

angstrom Unit measurement, 1/250 millionth of an inch (10^{-8} cm). Used to measure the elements in electronic components on a chip. There are 10,000 angstroms in one micron.

animated graphics Moving diagrams or cartoons often found in computer-based courseware.

animation   Process of making an object appear to move by rapidly displaying a series of pictures of it, each one in a slightly different position. Technique used for producing computer-generated movies.

annotation symbol   Symbol used to add messages or notes to a flowchart, attached to other flowcharting symbols by dashed lines.

ANS-COBOL   A version of COBOL standardized in 1974 by the American National Standards Institute.

ANSI   Acronym for American National Standards Institute, the organization that publishes standards for various aspects of the computer industry.

answer mode   Ability of a modem to accept an incoming call from another modem.

answer/originate   In telecommunications, the alternatives of receiving (answering) or sending (originating) a phone call.

anthropomorphism   Figure of speech used to describe computers, and devices controlled by computers, as though they were persons.

anti-aliasing   At low resolutions, diagonal lines in digitized images appear as stair-steps and are called "jaggies." This effect is called "aliasing." Anti-aliasing is the smoothing or removal of these "jaggies" to recreate smoother diagonal lines.

antistatic mat   Floor mat placed in front of a device, such as a disk unit, that is sensitive to static, to prevent shocks that could cause loss of data during human handling of the unit.

antivirus program   See vaccine.

APL   Acronym for A Programming Language, a mathematically structured programming language. The power of the language is demonstrated by its extended single operators that allow a user to perform directly such calculations as taking the inverse of a matrix or solving a set of linear equations.   APL was developed by Kenneth Iverson in the mid-1960s and originally designed for use on IBM mainframes. APL is very compact, hard to read, scientific programming language. It is used on a wide variety of computers from microcomputers to supercomputers.

Apollo   A manufacturer of high-performance workstations. Apollo was founded in 1980 and pioneered the concept of networked workstations. In 1989, Apollo became a division of the Hewlett-Packard Company.

append   Add on; such as to add new records to a database or to add to the end of a character string or list.

Apple Computer, Inc.   One of the first and certainly the most influential of the microcomputer manufacturers. Founded in 1976 by Steven P. Jobs and Stephen G. Wozniak, using the family garage as a base and $100 in capital, Apple made computers that became wildly successful. Because of excellent design principles, the early Apple II family of microcomputers is still useful, and later machines, such as the Macintosh family of microcomputers, have become extremely popular and have greatly affected the design of other machines and of software. The Macintosh computer, with its innovative software, is in a class by itself. Apple Computer, Inc. is a leader in high-performance personal computing.

Apple key   On keyboards produced by Apple Computer, Inc., a special key identified by the Apple logo symbol. The key is used by the operating system and certain applications programs.

Apple Macintosh   See Macintosh.

Applesoft BASIC   Extended version of the BASIC programming language used with the Apple II family of computers and capable of processing numbers in floating-point form. An interpreter for creating and executing programs is Applesoft BASIC is built into the computer.

AppleTalk   A network scheme designed primarily for the Apple Macintosh computer. The system often uses the relatively slow LocalTalk hardware, but has grown in popularity because of its low cost, ease of use and installation, and general reliability. It allows computers to share files and peripherals.

Apple II   A family of personal computers from Apple Computer, Inc. The first Apple II was introduced in 1977. The computer family now includes several models widely used in secondary schools, businesses and homes. The Apple II computers are based on the MOS Technology 6502 microcomputer.

AppleWorks   An integrated software package that runs on the Apple II family of microcomputers. The program combines word processing, spreadsheet, and database management. It was introduced in 1983.

application   Task to be performed by a computer program or system. Broad examples of computer applications are engineering design, numerical control, airline seat reservations, business forecasting, and hospital administration. Accounts receivable, mailing list, or electronic spreadsheet programs are examples of applications that run on small business computers.

application generator   A very high-level language that allows the user to give a detailed explanation of what data are to be processed, rather than how to process the data.

application-oriented language   Problem-oriented programming language whose statements contain or resemble the terminology of the computer user.

application-specific integrated circuit   An integrated circuit designed to fill the specific requirement of an application.

applications programmer Computer programmer who develops applications programs.

applications programming Preparation of programs for application to specific problems to find solutions.

applications programs Programs normally written by programmers within an organization that enable the computer to produce useful work, such as specific inventory control, attendance accounting, linear programming, or medical accounting tasks.

applied mathematics Mathematics put to practical use as in mechanics, physics, or computer science.

approximation Number that is not exact, but has been rounded off to a prescribed decimal place: 3.14 and 3.14159 are both approximations of pi.

APT Acronym for Automatic Programmed Tool, a programming system used in numerical control applications for the programmed control of machine functions. APT allows a user to define points, lines, circles, planes, conical surfaces, and geometric surfaces.

arcade game Computer video games popularized by coin-operated machines, characterized by high-resolution color graphics, high-speed animation, and sound. Players often use joysticks to control a screen object, and the computer scores points based on the game's rules.

architecture (1) Physical structure of a computer's internal operations, including its registers, memory, instruction set, and input/output structure. (2) The special selection, design, and inter-connection of the principal components of a system.

archival Pertaining to long-term storage of data.

archive (1) To copy programs and data onto an auxiliary storage medium, such as disk or tape, for long-term retention. (2) To store data for anticipated normal long-term use. (3) A procedure for transferring image information from an on-line optical storage medium to an off-line medium.

Arcnet A computer networking scheme.

area search Examination of a large group of documents to select those that pertain to one group, such as a specific category or class.

argument Variable to which either a logical or a numerical value may be assigned.

arithmetic (1) Branch of mathematics concerned with study of the positive real numbers and zero. (2) Pertaining to such operations as addition, subtraction, multiplication, and division, or to the section of the computer hardware that performs these operations.

arithmetic expression   One or more numbers, variables, functions, symbols, or any combination of these that represents a single value in an arithmetic operation or function. (3 + 48)/17, A + 10, X * Y - 82, and 6 are all arithmetic expressions.

arithmetic-logic unit   Basic element of the central processing unit where arithmetic and logical operations are performed.

arithmetic operation   Various manipulations of numerical quantities, including the fundamental operations of addition, subtraction, multiplication and division, as well as aggregation, exponentiation, and extraction of roots.

arithmetic operator   Symbol that tells a computer to perform addition, subtraction, multiplication, division, aggregation, or raising to a power—which, with negative powers, is tantamount to extracting roots.

arithmetic shift   To multiply or divide a quantity by a power of the number base. For example, if binary 1101, representing decimal 13, is arithmetically shifted twice to the left, the result is 110100, representing 52, which is also obtained by multiplying 12 by 2 twice; however, if decimal 13 is shifted to the left twice, the result would be the same as multiplying by 10 twice, or 1300.

arithmetic unit   Same as arithmetic-logic unit.

arrangement   Order of index terms or items of data in a system.\

array   (1) Series of related items. (2) Ordered arrangement or pattern of items or numbers, such as a determinant, matrix, vector, or table of numbers.

array processor   Processor that performs matrix arithmetic much faster than standard computers. Capable of performing operations on all the elements in large matrices at one time. Also called a vector processor.

arrival rate   Number of characters or messages arriving over a data communications medium per unit of time.

ART   PFS First Publisher graphics format used for clip art.

artificial intelligence (AI)   A group of technologies that attempt to emulate certain aspects of human behavior, such as reasoning and communicating, as well as to mimic biological senses, including seeing and hearing. Specific technologies include expert systems (also called knowledge-based systems), natural language, neural networks, machine translation and speech recognition. AI is the branch of computer science that is concerned with developing computer systems capable of simulating human reasoning and sensation. AI involves using computers and software that, like the human mind, use stored knowledge to make decisions involving judgement or ambiguity. See robotics.

artificial language Language based on a set of prescribed rules that are established prior to its usage.

Artline An illustrative graphics program for use with IBM-compatible microcomputers. Features include multi-layer editing, an autotrace facility, scalable fonts, 3-D shading effects, a blending function to change one image into another, and access to a large supply of clip art images.

Arts & Letters Graphics Editor An illustrative graphics program which runs on Windows and OS/2. A special effect function allows text, clip art, and freeform graphics to be warped, bent, stretched and twisted by specifying the shape into which the object is to fit. A Graduated Fill function allows colorful blends and the 3-D illusion of depth by a variety of linear and radial fill for text and graphic art work. The program has several thousand files of clip art and an autotrace feature.

artwork Visual and graphic elements on a page, such as line drawings, halftones, or solids.

ASCC Acronym for Automatic Sequence Controlled Calculator, one of the first electromechanical computers, developed under the direction of Howard Aiken at Harvard University. Completed in 1944, it followed instructions stored on paper tape.

ascender Portion of lower-case letters that extends above the main portion of the letter, such as the tops of b, d, and h.

ascending order Order that ranges from smallest to largest or first to last. Alphabets and counting numbers are in naturally ascending order. Contrast with descending order.

ASCII Acronym for American Standard Code for Information Interchange. Pronounced "ass-key." A 7-bit standard code adopted to facilitate interchange of data among various types of data processing and data communications equipment. Compare EBCDIC.

ASIS See American Society for Information Science.

ASM See Association for Systems Management.

aspect ratio In computer graphics, the relationship of the height and width of the video display screen frame or image area.

assemble To gather, interpret, and coordinate data required for a computer program, translate the data into computer language and project it into the final program for the computer to follow.

assembler Computer program that takes nonmachine-language instructions prepared by a computer user and converts them into a form that may be used by the computer. Computer program that assembles.

assembling Automatic process by which a computer converts a symbolic source-language program into a machine language, usually on an instruction-by-instruction basis.

assembly language Programming language that allows a computer user to write a program using mnemonics instead of numeric instructions. A low-level symbolic programming language that closely resembles machine-code language.

assembly listing Printed output produced by an assembler. Lists the original assembly-language program, the machine-language version of the program, storage assignments, error messages, and other information useful to the programmer.

assertions A concept referring to the storage of procedures as a part of an object-oriented database. An assertion is a property of the object with which it is associated, typically some condition that the object must satisfy. Assertions are like methods, but are not encapsulated along with the local data on which they operate.

assignment statement Source language statement that makes an assignment.

Association for Computing Machinery (ACM) World's largest educational and scientific society committed to the development of technical skills and professional competence of computer specialists. Founded in 1947, ACM has earned a reputation for technical excellence by publishing prestigious journals and sponsoring numerous conferences that promote an ongoing dialogue among students, educators, and practitioners. The association is dedicated to the development of information processing as a discipline, and to the responsible use of computers in an increasing diversity of applications.

Association for Systems Management (ASM) An international organization engaged in keeping its members abreast of the rapid growth and change occurring in the field of systems management and information processing. Founded in 1947, it has five technical departments: Data Communications, Data Processing, Management Information Systems, Organization Planning, and Written Communications. Members can belong to one or more of these departments.

Association for Women in Computing (AWC) Nonprofit professional organization comprised of people who have an interest in the field of computer data processing. Main goals are to promote communication among further the professional development and advancement of, and promote the education of women in computing.

Association of Computer Users An organization, founded in 1979, whose members are interested in the use of small computers for business purposes.

Association of Data Processing Service Organizations (ADAPSO) Association of commercial institutions that offers data processing services through systems that its members operate on their own premises. Founded in 1960, ADAPSO is oriented toward improving management techniques and defining performance standards for computer services.

Association of Information Systems Professionals (AISP) Organization of professionals involved in all aspects of information systems. Founded in 1972 as the International Word Processing Association, AISP now has members worldwide with organized chapters in more than 100 metropolitan areas of the United States and Canada.

associative storage Storage device whose storage locations are identified by their contents (rather than by names or positions, as in most computer storage devices).

asterisk Symbol (*) used in many programming languages to represent a multiplication operator.

asynchronous Pertaining to a mode of data communications that provides a variable time interval between characters during transmission.

asynchronous computer Computer in which each operation starts as a result of a signal generated by the completion of the previous operation or by the availability of the equipment required for the next operation.

asynchronous input Input data having no time-dependable pattern or cycle when related to the computer system.

asynchronous transmission Method in which data characters are sent at random time intervals. Limits phone-line transmission to about 2400 bps.

AT The first 80286-based personal computer introduced by the IBM Corporation in 1984. AT stands for Advanced Technology.

Atanasoff-Berry Computer (ABC) An early electronic digital computer, designed by John V. Atanasoff and Clifford Berry. It was completed in 1942.

Atanasoff, John V. Designer of an early electronic digital computer that was completed in 1942. The computer was named the ABC (Atanasoff-Berry Computer).

Atari Corporation Manufacturer of a popular line of personal computer systems. Atari produced several older home computers, and in 1985 introduced the Atari ST family of microcomputers. The ST computers are high-performance personal computers with capabilities for computer graphics in color.

Atari ST A personal computer series from Atari Corporation.

ATM Acronym for Automatic Teller Machine.

atom   (1) Elementary building block of data structures. Corresponds to a record in a file and may contain one or more fields of data. (2) In list processing programming languages, a basic element in a list. For example, in the list, "This is a list," each word is an atom.

atomic operation   An operation that cannot be divided into smaller operations.

attach   To connect a peripheral to a computer to increase its capacity.

attenuation   Decrease in the strength of a signal as it passes through a control system.

atto   Prefix meaning one quintillionth, or a billionth of a billionth; 10^{-18}. Abbreviated a.

attribute   (1) manner in which a variable is handled by the computer. (2) Characteristic quality of a data type, data structure, element of a data model, or system. (3) Feature of a device. (4) Column of a relation in a relational database.

audio   Sound that can be heard by a human (15 to 20,000 Hz).

audio device   Any computer device that accepts sound and/or produces sound.

audio output   Computer output generated through voice synthesizers that create audible signals resembling a human voice.

audio-response device   A device that converts data in internal storage to vocalized sounds understandable to humans. Also called a voice output unit or a voice synthesizer.

audiovisual   Pertaining to nonprint materials—such as films, tapes, and cassettes—that record information by sound and/or sight.

audit trail   Means for identifying the actions taken in processing input data or in preparing output. By use of the audit trail, data on a source document can be traced to a specific output, and an output can be traced to the source items from which it was derived. For example, it could reveal that Nancy Wilson changed the inventory figures in the Auto Supply account at 2:32 P.M. on October 8.

authentication   A process for verifying the correctness of a piece of data.

authenticity   Integrity of a message.

authoring system   Computer system capable of executing an author language.

authorization   System control feature that requires specific approval before processing can take place.

authorized program Computer program capable of altering the fundamental operation or status of a computer system.

author language Programming language used for designing instructional programs for computer-assisted instruction systems.

authors (1) People who design instructional material for computer-assisted instruction systems. (2) A person who creates a hypertext document.

auto-answer Modem that can automatically answer incoming telephone calls from computers and pipe the data into another computer.

autochart Type of documentor used for the automatic production and maintenance of charts, principally flowcharts.

auto-dial Modem capable of connecting to the telephone system and dialing a number. The modem and communications software perform the proper communications procedures so that computers may exchange data.

AUTODIN Acronym for AUTOmatic Digital Network, the data-handling portion of the military communications system.

auto-disconnect Automatic disconnecting by one modem when it receives a disconnect message or when the other party hangs up.

autoflow A setting found in many page layout programs that allows for continuous placement of blocked text from page to page without operator intervention.

autofont A self-training OCR system that automatically adjusts to the type designs of different typefaces in order to read a wide range of documents quickly and accurately.

auto indexing System of indexing that superimposes additional information at any of several given addresses.

auto-load Key on some computer keyboards that activates the computer. Essentially boots the operating system into internal storage and starts execution of the system.

automata Theory related to the study of the principles of operation, behavioral characteristics, and application of automatic devices.

automated data processing Largely self-regulating process in which information is handled with a minimum of human effort and intervention.

automated flowchart Flowchart drawn by a computer-controlled printer or plotter.

automated office Result of the merger of computers, office electronic devices, and telecommunications technology in an office environment.

automated teller machine (ATM) Banking terminal that provides customers with 24-hour deposit-and-withdrawal service. Special-purpose device connected to the bank's computer system. To use the automatic teller, the customer inserts a plastic identification card, enters a special password code and communicates with the system by using a numeric keypad and visual display.

automatic Pertaining to a process or device that, under specified conditions, functions without intervention by a human operator.

automatic carriage Control mechanism for a printer that can automatically control the feeding, spacing, skipping, and ejecting of paper or preprinted forms.

automatic check Equipment check built in specifically for checking purposes.

automatic coding Machine-assisted preparation of machine-language routines.

automatic controller Device or instrument capable of measuring and regulating by receiving a signal from a sensing device, comparing this data with a desired value, and issuing signals for corrective action.

automatic error correction Technique for detecting and correcting errors that occur in data transmission or within the system itself.

automatic hyphenation A feature that hypenates words automatically. Often found in word processor and page layout programs.

automatic loader Hardware loader program, usually implemented in a special ROM, that allows loading of an auxiliary storage unit (hard disk or floppy disk).

automatic pagination A feature that automatically breaks text into pages. Often found in word processing and page layout programs.

automatic programming (1) Process of using a computer to perform some stages of the work involved in preparing a program. (2) Production of a machine-language computer program under the guidance of a symbolic representation of the program.

automatic reformatting In word processing, automatic adjustment of text to accommodate changes.

automatic shutdown Ability of some systems software to stop a network or a computer system as a whole in an orderly fashion.

automatic teller machine See automated teller machine.

automation (1) Implementation of processes by automatic means. (2) Automatically controlled operation of an apparatus, process, or system by mechanical or electronic devices that take the place of human observaion, effort and decision.

automaton Machine designed to simulate the operations of living things.

automonitor (1) Computer's record of its functions. (2) Computer program that records the operating functions of a computer.

autopolling Contraction of automatic polling, a process whereby terminals in a computer network are scanned periodically to determine whether they are ready to send information. A combination of hardware and software that polls the terminals in a computer network.

auto-redial Modem feature for redialing a number until contact is established.

auto-repeat Feature of some keyboards that allows a key to repeat automatically when held down.

auto-restart Capability of a computer to perform automatically the initialization functions necessary to resume operation following an equipment or power failure.

autoscore In word processing, an instruction that causes text to be underlined.

autotrace A feature of many drawing programs that draws lines along the edges of a bitmapped image in order to convert the image into an object-oriented one. Using the autotrace tool you can transform low-resolution graphics (72 dots per inch bit-mapped image) into art that can print at substantially higher resolution (object-oriented graphics can print at the printer's maximum resolution).

auxiliary equipment Equipment not under direct control of the central processing unit.

auxiliary operation Operation performed by equipment not under control of the central processing unit.

auxiliary storage Storage that supplements the main storage of a computer, such as hard disks, floppy disks, magnetic tapes, and optical discs.

availability Ratio of the time that a hardware device is known or believed to be operating correctly to the total hours of scheduled operation.

available time Time that a computer is available for use but is not being used.

Avant Garde A modern sans serif typeface design owned by the International Typeface Corporation (ITC) and included as a built-in font with many PostScript laser printers.

axes In a two-dimensional coordinate system, lines used as references for vertical (Y) and horizontal (X) measurement. See Cartesian coordinate system.

b Abbreviation for bit or binary. For example, bps for bits per second and 1101b for the binary number 1101.

B Abbreviation for byte or baud. Used for bytes when referring to storage, or baud rate when referring to communications. For example, KB means 1 kilobyte (1024 bytes).

Babbage, Charles (1792-1871) British mathematician and inventor. Designed a difference engine for calculating logarithms to 20 decimal places and an analytical engine that was a forerunner of the digital computer. Babbage was ahead of his time, and the engineering techniques of his day were not advanced enough to build his machines successfully.

babble Cross talk from a large number of channels in a system.

background (1) In multiprogramming, the environment in which low-priority programs are executed. (2) That part of a display screen not occupied with displayed characters or graphics (foreground). (3) In large computers, the memory area for programs with low-priorities.

background noise In optical scanning, electrical interference caused by such things as ink tracking or carbon offsetting.

background processing Execution of lower-priority computer programs during periods when system resources are not required to process high-priority programs.

background program Program that can be executed whenever the facilities of a multiprogramming computer system are not required by other programs of higher priority. Contrast with foreground program.

backing store Backup memory to the computer main memory. More commonly called auxiliary storage.

backing-up Making backup copies of files to prevent loss of their contents in the event the originals are damaged or lost.

backlash   In a mechanical operation, the "play" between interacting parts, such as two gears, as a result of tolerance.

back panel   Back of a computer case, with a number of sockets for connecting peripheral devices to the computer.

backplane   Circuitry and mechanical elements used to connect the boards of a system. Main circuit board of a computer into which other circuit boards are plugged.

backspace   Keyboard operation that moves the cursor one place to the left. Allows modification of what has already been typed before it is entered into the computer.

backspace tape   Process of returning a magnetic tape to the beginning of the preceding record.

backtracking   Operation of scanning a list in reverse.

backup   (1) pertaining to procedures or standby equipment available for use in the event of failure or overloading of the normally used procedures or equipment. (2) To make a copy of a program or data in case the original is lost, damaged, or otherwise inaccessible.

backup copy   Copy of a file or data set kept for reference in case the original file or data set is destroyed.

backup disk   A duplicate copy of a floppy disk that preserves files in case of some disaster.

backup programmer   Programer who is an assistant to the chief programmer.

Backus Normal Form (BNF)   Notation for describing the syntax of programming languages. It was the first metalanguage to define programming language; developed by John Backus and Peter Naur in 1959. Also called Backus-Naur Form.

Backus, John   In 1957, at the IBM Corporation, developed the computer language FORTRAN (FORmula TRANslator), a high-level programming language used to perform mathematical, scientific, and engineering computations.

backward chaining   Goal-driven method of reasoning that proceeds from the desired goal to the facts already known. Contrast with forward chaining.

backward read   Feature available on some magnetic tape systems whereby magnetic tape units can transfer data to computer storage while moving in reverse.

badge reader   Terminal equipped to read credit cards or specially coded badges.

bad sectors During formatting of disks, all sectors are checked for usability. Unusable sectors are "flagged" as bad and are not used by the operating system. The remaining areas can still be used. Bad sectors are sometimes used by viruses to store the code outside the reach of the users and the operating system.

Baldwin, Frank Stephen In 1875, invented the first practical reversible four-process calculator in the United States.

ball printer Printer that has the printing elements on the face of a ball-like replacement element. Type fonts can easily be changed by changing the typeball.

band printer Impact printing device that uses a steel band or polyurethane belt to carry the character set. Can produce multiple carbon copies at speeds ranging from 300 to 2000 lines per minute.

bandwidth In data communications, difference between the highest and lowest frequencies of a band. Used as a measure of the capacity of a communication channel, expressed in bits per second, or bauds.

bank (1) In communications, a range of frequencies, as between two specified limits. (2) Range, or scope, of operation. (3) Group of circular recording tracks on a storage device such as a disk.

bar chart Widely used chart in business graphics. Used to display a time schedule.

bar code Code made up of a series of variable-width vertical lines which can be read by an optical bar reader. Bar codes are used to identify retail sales items, books, etc.

bar code reader A photoelectric scanner that reads bar codes by means of reflected light.

Bardeen, John Joined the Bell Laboratories in 1945, and shared with William Shockley and Walter Brattain the glory of the discovery of the transistor and the 1956 Nobel Prize in physics. Since 1951 he has been professor of physics at the University of Illinois and has been working on superconductivity.

bare board Printed circuit board with no electronic components on it.

bar graph A graph made up of filled-in columns or rows that represent the change of data over time.

bar printer Impact printing device that uses several type bars positioned side by side across the line.

base (1) Radix of a number system. (2) Region between the emitter and collector of a junction transistor that receives minority carriers ejected from the emitter. (3) On a printed circuit board, the portion that supports the printed pattern.

base address Specified address that is combined with a relative address to form the absolute address of a particular storage location.

baseband transmission Method of using low-frequency transmission of signals across coaxial cables for short-distance, local area network transmission.

base class In object-oriented programming, the most generalized class in a class structure. Most applications have many such base classes. Some languages define a primitive base class, which serves as the ultimate superclass of all classes.

base 8 See octal.

baseline An imaginary horizontal line with which the base of each character, excluding descenders, is aligned.

baseline document Reference document for changes to a data processing system.

base 16 See hexadecimal.

base 10 See decimal.

base 2 See binary.

BASIC Acronym for Beginner's All-purpose Symbolic Instruction Code, an easy-to-learn, easy-to-use, algebraic programming language with a small repertory of commands and simple statement formats. Developed at Dartmouth College by John Kemeny and Thomas Kurtz. Widely used in programming instruction, in personal computing, and in business and industry. The language has changed over the years. Early versions are unstructured and interpreted. Later versions are structured and often compiled. Implementations of BASIC include Applesoft BASIC, BASICA, CBASIC, GW-BASIC, Microsoft BASIC, Turbo BASIC and QuickBASIC.

BASICA A version of the BASIC programming language developed by Microsoft Corporation for the IBM PC family of computers.

basic input-output system (BIOS) A set of programs encoded in read-only memory (ROM) in IBM-compatible microcomputers. These programs facilitate the transfer of data and control instructions between the computer and peripherals.

basic linkage Linkage used repeatedly in one routine, program, or system that follows the same set of rules each time.

batch (1) Group of records or programs considered as a single unit for processing on a computer. (2) To use batch processing.

batch processing (1) Technique by which programs to be executed are coded and collected together for processing in groups or patches. The user gives the job to a computer center, where it is put into a batch of programs and processed, and then returned. The user has no direct access to the machine. See remote batch processing. (2) Processing as a group data that has been accumulated over a period of time or must be done periodically, as in payroll and billing applications.

batch total Sum of a set of items in a batch of records. Used to check the accuracy of operations involving the batch.

battery backup Auxiliary power provided to a computer so volatile information is not lost during a power failure.

baud rate The speed at which telecommunicated data is transmitted, measured in bits per second. Common baud rates are 300, 1200 and 2400.

Baudot code Code for the transmission of data in which five bits represent one character. Usually applied to the code used in many tele-printer systems. Also called International Telegraph Code Number 1. By 1950 this code had become one of the standards for international tele-graph communications.

Baudot, Emile (1845-1903) Pioneer in printing telegraphy who invented the Baudot code in 1880.

bay Cabinet or rack in which electronic equipment is installed. Also called equipment bay.

BBS Acronym for Bulletin Board Service. Enables users to log into another computer system from remote terminals. Many of these BBS's can be used free of charge and can be reached by modem.

BCD Acronym for Binary Coded Decimal.

beacon In a network, a special message sent by a node indicating a serious network problem.

beam penetration CRT A vector display system which produces color by varying the strength of an electron beam directed at a screen coated with (typically) both red and green phosphor layers.

bebugging Intentional seeding of a program with known mistakes to measure the rates of debugging by student programmers.

beep Audible sound produced by a computer's speaker. Also a command in some programming languages which causes the computer's speaker to emit a sound.

behavior In object-oriented programming, how an object acts and reacts, in terms of its state changes and message passing.

bell 103 Standard for 300-baud modems.

Bell Laboratories The research and development center of the AT&T Company and one of the most renowned scientific laboratories in the world. Many computer hardware developments and software concepts and programs were generated at Bell Laboratories.

bells and whistles Informal description of the special or extra features of a computer system, including graphics, color displays, sound, and many peripherals.

bell 212A Standard for 1200-baud modems.

belt-bed plotter A pen plotter which uses a wide continuous belt for holding the paper.

benchmark Point of reference from which measurements can be made, such as use of a program to evaluate the performance of a computer. Any standard against which products can be compared.

benchmark problem Problem designed to evaluate and compare the performance of digital computers.

benchmark tests Tests used in the measurement of computer equipment performance under typical conditions of use, such as a computer program run on several different computers for the purpose of comparing execution speed, throughput, and so forth.

Bernoulli™ box A removable hard disk system for microcomputers, manufactured by Iomega Corporation. The main advantage of this cartridge system is that one hard disk system can be used for multiple libraries of hard disk data.

Berry, Clifford In 1939, with John Atanasoff, invented an early electronic digital computer—the ABC (Atanasoff-Berry Computer).

beta test The product test stage following alpha test during which a new product is tested under actual usage conditions in a customer environment. Software testing by first-time users.

Bezier curve A type of curve generated by an algorithm. Named after French mathematician Pierre Bezier, it is used to display nonuniform curves based upon a fitting algorithm. Bezier curves need only a few points to define a large number of shapes, hence their usefulness over other mathematical methods for approximating a given shape. Within drawing programs, Bezier curves are typically reshaped by moving the handles that appear off of the curve.

bias Amount by which the average of a set of values departs from a reference value.

bibliography (1) Annotated catalog of documents. (2) Enumerative list of books. (3) List of documents pertaining to a given subject or author. (4) Process of compiling catalogs or lists.

bidirectional Data flow may go in either direction on a wire. Transceivers at each end both receive and transmit. Common bidirectional buses are tristate or open collector transistor-transistor logic.

bidirectional printer Printer that prints from left to right as well as from right to left, avoiding carriage-return delay.

biform In typography, a typeface that combines lowercase and small cap characters to form the lower case alphabet.

bifurcation Condition whereby two, and only two, outcomes can occur, such as on or off, 1 or 0, true or false.

Big Blue Nickname for International Business Machines Corporation (IBM), derived from the company's use of a distinctive blue paint on its mainframes and other equipment.

BINAC Acronym for BINary Automatic Computer, built by the Eckert-Mauchly Corporation in 1949.

binary Mathematical representation of a number to the base 2, i.e., with only two states, 1 and 0; ON and OFF; or HIGH and LOW. Requires a greater number of digits than base 10, i.e. 254 = 11111110.

binary arithmetic (1) Mathematical numeration system equivalent to our decimal arithmetic system but involving only two digits: 1 and 0. (2) Expression recognizing that all arithmetic calculations are done with two values at a time.

binary code Coding system in which the encoding of any data is done through the use of bits, 0 or 1, in which 0 represents off and 1 represents on. ASCII and EBCDIC are two such systems.

binary coded character One element of a notation system representing alphanumeric characters—such as decimal digits, alphabetic letters, and special symbols—by a predetermined configuration of consecutive binary digits.

binary coded decimal (BCD) Computer coding system in which each decimal digit is represented by a group of four binary 1s and 0s.

binary coded decimal number Any number, usually consisting of successive groups of figures, in which each group of four figures is a binary number that represents, but does not necessarily equal arithmetically, a particular figure in an associated decimal number; for example, the decimal number 264 is represented as the binary coded number 0010 0110 0100.

binary device (1) Device that can register two conditions, such as an electrical switch that can be on or off. (2) In computer science, equipment that records data in binary form or that reads the data so coded.

binary digit   Either of the characters 0 or 1. Abbreviated bit.

binary file   File containing programs in machine code.

binary notation   Numeral system written in base 2 notation.

binary number   Any numeral, usually of more than one digit, expressing a sum in which the quantity represented by each digit is based on a radix of 2. The digits used are 0 and 1.

binary point   Radix point in a mixed binary numeral, separating the fractional part from the integer part. In the binary numeral 110.011, the binary point is between the two 0s.

binary search   Search method in which a series of items is divided into two parts, one of which is rejected, and the process is repeated on each unrejected part until the item with the desired property is found. Often the best method when the list to be searched is known to be in order and relatively uniform. Many database systems use this method for locating items in their indexes.

binary system   Numeral system with a base or radix of 2. The numeral 111 in the binary system represents the quantity 1, plus 1 x 2^1, plus 1 x 2^2—that is, 7 in the decimal system.

binary-to-decimal conversion   Process of converting a numeral written in base 2 to the equivalent numeral written in base 10.

binary-to-hexadecimal conversion   Process of converting a numeral written in base 2 to the equivalent numeral written in base 16.

binary-to-octal conversion   Process of converting a numeral written in base 2 to the equivalent numeral written in base 8.

binary tree   A data structure in which each node contains one parent and no more than two children.

binding   In object-oriented programming, the process of weaving a program together to resolve all the connections among its components. Static, or early, binding resolves these connections before the program is run. Dynamic, or late, binding occurs while the program is running.

binding time   Stage at which a compiler replaces a symbolic name or address with its machine-language form.

biochip   An organic device that assembles itself and requires no electricity to operate. If biochip research proves to be successful, one billion times as much data as that now stored on a silicon chip will be able to be stored on a biochip.

biocomputer   A computer that will have its central processor and memory stored on biochips.

biometrics   The science of measuring individual body characteristics; used in some security systems.

bionics   Study of living systems for the purpose of relating their characteristics and functions to the development of mechanical and electronic hardware.

BIOS   Acronym for Basic Input/Output System. In some operating systems, the part of the system that customizes it to a specific computer.

bipolar   Pertaining to the most popular fundamental kind of integrated circuit, formed from layers of silicon with different electrical characteristics. Bipolar literally means "having two poles," unlike the earlier MOS Field Effect Transistor (MOSFET), which is unipolar ("having one pole"). As in MOSFET, the current flow of majority carriers goes in one direction only, such a from source to drain. In a bipolar transistor, the current in the emitter region splits and flows toward two terminals (poles), the base and the collector.

bipolar read only memory   See BROM.

biquinary code   A 7-bit weighted code used primarily to represent decimal numbers. A redundant code that may be used to provide error-checking features. A pair of bits represents the decimal number 5 or 0, and the remaining 5 bits are used to represent the decimal numbers 0 through 4.

bistable device   Device with only two stable states, such as on and off.

bi-state   Situation in which a computer component takes on one of only two possible conditions.

bit   (1) Binary digit; a digit (1 or 0) in the representation of a number in binary notation. (2) Smallest unit of information recognized by a computer and its associated equipment. Several bits make up a byte, or a computer word.

bit control   Means of transmitting serial data in which each bit has a significant meaning, and a single character is surrounded with start and stop bits.

bit density   Measure of the number of bits recorded per unit of length or area on magnetic tape or disk.

bit flipping   Process of inverting bits—changing 1s to 0s and vice versa. For example, in a graphics program, to invert a black-and-white bit-mapped image (to change black to white and vice versa), the program could simply flip the bits that makeup the bit map.

bit image   Collection of bits stored in a computer's memory, arranged into a rectangular matrix. The computer's display screen is a bit image that is visible to the user.

bit manipulation   Act of turning bits on and off. Sometimes called bit-flipping.

bit map   A data structure that describes a bit image being held in computer storage. Each picture element (pixel) is represented by bits stored in the memory. Bit-mapped graphics are notorious for using lots of memory. Up to 1 million bytes of memory may be required to store a bit map for a high-resolution screen display or to store a full page scanned image.

bitmap file formats   See ART, CUT, GIF, IFF, IMG, MacPaint, NEO, PCX, TGA and TIFF. Contrast with object file formats.

bit-mapped font   A set of characters in a particular size and style, in which each character is described in a unique bit map (pattern of dots). Bit-mapped screen or printer fonts represent characters with a matrix of dots. To display or print bit-mapped fonts, the computer or printer must keep a full representation of each character in memory.

bit-mapped graphics   A method of generating screen images by creating a one-for-one correspondence between bits in memory and pixels on the screen. In color graphics, three or more bits are required in the bit map to represent the red, green, and blue values of an individual pixel. Bit-mapped graphics are created by paint programs and some scanners.

bit rate   Rate at which binary digits, or pulse representations, appear on communication lines or channels.

bit stream   Binary signal without regard to groupings by character.

bit test   Program check to determine whether a specific bit is on (1) or off (0).

bit transfer rate   Number of bits transferred per unit of time, usually expressed in bits per second.

bit twiddler   (1) Hacker. (2) Person who enjoys working with computers.

black box   Electronic or mechanical device that alters input signals in a predictable manner but whose inner workings are often a mystery to the user.

blank   (1) Part of a medium in which no characters are recorded. (2) In electronic spreadsheets, a command that will erase the contents of a cell or range of cells. (3) Empty space with dimension of one character of data.

blanking   On a display screen, not displaying a character although it is present; leaving a space.

bleed   In a printed document, any element that runs off the edge of the page.

blind search   Time-consuming type of search that uses an orderly scheme, but no prescience, to exhaust all possibilities.

blinking   Graphics aid that makes a predefined graphic entity blink on the CRT to attract the designer's attention.

block device   A device such as a disk drive that can read and write data only in chunks at a time, rather than byte by byte or bit by bit. The number of bytes in each chunk is normally called the block size. Almost all mass-storage devices are either inherently block devices or made in software to appear as if they were.

block diagram   Graphic representation of the logical sequence by which data is processed.

block graphics   Graphics images created by using block graphics characters. Because the block graphics characters are handled the same way as ordinary characters, the computer can display block graphics considerably faster than bit-mapped graphics.

block header   Brief record of data that describes a block of memory and its contents.

blocking   The process of grouping a specified number of logical records into one contiguous unit of storage called a block, usually to increase the efficiency of computer input and output operations.

blocking factor   Number of logical records per physical record on a magnetic tape or disk.

blocking object   In object-oriented programming, a passive object whose semantics are guaranteed in the presence of multiple threads of control.

block length   Measure of the size of a block, usually specified in units such as records, words, characters, or bytes.

block move   (1) Process in which a block of text is moved from one part of a document or file to another, or from one document or file to another. (2) In word processing, a feature that allows the user to identify a block of text and move it anywhere in a file. Electronic equivalent of "cut and paste."

block sorting   Sorting technique used to break down a file into related groups.

blocks world   Artificially created environment of blocks used in the study of robotics and natural language.

block transfer   Relocation of an entire block of data from one area of storage to another.

blow up   (1) Unexpected halt to a program due to a bug or because it encounters data conditions it cannot handle. (2) To enlarge a picture.

blue ribbon program   Computer program that executes properly on the first try and does not require any debugging.

BNF   Acronym for Backus Normal Form.

board   Short for printed circuit board. A flat, thin, rectangular component of a computer or peripheral that includes one or more layers of printed circuitry and to which chips and other electronic parts are attached. Sometimes called a card.

board computer   Computer in which all electronic components are laid out on a single circuit board.

board exchange warranty   Warranty that provides a customer with a new replacement board when the original needs repair.

boilerplate   Pieces of text that get used over and over again, word for word, in different documents.

boilerplate document   Document created by combining selected paragraphs from a set of standard paragraphs with a small amount of original information.

boldface   Printed characters in darker type than the surrounding characters.

boldface font   A set of type characters that are darker and heavier than normal type.

bold printing   Ability to make certain letters darker than the surrounding text. Some printers produce bold characters by overstriking or shadow printing.

Bollee, Leon   Frenchman who in 1886, designed the first machine to perform multiplication successfully by a direct method instead of repeated addition.

bomb   (1) A concealed fault that can cause a system to crash. (2) To sabotage a system by deliberately writing a program that will disrupt the system.

bookkeeping   See housekeeping.

Bookman   A serif typeface frequently used for body type. Bookman, a design owned by the International Typeface Corporation (ITC), is included as a built-in font with many PostScript laser printers.

Boolean algebra   Branch of symbolic logic similar in form to algebra, but dealing with logical relationships instead of numerical relationships. Lay dormant until it could be usefully applied to the fields of relay switching and electronic computers. Has now become an important subject in logic design of electronic computers. Named for George Boole.

Boolean operator   Logic operator, each of whose operands and whose result has one of two values.

Boole, George (1815-1864)   British logician and mathematician. In 1847, wrote a pamphlet called "Mathematical Analysis of Logic." In 1851, wrote a more mature statement of his logical system in a larger work, "An Investigation of the Laws of Thought," in which are founded the mathematical theories of logic. See Boolean algebra.

boot   To start up a computer. Microcomputers have a bootstrap routine in a ROM chip that is automatically executed when the computer is turned on or reset. It searches for the operating system, loads it and then passes control over to it.

bootstrapping   Starting a computer system. "Cold boot" means complete restarting after switching the power on, while "warm boot" means partial restarting under operating system control.

boot virus   A type of computer virus which modifies one or more of those parts of the operating system which are read in during the bootstrapping process.

border   (1) In on-screen windows, the edge surrounding the user's workspace. Window borders provide a visible frame around a document or graphic. (2) In printing, a decorative line or pattern along one or more edges of an illustration or page.

bore   Diameter of a hole; such as on a floppy disk or magnetic tape reel.

Borland International Inc.   A leading microcomputer software company. Founded in 1983 by Philippe Kahn, Borland introduced Turbo Pascal, which instantly became a popular commercial product. Borland has continued to develop popular software products.

borrow   Arithmetically negative carry. It occurs in direct subtraction by raising the low-order digit of the minuend by one unit of the next higher-order digit.

BOT   Acronym for Beginning Of Tape, a mark that shows where to start recording on a magnetic tape.

bottleneck   See limiting operation.

bottom-up technique   Implementation technique wherein the bottom-level modules are written and tested, after which the next-lowest level of modules are written and tested. This process continues until all of the modules have been completed. Contrast with top-down development.

bound   Pertaining to whatever limits system performance, such as processor bound or I/O bound, indicating which component of a system is the bottleneck preventing faster performance.

boundary fill   Filling a region with color by switching to a new value all pixels that are bounded by other pixels having boundary values.

bpi   Abbreviation for bits per inch; sometimes bytes per inch, which is also abbreviated BPI.

bps   Abbreviation for bits per second; sometimes bytes per second, which is also abbreviated BPS. 1 bps = 1 baud.

braindamaged   Refers to a program that performs in an ill-behaved or destructive manner. For example, a program that fails to respond predictably to commands is said to be a braindamaged program.

brain-wave interface   Capability of hardware and software to enable the computer to read and act upon the thoughts of humans.

branch   Selection of one or more possible paths in the flow of control, based on some criterion. Programming instruction that causes transfer of control to another program sequence.

branch instruction   Instruction to a computer that enables it to choose between alternative program paths, depending upon the conditions determined by the computer during the execution of the program.

branchpoint   Place in a program where a branch is selected.

Brattain, Walter Houser   Joined the Bell Laboratories in 1929, and shared with John Bardeen and William Shockley the discovery of the transistor and the 1956 Nobel Prize in physics.

breadboard   Experimental or rough construction model of a process, device, or construction.

break   (1) Interruption of a transmission. (2) To interrupt execution of a program.

break key   On some computers, a keyboard key that will interrupt what the computer is doing.

breakpoint   Specified point in a program at which the program may be interrupted by manual intervention or by a control routine. Generally used as an aid in testing and debugging programs.

Bricklin, Daniel   Developed the first electronic spreadsheet, VisiCalc, in 1978. The spreadsheet concept was so popular in the early 1980s that it actually helped sell personal computers. Today, electronic spreadsheets are one of the most popular programs used with personal computers.

bridge   A device that connects networks of the same type, allowing equipment on one local area network (LAN) to communicate with devices on another.

bridgeware Computer programs used to translate instructions written for one type of computer into a format that another type of computer understands.

briefcase computer Portable computer that will fit inside a briefcase.

brightness In the HSB color model, one of the three characteristics used to describe a color. Brightness refers to the color's percentage of black. (2) In computer graphics, the relative presence or absence of shading (whiteness to grayness to blackness). (3) On some CRT terminals, the ability to vary the intensity of the screen display. Especially useful in highlighting selected segments.

broadband Data communications transmission facilities capable of handling frequencies greater than those required for voice-grade communications. Broadband communication channels—such as microwaves, fiber optics, laser beams, and satellite transmission—can transmit data at rates up to five million baud.

broadcast In data communications, the dissemination of information to a number of stations simultaneously.

BROM Acronym for Bipolar Read Only Memory, a read only memory with no write function, that uses bipolar semiconductor devices.

brownout A period of low-voltage electrical power caused by unusually heavy demand. Brownouts can cause computers to operate erratically or to crash.

browser A tool supplied with the programming language that lets the programmer view the hierarchy and edit code in object-oriented languages.

browsing Looking at files or computer listings in search of something interesting, often without authorization to do so.

brush In computer paint programs, a tool used to produce brushstrokes of varying width, and in some cases calligraphic or shadowing effects.

brute-force technique Any mathematical technique that depends on the raw power of a computer to arrive at a nonelegant solution to a mathematical problem. Most computer users try to avoid brute-force techniques unless they have no practical alternative.

BSC Acronym for Binary Synchronous Communication, a procedure used for data transmission.

BTAM Acronym for Basic Telecommunications Access Method, an access method that permits read/write communications with remote devices.

B-tree Short for balanced tree, a way of organizing the pointers to information in databases that allows quick retrieval of any single specified record.

bubble chart   A type of chart in which annotated circles (bubbles) connected by lines represent connections between concepts or parts of a whole without emphasizing a structural, procedural or sequential relationship between the parts.

bubble memory   Method by which information is stored as magnetized dots (bubbles) that rest on a thin film of semiconductor material. Offers a compact, nonvolatile storage capability.

bubble sort   Sort achieved by exchanging successive pairs of keys until the list is ordered. Also called ripple sort.

bucket   Specific portion of storage used to hold a group of records that are addressed jointly. Could be hardware-related or determined by hashing.

buffer   Temporary storage area used to equalize or balance different operating speeds. Can be used between a slow input device, such as a terminal keyboard, and the main computer, which operates at a very high speed.

buffered computer   Computer that provides for simultaneous input/ output and process operations.

buffering   Delaying and temporary storing of data in a data communications path.

bug   Mistake in a computer program or system or a malfunction in a computer hardware component. To debug means to remove mistakes and correct malfunctions.

building block principles   System design that permits addition of other equipment units to form a larger system. See modularity.

built-in check   See automatic check.

built-in font   A printer font encoded permanently in the printer's read-only memory (ROM).

bulk eraser   Device used to erase information from a storage medium such as a floppy disk or tape.

bulk storage   Large-capacity data storage, generally long term.

bullet   An open or closed circle used to set off items in a list.

bulletin board service   A service that permits individuals who have personal computers to communicate with others who have similar interests. Individuals who subscribe to the service can retrieve information from a common database. Called BBS.

bundle   To include software, peripherals, and services as part of the purchase price of a computer system.

bundled software   Software included with a computer system as part of the system's total price. Contrast with unbundled.

bunny suit   The protective clothing worn by an individual in a clean room that keeps human bacteria from infecting the computer chip-making process.

burn   To ruin circuitry by subjecting it to excessive current or heat.

burn-in   Process of testing electronic circuits and components by running the circuits at elevated temperatures in an oven. A typical test might be to run components continuously for a week at 50°C (122°F). This testing process causes weak links in the circuit to burn out, the failed circuitry is replaced with components that will withstand the test.

burning   Process of programming a read only memory.

Burroughs' adding machine   First commercially practical adding-listing machine. Invented in 1884 by William Burroughs. The keyboard and mechanism remain practically unchanged in some of today's manual machines.

Burroughs, William Seward (1857-1898)   Invented the first commercial adding machine.

burst   (1) In computer operations, to separate continuous-form paper into discrete sheets. (2) In data transmission, a sequence of signals counted as one unit.

burster   Mechanical device that takes apart a multipage computer printout. Separates copies and removes carbon paper.

burst mode   Method of reading or writing data that does not permit an interrupt to occur.

bus   Channel or path for transferring data and electrical signals.

Bushnell, Nolan   In 1972, started Atari Corporation and introduced computerized game playing. Although his first game, Computer Space, was a commercial flop, he then developed many successful games: Pong, Pac Man, Space Invaders, Asteroids and Missile Command.

Bush, Vannevar (1890-1974) Trying to solve differential equations associated with power failures, he built, in 1930, the first automatic computer general enough to solve a wide variety of problems. Called a "differential analyzer," this forerunner of present-day analog computers weighed 100 tons and used thousands of vacuum-tubes.

business data processing   Data processing for business purposes, such as payroll, scheduling, and accounting.

business graphics   (1) Pie charts, bar charts, scattergrams, graphs, and other visual representations of the operational or strategic aspects of a business, such as sales vs. costs, sales by department, comparative product performance, and stock prices. (2) Applications programs that allow the user to display data as visual presentations.

business-oriented programming language   Language designed for handling large data files in business applications. See COBOL.

business programming   Branch of computer programming in which business problems are coded for computer solution. Usually involves relatively few calculations but extensive files with a large number of data inputs and outputs.

business software   Programs specifically designed for business applications. Examples are electronic spreadsheets, database management systems, business graphics packages, payroll programs, and accounting programs.

bus network   System in which all stations, or computer devices, communicate by using a common distribution channel, or bus.

bus system   Network of paths inside the computer that facilitate data flow. Important buses in a computer are identified as data bus, control bus, and address bus.

buzzwords   Words or phrases that happen to be the popular cliches of a group of people.

bypass   Parallel path around one or more elements of a circuit.

bypass capacitor   Capacitor used to reduce electrical noise from the power supply.

Byron, Ada   See Lovelace, Ada Augusta.

byte   (1) Eight binary bits of data grouped together to represent a character, digit or other value.

bytes per inch (BPI)   Number of bytes that can be contained on one inch of magnetic tape. Common measure of recording density.

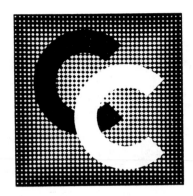

C Full name of a programming language designed for use on microcomputers. Combines high-level statements with low-level machine control to deliver software that is both easy to use and highly efficient. It is very popular with system programmers because of its transportability between computer systems. C was developed by Dennis Ritchie at Bell Laboratories in the early 1970s.

C++ An object-oriented version of the C programming language, developed by Bjarne Stroustrup in the early 1980s at Bell Laboratories. The language has been chosen by several large software publishers for major development projects. The term C++ means "more than C."

cable Electrical wire or bundle of wires used to connect two parts of the system together. Carries electrical power of electrical signals.

cable connector Male/female plug used for connecting cables between a computer and peripherals.

cache A faster memory in which parts of the information in the main (slower) memory or disk are copied. Information that is likely to require reading or alteration goes to the cache, where the system can access it more quickly. Caching can significantly speed processing of some programs, especially if floppy disks are used for mass storage.

caching Retaining data in cache memory for rapid access.

CAD Acronym for Computer-Aided Design, a term applied to programs and computer systems used in designing engineering, architecture and scientific models. The process involves direct, real-time communication between a designer and a computer, generally by the use of a CRT display and a light pen, mouse, or graphics tablet. Some CAD applications create objects in two or three dimensions, presenting the result as wire-frame "skeletons," as models with shaded surfaces, or as solid objects.

CADAM Acronym for Computer Augmented Design And Manufacturing, the process of or methods for using computer systems as tools in design and manufacturing applications.

CAD/CAM Acronym for Computer-Aided Design/Compute-Aided Manufacturing.

CADD See Computer-Aided Design and Drafting.

CAE Computer-Aided Engineering; analyzes a design for basic error-checking, or to optimize manufacturability, performance, and economy. Information drawn from the CAD/CAM design database is used to analyze the functional characteristics of a part, product, or system under design, and to simulate its performance under various conditions.

cage See card cage.

CAI Acronym for Computer-Assisted Instruction.

CAL Acronym for Computer-Augmented Learning.

calculating Reconstructing or creating new data by compressing certain numeric facts.

calculations Mathematical processes performed on data.

calculator Any mechanical or electronic machine used for performing calculations. Calculators, as distinguished from computers, usually require frequent human intervention.

calculator mode Operating mode on come interactive computer systems that allows the terminal (or keyboard/display in the case of microcomputer systems) to be used as a desk calculator. The user types an expression; the computer then evaluates it and returns the answer immediately.

calibration Process of determining by measurement or by comparison with a standard the correct value of each scale reading on a meter or the correct value of each setting of a control knob.

call (1) To transfer control to a specific closed subroutine. (2) In communications, the action performed by the calling party, or the operations necessary in making a call, or the effective use made of a connection between two stations.

callback PPD A port protection device that screens incoming calls.

calligraphic graphics Method of forming an image from scan lines oriented in arbitrary directions and drawn in an arbitrary order. Expensive electronics are required, but spatial anti-aliasing is not. Typical of this style of graphics are the "wire-frame" models that were considered synonymous with computer graphics in the early days.

calling sequence Specified set of instructions and data necessary to call a given subroutine.

call instruction Instruction that, after diverting execution to a new sequence of instructions, permits return to the program's original sequence.

Canadian Information Processing Society (CIPS) Organization formed to bring together Canadians with a common interest in the field of information processing. Has a membership of scientists, business people, and others who make their careers in computing and information processing.

cancel Keyboard operation that deletes the line currently being typed.

candidates Alternative plans offered in the preliminary design phase of a project.

canned software Programs prepared by computer manufacturers or software developers and provided to a user in ready-to-use form. General enough to be used by many businesses and individuals. Contrast with custom software.

Canon engine The internal mechanism of a Canon office photocopier, used in many laser printers.

Canvas A power-packed multi-purpose drawing and painting program for the Apple Macintosh computer. With 24-bit color, unlimited layers, Bezier curves, precision tools, bit-mapped editing at high resolutions, and full color separation, it combines color capabilities and powerful object-editing options with a friendly interface and ease of use. Other features include fractional leading and kerning, tab support within a text block, text-wrapping around irregular objects and binding text to any curve/shape. It also includes object-blending from one shape to another, splitting/combining of objects, custom gradient color fills, the ability to edit multiple Bezier curve anchor points simultaneously and EPSF, CGM, and Illustrator import/export translators.

CAP Acronym for Computer Aided Publishing.

capacitance Measure of the ability to store electric charge, the basic unit of measurement being a farad.

capacitor Electronic component that stores a charge of static electricity and, when properly stimulated, releases this charge. This is the way bits are written to and read from computer storage.

capacitor storage Storage device that utilizes the capacitance properties of materials to store data.

capacity Number of items of data that a storage device is capable of containing. Frequently defined in terms of computer words, bytes, or characters.

cap height The height of a capital letter from the baseline.

caps Capital letters. All caps means that all letters are capitalized; initial caps means the capitalization of the first letter of each significant word.

capstan Rotating shaft within a magnetic tape drive that pulls the tape across the recording heads at a constant speed.

capture (of data)   Recording of data on a form or its entry into a computer.

carbon ribbon   Ribbon used with printers to produce extremely sharp characters with excellent definition.

card   (1) Printed circuit board. (2) Storage medium in which data are represented by means of holes punched in vertical columns in an 7.37 inch by 3.25 inch (18.7 cm by 8.3 cm) paper card.

card cage   Chassis inside the computer housing on which printed circuit boards are mounted.

card code   Combinations of punched holes that represent characters in a punched card.

card column   One of the vertical lines of punching positions on a punched card.

card field   Fixed number of consecutive punched card columns assigned to a unit of information.

card hopper   Device that holds punched cards and makes them available for the feeding mechanism of card handling equipment.

cardinality   In object-oriented programming, the number of instances that a class may have; the number of instances that participate in a using class relationship.

cardinal number   A number that indicates how many items there are in a set. For example, if "file 21 contains 10 graphic images," 21 is ordinal; 10 is cardinal. See ordinal number.

card punch   Output device that accepts information from the computer's memory and punches it into cards.

card reader   (1) Input device that reads information punched into cards and transfers it into the computer's memory. (2) A device designed to read the magnetic strip on the back of credit cards.

card row   One of the horizontal lines of punching positions on a punched card.

carriage   Control mechanism for a printer that automatically feeds, skips, spaces, and ejects paper forms.

carriage return (CR)   In a character printer the operation that causes the next character to be printed at the left margin.

carrier frequency   Constant signal transmitted between communicating devices that is modulated to encode binary information.

carry (1) Process of bringing forward. Special condition that occurs when the sum of two digits in a single column is equal to or greater than the number base. (2) Carry digit, or the digit to be added to the next higher column.

CARS Acronym for Computer Assisted Retrieval System. A system locating off-line archival document storage on microfiche cartridges or microfilm rolls.

Cartesian coordinate system System named for French mathematician Rene Descartes whereby, in a flat plane, a point can be located by its distances from two intersecting straight lines, called the axes, the distance from one axis being measured along a parallel to the other axis. The numbers associated with the point are called the coordinates of the point.

cartridge A generic term that can refer to any of several devices that are self-contained, usually in some kind of plastic housing. For example, ROM cartridge, disk cartridge, toner cartridge, memory cartridge, tape cartridge, or font cartridge.

cartridge font A series of typefaces contained in ROM chips mounted within a plastic module called a cartridge. The cartridge is placed in a compatible laser printer to allow it to use the typefaces.

cascade connection Two or more similar component devices arranged in tandem, with the output of one connected to the input of the next.

cascade control Automatic control system in which the control units are linked chain fashion, each feeding into, as well as regulating, the next stage.

cascade sort External tape sort that sorts by merging strings from all but one tape onto the remaining tape. Subsequent passes merge fewer tapes until one tape contains all items.

CASE An acronym for Computer-Aided Software Engineering. A combination of techniques and tools aimed at building and maintaining software systems of all types—large and small, commercial and scientific, on-line and real-time. CASE tools provide coverage of the software life cycle by providing auto analysis, design, implementation and maintenance as well as project management of software systems.

cashless society Computerized system in which purchase transactions would be settled instantaneously by transferring credits from the buyer's bank account to the seller's account. No cash would ever be exchanged, with EFT deposits replacing paychecks as well as payments for goods and services.

cassette recorder Device designed to use cassettes to record and store digital data and at a later time, reload this data into the computer's internal storage. Used with early microcomputer systems.

catalog Ordered compilation of item descriptions and sufficient information to afford access to the items, such as a listing of programs or data file names that are stored on a diskette. To catalog a disk is to instruct the computer to print out a list of all of the files on the disk.

catena Connected series.

cathode ray tube (CRT) Electronic tube with a screen upon which information may be displayed.

CBASIC A compiler BASIC programming language. A CBASIC program is translated into object code before it is executed. Program execution time is much faster than the more popular interpreter BASIC.

CBEMA See Computer and Business Equipment Manufacturers Association.

CCP Acronym for Certificate in Computer Programming. CCP examinations are given annually at test centers in colleges and universities in the United States, Canada, and several international locations. Three separate full-day examinations test a common core of programming knowledge and an area of specialization: business programming, scientific programming, or systems programming. The common core of knowledge emphasizes such areas as data and file organization, techniques of programming, programming languages, interaction with hardware and software, and interaction with people. The certificate is awarded by the Institute for Certification of Computer Professionals.

CD Acronym for Compact Disc, a 4 5/8-inch silver platter used for audio recordings. Compact, durable, and capable of extraordinary fidelity, the CD is an excellent long-lasting recording medium. See CD-ROM.

CD-I Acronym for Compact Disc-Interactive. A small optical disc system that is under the interactive control of the user.

CDP Acronym for Certificate in Data Processing. CDP examinations are given annually at test centers in colleges and universities in the United States, Canada, and several international locations. This broad-based examination consists of five sections and requires half a day to complete. In addition to having experience requirements and espousing the Code of Ethics, CDP candidates must successfully complete all five sections of the examination to receive the certificate. The certificate is awarded by the Institute for Certification of Computer Professionals.

CD player A device that reads the information stored on a compact disc.

CDR A CoralDraw object file format.

CD-ROM An acronym for compact disc read-only memory, a type of optical disc that uses the same basic technology as do the popular CD audio discs. Although a CD-ROM drive can only read data (the data is permanently stamped onto the discs during manufacturing), the discs are

44

inexpensive to make and can each hold about 650 megabytes of data. Contents are typically an entire encyclopedia on a single CD, a set of reference works, a clip-art library, a collection of fine art or any other publication which is for reading only.

cell (1) Storage for one unit of information, usually one character, one byte, or one word. A binary cell is a cell of one binary digit capacity. (2) Single coordinate location within the grid, or matrix, that constitutes the basic form of an electronic spreadsheet.

cell address In a spreadsheet, the column and row coordinates of a cell.

cell animation An animation technique in which a background painting is held stationary while animated images are moved over the painting, producing the illusion of movement. Animation programs are available that perform cell animation.

cell contents The label, value, formula, or function contained in a spreadsheet cell.

centering Word processing and page layout program feature that places a line of text midway between the left and right margins.

centralized data processing Concept by which a company has all its computing equipment located at the same site, and field-office operations have no effective data processing capability. Contrast with distributed data processing.

centralized network configuration Structure of a computer network whose dominating feature is a central computer that, one way or another, is involved in everything that happens in the system.

central processing unit (CPU) Major component of a computer system with the circuitry to control the interpretation and execution of instructions.

Centronics interface A defacto facto standard for parallel data exchange paths between computers and peripherals. Centronics Corporation was one of the original printer manufacturers to use the parallel scheme for communications between computers and printers. The 36-pin parallel interface was introduced in 1970.

Certificate in Computer Programming See CCP.

Certificate in Data Processing See CDP.

certification (1) Acceptance of software by an authorized agent, usually after the software has been validated by the agent, or after its validity has been demonstrated to the agent. (2) Voluntary system of attesting that a person has achieved a certain professional status, usually by passing a rigorous examination. See CCP and CDP.

CG An acronym for Computer Graphics, any graphical element created with the aid of a computer.

CGA   Acronym for Color/Graphics Adapter. The original low-resolution color standard for IBM compatible microcomputers, introduced by the IBM Corporation in 1981. The CGA is capable of several character and graphics modes. CGA has been superceded by EGA and VGA.

CGM   Acronym for Computer Graphics Metafile. A standard object oriented graphics file format. CGM stores images primarily in vector graphics, but also provides a raster format.

chain   (1) Linking of records by means of pointers in such a way that all like records are connected, the last record pointing to the first (2) Set of operations that are to be performed sequentially.

chained files   Data files where data blocks are chained together by using pointers.

chained list   List in which each item points to the next item and the order of retrieval need not have any relation to the storage order.

chain field   Field in a record that defines the location and storage device of other data items logically related to the original record but not physically attached.

chaining   (1) Process of linking a series of records, programs, or operations together. (2) Method of allowing the execution of programs larger than the main memory of a computer by loading and executing modules of the same program sequentially.

chaining search   Technique used for retrieving data from a file by using addresses in the records that link each record to the next in the chain.

chain printer   Impact line printer that has its character set assembled on a chain revolving horizontally past all print positions; it prints when a print hammer (one for each column on the paper) presses the paper against an inked ribbon that in turn presses against the appropriate characters on the aligned print chain.

chamfer   A beveled edge between two intersecting lines.

change agent   The role of the systems analyst in overcoming resistance to change within an organization.

channel   (1) Path for electrical or electronic transmission between two or more points. Also called a path, link, line, facility, or circuit. (2) Transmission path that connects auxiliary devices to a computer.

channel adapter   Device that enables data communications between channels on different hardware devices.

channel capacity   In data communications, an expression of the maximum number of bits per second that can be accommodated by the channel. This maximum number is determined by the bandwidth modulation scheme and certain types of noise. The channel capacity is most often measured in bauds, or bits per second.

character Any symbol, digit, letter, or punctuation mark—including the blank character—stored or processed by computing equipment.

character checking Checking of each character by examining all characters as a group or field.

character code Code designating a unique numerical representation for a set of characters.

character density See density.

character generator Circuit that forms the letters or numbers on a screen or printer.

character graphics A set of special symbols that are placed together to create graphics.

characteristic That part of a floating-point number that represents the size of the exponent. See mantissa.

character pitch In a line of text, the number of characters per inch.

character printer Printer in which only a single character is composed and determined within the device prior to printing.

character recognition Technology of using machines to identify human-readable symbols automatically, and then to express their identities in machine-readable codes. This operation of transforming numbers and letters into a form directly suitable for electronic data processing is an important method of introducing information into computing systems.

character set All of the numbers, letters, and symbols associated with a given device or coding system. All of the characters recognized by a computer system.

characters per inch Method of expression the output from dot matrix and daisy wheel printers as determined by type size and style. Abbreviated cpi.

characters per second Unit for measuring output of low-speed serial printers. Abbreviated cps.

character string String of alphanumeric characters.

charge coupled device (CCD) Semiconductor memory device within which stored information circulates rather than remains in fixed locations.

Charles Babbage Institute Organization for the study of the information revolution from a historical perspective. Intended as a clearinghouse for information about research resources related to this history and a repository for archival materials.

chart (1) Visual representation of quantitative information—such as a bar graph, in which the information is made visual by heavy horizontal or vertical lines, or a circle graph or pie chart, in which the information is pictured as slices of an imaginary pie. (2) See flowchart and structure chart.

chassis Metal frame upon which the wiring, sockets, and other parts of an electronic assembly are mounted.

check bit A bit added to each byte to alert the computer to an error in data transmission. Also called a parity bit.

check digits One or more digits carried within a unit item of numerical data to provide information about the other digits in the unit in such a manner that, if a transcription or transposition error occurs in subsequent data entry, the check fails, and an indication of error is given.

checkout See debug.

checkpoint Specified point at which a program can be interrupted, either manually or by a control routine. Used primarily as an aid in debugging programs.

check problem Testing problem designed to determine whether a computer or a computer program is operating correctly.

check sum Summation of digits or bits used primarily for checking purposes and summed according to an arbitrary set of rules. Used to verify the integrity of data.

chiclet keyboard A type of microcomputer keyboard. The name was derived from the chewing gum because the keys are small and square, resembling the gum pieces. Chiclet keys are much smaller and typically spread out, so touch typing is more difficult than on a conventional keyboard. An undesirable keyboard used in older low-cost microcomputers; however, a useful keyboard in systems for children and handicapped people.

chief information officer Manager of an MIS department.

chief programmer team A software development team structure in which one programmer is assigned overall responsibility for the project.

child Data record that can be created only based upon the contents of one or more other records (parents) already in existence.

chip Small component that contains a large amount of electronic circuitry. Thin silicon wafer on which electronic components are deposited in the form of integrated circuits. Chips are the building blocks of a computer and perform various functions, such as doing arithmetic, serving as the computer's memory, or controlling other chips.

chip-carrier The intermediate physical package into which the die is mounted.

chip family Group of related chips, each of which (except the first) evolved from an earlier chip in the family. For example, the Intel Corporation's family of 80x86 microprocessors: 80286, 80386, 80486.

chooser In the Apple Macintosh environment, a desktop accessory that allows the user to select a device driver to be used by the system.

chop To discard unneeded data.

chroma Color attributes, such as saturation, shade, and hue.

chromaticity Dominant wavelength and purity of a color as objectively measured; corresponds to hue and saturation of the color without regard to brightness.

chrominance Portions of composite video signal controlling color.

chunking along Slang term referring to the operation of a long running, dependable program.

churning See thrashing.

CIM Acronym for Computer Input Microfilm.

cipher Secret method of representing information to ensure computer security.

ciphertext A term used to describe data that has been encrypted.

circuit (1) Pathway designed for the controlled flow of electrons. (2) System of conductors and related electrical elements through which electrical currents flow. (3) Communication link between two or more points.

circuit board Thin insulating board used to mount and connect various electronic components and microchips in a pattern of conductive lines. This circuit pattern is etched into the board's surface.

circuit capacity Number of channels in a circuit that can be dealt with simultaneously.

circuit card See circuit board.

circuitry Complex of circuits describing interconnection within or between systems.

circuit switching Physical connection between two nodes in a communication network that dedicates bandwidth of that circuit until the connection is dropped.

circular list Linked list, usually of data elements, in which the last element points to the first one.

circular shift Shifting operation whereby bits or characters shifted off one end of a register enter the register on the opposite end.

CIU Acronym for computer interface unit.

cladding A glass or plastic sheath that surrounds the core of an optical fiber. It keeps the light waves inside the core by bouncing the light waves back into the core of the unit.

Claris CAD A full-featured, easy-to-use, two-dimensional computer-aided design program for the Apple Macintosh computer from Claris Corporation. Claris CAD gives one the power to create accurate, professional illustrations and drawings.

class In object-oriented programming, the description of a set of nearly identical objects that share common methods and general characteristics. The terms "class" and "type" are usually interchangeable; a class is a slightly different concept than a type, in that it emphasizes the importance of hierarchies of classes.

class category In object-oriented programming, a collection of classes, some of which are visible to other class categories, and others of which are hidden.

class diagram In object-oriented programming, part of the notation of object-oriented design, used to show the existence of classes and their relationships in the logical design of a system. A class diagram may represent all or part of the class structure of a system.

classify To categorize or place data with similar characteristics into the same category.

class library In object-oriented programming, a collection of generic classes that can be adapted and tailored for a particular application.

class structure In object-oriented programming, the "kind of" hierarchy of a system; a graph whose vertices represent classes and whose arcs represent relationships among these classes. The class structure of a system is represented by a set of class diagrams.

class variable In object-oriented programming, a placeholder for part of the state of a class. Collectively, the class variables of a class constitute its structure. A class variable is shared by all instances of the same class.

clean room A room in which dust and other small particles are filtered from the air and in which protective clothing is worn to avoid contaminating electronics components and other delicate, sensitive equipment.

clear (1) Keyboard function that removes the contents from the display screen. (2) Same as zap.

clearing Replacing the information in a register, storage location, or storage unit with zeros or blanks.

click Means to point the mouse pointer at a word or icon on the screen, press the mouse button, and then release it quickly. Clicking is usually performed to select or deselect an item or to activate a program or program feature.

click art Clip art on a diskette or CD-ROM. A floppy disk or CD-ROM of professionally drawn pictures that are ready to copy and use in computer produced documents.

client (1) In object-oriented programming, an object that uses the resources of another, either by operating upon it or by referencing its state. (2) An individual or organization contracting for systems analysis.

client/server A relationship between machines in a communications network. The client is the requesting machine; the server is the supplying machine.

clip art Collections of pictures and design elements (such as borders, symbols, drawings, etc.). The collections may be in printed form or stored on diskettes or CD-ROM. This pre-drawn artwork can be used in designing newsletters, brochures, flyers, books, magazines and incorporated into other documents.

clipboard A temporary holding place that facilitates the cutting and pasting of text and graphics. Clipboard information is held in memory only while the computer is turned on. A clipboard allows information to be transferred from one program to another. A clipboard stores a copy of the last information that was "copied" or "cut." A "paste" operation passes data from the clipboard to the current program.

clipping Removing portions of an image that are outside the boundaries of the edge of a window or display screen. Certain graphics programs also support clipping as a means of masking everything but a certain object so that painting tools, for example, can be applied to the object alone.

clipping path A curve or polygon that is used to mask an area in a document. Only what is inside the clipping path appears when the document is printed.

clobber To write new data over the top of good data in a file or otherwise damage a file so that it becomes useless. To wipe out a file.

clock (1) Timing device that generates the basic periodic signal used to control the timing of all operations in a computer. (2) Device that records the progress of real time, or some approximation of it, and whose contents are available to a computer program.

clocking Technique used to synchronize a sending and a receiving data communications device. Permits synchronous transmission at high speeds.

clock pulse Synchronization signal provided by a clock.

clock rate Time rate at which pulses are emitted from a clock.

clock track Track on which a pattern of signals has been recorded to provide a time reference.

clockwise Moving from left to right.

clone In nonbiological terms, a product or idea that is an exact duplicate or copy of another. A computer or a software program that duplicates another program exactly (e.g., a personal computer that closely imitates the operation and architecture of the IBM PS/2 computer).

CLOS An acronym for Common Lisp Object System, a system where the user can experiment not only with object-oriented progamming (OOP), but with the design of object-oriented programming systems.

close box A small box at the upper left-hand corner of a window used to close the window.

closed architecture Personal computer design that limits add-ons to those that can be plugged into the back of the machine.

closed file File that cannot be accessed for reading or writing. Contrast with open file.

closed loop Loop that is completely circular.

closed routine See closed subroutine

closed shop Operation of the data processing center by professional operators. Programs and data are carried by messengers or transmitted over telephone lines, avoiding the necessity of users entering the computer room and enabling a much more efficient use of the computer. Contrast with open shop.

closed subroutine Subroutine stored at one place and linked to one or more calling routines. Contrast with open subroutine.

cluster controller Down-line processor that collects data from a number of low-speed devices then transmits concentrated data over a single communications channel.

clustered devices Group of terminals connected to a common controller.

clustering (1) In object-oriented progamming, the storing of objects contiguously on a disk for efficient accessing. (2) Grouping things with similar characteristics.

CLV An abbreviation for Constant Linear Velocity, a method of packing more data onto a disk by making sure the rate at which the disk passes the head stays the same on the outer tracks as on the inner tracks. In practice, that means changing the disk's rotation speed as the head moves in and out.

CMI Acronym for Computer-Managed Instruction.

CML Acronym for Current Mode Logic.

CMOS An abbreviation for Complementary Metal-Oxide Semiconductor, a technology for making integrated circuits that use very little power. This technology is popular both for portables and for desktop computers, partly because it produces less heat than other integrated circuits. Invented by Frank Wanlass in the mid-1960s.

CMY Abbreviation for Cyan, Magenta, Yellow. Color mixing system used to print colors.

CMYK Abbreviation for Cyan, Magenta, Yellow, Key/Black. The color model used in the printing color separation process. The colors of this model are also known as process colors, and are based on the three main tones of printing inks used in much color reproduction.

coaxial cable Special type of communications cable that permits transmission of data at high speed. Usually employed in local networks.

COBOL Acronym for COmmon Business-Oriented Language, a high-level language developed for business data processing applications. Every COBOL source program has four divisions: (1) Identification Division identifies the source program and output of a compilation; (2) Environment Division specifies those aspects of a data processing problem that are dependent upon the physical characteristics of a particular computer; (3) Data Division describes the data that the object program is to accept as input, manipulate, create, or produce as output; and (4) Procedure Division specifies the procedures to be performed by the object program, using English-like statements. COBOL was formally adopted in 1960; it stemmed from FLOWMATIC, a language developed by Grace Hopper in the mid-1950s.

CODASYL Acronym (pronounced code-a-sill) for Conference On Data Systems And Languages, a federally sponsored industry committee that developed standards that led to the COBOL language and many of the more complex types of databases. Founded in 1959, it is made up of individuals and institutions that contribute their own time and effort.

code (1) Set of rules outlining the way in which data may be represented. (2) Rules used to convert data from one representation to another. (3) To write a program or routine. Same as encode.

code conversion   Process for changing the bit groupings for characters in one code into the corresponding character bit groupings for a second code.

coded decimal number   Number consisting of successive characters or a group of characters that usually represents a specific figure in an associated decimal number.

Code of Fair Information Practices   The code published in a report prepared by the Department of Health, Education, and Welfare resulted in the passage of the Privacy Act of 1974.

coder   One who expresses a problem design, or part of a problem, in a computer language."Coder" is often used in the derogatory sense of a person who does little analysis and planning, but merely expresses someone else's design in a computer language.

code set   Complete set of representations defined by a code. All of the two-letter post office identifications for the 50 states constitute a code set.

coding   (1) Writing a list of instructions that will cause a computer to perform specified operations. (2) Ordered list or lists of the successive instructions that will cause a computer to perform a particular process.

coding form   Form on which the instructions for programming a computer are written. Each programming language has its own coding form.

coercion   In programming language expressions, an automatic conversion from one data type to another.

COGO   Acronym for COordinate GeOmetry, a problem-oriented programming language used to solve geometric problems. Used primarily by civil engineers.

coherence   Assumption used in raster scan display technology that attributes the same value of an individual pixel to its adjacent pixel.

cohesion   A measure of the inner strength of a program module.

cold boot   Act of turning a computer on and loading an operating system into it.

cold fault   Computer fault that is apparent as soon as the machine is switched on.

cold site   An environmentally suitable empty shell in which a company can install its own computer system.

cold start   Restart activity used when a serious failure has occurred in a system, making the contents of the direct access storage inaccessible so that no trace of the recent processing can be used. The system must be reloaded and activity restarted as though at the beginning of a day. More simply, restarting the computer by turning it off and then on again—all programs and data in memory are lost.

collate To merge two or more sequenced data sets to produce a resulting data set that reflects the sequencing of the original sets.

collating sort Sort that uses a technique of continuous merging of data until one sequence is developed.

collation sequence Order that the computer will use when it arranges items from first to last. Typically, this order is alphabetical for words and numerical for numbers. However, the question becomes complex when one must take into account upper-case and lower-case, mixed numbers and words, punctuation, numbers that are not filled to the same length with leading zeros, and other factors.

collection Process of gathering data from various sources and assembling it at one location.

collector Section of a semiconductor device towards which electricity flows.

collision (1) Result of keys colliding at the same address when two keyboard operations are ordered simultaneously. Programming in the computer's operating system defines which operation will be performed. (2) The problem that occurs when two records have the same disk address.

collision detection (1) In computer graphics, particularly in arcade-type games, a program often must determine when two objects have collided. Several programming techniques may be used to detect a collision. (2) Task performed in a multiple-access network to prevent two computers from transmitting at the same time.

color The hue perceived for different wavelengths in the portion of the electromagnetic spectrum to which the human eye responds. It is possible to create almost all visible colors using two systems of primary colors. Transmitted colors use red, green and blue (RGB), and reflected colors use cyan, magenta, and yellow (CMY). Color displays use RGB and color printers use CMY.

color bits A predetermined number of adjacent bits assigned to each displayable pixel that determines its color when it is shown on a display screen. For example, 2 color bits are required for 4 colors, 4 color bits are required for 16 colors, 8 color bits are required for 256 colors, and 24 color bits are required for over 16 million colors.

color burst signal Signal present in composite video output that provides color information. Sometimes turning off the color burst signal improves the quality of pictures on black-and-white monitors.

color coding Process of identifying records by using different colors for different types of records.

color graphics Any type of computer graphic in which the images displayed on a visual display screen, printed copy, or other type of display are shown in more than one color.

color model Any method for representing color in graphic arts and desktop publishing. In the graphic arts and printing areas, colors are often specified with the Pantone system. In computer graphics, colors can be described using any of several different color systems: RGB (red, green, blue), CMY (cyan, magenta, and yellow), and HSB (hue, saturation, and brightness).

color monitor A computer display designed to work with a video card or adapter to produce text or graphics image in color. A color monitor has a screen coated internally with three phosphors—one each for red, green and blue. To light the phosphor and produce a spot of color, such a monitor also usually contains three electron guns—again, one for each of the three colors.

color printer Output device that can produce text, charts, graphics, and artwork in several colors. Dot matrix, ink-jet, thermal-transfer and laser printers can print full-color output.

color resolution The number of different colors or gray-scale values a system can produce or work with. A value is usually given in bits.

ColorRIX A draw/paint program for IBM-compatible microcomputers. In addition to the usual draw/paint tools, the program includes several scalable bit-mapped fonts, a printing/screen capture feature, a presentation slide show, an application/language independent screen loader and sophisticated animation effects.

color saturation The amount of a hue contained in a color; the more saturation, the more intense the color.

color separation The creation of a multicolor graphic by creating several layers, with each layer corresponding to one of the colors that will be printed when the graphic is reproduced by a commercial printer.

ColorStudio An Apple Macintosh 24-bit true color imaging program for graphics arts professionals. It allows for merging high-resolution color photos, video captures, pixel artwork and PostScript type. Features include powerful paint and retouching tools, a full density gray scale mask and six pressure tools: airbrush, charcoal, paintbrush, pencil waterdrop, and finger tip. Painting and selection tools can be customized for photo-retouching, masking and special effects. It allows for precise calibrating its own color balance as well as that of other applications.

COLOSSUS Special-purpose computer developed in 1943 to crack German codes.

column (1) Vertical numbers of one line of an array. (2) One of the vertical lines of punching positions on a punched card. (3) Position of information in a computer word. (4) Horizontal division of an electronic spreadsheet. Together with rows, columns serve to form the spreadsheet matrix. Contrast with row.

COM Acronym for Computer Output Microfilm.

combination logic Circuit arrangement in which the output state is determined by the present state of the input. Digital system not utilizing memory elements.

combinatorial explosion Condition that occurs in problem solving when the possibilities to be examined become too numerous for the computer. Can occur even with very large computers.

combinatorics Study of methods of counting how many objects there are of some type, or how many ways there are to do something—combinations and permutations.

COMDEX The largest computer trade show in the world. Held semi-annually in Atlanta and Las Vegas in the United States and in other locations throughout the world.

COMIT One of the string processing languages.

command (1) Control signal. (2) Loosely, a mathematical or logic operator. (3) Loosely, a computer instruction.

command-chained memory Technique used in dynamic storage allocation.

command-driven software Software that takes action as a result of the user typing single letter, word, or line commands.

command key Any keyboard key used to perform specific functions.

command language Language used to give instructions to an operating system.

command menu The list of commands in an applications software program.

command processing Reading, analyzing, and performing of computer instructions.

command processor The part of an operating system that accepts commands from the user for operating system tasks. Also called a shell.

command tree A hierarchical diagram that shows all the choices from a main command menu and the associated submenus.

comments English prose that may be interspersed among the computer-language statements of a computer program to explain their action to human readers of the program. Special markers on the comments cause the computer to ignore them. Properly done comments are a valuable form of internal documentation because they are embedded in the program itself, therefore they stay with the program. Comments provide helpful notes for future users who may later attempt to understand or alter the program.

Commodore 64/128 The Commodore 64 is a home computer introduced in 1982 by Commodore Business Machines, Inc. Over 10 million of these machines have been sold worldwide. The Commodore 128 was an upgraded Commodore 64 that was introduced in 1986.

Commodore Business Machines, Inc. Manufacturer of the Amiga family of microcomputers and several older microcomputers including the popular Commodore 64.

common carrier Government-regulated private company that provides telephone, telegraph, and other telecommunications facilities for public use.

common language Computer programming language sensible to two or more computers with different machine languages. BASIC, COBOL, FORTRAN, and Pascal are common languages.

Common Lisp Object System (CLOS) An object-oriented version of the artificial intelligence language, LISP.

common storage Section of memory for each user that holds data or parameters that are accessible to all programs.

communicating Process of transmitting information to a point of use.

communicating word processors Network of word processors used to transmit electronic mail.

communication (1) Flow of information from one point (the source) to another (the receiver). (2) Act of transmitting or making known. (3) Process by which information is exchanged between individuals through the use of a commonly accepted set of symbols.

communications channel Physical means of connecting one location or device to another for the purpose of transmitting and receiving data. Coaxial cables, fiber optics, microwave signals, telephone lines, and satellite communications all serve as communications channels.

communications control unit Usually, a small computer whose only job is to handle the flow of data communications traffic to and from a mainframe computer.

communications link Method by which information is transmitted between computer devices.

communications processor Computer that provides a path for data transfer between the computer system and the data communications network.

communications protocol Set of communication rules that provides for error checking between devices and ensures that transmitted data are not lost.

Communications Satellite Corporation (COMSAT) Privately owned U.S. communications carrier company operating under a mandate from Congress. American representative in the INTELSAT organization, it provides technical and operational services for the global communications system. Traffic on the system is coordinated through an operations center in Washington, D. C.

communications satellites Earth satellites placed in different spots in the geostationary orbit 22,250 miles (36,000 km) above the equator that serve as relay stations for communications signals transmitted from Earth stations. These satellites orbit Earth once every 24 hours, giving the impression that they are "parked" in one spot over the equator. Once in this orbit, a satellite is capable of reaching 43 percent of Earth's surface with a single radio signal.

communications server Device that connects local area networks to wide area or telecommunications networks.

communications software Programs that allow computers to communicate through a modem. Some communications programs are capable of automatic telecommunications, such as auto-answering, auto-dialing, and even dialing another computer at a preset time to establish communication and send and receive information. Some programs allow operation of an unattended remote computer—accessing disk files, operating peripherals, and so forth.

communications system System that consists of senders, physical channels, and receivers of data communications.

compact disc An optical disc, a nonmagnetic, shiny metal disc used to store digital information.

compaction Packing of data structures to make room in storage.

compact keyboard A keyboard with reduced-size keys or reduced spacing between keys.

Compaq Computer Corporation A manufacturer of IBM-compatible microcomputers. Founded in 1982, Compaq has become an industry leader and is known for producing reliable computers.

comparative sort Sort by comparison of two or more keys.

comparator Device for checking the accuracy of transcribed data by comparing it with a second transcription, noting any variation between the two.

compare operation An operation in which the computer compares two data items and performs alternative operations based on the comparison.

compart Computer art.

compatibility (1) Property of some computers that allows programs written for one computer to run on another (compatible) computer, even though it is a different model. (2) Ability of different devices, such as a computer and a printer, to work together. (3) Refers to the ability of specific software to work with a specific brand and model of computer. All software is not "compatible" with all computers.

compatible (1) Pertains to the degree of interworking possible between two devices or systems. If an element in a system is fully compatible with the functional and physical characteristics of a system, it can be incorporated into the system without modification (2) Personal computer that can run software designed for the IBM PC and/or IBM PS/2 computers.

compatible software Programs that can be run on different computers without modification.

compilation One of two principal means of translating programs written in high-level languages into machine-language instructions that can be directly executed by the processor. Entails translating a complete program before any execution. Contrast with interpretation, in which each instruction is translated when it is to be executed.

compilation time Time during which a source-language program is translated (compiled) into an object program (machine language).

compile To prepare a machine-language program or a program expressed in symbolic coding from a program written in high-level programming language such as COBOL, or Pascal.

compile-and-go Operating technique by which the loading and execution phases of a program compilation are performed in one continuous run. Especially useful when a program must be compiled for a one-time application.

compiler Computer program whose purpose is that of translating high-level-language statements into a form that can directly activate the computer hardware. Translates a complete program before any execution.

compiler-compiler Same as metacompiler.

compiler language Source language that uses a compiler to translate the language statements into an object language.

compiler program See compiler.

compile time Time required to compile a program. The point in the processing of a program when it is being translated from source code to object code by a translator (compiler).

complement Number used to represent the negative of a given number.

Obtained by subtracting each digit of the number from the number representing its base and, in the case of two's complement and ten's complement, adding unity to the last significant digit.

complementary constant current logic   See C^{3}L.

complementary MOS (CMOS)   Method of making metallic oxide semiconductor (MOS) chips that uses almost no power and works faster than MOS. Not very good for LSI, but used in electronic watches and clocks where power has to come from a battery.

completeness check   Establishes that none of the fields is missing and that the entire record has been checked.

component   Basic part; element; part of a computer system; portion of an application.

composite   Type of video signal in which all three primary video color signals (red, green, blue) are combined, which limits the sharpness of the monitor image. Used in some monitors and TV set that use only one electron gun to generate the three primary colors.

composite symbol   Symbol consisting of more than one character, such as the composite symbol < >, which stands for "not equal to" in some software systems.

composite video   Color output from a computer color display described in terms of its hue and its brightness and encoded in a single video signal. The color control signal is a single data stream that must be decoded into three colors (red, green, and blue). Inexpensive color monitors, called composite monitors, use composite video and produce a slightly better picture than a TV set but not the high quality of RGB monitors.

composition   The selection of type sizes and styles and the positioning of type on a page.

compound statement   Single instruction that contains two or more instructions that could otherwise be used separately.

compressed file   A file that a file compression utility has written to a special disk format that minimizes the storage space required.

CompuServe   Major information service network used by individuals as well as businesses. Carries timely news features, stock market reports, electronic mail, educational programs, legal advice, travel reservations, encyclopedia references, games, programming aids, and more. Personal computer owners can reference the CompuServe network via the common telephone system.

computability   Property by which computational problems are classified.

computation   Result of computing.

compute-bound Pertaining to a program or computer system that is restricted or limited by the speed of the central processing unit. Same as processor bound.

computed field A file field that is based on the values of other fields.

computed radiography A diagnostic imaging technique that directs X-rays at the patient as conventional X-ray units do, but develops the image immediately by scanning with a laser beam, a process that also digitizes the image.

computed tomography A diagnostic imaging technique that directs X-rays axially around a patient and computes a two-dimensional image of the body slice that is displayed on a cathode ray tube.

computer Device capable of solving problems or manipulating data by accepting data, performing prescribed operations (mathematical or logical) on the data, and supplying the results of these operations.

computer accessories The equipment that can be attached to a computer, such as mouse, disk drive, visual display device, keyboard, or printer.

computer-aided design (CAD) Computer systems and programs used in designing tools, automobiles, buildings, aircraft, molecules, farm equipment, integrated circuits, and thousands of other products. Computer-aided design has become a mainstay in a variety of design related fields, such as architecture, mechanical engineering, interior design, civil engineering and electrical engineering. CAD applications are graphics and calculation-intensive, requiring fast computers and high-resolution video displays.

computer-aided design and drafting (CADD) The use of a computer system for industrial design and technical drawing.

computer-aided design/computer-aided manufacturing (CAD/CAM) Efforts to automate design and manufacturing operations, a rapidly-growing branch of computer graphics, currently relying primarily on calligraphic graphics but branching out to incorporate raster graphics. Wide-ranging uses include designing auto parts, buildings, and integrated circuits.

computer-aided factory management System for managing a production facility in which computers schedule operations, keep accurate accounts on parts inventories, and order new supplies as required from supply houses.

computer-aided manufacturing (CAM) Use of computer technology in the management, control, and operation of manufacturing.

computer aided publishing (CAP) The use of software packages to facilitate the layout of text and graphics in publishing applications.

Computer and Business Equipment Manufacturers Association An organization for computer vendors, business equipment manufacturers, and suppliers. Founded in 1916, CBEMA is involved in the development of standards for the data processing and business equipment industries.

computer anxiety Fear of computers.

computer architecture Area of computer study that deals with the physical structure (hardware) of computer systems and the relationships among these various hardware components.

computer art A broad term that can refer either to art created on a computer or to art generated by the computer, the difference being whether the artist is human or electronic. When created by human beings, computer art is done with painting and drawing programs that offer a range of drawing tools, brushes, pencils, patterns, shapes, and colors. The artist can dream lovely images and use the computer to bring them to vivid reality.

computer artist Person who uses computers as tools in producing art.

computer-assisted instruction (CAI) Use of computers to augment individual instruction by providing students with programmed sequences of instruction under computer control. Manner of sequencing the materials permits students to progress at their own rate. Responsive to students' individual needs.

computer-augmented learning (CAL) Method of using a computer system to augment, or supplement, a more conventional instructional system, such as by using simulation programs to aid in problem solving in a course of instruction.

computer awareness Generally, an understanding of what a computer is, how it works and the role and impact of computers in society.

computer-based learning (CBL) Term used to embrace all the present forms of educational computing.

computer center Facility that provides computer services to a variety of users through the operation of computer and auxiliary hardware, and through ancillary services provided by its staff.

computer center director Individual who directs the activities, operations, and personnel in a computer center.

computer chess A computer program that plays the game of chess. Since 1970, the ACM North American Computer Chess Championships have served both as a catalyst for progress and as a historical record of this most exciting area of artificial intelligence research. During these 20+ years, programs have improved from the level of rank club players to among the best in the world. The names of some of the popular chess programs are: CHESS, RIBBIT, BELLE, CRAY BLITZ, HITECH and DEEP THOUGHT.

computer circuits Circuits used in digital computers, such a gating circuits, storage circuits, triggering circuits, inverting circuits, and power amplifying circuits.

computer classifications Digital computers are broken down into three classifications: mainframes (which includes supercomputers), minicomputers and microcomputers.

computer conferencing A method of sending, receiving, and storing typed messages within a network of users.

computer coordinator An educational professional who has the responsibility of teaching information technology in a specific school or school district.

computer crime The unauthorized use of computer systems, including software or data, for unlawful purposes.

computer curriculum The use of computers in schools to enhance the learning process.

computer doctor Jargon for a computer repairperson.

computer drawing A graphic image prepared on a computer.

computer enclosure Cabinet or housing for a computer's circuit boards and power supply.

computer engineering Field of knowledge that includes the design of computer hardware systems. Offered as a degree program in several colleges and universities.

computer equity Equal opportunity for computing for all social groups.

computerese Jargon and other specialized vocabulary of people working with computers and information processing systems.

computer family A term commonly used to indicate a group of computers that are built around the same central processing unit, same microprocessor, or around a series of related microprocessors and that share significant design features. For example, the IBM PC and IBM PS/2 models represent a family designed by IBM Corporation around the Intel 80x86 series of microprocessors (80286, 80386 and 80486).

computer flicks Movies made by a computer.

Computer Fraud and Abuse Act A law passed by congress in 1984 to fight computer crime.

computer game Interactive software or firmware in which the input data consists of the human player's physical actions and the output is an interactive graphics display.

computer graphicist Specialist who uses computer graphics systems to produce graphs, charts, animated diagrams, art forms, and graphics designs.

computer graphics General term meaning the appearance of pictures or diagrams, as distinct from letters and numbers, on the display screen or hard-copy output device. The term computer graphics encompasses different methods of generating, displaying, and storing information.

computer graphics metafile (CGM) An international device-independent file format for storage of object-oriented graphics images. CGM files can be exchanged among users of different systems and different programs.

computer-independent language High-level language designed for use in any computer equipped with an appropriate compiler.

computer industry Industry composed of businesses and organizations that supply computer hardware, software, and computer-related services.

computer information system (CIS) Coordinated collection of hardware, software, data, people, and support resources to perform an integrated series of functions that can include processing, storage, input, and output.

computer input microfilm (CIM) Technology that involves using an input device to read the contents of microfilm or microfiche directly into the computer.

computer instruction See instruction.

computer integrated manufacturing (CIM) Concept of totally automated factory in which all manufacturing processes are integrated and controlled by a CAD/CAM system. CIM enables production planners and schedulers, shop/floor foremen, and accountants to use the same database as do product designers and engineers.

computer interface unit (CIU) Device used to connect peripheral devices to a computer.

computerization (1) Application of a computer to an activity formerly done by other means. (2) Actual reshaping of society by the widespread adoption and use of computers.

computerized axial tomography (CAT) Computer controlled X-ray technique that shows a picture of a site through the body at a given depth. The computer is used to bring out the details of this picture, recording X-rays passing through the body in changing directions and generating an image of the body's structure.

computerized database Set of computerized files on which an organization's activities are based and upon which high reliance is placed for availability and accuracy.

computerized game playing Recreational use of computers that have been programmed to play a wide variety of games.

computerized mail Technique of delivering mail in electronic form directly to homes and businesses through computer equipment. See electronic mail.

computerized numerical control See numerical control.

computer jargon Technical vocabulary associated with the computer field. See computerese.

computer language See programming language.

computer leasing company Company that specializes in leasing computer equipment that it purchases from a computer manufacturer.

computer letter Personalized form letter produced by a word processing system or a special form-letter program.

computer literacy A broad knowledge of how to use computers to solve problems, general awareness of the functioning of the software and hardware, and an understanding of the societal implications of computers. It is the nontechnical study of the computer and its effect upon society that provides one with some of the knowledge, tools, and understanding to live in a computer-oriented society. It is a state of being able to function comfortably as a user in a computerized environment but not necessarily possessing technical comprehension.

computer-managed instruction (CMI) Application of computers to instruction in which the computer is used as a record keeper, manager, and/or prescriber of instruction.

Computer Museum Archive for computer history, located in Boston, Massachusetts, whose collection contains many early computer systems and taped presentations of computer pioneers.

computer network Complex consisting of two or more interconnected computer systems, terminals, and communication facilities.

computernik Avid computer user who chooses to spend a large amount of time using computers.

computer numerical control Technique by which a machine-tool control uses a computer to store numerical control instructions generated earlier by CAD/CAM for controlling the machine.

computer-on-a-chip Complete microcomputer on an integrated circuit chip.

computer operations That part of a computer installation responsible for the day-to-day collection, production, distribution, and maintenance of data.

computer operations manager Person who oversees the computer operations area in an organization. Responsible for hiring personnel and scheduling work that the system is to perform.

computer operator Person skilled in the operation of the computer and associated peripheral devices. Performs other operational functions that are required in a computer center, such as loading a disk drive, removing printouts from the line printer rack, and sometimes bursting and decollating.

computer output microfilm (COM) Technology that involves recording computer output on microfilm or microfiche.

computer output microfilm (COM) recorder Device that records computer output on photosensitive film in microscopic form.

computer phobia Fear of computers.

computer process control system System that uses a computer connected to sensors that monitor a process in order to control that process and its modification so that a product can be produced at a profit.

computer processing cycle (1) Steps involved in using a computer to solve a problem: write the program in a programming language; input the program into the computer; compile and execute the program. (2) Basic processing cycle of input, process, and output.

computer program Formal expression of the sequence of actions required for a data processing task. The programmer's specification of the task(s) to the computer in a formal notation that can be processed by the computer. Consists of a series of statements and instructions that cause a computer to perform a particular operation or task.

computer programmer Person whose job is to design, write, and test programs that cause a computer to do a specific job.

computer revolution See information revolution.

computer science Field of knowledge embracing all aspects of the design and use of computers. Aspects of computer science range from programming and computer graphics to artificial intelligence and robotics. Offered as a degree program in many colleges and universities.

computer security Preservation of computing resources against abuse or unauthorized use, especially the protection of data from accidental or deliberate damage, disclosure, or modification.

computer services company Company that provides computer services to other individuals and organizations.

computer simulation Representation of a real or hypothetical system, constructed from a computer program.

computer specialist   Individual, such as a systems analyst or a programmer, who provides computer services to computer-using organizations, usually as an independent contractor or consultant.

computer store   Retail store where customers can select, from the shelf or the floor, a full computer system or just a few accessories. These stores typically sell software, books, supplies, and periodicals. In a broad-based computer store, one can examine and operate several types of microcomputer systems.

computer system   System that includes computer hardware, software, and people. Used to process data into useful information.

computer user   Any person who uses a computer system or its output.

computer users group   Group whose members share the knowledge they have gained and the programs they have developed on a computer or class of computers of a certain manufacturer. Most groups hold meetings and distribute newsletters to exchange information, trade equipment, and share computer programs.

computer utility   Service that provides computational ability, usually a time-shared computer system. Programs, as well as data, may be made available to the user. The user also may have her or his own programs immediately available in the central processing unit, or have them on call at the computer utility, or load them by transmitting them to the computer prior to using them. Certain data and programs are shared by all users of the service; other data and programs, because of their proprietary nature, have restricted access. Computer utilities are generally accessed by means of data communications subsystems.

computer vendor   Organization that manufactures, sells, or services computer equipment.

computer virus   A program that attaches itself to other programs or data. A virus' typical purpose is to disrupt the processing of information on an infected system. When an infected program is executed, the virus reproduces and spreads by searching for other software that is not infected, and then attaching itself to previously "clean" software.

computer vision   The processing of visual information by a computer.

computer word   Fixed sequence of bits, bytes, or characters treated as a unit and capable of being stored in one storage location.

computer work table   The average desk or work table is about 30 inches (76 cm) from the floor. The chair height should be adjusted to leave a gap of at least 8 inches (20 cm) for your knees; the seat will then be about 16 inches (40 cm) from the floor.

Computerworld   A weekly publication that provides articles and advertisements regarding topics of interest, such as word processing, robotics, office automation, programming languages, computer equipment, computer personnel, and general computer information.

computing Act of using computing equipment for processing data. Art or science of getting the computer to do what the user wants.

computing power The relative speed of computing. One computer is described as being more powerful than another if it can handle more work at a faster speed.

computing system See computer system.

COM recorder Device that records computer output on photosensitive film in microscopic form. See computer output microfilm.

concatenate To link together or join two or more character strings into a single character string, or to join one line of a display with the succeeding line. To compress.

concatenated data set Collection of logically connected data sets.

concatenated key More than one data item used in conjunction to identify a record.

concentrator Device that allows a number of slow-speed devices to utilize a single high-speed communications line. Also called multiplexer.

conceptual tool Tool for working with ideas instead of things.

concordance Alphabetical list of words and phrases appearing in a document, with an indication of where those words and phrases appear.

concurrency In object-oriented programming, the property that distinguishes an active object from one that is not active. Concurrency is one of the fundamental elements of the object model.

concurrent Pertaining to the occurrence of two or more events for activities within the same specified interval of time.

concurrent language A language that supports the simultaneous execution of multiple objects, usually on parallel architecture hardware.

concurrent object In object-oriented programming, an active object whose semantics are guaranteed in the presence of multiple threads of control.

concurrent processing Performance of two or more data processing tasks within a specified interval.

concurrent program execution Two or more programs being executed at the same time.

condensed type Type narrowed in width so that more characters will fit a linear inch.

condition (1) Given set of circumstances. (2) Definite state of being.

conditional branching See conditional transfer.

conditional paging Word processing feature that causes printing to begin on the next page if a specified block of text will not fit completely within the remaining space on a page.

conditional replace A word processing function that asks the user whether to replace copy each time the program finds a particular item.

conditional statement Statement that is executed only when a certain condition within the routine has been met.

conditional transfer Instruction that may cause a departure from the sequence of instructions being followed, depending upon the result of an operation, the contents of a register, or the settings of an indicator. Contrast with unconditional transfer.

condition code Limited group of program conditions—such as carry, borrow, and overflow—pertinent to the execution of instructions.

condition entry One of the four sections of a decision table. Answers all questions in the condition stub.

conditioning Improvement of the data transmission properties of a voiceband transmission line by correction of the amplitude phase characteristics of the line amplifiers.

condition stub One of four sections of a decision table. Describes all factors (options) to be considered in determining a course of action.

CONDUIT Nonprofit publisher of educational software. Reviews, tests, packages, and distributes instructional computer programs and related printed materials.

conference tree Type of bulletin board structured around topics and user comments, with each main branch being a broad topic that the user can then elaborate on as the branch lengthens.

confidentiality Quality of protection against unauthorized access to private or secret information.

configure To assemble a selection of hardware or software into a system and to adjust each of the parts so that they all work together.

configuration Assembly of machines that are interconnected and are programmed to operate as a system. Layout or design of elements in a hardware or information processing system.

configuration management Task of accounting for, controlling, and reporting the planned and actual design of a product throughout its production and operational life.

connecting cable Cable used to transfer electrical impulses between two pieces of equipment.

connector (1) Coupling device that provides an electrical and/or mechanical junction between two cables, or between a cable and a chassis or enclosure. (2) Device that provides rapid connection and disconnection of electrical cable and wire terminations.

connector symbol Flowcharting symbol used to represent a junction in a line of flow. A small circle, possibly containing some identifier, connects broken paths in the line of flow on the same page. A pentagonal shape connects the flow on different pages of the same flowchart.

connect time In time-sharing, the length of time you are "on" the computer; duration of the telephone connection. Usually measured by the duration between sign-on and sign-off.

consecutive Pertaining to the occurrence of two sequential events without the intervention of any other such event.

consistency check Check to ensure that specific input data fall within a predetermined set of criteria. Control method wherein like data items are checked for consistency of value and form.

console That part of a computer system that enables human operators to communicate with the system.

console operator Same as computer operator.

consortium A joint venture to support a complete computer facility to be used in an emergency.

constant Value that does not change during the execution of the program. Also called literal.

constraint Condition that limits the solutions to a problem.

constructor In object-oriented programming, an operation that creats an object and/or initializes its state.

consultant Expert in the use of computers in specific applications environments, such as business data processing, education, military systems, or health care. Often helps to analyze and solve a specific problem.

container class In object-oriented programming, a class whose instances are collections of other objects.

content-addressable memory Same as associative storage.

contention Condition on a multipoint communications channel when two or more locations try to transmit at the same time. Also occurs when two CPUs attempt to control the same device at once.

contents directory   Series of queues that indicate the routines in a given region of internal storage.

context sensitivity   Software feature that allows a user to access information about the application or command the user is currently using.

contiguous   Adjacent or adjoining.

contiguous data structure   See sequential data structure.

contiguous graphics   Making diagrams with certain characters that touch each other.

contingency plan   Plan for recovery of a computer information system following emergencies or disasters.

continuous forms   Fanfold paper or roll paper that has small holes on the outer edges for automatic feeding into printers. Can be blank sheets or preprinted forms such as checks, invoices, or tax forms.

continuous processing   Input of transactions into a system in the order they occur and as soon after they occur as possible.

continuous scrolling   Moving text, line by line, forward or backward, through a window.

continuous tone   Any photograph or art work that is not yet screened for printing. A very close look at a photograph or piece of artwork reveals the colors or grays blending smoothly into one another. A newspaper photo shows the image mode of various-sized dots, called a line screen. This must be done to all photographs, black-and-white or color, before they are printed. Magazines and books use a finer screen and it is harder to see the individual dots.

continuous-tone image   Color or black-and-white image formed of combinations of separate areas made up of different color tones or gray tones.

contouring   (1) In computer graphics, the creation of the outline of a body, mass, or figure. For example, in a CAD model, the representation of the surface of an object—its bumps and crannies. (2) In image processing, contouring refers to the loss of detail that occurs in a shaded image when too few gradations of gray are used to reproduce a graphic such as a photograph.

contrast   In optical character recognition, the differences between color or shading of the printed material on a document and the background on which it is printed.

contrast enhancement   Improvement of light-to-dark distinctions. A real digitizing process typically involves some kind of nonlinear detector that destroys the light-to-dark relationships of the object scanned. Correct contrast can be reintroduced if the characteristics of the detector are known. Contrast can even be heightened if desired.

control   Function of performing required operations when certain specific conditions occur or when interpreting and acting upon instructions. See control section and control unit.

control block   Storage area through which a particular type of information required for control of the operating system is communicated among its parts.

control break   Point during program processing at which some special processing event takes place, based upon change in value of a control field.

control bus   In a computer, the path linking the CPU's control register to memory.

control character   Character whose occurrence in a particular context initiates, modifies, or stops a control operation.

control circuits   Electrical circuits within a computer that interpret the program instructions and cause the appropriate operations to be performed.

control clerk   Person who has responsibility for performing duties associated with the control over data processing operations.

control console   That part of a mainframe system used for communication between the console operator or service engineer and the computer.

control data   One or more items of data used as a control to identify, select, execute, or modify another routine, record, file, operation, or data value.

Control Data Corporation (CDC)   One of the first major manufacturers of computer equipment. It was founded in 1957 by William Norris. CDC's first computer was the CDC 1604; introduced in 1957. Since then, CDC has produced several mainframes including many supercomputers. CDC is also the developer of the computer-based education system, PLATO.

control field   Field in a data record used to   identify and classify the record. Same as key.

control key   Special-function key on a computer keyboard. Used simultaneously with another key to enter a command instructing the system to perform a task.

controlled variable   Variable that takes on a specific set of values in an iterative structure in a programming language.

controller   The electronic board or unit that regulates the operation of a peripheral device. There are disk controllers, printer controllers, tape controllers, and so on. The controller takes the general commands from the computer system, converts them into the actual signals for controlling the device, and brings the data and status signals from the device into the computer in the appropriate form.

control logic Order in which processing functions will be carried out by a computer.

control panel That part of a computer control console that contains manual controls.

control program Operating system program responsible for the overall management of the computer and its resources.

controls Methods and procedures for ensuring the accuracy, integrity, security, reliability, and completeness of data or processing techniques.

control section That part of the central processing unit responsible for directing the operation of the computer in accordance with the instructions in the program.

control sequence Normal order of selection of instructions by a computer wherein it follows one instruction order at a time.

control signal Computer-generated signal for automatic control of machines and processes.

control statement Operation that terminates the sequential execution of instructions by transferring control to a statement elsewhere in the program.

control station Network station that supervises control procedures, such as addressing, poling, selecting, and recovery. Also responsible for establishing order on the line in the event of contention or any other abnormal situation.

control structures Facilities of a programming language that specify a departure from the normal sequential execution of statements.

control total Accumulation of numeric data fields that are used to check on the accuracy of the input, processed data, or output data.

control unit Portion of the central processing unit that directs the step-by-step operation of the entire computing system.

control words Series of reserved character sequences that have a special meaning to the program that reads them.

convention Standard and accepted procedures in computer program development and the abbreviations, symbols, and their meanings as developed for particular programs and systems. Any programming style rule, providing consistency among different programs.

conversational Pertaining to a program or a system that carries on a dialogue with a terminal user, alternately accepting input and then responding to the input quickly enough for the user to maintain his or her train of thought.

conversational interaction   Interaction with a computer that takes the form of a dialogue between the user and the machine.

conversational language   Programming language that uses a near-English character set that facilitates communication between the user and the computer. BASIC is a conversational language.

conversational mode   Mode of operation that implies a dialogue between a computer and its user in which the computer program examines the input supplied by the user and formulates questions or comments that are directed back to the user.

conversational system   See interactive system.

conversion   (1) Process of changing information from one form of representation to another, such as from the language of one type of computer to that of another or from a scanned image to magnetic disk. (2) Process of changing from one data processing method to another or from one type of equipment to another. (3) Process of changing a number written in one base to the base of another numeral system.

conversion table   Table comparing numerals in two different numeral systems.

convert   (1) To change data from radix to radix. (2) To move data from one type of storage to another, such as from CD-ROM to floppy disk.

converter   (1) Device that converts data recorded on one medium to another medium, such as a unit that accepts data from MICR documents and records it on magnetic disks. (2) Device that converts data in one form into data in another form, such as from analog to digital.

cookbook   Step-by-step book or manual that describes a program, a system or some other topic.

cooling fan   A small fan that keeps the circuit boards and ICs cool.

coordinate indexing   (1) System of indexing individual documents by descriptors of equal rank so that a library can be searched for a combination of one or more descriptors. (2) Indexing technique whereby the interrelationships of terms are shown by coupling individual words.

coordinate paper   Continuous-feed graph paper used for graphs or diagrams produced on a digital plotter.

coordinates   (1) Ordered set of absolute or relative data values that specify a location in a Cartesian coordinate system. (2) In an electronic spreadsheet, the intersection of two numbers and/or letters that uniquely identify the column and row of a cell. (3) Two numbers used to position the cursor, or pointer, on the screen.

coprocessor   Device that performs specialized processing in conjunction with the main microprocessor of a system. It works in tandem with another central processing unit to increase the computing power of a system. An extra microprocessor to handle some things faster than the main processor, i.e., a math coprocessor or a graphics coprocessor.

copy   (1) To reproduce data in a new location or other destination, leaving the source data unchanged, although the physical form of the result may differ from that of the source; for example, to make a duplicate of all the programs or data on a disk, or to copy a graphic screen image to a printer. (2) To reproduce text or a graphic image onto the clipboard.

copy buster   A program that is able to make copies of "so-called" copy protected floppy disks.

copyfit   To get text to fit within the available area.

copy holder   Device used to hold papers so the user can easily read them when typing on a keyboard. Its purpose is to reduce back, shoulder, neck, and eye strain.

copy program   (1) A program designed to duplicate one or more files to another disk. (2) A program that circumvents the copy-protection device on a computer program so that the software can be copied to another disk.

copy protection   Methods used by software developers to prevent any copying of their programs. To protect against illegal copying of software, many software developers build copy-protection routines into their programs. Copy-protection techniques are sometimes sophisticated, although several commercial programs exist that allow users to override many standard copy-protection techniques. Now that hard disks are common to many microcomputer systems, copy protection has been abolished.

copyright   Recognized ownership of creative work; protection against unauthorized use of work.

copyright notice   A notification of copyright that is part of a program and is often printed on the display screen at the start of the program. It reminds the user that the program has a copyright, and that making copies for any purpose other than for backup is illegal.

copyrighted software   Software that costs money and must not be copied without permission from the software developer.

Corbato, Fernando J.   Organized the concepts and led the development of the general-purpose large-scale time-sharing and resource-sharing computer systems CTSS and Multics.

Corel Draw   An illustrative graphics program which runs on Windows.

Has an advanced autotracing feature that quickly and easily builds a vector-based image from an entire bit-mapped black/white, gray scale, or color clip art, paint program or scanned image file. Introduced in 1989 by Corel Systems Corporation, Corel Draw includes over 100 precision fonts and is known for its speed and ease of use.

core storage Form of storage device that utilizes magnetic cores usually strung through wires in the form of an array. Used in older computers.

corrective maintenance Activity of detecting, isolating, and correcting failures after they occur.

cost analysis Technique used to determine the overall costs of a given system and to compare them to cost factors estimated for a new design.

cost/benefit analysis Quantitative form of evaluation in which benefits are assessed and costs associated with achieving the benefits are determined.

cost-effectiveness Effectiveness of a system or an operation in terms of the relationship of the benefits received to the resources expended to attain them. A system in which the received benefits exceed the associated costs is considered cost-effective.

costing Method of assigning costs to a project, job, or function.

cottage key people People who work at home and transmit work to the company by telecommunications, diskettes, or other means.

count Successive increase or decrease of a cumulative total of the number of times an event occurs.

counter Device, such as a register or computer storage location, used to represent the number of occurrences of an event.

counting loop Program loop used to perform some action a fixed number of times.

coupling Interaction between systems or between properties of a system.

courier Monospaced typeface which resembles typewriter text. Commonly a built-in font on laser printers.

courseware Name given to computer programs written especially for educational applications, such as teaching chemistry, history, mathematics, Spanish, or reading skills. See computer-assisted instruction.

cpi Abbreviation for characters per inch.

CPM Acronym for Critical Path Method.

CP/M Acronym for Control Program for Microcomputers, an operating system for older microcomputer systems. Created by Gary Kildall of Digital Research Inc. It was very popular in the early 1980s.

cps Abbreviation for characters per second.

CPU Acronym for Central Processing Unit.

CR Acronym for Carriage Return.

cracker A programmer who gains access to a system without authorization.

crash System shutdown caused by a hardware malfunction or a software mistake. When a computer fails to respond to any commands, it is said to have undergone a crash. It can be caused by human error, incompatibility between the software and operating system, or even by static electricity.

Cray Brand name for a series of supercomputers manufactured by Cray Research, Inc.

Cray Research, Inc. A manufacturer of supercomputers founded in 1972 by Seymour Cray, a leading designer of mainframes at Control Data Corporation. In 1976, Cray Research sold its first supercomputer, the Cray 1, to Los Alamos National Laboratories. Other supercomputers manufactured by Cray Research include the Cray X-MP, the Cray 2, and Cray Y-MP. The Cray Y-MP, introduced in 1988, costs 20 million dollars and can perform over a billion calculations per second.

Cray, Seymour Founded Cray Research, Inc. in 1972 for the purpose of developing supercomputers. Introduced the world's first commercial supercomputer, the Cray 1, in 1976. It could perform 160 million calculations per second. He designed the Cray 2, twelve times faster than the Cray 1, and released it in 1985. In 1989, Seymour Cray left Cray Research and founded Cray Computer Corporation.

CRC Acronym for Cyclic Redundancy Check, a method for checking for errors in transmitted data.

create (1) To make a new file on a disk as opposed to modifying an existing file. (2) To define the fields for a database record, specifying field name, length, field type, and so on.

creative designer In desktop publishing, the individual who lays out and designs a page.

Cricket Stylist A popular object-oriented drawing program for the Apple Macintosh computer. Using Cricket Stylist you can create drawings using the familiar line, rectangle, and oval tools. The program offers black-and-white, gray scale and full color support. A full set of drawing tools is provided, including a novel starburst tool to create starburst objects.

crime, computer See computer crime.

critical path That path through a network that defines the shortest possible time in which the entire project can be completed.

critical path method (CPM) Management technique for control of large-scale, long-term projects involving the analysis and determination of each critical step necessary for project completion.

CROM Acronym for Control ROM, an integral part of most CPU chips. Storage for the micro instructions that the CPU assembles into a sequence to form the complex macro instructions, such a Multiply or Branch-On-Negative Accumulator, available to the computer user.

crop To trim a graphics image for a better fit or to eliminate unwanted portions. In preparing an illustration for traditional printing, cropping is used to clean up a graphic for placement in a document.

cross-assembler Assembler run on one computer for the purpose of translating instructions for a different computer.

cross-check To check the computing by two different methods.

cross-compiler Compiler that runs on a machine other than the one for which it is designed to compile code.

cross-compiling/assembling Technique whereby one uses a minicomputer, mainframe, or time-sharing service to write and debug programs for subsequent use on microcomputers.

cross-footing check Process of cross-adding, or subtracting, then zeroing-out the results.

cross hairs On an input device, two intersecting lines—one horizontal and one vertical—whose intersection marks the active cursor position of a graphics system.

crosshatching In computer graphics, the shading of some portion of a drawing with a pattern of intersecting lines or figures repeated across the area being shaded. Crosshatching is one of several methods for filling in areas of a graphic.

cross-reference dictionary Printed listing that identifies all references of an assembled program to a specific label. In many systems, this listing is provided immediately after a source program has been assembled.

cross talk Unwanted energy transferred from one circuit, called the "disturbing circuit," to another circuit, called the "disturbed circuit." Generally occurs when signals from one circuit emerge onto another circuit as interference.

crowbar Circuit that protects a computer system from dangerously high voltage surges.

CRT Acronym for Cathode Ray Tube, the picture tube of the standard computer display screen. A CRT display is built around a vacuum tube containing one or more electron guns whose electron beams rapidly sweep horizontally across the inside of the front surface of the tube, which is coated with a material that glows when irradiated.

CRT plot Computer-generated drawing or graph projected onto the screen of a cathode ray tube.

CRT terminal (1) Visual display unit (VDU). (2) Display device with keyboard as used by an operator to communicate with a computer. As the operator types a message or text on the keyboard, the characters are displayed on the screen.

crunch Nontechnical term used by computer people to refer to the computer's capacity to process numbers and perform routine arithmetic functions. Computers can process, or crunch a lot of numbers quickly. See number cruncher.

cryoelectronic storage Storage device consisting of materials that become superconductors at extremely low temperatures.

cryogenics Study and use of devices that utilize the properties assumed by materials at temperatures near absolute zero.

cryosar Two-terminal semiconductor switching device that operates at very low temperatures.

cryotron Current-controlled switching device based on superconductivity; used primarily in computer circuits.

cryptanalysis Operation of converting encrypted messages to the corresponding plaintext without initial knowledge of the key employed in the encryption.

cryptographic techniques Methods of concealing data by representing each character or group of characters by others.

cryptography Any of various methods for writing in secret code or cipher. As society becomes increasingly dependent upon computers, the vast amounts of data communicated, processed, and stored within computer systems and networks often have to be protected, and cryptography is a means of achieving this protection. It is the only practical method for protecting information transmitted through accessible communications networks, such as telephone lines, satellites, or microwave systems.

crystal Quartz crystal that vibrates at a specific frequency when energy is supplied to it. These vibrations provide an accurate frequency by which to time the clock within a computer system.

CSMA Acronym for Carrier-Sensed Multiple-Access. A protocol that controls access to a network's bus.

CT Acronym for Computed Tomographic. See computerized axial tomography.

CTRL Acronym for control.

cue See call.

current Flow of electrons through a conductor. Measured in amperes, where 1 ampere equals 6.25×10^{18} electrons per second.

current awareness system Process whereby a user is notified periodically by a central file or library when selected items of information have been acquired.

current cell The cell currently available for use on a spreadsheet.

current drive The disk drive currently being used by the computer system.

current location counter Counter kept by an assembler to determine the address that has been assigned to either an instruction or constant being assembled.

current loop Type of serial communication in which the presence or absence of an electrical signal indicates the state of the bit being transmitted.

current mode logic (CML) Logic circuit that employs the characteristics of a differential amplifier circuit in its design.

current page box In desktop publishing programs, an area that displays the current page being worked on.

cursive scanning Scanning technique used with video display terminals in which the electrons being sent toward the screen are deflected to form the outlines of the picture one line at a time in the same way an artist might draw the same image.

cursor (1) Moving, sliding, or blinking symbol on a CRT screen that indicates where the next character will appear. (2) Position indicator used on a video display terminal to indicate a character to be connected or a position in which data is to be entered. (3) On graphic systems, it can take any shape (arrow, square, paintbrush, etc.) and is used to mark where the next graphic action is to take place.

cursor control Ability to move a video display prompt character to any position on the screen.

cursor control keys Keys that, when pressed, move the cursor in a designated direction. Cursor movement keys generally have directional arrows on their keytops.

cursor tracking Positioning a cursor on a display screen by moving a stylus on a graphics tablet connected to the computer.

curve fitting Mathematical technique for finding a formula that best represents a collection of data points. Usually the formula is used to plot the best-fit line through the points.

custodian Person or organization responsible for physical maintenance and safeguarding of data stored on disk packs, tape reels, diskettes, removable hard disks, and so forth. See librarian.

customer engineer (CE) A person who repairs or does preventive maintenance on a computer or on its input/output devices and other off-line equipment. Also called field engineer.

custom IC Integrated circuit (IC) manufactured to a specific customer's design and specification.

customize Process of altering a piece of general-purpose software or hardware to enhance its performance, usually to fit a specific user's need.

customized form letters Personalized form letters produced by word processing systems and special form-letter programs.

custom software Programs prepared specifically for a business or organization and tailored to the business's needs.

cut Act of removing text or graphics from a document. Compare paste.

CUT A bitmap format used by Dr. Halo and a few other graphics programs.

cut and paste Method employed by some systems to move graphics and/or text from one location to another. Such systems usually permit the performance of other operations between the cut and the paste steps. Cut and paste enables compatible programs to share text and graphics.

cut form Data-entry form, such as a utility bill, used by OCR devices.

cut-sheet feeder Device that feeds sheets of paper to the printer, one at a time. Usually a friction-feed device.

cutter path Line described by the motion of a cutting tool controlled by a computer-aided manufacturing system.

cyan Shade of blue frequently used on VDTs for color graphics.

Cyber Brand name for a line of mainframes and supercomputers manufactured by Control Data Corporation.

cybernetics Branch of learning that seeks to integrate the theories and studies of communication and control in machines and living organisms.

cyberphobia Fear of computers.

cycle As related to computer storage, a periodic sequence of events occurring when information is transferred to or from the storage device or a computer. Time it takes to reference an address, remove the data, and be ready to select it again.

cycle stealing Technique that allows a peripheral device temporarily to disable computer control of the I/O bus, thus allowing the device to access the computer's internal memory.

cycle time (1) Minimum time interval between the starts of successive accesses to a storage location. (2) Time required to change the information in a set of registers.

cyclic reduncandy check (CRC) Error-detection scheme often used in disk devices. When data are stored, a CRC value is computed and stored. Whenever it is reread, the CRC value is computed once again. If the two values are equal, the data is assumed to be error-free.

cyclic shift Shift in which the digits dropped off at one end of a word are returned at the other in a circular fashion. If a register holds eight digits, 23456789, the result of the cyclic shift two columns to the left would be to change the contents of the register to 45678923.

cylinder As related to magnetic disks, a vertical column of tracks on a magnetic disk pack. The corresponding tracks on each surface of a disk pack.

cylinder method Method or concept that data on all tracks above and below the one currently being used are available by merely switching read/ write heads. Allows access to large amounts of information with no extra movement of the access device.

cypher Form of cryptography in which the plaintext is made unintelligible to anyone who intercepts it by a transformation of the information itself, based on some key.

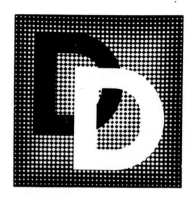

D Acronym for Direct Access.

D-A converter See digital-to-analog converter.

daisy chain Specific method of propagating signals along a bus that permits the assignment of device priorities based on the electrical position of the device along the bus.

daisy wheel printer Printer that uses a metal or plastic disk with printed characters along its edge. The disk rotates until the required character is brought before a hammer that strikes it against a ribbon. Popular letter-quality printer used with personal computers.

dark bulb Type of cathode ray tube, almost black in appearance when turned off, that gives good contrast to video displays.

darkness Intensity, especially low intensity or limited brightness.

DASD Acronym for Direct Access Storage Device.

DAT Acronym for Dynamic Address Translation.

data Formalized representation of facts or concepts suitable for communication, interpretation, or processing by people or by automatic means. Raw material of information. Individual pieces of quantitative information, such as dollar sales of carpets, numbers of building permits issued, units of raw material on hand. Historically, data is a plural noun while datum is singular—a distinction now generally ignored in data processing terminology.

data acquisition Retrieval of data from remote sites initiated by a central computer system. Collection of data from external sensors.

data administrator See database administrator.

data aggregate Any collection of data items within a record that is given a name and referred to as a whole, such as an array.

data bank (1) Comprehensive collection of libraries of data. (2) Loosely, a database.

database Most generally, any clearly identified collection of data, such as a telephone book or the card catalog at a library. In theory, a database should contain all its information in one central store or file, each record in the file containing roughly the same type of information—such as name, address, city, state, zip code, area code, and telephone number. Each of these categories is called a field, while a record consists of a set of fields pertaining to one person or item. The database file is made up of a number of related records. Some people differentiate between a data base (two words), meaning an underlying collection of data in the real world, and a database (single word) as a coherent collection of data entered into a computer system. As applied to data in the computer, it particularly means data organized so that various programs can access and update the information.

database administrator Person responsible for the creation of the information system database and, once it is established, for maintaining its security and developing procedures for its recovery from disaster.

database analyst Key person in the analysis, design, and implementation of data structures in a database environment.

database environment That environment resulting from the integration of users, data, and systems by implementing the database.

database management Systematic approach to storing, updating, and retrieving of data items, usually in the form of records in a file, by which many users, or even many remote installations, will use common databases.

database management system (DBMS) Collection of hardware and software that organizes and provides access to a database. The computer program provides the mechanisms needed to create a computerized database file, to add data to the file, to alter data in the file, to organize data within the file, to search for data in the file, and so forth. In other words, it manages data. Popular database management programs are dBASEIII and Paradox.

database manager Program that allows the user to enter, organize, sort, and retrieve information.

database server Intelligent way of storing database files. The server can sort and manipulate data prior to sending to node.

database specialist Person who works with databases.

data bus Bus system that interconnects the CPU, storage, and all the input/output devices of a computer system for the purpose of exchanging data.

data byte Eight-bit binary number representing one character of data the computer will use in an arithmetic or logical operation, or store in memory.

data capturing Gathering or collecting information for computer handling, the first step in job processing. Also called data collection.

data catalog Organized listing by full name of all data elements used by an organization.

data center The department that houses the computer systems, related equipment and data files.

data chaining Process of linking data items together. Each data item contains the location of the next data item.

data channel Communications link between two devices or points.

data clerk Person who does clerical jobs in a computer installation.

data collection (1) Gathering of source data to be entered into a data processing system. Also called data capturing. (2) Act of bringing data from one or more points to a central point.

data command A command that consists of a period followed by letters. Used in some older types of word processing programs for embedded commands.

data communications (1) Movement of encoded information by means of electrical transmission systems. (2) Entire process and science of enabling digital devices, such as computers, to communicate with each other.

data communications equipment Equipment associated with the transmission of data from one device to another. Examples are modems, remote terminals, and communications processors.

data communications system System consisting of computers, terminals, and communications links.

data compatibility The ability of two or more computers to read from and write to each other's data disks or use each other's data files, even if they cannot run the same programs.

data compression Technique that saves computer storage space by eliminating empty fields, gap redundancies, or unnecessary data to reduce the size or the length of records.

data concentration (1) Collection of data at an intermediate point from several low-and medium-speed lines for retransmission across high-speed lines. (2) Addition of one item at the end of others to produce one longer data item.

data control section   Organization or group responsible for meeting quality control standards for processing and for collecting input from, and delivering output to, computer users.

data conversion   Process of changing the form of data representation.

data definition   In programming, a statement that gives the size, type, and often the content of a field or record. That portion of a program that identifies the data to be used in analysis.

data definition language (DDL)   Language used by a database administrator to create, store, and manage data in a database environment. Also called data description language.

data description language (DDL)   Language that specifies the manner in which data are to be stored and managed in a database environment by a database management system. Also called data definition language.

data dictionary   List of all the files, fields, and variables used in a database management system. A data dictionary helps users remember what items they have to work with and how they have been defined. Particularly helpful when writing a large number of linked procedures or programs that share a database.

data diddling   Technique whereby data is modified before it goes into a computer file where it is less accessible.

data directory   Ordered collection of data element names and/or identifiers and their attributes that provides the location of the elements.

data directory/dictionary   Ordered collection of data elements that combines the features of a data catalog, data dictionary, and data directory. Describes and locates each data element.

data division   Third of four main parts of a COBOL program.

data editing   Procedure to check for irregularities in input data. Typical checks are a range check, reasonableness check, and checks to determine whether data is properly alphabetic or numeric, as required.

data element   Combination of one or more data items that forms a unit or piece of information, such as the social security number in an employee/ payroll database.

data encryption   Coding technique used to secure sensitive data by mixing or jumbling the data according to a predetermined format.

data encryption standard   The standardized public key by which senders and receivers can scramble and unscramble their messages.

data entry   (!) Process of converting data into a form suitable for entry into a computer system, such as by keying from a terminal onto magnetic disk or tape. (2) Process of entering data directly into a computer system.

data entry device   Equipment used to prepare data so the computer can accept it.

data entry operator   Person who uses a keyboard device to transcribe data into a form suitable for processing by a computer. Often a member of a computer operations staff who is responsible for keying data into a computer system.

data entry specialist   Person responsible for inputting information into the computer for processing.

data export   Capacity to transport (write) information from one database in a form that can be used (read) by another program, such as a word processor for form letters and reports, a spreadsheet, or a different database. Opposite of data import.

data field   (1) One column or consecutive columns on a coding form or punched card used to record a particular piece of data. (2) Part of a data record.

data field masking   Using special characters to offset or divide data fields. For date fields, the slash or hyphen characters are often used to divide the month, day, and year: 09/23/91. For telephone numbers, the parentheses and hyphen characters may be desired: (999) 999-9999. Similar types of characters may be used for part numbers or in other fields where such offsets improve the readability of character strings. These masks can be inserted by the computer, so an operator does not have to enter the hyphen or other character manually. Only the numbers 092391 are entered in the above data field, with the slashes inserted automatically by the computer program. This feature greatly simplifies data entry and ensures standardization. Some programs routinely mask such fields as date and telephone number.

data file   Collection of related data records that have been organized in a specific manner. Also called text file.

data file processing   Updating of data files by adding, changing, or deleting records to reflect the effects of current data.

dataflow   Generic term that pertains to algorithms or machines whose actions are determined by the availability of the data needed for these actions.

dataflow analysis   Study of the movement of data among processing activities.

dataflow diagram   Graphic systems analysis and design tool that enables a systems analyst to represent the flow of data through a system.

data gathering   Task of collecting data from internal and/or external sources.

Data General Corporation (DGC) A computer manufacturer founded in 1968 by Edson de Castro. In 1969, the company introduced the Nova, an advanced minicomputer. During its early years, the company was successful in marketing its minicomputers in university, scientific and OEM markets. Over the years, DGC has developed a variety of minicomputer systems.

data import Ability to use (read) information developed with another program. Particularly important in the use of integrated software where several programs will use the information gathered or produced by one program. Opposite of data export.

data independence Status of a database system with storage structure and accessing strategy that can be changed without significantly affecting the application.

data integrity Performance measure based on the rate of undetected errors.

data interchange format (DIF) Standard among software developers that allows data from one program to be accessible to another program.

data item Item of data used to represent a single value. Smallest unit of named data.

data leakage Illegal removal of data from a computer facility.

data librarian Person who maintains custody and control of disks, tapes, and procedures manuals by cataloging and monitoring the use of these data resources.

data link Equipment that permits the transmission of information in data format.

data logging Recording of data about events that occur in time sequence.

data management (1) General term that collectively describes those functions of a system that provide access to hardware, enforce data storage conventions, and regulate the use of input/output devices. (2) Major function of operating systems that involves organizing, cataloging, locating, retrieving, storing, and maintaining data.

data management system (1) System that provides the necessary procedures and programs to collect, organize, and maintain the data required by information systems. (2) System that assigns the responsibility for data input and integrity to establish and maintain the databases within an organization.

data manipulation Process of using language commands to add, delete, modify, or retrieve data in a file or database.

data manipulation language (DML) Language that allows a user to interrogate and access the database of a computer system by using English-like statements.

data medium Material in or on which a specific physical variable may represent data, such as magnetic disk or CD-ROM.

data model Formal language for describing data structures and operations on those structures. Usually divided into a data description language and a data manipulating language.

data movement time Time taken to transfer data to or from a disk once the read/write head is properly positioned on a disk track.

data name Name of the variable used to indicate a data value, such as pi for 3.14159...

data origination Translation of information from its original form into machine-sensible form.

data packet Means of transmitting serial data in an efficient package that includes an error-checking sequence.

data point Numeric value for charting purposes. In a simple line chart, time may be plotted across the X axis and another value against the Y axis, the intersection being a data point.

data preparation Process of organizing information and storing it in a form that can be input to the computer.

data preparation device Device that permits data capture in which the source data is collected and transformed into a medium or form capable of being read into a computer.

Datapro Research/publishing company that provides in-depth information about computer hardware and software products.

data processing (1) One or more operations performed on data to achieve a desired objective. (2) All functions of a computer center. (3) Operations performed by data processing equipment. (4) Operations performed on data to provide useful information to users.

data processing center Computer center equipped with devices capable of receiving information, processing it according to human-made instructions, and producing the computed results. Same as information processing center.

data processing curriculum Course of study, normally offered by a business school or college, that prepares students for entry level jobs as applications programmers or systems analysts.

data processing cycle Combined functions of input, processing, and output.

data processing management Managing the data processing function, its people, and its equipment. Since this activity follows the well-recognized principles of planning, control, and operation, its basic prerequisites are the same skills that are needed to manage any other enterprise.

Data Processing Management Association (DPMA) Largest professional association in the field of computer management. Its purpose is to engage in education and research activities focused on the development of effective programs for the self-improvement of its worldwide membership. Seeks to encourage high standards of competence and promotes a professional attitude among its members. Sponsors high school clubs and college chapters. DPMA was founded in 1951.

data processing manager Person who runs the data processing center, usually including the operation of the computer. The biggest part of the manager's job is concerned with developing new systems and keeping them running.

data processing system Network of data processing hardware, software, people, and procedures capable of accepting information, processing it according to a plan, and producing the desired results.

data processing technology Science of information handling.

data processor Any device capable of performing operations on data, such as a desk calculator or a personal computer.

data protection Measure to safeguard data from undesired occurrences that intentionally or unintentionally lead to destruction, modification, or disclosure of data.

data rate Rate at which a channel carries data, measured in bauds (bits per second)..

data record Collection of data fields, pertaining to a particular subject. Part of a data file.

data reduction Process of transforming raw data into useful, condensed, or simplified intelligence. Often adjusting, scaling, smoothing, compacting, editing, and ordering operations are used in the process.

data scope Special display device that monitors a data communications channel and displays the content of the information being transmitted over it.

data security Protection of data from accidental or malicious destruction, disclosure, or modification.

data set (1) Device that permits transmission of data over communications lines by changing the form of the data at one end so it can be carried over the lines; another data set at the other end changes the data back to its original form so it is acceptable to the computer or other machine. See modem. (2) Collection of related data items, especially as grouping of related records, called a file.

data sharing Ability of computer processes or of computer users at several nodes to access data at a single node.

data sink Memory or recording device capable of accepting signals from a data transmission device and storing data for future use.

data source Device capable of originating signals for a data transmission device.

data storage techniques Methods used by a program to store data files.

data stream Serial data transmitted through a channel from a single input/output operation.

data structure Structure of relationships among files in a database and among data items within each file.

data switch box A device that allows you to connect multiple peripherals to one computer or multiple computers to one peripheral.

data tablet Manual input device for graphic display consoles.

data terminal Point in a computer system or data communications network at which data can be entered or retrieved.

data transfer operations Operations that move data, whether externally through data communications or within main computer storage by copying from one location to another.

data transfer rate Rate of transfer of data from one place to another, such as from computer main memory to disk or from one computer's memory to another computer's memory.

data transmission Sending of data from one part of a system to another part. See data communications.

data type Interpretation applied to a string of bits, such as integer, real, or character.

data validation Measures taken to ensure that data fields conform to desired specifications. Fields may be checked for inappropriate characters or for deviation from specified lengths or values. See edit.

data value Any string of symbols that serves as the representative of some item of information.

data word Ordered set of characters, usually of a preset number, that is stored and transferred by the computer's circuits as a fundamental unit of information.

data word size Specific length of data word that a particular computer is designed to handle.

datum Unit of information, such as a computer word.

daughter board A small circuit board that adds capability to another circuit board (motherboard).

da Vinci, Leonardo A towering Renaissance figure of fifteenth-century Italy. Not only was he a great painter but also a genius who could bring an artist's discipline, training and insight to the pursuit of scientific achievement. He designed a calculator that had 13 decimal wheels and a carry mechanism. Nobody knows whether he ever made a model or whether later inventors knew about his design.

dBASE A relational database management system for IBM-compatible microcomputer systems from Ashton-Tate Corporation. It was the first comprehensive database system for personal computers. It was created by Wayne Ratliff to manage a company football pool. Renamed dBASE II after George Tate and Hal Lashley formed Ashton-Tate Corporation to market it.

dBASE III A relational database management package that can open (access) more than one file at a time as opposed to a file manager that can open only one file at a time. With its built-in command-processing language, the relational capabilities let the user create complex databases and reports, along with screens that ask questions when input is needed. This enables experienced programmers to set up systems for use by less-experienced users.

DB-9 connector Plug with either 9 pins (male) or 9 slots (female).

DB2 A mainframe-based relational database management system from the IBM Corporation.

DB-25 connector Plug with either 25 pins (male) or 25 slots (female). Most commonly used with an RS-232C interface connection.

DBMS Acronym for Database Management System.

DC Acronym for (1) Data Conversion, (2) Design Change, (3) Digital Computer, (4) Direct Current, (5) Direct Cycle, (6) Display Console.

DCE The abbreviation for data circuit terminating equipment, the name used by the RS-232 standard for modems and other devices that connect terminals or computers to communication lines.

DCTL Acronym for Direct Coupled Transistor Logic.

DDD Acronym for Direct Distance Dialing, the facility used for making long-distance telephone calls without the assistance of a telephone operator.

DDL Language for declaring data structures in a database. See data definition language and data description language.

dead halt Halt situation in which the system cannot return to the point at which it halted.

dead letter box In message switching systems, a file capturing undeliverable messages.

deadlock The condition in which each of two programs needs resources held captive by the other, and neither is willing to release the resource it is holding until it gets the one the other is holding.

deallocation Release of a resource by a program when the program no longer needs it. Opposite of allocation.

deblocking Extracting a logical record from a block or group of logical records.

debounce To prevent spurious closures of a key or switch from being recognized. One method is to introduce time delays that give the switch contacts time to settle down.

debug To detect, locate, and remove all mistakes in a computer program and any malfunctions in the computing system itself.

debugging aids Computer routines—such as a tracing routine, snapshot dump, and post mortem dump—that are helpful in debugging programs.

DEC Acronym for Digital Equipment Corporation, a large manufacturer of minicomputer systems.

decatenate To separate into two or more paths. Contrast with concatenate.

deceleration time Time required to stop a magnetic tape after reading or recording the last piece of data from a record on that tape.

decentralized computer system System in which the computer and some storage devices are in one location, but the devices that access the computer are elsewhere.

decimal (1) Characteristic or property involving a selection, condition, or choice in which there are ten possibilities. (2) Pertaining to the number system with a radix of 10. (3) Decimal point.

decimal code Form of notation by which each decimal digit is expressed separately in some other number system.

decimal digit Numeral in the decimal numeral system. The radix of the decimal system is 10, and the following symbols are used: 0, 1, 2, 3, 4, 5, 6, 7, 8, and 9.

decimal number Any number usually of more than one digit, in which the quantity represented by each digit is based on the radix of 10.

decimal point Radix point in a mixed decimal numeral, separating the fractional part from the integer part. In the decimal numeral 741.12, the decimal point is between the two 1s.

decimal system Base-10 positional numeration system.

decimal-to-binary conversion Process of converting a numeral written in base 10 to the equivalent numeral written in base 2.

decimal-to-hexadecimal conversion Process of converting a numeral written in base 10 to the equivalent numeral written in base 16.

decimal-to-octal conversion Process of converting a numeral written in base 10 to the equivalent numeral written in base 8.

decision Computer operation of determining if a certain relationship exists between data in storage or registers and of taking alternative courses of action. Determination of future action.

decision instruction Instruction that affects the selection of a branch of a program.

decision structure Same as selection structure.

decision symbol Diamond-shaped flowcharting symbol used to indicate a choice or a branching in the formation processing path.

decision table Table listing all contingencies to be considered in the description of a problem, with corresponding actions to be taken. Sometimes used instead of flowcharts to describe operations of a program.

decision theory Broad spectrum of concepts and techniques that have been developed both to describe and to rationalize the process of making a choice among several possible alternatives.

decision tree Pictorial representation of the alternatives in any situation.

declaration statement Part of a computer program that defines the nature of other elements of the program or reserves parts of the hardware for special use.

declarative language A programming language that frees the programmer from specifying the exact procedure the computer needs to follow to accomplish a task. Instead, you inform the program what you want to accomplish.

DECnet A networking architecture that links Digital Equipment Corporation systems, from large minicomputers to workstations, and is based on Ethernet hardware.

decode To translate or determine the meaning of coded information. Reverse of encode.

decoder (1) Device that decodes. (2) Matrix of switching elements that selects one or more output channels according to the combination of input signals present.

decollate To arrange copies of continuous forms in sets and remove the carbon paper from them.

decrement Amount by which a value or variable is decreased. Contrast with increment.

decryption Process of taking an encrypted message and reconstructing from it the original meaningful message, or plaintext. Opposite of encryption.

DECUS Acronym for the Digital Equipment Computer (DEC) Users Society, a user group whose objective is the exchange and dissemination of ideas and information pertinent to DEC computers.

dedicated Pertaining to programs, machines, or procedures that are designed or reserved for special use.

dedicated chip A chip which performs one task only, such as a memory chip.

dedicated computer Computer whose use is reserved for a particular task. Compare special-purpose computer.

dedicated device Device designed to perform only certain functions and that cannot be programmed to perform other functions.

dedicated lines Telephone lines leased for exclusive use by a group or individual for telecommunications. Users pay a set fee for leased lines rather than the per-call or per-minute charges for switched lines.

dedicated system Computer-based device with one primary function, such as word processing. Usually easier to use for its intended task than for any other. General-purpose systems are usually more flexible.

de facto standard A programming language, product, design or program that has become so widely used and imitated that it has little competition but those whose status has not officially been declared by a recognized standard establishing organization. For example, the enhanced 101/102-key keyboard introduced by IBM partway through the life of the IBM PC/AT computer has become the de facto standard keyboard for most newer IBM-compatible microcomputers.

default Assumption made by a system or language translator when no specific choice is given by the program or the user. A choice that has been pre-set for you. You can override it or simply accept the setting which the manufacturer or developer has deemed most likely appropriate.

default drive Disk drive assigned by a system when no drive number is specified by the user.

default settings Settings automatically used by a program unless the user specifies otherwise.

deferred address Indirect address.

deferred entry Entry into a subroutine that occurs as a result of a deferred exit from the program that passed control to it.

deferred exit Passing of control to a subroutine at a time determined by an asynchronous event rather than at a predictable time.

defragmentation A process in which all the files on a hard disk are rewritten so that all parts of each file are written to contiguous sectors.

degausser Device used to erase information from magnetically recorded media such as a floppy disk or magnetic tape.

degradation Condition in which a system continues to operate but at a reduced level of service. Unavailability of proper equipment maintenance, and computer programs not maintained to accommodate current needs, are the two most common causes.

deinstall To remove a program or hardware device from active service.

dejagging Computer graphics technique for drawing smooth lines, characters, and polygons.

de jure standard Standards that exist in the marketplace due to their adoption by standard approving bodies, such as the American National Standards Institute (ANSI) and International Standards Organization (ISO).

delay circuit Electronic circuit that deliberately delays the delivery of a signal for a present interval.

delay line storage Storage device that consists of a delay line and a means for regenerating and reinserting information into the delay line. Used in early computers.

delete (1) To remove or eliminate. To erase data from a field or to eliminate a record from a file. (2) Method of erasing data.

deletion record New record that will replace or remove an existing record of a master file.

delimit To fix the limits of something, such as to establish maximum and minimum limits of a specific variable.

delimiter Special character, often a comma or space, used to separate variable names or items in a list or to separate one string of characters from another, as in the separation of data items.

delivery Final step in the program development cycle where the program or system is given to the users for execution against actual data.

Dell Computer Corporation A manufacturer of IBM-compatible microcomputers that was founded in 1984 by Michael Dell in Austin, Texas. Dell provides a complete line of microcomputers from laptops to high-end machines.

Deluxe Paint A popular paint program for Commodore Amiga and IBM-compatible microcomputers.

demagnetization Process of erasing information stored on magnetic disks or tapes. See degausser.

demand paging In virtual storage systems, the transfer of a page from external page storage to real storage at the time it is needed for execution.

demand report Report produced only upon request and used in strategic decision making to provide responses to unanticipated queries.

demo A demonstration program designed to emulate some of the functions of an application program for advertising and marketing purposes.

democratic team A software development team structure in which team members share responsibility.

demodulation In data communications, the process of retrieving an original signal from a modulated carrier wave. Used in data sets to make communications signals compatible with computer terminal signals. Counterpart to modulation.

demodulator Device that receives signals transmitted over a communications link and converts them into electrical pulses, or bits, that can serve as inputs to a data processing machine. Contrast with modulator.

demon (1) In object-oriented programming, an active object. (2) A section of a compiuter program or a complete program that waits until an event occurs before running.

demount To remove a magnetic storage medium from a device that reads or writes on it, such as to remove a disk pack from the disk drive.

demultiplexer Circuit that applies the logic state of a single input to one of several outputs. Contrast with multiplexer.

dense binary code Code in which all possible states of the binary pattern are used.

dense list See sequential list.

density Number of characters that can be stored in a given physical space. Measures how close together data are recorded on a magnetic medium, usually in bytes per inch. As recording density increases, the capacity of a storage device increases. See double density.

dependency Relationship where the execution of one job has to be completed before another can begin.

dependent variable Output of a model, so called because it depends on the inputs.

depth queuing Technique, such as shading, used to enhance the three-dimensional appearance of a two-dimensional object.

deque Double-Ended QUEue that allows insertions and deletions at both ends of a list.

descender Portion of lower-case letters (g, j, p, q, and y) that extends below the baseline of other characters.

descending order Order that ranges from highest to lowest in numeric value or alphabetically. Contrast with ascending order.

descriptor Significant word that helps to categorize or index information. Sometimes called a keyword.

design aids Computer programs or hardware elements intended to assist in implementing a computer system. See debugging aids and programming aids.

design automation Use of computers in the design and production of circuit packages, new computers, and other electronic equipment.

design costs Costs associated with systems design, programming, training, conversion, testing, and documentation.

design cycle (1) In a hardware system, the complete cycle of development of equipment, which includes breadboarding, prototyping, testing, and production. (2) In a software system, the complete plan for producing an operational system, which includes problem description, algorithm development, flowcharting, coding, program debugging, and documentation. See program development cycle.

design engineer Person involved in the design of a hardware product, such as a disk unit or microprocessor chip.

Designer An illustrative graphics program for IBM-compatible microcomputer systems. Features include color bitmapping, text wrapping, autotracing, Bezier curve controls, slideshow, scalable fonts, color separations, several fill patterns, and a large clip art library.

design heuristics Guidelines that can be followed when dividing a larger problem or program into smaller, more manageable modules.

design language Programming language whose statements and syntax facilitate its use in design work.

design phase Process of developing an information system based upon previously established system requirements.

design specifications Result of an analysis of information needs of a specific system within the organization. Included are specifications for input, processing, and output.

design walkthrough An overview of a system design by users, programmers, and consultants.

desk accessory (DA) In a graphical user interface, helpful utilities (e.g., calculator, notepad, thesaurus, paint program, word processor, etc.) that you can open when you are in the middle of any program. Desk accessories are accessed by selecting them from a special pull-down menu. Desk accessories are conveniences that can be activated when needed and then either put away or moved to a small part of the display screen.

desk checking Manual checking process in which representative sample data items, used for detecting errors in program logic, are traced through the program before it is executed on the computer.

DeskPaint/DeskDraw An Apple Macintosh paint/draw application in desk accessory form. The application features a full set of paint and draw tools that allow creation or editing of black and white, gray scale and color images, and work with MacPaint, PICT and TIFF file formats. Users can convert from one pixel depth to another, auto-trace black and white bit maps and create graduated fills.

desktop Screen display containing icons that represent programs, files or resources available to the user.

desktop computer A computer that will fit on the top of a standard size office desk. Most personal computers and lap computers can be considered desktop computers. A desktop computer is equipped with sufficient internal memory and auxiliary storage to perform business computing tasks.

desktop presentation Presenting text, video, and graphics on the computer for display to others.

desktop publishing When printed pieces including words and pictures (ads, newsletters, magazines, brochures, books) are created almost entirely on a computer. Desktop publishing programs convert normal text into professional quality documents that can be printed on laser printers or imagesetters. The term "desktop publishing" was coined by Paul Brainerd, president of Aldus Corporation, the developer of PageMaker.

desktop publishing template Already prepared page layouts stored on disk.

desktop video   Using a computer to create and edit video images.

destination   Device or address that receives the data during a data transfer operation.

destructive operation   Process of reading or writing data that erases the data that is read or that was stored previously in the receiving storage location.

destructive read   Process of destroying the information in a location by reading the contents.

destructor   In object-oriented programming, an operation that frees the state of an object and/or destroys the object itself.

detachable keyboard   Keyboard not built into the same case as the video display or desk unit. Connects to the system with a cable and allows greater flexibility in positioning of the keyboard display—one result of ergonomics.

detail   Small section of a larger file or graphics picture.

detail diagram   Diagram used in HIPO to describe the specific function performed or data items used in a module.

detail file   File containing relatively transient information, such as records of individual transactions that occurred during a particular period of time. Contrast with master file.

detail printing   Operation in which a line of printing occurs for each record read into the computer.

detail report   Printed report in which each line usually corresponds to one input record that has been read.

detection   Passive monitoring of an event for the purpose of discovering a problem.

developer   A person who designs, writes, and tests software. Also called a programmer.

development time   Time used for debugging new programs or hardware.

development tools   Hardware and software aids intended for use in developing programs and/or hardware systems.

device   (1) Mechanical or electrical device with a specific purpose. (2) Any computer peripheral. (3) Any piece of physical equipment within or attached to a computer.

device cluster   Group of terminals or other devices that share a communications controller.

device code   Eight-bit code for a specific input or output device.

device dependent   Pertaining to a program or language that must be used with a particular computer or a particular peripheral, such as a printer or modem, or it will not function.

device driver   A special section of computer code that translates the general commands from an operating system or user programs into the exact code a specific peripheral device needs. Often, device drivers for a few standard peripherals are built into the operating system, but others must be added in installation. For example: your printer needs a driver, your mouse needs a driver. Generally speaking, drivers come with the new hardware or as part of any major software package. Once installed, you can forget about them.

device flag   One-bit register that records the current status of a device.

device independence   Ability to command input/output operations without regard to the characteristics of the I/O devices.

device level   A description of the cable, bus, or other connection that goes between peripherals and their controller, or a standard that applies to peripherals. For example, the interface that commonly goes between a hard disk drive and its controller is a device level interface.

device media control language   Language used by the database administrator to create the physical description of a database on a disk storage device.

device name   (1) The label by which a computer system component is identified by the operating system. (2) General name for a kind of device, such as a NEC Silentwriter 2 Model 90 laser printer.

device number   A number assigned to a particular peripheral device, used to identify it in the computer.

Devol, George   In 1952, an electromechanical feedback device called the "servo" was patented by Devol. His patents were to become the technical basis for the formation of Unimation, Inc., the first major robot manufacturer. Devol's forty patents earned him the title "Grandfather of Industrial Robots."

DFX   A common object format for CAD files from several CAD programs.

DGS Paint   A professional PC-based program for doing painting, composition, image retouching and image processing. The program is intuitive, designed to let the user build and customize on-screen functionality by choosing from a vast number of effects and tools. Up to seven brushes paint in 32-bits. Other features include multiple masks and stencils, digital compositing with pixel-by-pixel manipulation, patterns, texture mapping, and an extensive set of image processing functions including edge detection.

diagnosis Process of isolating malfunctions in computing equipment and of detecting mistakes in programs and systems. See debug.

diagnostic routine Routine designed to locate a malfunction in the central processing unit or a peripheral device.

diagnostics Message to the user, automatically printed by a computer, that pinpoint improper commands and errors in logic. Sometimes called error messages.

diagram Schematic representation of a sequence of operations or routines. See flowchart.

dialect Particular version of a computer language. Usually a minor modification of some base language like BASIC or Pascal, but because of vast differences in modifications it may be significantly different from other dialects of the same language.

dialog Question-and-answer session between a computer system and a human.

dialog box Interactive message box. A temporary window on the screen that contains a set of choices whenever the executing program needs to collect information from the user.

dial-up In data communications, the use of a dial or push-button telephone to initiate a station-to-station telephone call.

dial-up line Normal switched telephone line used as a transmission medium for data communications. Contrast with leased line.

dichotomizing search See binary search.

dictionary program Spelling-check program, often used with word processing systems.

diddle To tamper with data.

die Tiny rectangular piece of a circular wafer of semiconductor silicon, sawed or sliced during the fabrication of integrated circuits. After sawing, leads are bonded to the die and it is mounted in a chip-carrier. Also, referred to as a chip when it is mounted in a chip-carrier.

dielectric A electrostatic printing process in which an electrical charge is placed on a surface that is nonconductive and therefore holds the charge. Commonly, a coated, dielectric paper is used, and no intermediary is needed. In ionography (Delphax), there is a dielectric drum that accepts a charged image, is toned and transfers the image to uncoated paper.

DIF An acronym for Data Interchange Format, a particular standard for data files. It is used by many programs involving forecasting and it allows files created on one software package to be read by another software package—perhaps one produced by an entirely different company. DIF files are not interchangeable between different machines; an Apple DIF file disk cannot be read directly into an IBM machine. While the files are compatible, the disks are formatted differently for different machines.

difference   Amount by which one quantity or number is greater or less than another.

difference engine   Machine designed by Charles Babbage in 1822 that mechanized a calculating function called the "method of differences."

diffusion   High-temperature process by which impurity atoms deposited on the surface of a material, such as a silicon wafer, have sufficient thermal energy to penetrate the material, seeking to equalize their densities by displacing the host atoms and altering the electrical properties of the material in desired ways. Normal diffusion temperatures are between 900 and 1200° C for the most frequently used impurities in silicon.

digit   One of the symbols of a numbering system used to designate a quantity. The decimal system has the ten digits 0-9.

digital   Pertaining to representation of information by encoding as bits of 1s or 0s that indicate on or off states. Highly important in the technology of computers and data communications. Contrast with analog.

digital communications   Transmissions of information by coding it into discrete on/off electronic signals.

digital computer   A computer that operates on discrete data. A device that performs arithmetic, logical, and comparative functions upon information represented in digital form and that operates under control of an internal program. Digital means that the computer uses data in the form of discrete numbers; for example, binary ones and zeros. Most computers used today (mainframes, minicomputers and microcomputers), are digital. Contrast with analog computer.

digital control   Use of digital technology to maintain conditions in operating systems as close as possible to desired values despite changes in the operating environment.

Digital Darkroom   An image processing program from Silicon Beach Software that acts as a computerized darkroom to compose images. The program uses computer processing techniques to edit and enhance scanned images.

digital data   Data represented in discrete, discontinuous form, as contrasted with analog data, which is represented in continuous form.

Digital Equipment Corporation (DEC)   A major manufacturer of minicomputer systems, founded in 1957 by Kenneth Olson. DEC pioneered the minicomputer business with its PDP computers in 1959. The popular PDP-8 was introduced in 1965, and the PDP-11 was introduced in 1970. In 1977, DEC announced the VAX series minicomputer systems and gained a strong foothold in commercial data processing.

digital mapping   The digitizing of geographic information for a geographic information system.

digital plotter   Output device that uses an ink pen (or pens) to draw graphs, line drawings, and other illustrations.

digital recording   Technique for recording information as discrete points onto magnetic recording media.

digital repeater   Unit placed in a data communications path to reconstruct digital pulses, which tend to deteriorate as they travel through long conductors.

digital signal   Two electrical states that communicate a code in binary data (1s and 0s) the computer can understand. Each 1 or 0 is a bit, while eight bits equal a byte, or one character. The digital signal is converted by a modem into an analog signal (modulated) that may be transmitted over phone lines. Incoming analog signals detected by the modem are converted into digital signals (demodulated) the computer can understand.

digital speech   Recorded speech broken into tiny units of sound. Each tiny unit has characteristics—such as pitch, loudness, and tembre—that can be represented by numbers, which become the digital code for speech.

digital-to-analog converter (D-A converter)   Mechanical or electronic devices used to convert discrete digital numbers to continuous analog signals. Opposite of analog-to-digital converter.

digital tracer   A special hinged arm which can be used to trace over drawings and graphs and which sends the information to the computer.

digital transmission   Transmission of data as discrete impulses.

digitize   To register a visual image or real object in a format that can be processed by the computer. Digitized data are read into the system with graphics input devices. It includes scanning an image, tracing a picture on a graphics tablet or converting camera images into the computer.

digitized type   Type stored in comptuer readable form as a collection of dots or line elements.

digitizer   A graphics input device that converts images into digital data that the computer can accept.

digitizing   Process of converting graphic representations, such as pictures and drawings, into digital data that can be processed by a computer system.

digitizing camera   A camera coupled with a processor used for encoding highly detailed images such as pictures or three-dimensional objects into digital data.

digitizing tablet A graphics input device that allows the user to create images. It has a special stylus that can be used to draw or trace images, which are then converted to digital data that can be processed by the computer.

digit place In positional notation, the site where a digit is located in a word representing a numeral. The decimal system has the units place, the tens place, and so on.

Dijkstra, Edsger W. A Dutchman, born in 1930, who entered the programming profession in 1952, and three years later, decided to help make programming a respectable discipline in the years to come. The working vocabulary of programmers everywhere is studded with words originated or forcefully promulgated by Dijkstra—display, semaphore, deadly embrace, go-to-less programming, and structured programming. Dijkstra has had a strong influence on programming.

dimension Maximum size, or the number and arrangement of the elements, of an array.

dimmed command A command in a pull-down menu that is grayed-black. A dimmed command means that choice is not currently available to you; perhaps because another function needs to be accomplished before that selection can be made.

dimmed icon A grayed-black icon indicates that the object it represents, such as a disk, or a folder, or document on a disk, has either been opened or been ejected from the disk drive.

DIN Acronym for Deutsche Industrie Norm, the German industry standard.

DIN connector A round connector used on several computers manufactured by Apple Computer, Inc. DIN stands for Deutsche Industrie Norm, a German committee that establishes standards.

dingbats Small graphical elements used for decorative purposes in a document. Some fonts, such as Zapf Dingbats, are designed to present sets of dingbats.

diode Electronic device used to permit current flow in one direction and to inhibit current flow in the opposite direction.

diode transistor logic See DTL.

DIP Acronym for Dual In-line Package. A switch found on many computers and peripherals, used to set up or adjust the equipment. Dual In-line Package refers to the switch's plastic housing designed to be attached directly to a circuit board or to an equipment component case.

direct access Process of storing data in, or getting data from, a storage device in such a manner that surrounding data need not be scanned to locate the desired data. The time required to get desired data from the storage device is independent of the location of the data.

direct access processing   Same as direct processing and random processing. Contrast with sequential processing.

direct access storage device (DASD)   Basic type of storage medium that allows information to be accessed by positioning the medium or accessing mechanism directly to the information required, thus permitting direct addressing of data locations.

direct address   Address that specifies the storage location of an operand. Contrast with indirect address.

direct-connect modem   Modulator/demodulator that plugs directly into a modular telephone jack for use in data transmission.

direct conversion   Method of converting from one system to another by ceasing to operate the old system when the new one is implemented.

direct current   Flow of electrons in one direction such as supplied by a battery. Contrast with alternating current.

direct data entry   Entry of data directly into the computer through machine-readable source documents or through the use of on-line terminals.

direct distance dialing   See DDD.

direct file organization   Organization of records so each is individually accessible.

direct file processing   Processing that allows the user to access a record directly by using a record key.

direct memory access (DMA)   Method by which data can be transferred between peripheral devices and internal memory without intervention by the central processing unit.

directory   (1) In a partition by software into several distinct files, a directory is maintained on a device to locate these files. (2) Index file containing the names and locations of all the files contained on a storage medium. (3) Major section of a hard disk drive. As many directories as needed can be named and sub-directories can be created within them. As files are created, their names and disk locations are stored in the directory.

direct processing   Technique of handling data in random order, without preliminary sorting, and utilizing files on direct access storage devices.

disable   To remove or inhibit a normal capability. To use a command that prevents further operation of a peripheral device. Opposite of enable.

disassembler   Program that takes machine-language code and generates the assembler-language code from which the machine language was produced. See assembly language.

disaster dump Computer storage dump that occurs as a result of a nonrecoverable mistake in a program.

disaster recovery plan A method of restoring data processing operations if those operations are halted by major damage or destruction.

disc A round, flat circular piece of nonmagnetic, polished metal designed to be read from and written to by optical (laser) technology. Optical discs use the disc spelling. Floppy disks and hard disks are spelled disk.

disclaimer Clause associated with many software products that states the vendor is not responsible for any business losses incurred due to the use of the product.

discrete Pertaining to distinct elements or to representation by means of distinct elements, such as characters or bits.

discrete component Electrical component that contains only one function, as opposed to an integrated circuit.

disk Magnetic device for storing information and programs accessible by a computer. Can be either a rigid platter (hard disk) or a sheet of flexible plastic (floppy disk). Disks have tracks where data is stored.

disk access time Time required to locate a specific track on a disk. Also called seek time. Part of total access time.

disk buffer Area of a computer's memory set aside to hold information not yet written to disk.

disk cartridge A removable hard disk enclosed in a protective case. Disk cartridges are used by certain types of hard disk drives.

disk cache A section of random access memory (RAM) set aside by the operating system to store frequently accessed data and program instructions.

disk controller card Peripheral circuit card that connects disk drives to a computer and controls their operation.

disk copying Process of transferring the entire contents of one disk to another disk.

disk crash Condition of a disk unit that makes it unusable. Usually caused by contact between the read/write head of the disk drive and the surface of the disk.

disk directory A catalog. This is the computer's own record of where each file or program is stored on the disk. The directory usually takes up a few tracks at the beginning of a disk.

disk doctor A program that enables the user to investigate directly what is stored on a disk. The use of a disk doctor may be the only way of recovering valuable data following a disk crash.

disk drive Device that reads data from a magnetic disk and copies it into the computer, and that writes data from the computer's memory onto a disk so it can be stored.

disk duplication Process of copying information recorded on one magnetic disk onto another disk.

disk duplicator A device that formats and makes identical copies of floppy disks for software distribution.

disk envelope Removable protective paper sleeve used when handling or storing a 5.25-inch diskette. Must be removed before inserting the diskette in a disk drive.

diskette A single magnetic disk on which data is recorded as magnetic spots. Available in both 3.5-inch and 5.25-inch formats.

diskette tray Container used to protect and store diskettes.

disk file File that resides on a magnetic disk. Organized collection of data stored on a disk.

disk jacket Permanent protective covering for a disk, usually made of plastic. The disk is never removed from the jacket, even when inserted in a disk drive.

disk library Special room that houses a file or disk packs under secure, environmentally controlled conditions or a storage facility that houses a file of diskettes.

disk memory Storage using rotating disks as its storage element.

disk operating system (DOS) A collection of software stored on disk that controls the operation of the computer system. A computer cannot function unless it has access to its own operating system. Typically, it keeps track of files, saves and retrieves files, allocates storage space, and manages other control functions associated with disk storage.

disk pack Group of removable tiered hard disks mounted on a shaft and treated as a unit. Must be placed on a disk storage unit to be accessed.

disk partition Logical portion of a disk that provides an organization allowing smaller blocks of data to be handled more conveniently.

disk sector Corresponds to a block of data storage area between two successive radials on the disk. The cutting of a disk into sectors is analogous to the way a pie would be sliced.

disk unit See magnetic disk unit.

disk unit enclosure Cabinet designed to hold one or more disk drives and a power supply.

dispatch To select the next task and get it ready for processing.

dispatching priority Numbers assigned to tasks and used to determine precedence for use by the central processing unit in a multitask situation.

dispersed data processing Same as distributed data processing.

dispersed intelligence Network system in which the computing power is scattered or dispersed throughout the computer network.

displacement Difference between the base address and the actual machine-language address.

display (1) Physical representation of data, as on a screen or display. (2) Lights or indicators on computer consoles. (3) Process of creating a visual representative of graphic data on an output device.

display adapter Adapter board that electronically links the computer to a display screen and determines its capabilities, such as degree of resolution, color vs. monochrome, and graphics vs. no graphics.

display background That part of displayed graphic data that is not part of the image being processed and is not subject to change by the user. Used to highlight the image part of the display, called the display foreground.

display composition In desktop publishing, lines of type that are in bold, ornamental, or contrasting typefaces; used to attract attention.

display console Input/output device consisting of a display screen and an input keyboard.

display cycle Time it takes a visual display screen to be completely refreshed.

display device Device capable of producing a visual representation of data, such as a graphics printer, digital plotter, and video display terminal.

display face A typeface suitable for titles and headings in a document, distinguished by its ability to stand out from other text on the page.

display font The font as it appears on the display screen. Ideally, it closely represents the printer font of the same name and size specification.

display foreground That part of graphic data being displayed on a visual display device that is subject to alteration by the user. Contrast with display background.

display frame   One image in an animation sequence.

display highlighting   Ways of emphasizing information on a display screen by using such enhancers as blinking, boldface, high contrast, reverse video, underlining, or different colors.

display image   That portion of a displayed graphics file that is currently visible on the display device.

display menu   Onscreen series of a program options that allows the user to choose the next function or course of action to be executed, such as to print the contents of the visual display or to save a graphic display on a disk.

display PostScript (DPS)   A display language from Adobe Corporation that translates elementary commands in an application program to graphics and text elements on screen. The screen counterpart of the PostScript printer language. See PostScript.

display screen   The part of a display unit on which images and text are shown.

display surface   Medium upon which a visual representation of graphic data is made, such as a visual display screen, printer paper, plotter paper, or film.

display terminal   Any output device capable of producing a visual representation of graphic data.

display tolerance   Measure of accuracy with which graphic data can be output.

display type   Technology of the display, such as cathode ray tube (CRT), light-emitting diode (LED), and liquid crystal display (LCD).

display unit   Device that provides a visual representation of data.

DisplayWrite   A full-featured word processing program for IBM microcomputer systems.

distortion   Any undesired change in the waveform of an electric signal passing through a circuit, including the transmission medium. In the design of any electronic circuit, one important problem is to modify the input signal in the required way without producing distortion beyond an acceptable degree.

distributed database   Database spread throughout the computer systems of a network.

distributed computing   Concept of performing operations in a computer system whose terminals and central processing unit are separated geographically but are linked together functionally in a communications network. Contrast with centralized data processing.

distributed design   Information structure that identifies the existence of independent operating units but recognizes the benefits of central coordination and control.

distributed information processing system   Set of interacting computer systems of databases situated in different locations.

distributed network   Network configuration in which all node pairs are connected either directly or by redundant paths through intermediate nodes.

distributive sort   Sort formed by separating the list into parts and then rearranging the parts in order.

disturbance   Any irregular phenomenon that interferes with the interchange of intelligence during transmission of a signal. See noise.

dithering   The creation of additional colors or shades of gray to create special effects or to make "hard edges" softer. Dithering takes advantage of the eye's tendency to blur spots of different colors by averaging their effects and merging them into a single perceived shade or color. Dithering is used to add realism to computer graphics, and to create a wide variety of patterns for use as backgrounds, fills and shading.

division check   Multiplication check in which a zero-balancing result is compared against the original dividend.

DMA   Acronym for Direct Memory Access.

DML   Acronym for Data Manipulation Language.

DOA   Acronym for Dead On Arrival. Used to describe a product that does not work when received from the manufacturer or supplier.

document   (1) Handwritten, typewritten, or printed sheet or sheets of paper containing data. (2) Any representation or collection of information or text, whether human-readable or machine-readable.

documentation   (1) During systems analysis and subsequent programming, the preparation of documents that describe such things as the system, the programs prepared, and the changes made at later dates. See program development cycle. (2) Internal documentation in the form of comments or remarks.

documentation aids   Aids that help automate the documentation process, such as program description write-ups, flowcharts, HIPO, program runs, and pseudocode.

documentor   Program designed to use data processing methods in the production and maintenance of program flowcharts, text material, and other types of tabular or graphic information.

document reader   Any OCR or OMR equipment that reads a limited amount of information.

document retrieval Process of acquiring data from storage devices and, possibly, manipulating the data and subsequently preparing a report.

domain (1) Set of data values from which a relational attribute may draw its values. (2) Any problem area of interest.

domain expert A human expert who contributes to the development of an expert system.

domain knowledge Knowledge of the application environment.

dongle A slang term for the I/O device used to protect software. The dongle attaches to the port of a computer and acts as a key.

dopant Any substance added in the doping process, such as arsenic or phosphorus. See semiconductor device.

dope vector Vector wherein an atom of a linked list describes the contents of the other atoms in the list.

doping Process of introducing impurity elements into the crystalline structure of pure silicone during semiconductor fabrication. See semiconductor device.

DOS Operating system for IBM-compatible microcomputers. DOS is available in both generic MS-DOS and IBM-specific PC DOS versions. DOS is an acronym for Disk Operating System.

dot matrix Technique for representing characters by composing them out of selected dots from within a rectangular matrix of dots.

dot matrix printer Printer that creates text characters and graphs with a series of closely spaced dots. Uses tiny hammers to strike a needle mechanism against the paper at precise moments as the print head moves across the page. Some produce dot patterns fine enough to approach the print quality of a daisy wheel printer.

dot pitch The resolution of a dot matrix. (1) For display screens, it is expressed as the width of an individual dot; for example, a .28 dot pitch refers to a dot that is 28/100 of a millimeter in diameter. The smaller the number, the higher the resolution. (2) For printers, it is expressed as the number of dots per linear inch; for example, a desktop laser printer prints at least 300 dpi. The larger the number, the higher the resolution.

dots per inch (1) A linear measure of the number of dots a printer can print in an inch. For example, a 300 dpi laser printer can print up to 300 dots for each horizontal or vertical inch on the paper. (2) A measure of screen resolution that counts the dots that the device can produce per linear inch.

double buffering Software or hardware technique to transfer information between the computer and peripheral devices. Information in one buffer is acted on by the computer while information in the other is transferred in or out.

double-click Method to invoke a command by using the mouse button. The pointer or cursor is placed in the correct position on a display screen and the mouse button is pressed twice in rapid succession. A double-click is used to open a file, disk, or folder.

double density Having twice the storage capacity of a normal disk or tape. Ability to store twice as much data in a given area on a disk or tape as single density. In IBM-compatible microcomputers, a double density 5.25-inch disk has a capacity of 360K bytes, while the double density 3.5-inch disk has a capacity of 720K bytes.

double precision Pertaining to the use of two computer words to represent a number to gain increased precision.

double quote Another name for the quote mark (").

double-sided disk Magnetic disk capable of storing information on both of its surfaces. Contrast with single-sided disk.

doublestriking See overstriking.

double word Entity of storage that is two words in length.

doubly linked list List in which each atom contains one pointer that relates to the successor atom.

do until One of the the variations of the primitive loop construct of structured programming.

do while Variation of the primitive loop construct of structured programming.

Dow Jones Information Service A computer database containing current information on stock prices and other financial news. It can be accessed by subscribers with microcomputers and modems.

down Condition that exists when the hardware circuits of a computer are inoperable or there is a failure in the software system. When a computer is down, it is simply not functioning.

down-line processor Processor at or near the terminal point in a data communications network that facilitates the transmission of data.

downlink A communications channel from a satellite to an earth station.

download (1) Process of transferring data (files) from a large computer to a smaller one. (2) To transfer information to a laser printer from a computer. Opposite of upload.

downloadable font A set of characters of the same typeface and size stored on disk and sent (downloaded) to a printer's memory when needed for printing a document.

downtime Length of time a computer system is inoperative due to a malfunction. Contrast with available time and uptime.

downward compatible Pertaining to a computer compatible with a smaller or previous-generation computer.

dpi Acronym for dots per inch. The density of a printer's output; determines the overall appearance/quality of printed output. Laser printers offer 300 dpi and up. True typesetting starts at 1000 dpi. Dot matrix printers, on the low end, range from 72 to 150 dpi.

DPMA Acronym for Data Processing Management Association.

DPMA certificate Certificate formerly given by the Data Processing Management Association indicating that a person has attained a certain level of competence in the field of data processing. This Certificate in Data Processing is obtained by passing an examination offered yearly and now administered by the Institute for Certification of Computer Professionals.

draft mode Low-quality printing mode available on some printers.

draft quality Measure of quality for printed output. Usually refers to the result of top-speed printing and therefore not the most precisely defined or fully filled-in characters. Considered acceptable for working copies but not final work. Contrast with letter quality.

drag Action of moving the mouse while holding the button down; used to move or manipulate objects on a computer's display screen.

drain One of three connecting terminals of a field effect transistor, the other two being the source and the gate. If the charge carriers are positive, conventional current flows from source to drain.

DRAM Short for Dynamic RAM, meaning a type of memory chip that keeps its contents only if supplied with regular clock pulses and a chance to periodically refresh the data internally. DRAM is far less expensive than static RAM (which needs no refreshing) and is the type found in most personal computers.

DRAW A graphics instruction in many versions of the BASIC programming language, which is useful for high-resolution graphics.

drawing Process of creating a graphic image with an object-oriented drawing program.

drawing program A program for creating and manipulating object-oriented graphics, as opposed to creating and manipulating pixel images. For example, in a drawing program the user can manipulate an element such as a triangle, or a block of text as an independent object simply by selecting the object and moving it.

DrawPerfect   A drawing program for IBM-compatible microcomputers. This charting, drawing and presentation program provides 256 colors. It creates 2-D bar, pie, and graph charts.

Dr. Halo   A paint program for IBM-compatible microcomputers.

drift   Change in the output of an electric circuit. Occurs slowly over a period of time.

drill-and-practice program   Teaching software that reinforces old lessons.

drive   Physical components necessary for writing data to, and reading data from, a diskette or disk. Short name for disk drive.

drive number   The naming convention for disk drives. For example, in a two-drive Apple Macintosh system its drives are 0 and 1; in a two-drive IBM-compatible microcomputer system the drives are A and B.

driver   Series of instructions the computer follows to reformat data for transfer to and from a particular peripheral device. Electrical and mechanical requirements differ from one kind of device to another, and software drivers are used to standardize the format of data between them and the computer.

DRO   Acronym for Destructive Read Out. See destructive read.

drop   (1) In a network, remote terminal location. (2) Distance between top and bottom of a sheet of computer stationery, measured in millimeters or inches.

drop cap   An initial letter of a chapter or paragraph enlarged and positioned so that the top of the character is even with the top of the first line and the rest of the character descends into the second and subsequent lines.

drop dead halt   Halt from which there is no recovery.

drop-down menu   A type of menu that drops from the menu bar when requested and remains open without further action until the user closes it or chooses a menu item. Same as pull-down menu.

drop in   Character that appears erroneously—on a display screen, on a printout, or in a file—because the disk drive or tape drive misstored or misread one or more bits.

drop out   (1) In data transmission, a momentary loss in signal, usually due to the effect of noise or system malfunction. (2) Character that vanishes from a display, printout, or file because the disk drive or tape drive misstored or misread one or more bits.

drop shadow A shadow placed behind an image, slightly off-set horizontally and vertically, that creates the illusion that the topmost image has been lifted off the surface of the page.

drum See magnetic drum.

drum plotter Output device that draws schematics, graphs, pictures, and so forth on paper with automatically controlled pens. The paper is wrapped around a cylindrical drum that turns forward and backward at various speeds under one or more pens that slide to and fro, marking the paper.

drum printer Printing device that uses a drum embossed with alphanumeric characters. Type of line printer, that can print several thousand lines per minute. Each print position has a complete set of characters around the circumference of the drum.

dry plasma etching Method for developing a mask on a wafer.

dry run Program-checking technique of examining the logic and coding of a program from an algorithm and written instructions and recording the results of each step of the operation before running the program on the computer.

DSL Acronym for Dynamic Simulation Language.

DTL Acronym for Diode Transistor Logic, microelectronic logic based on connections between semiconductor diodes and the transistor.

DTP See desktop publishing.

dual channel controller Controller that enables reading from, and writing to, a device to occur simultaneously.

dual density (1) Pertaining to tapes or disks on which data is densely recorded. (2) Floppy disk with double-sided recording capability.

dual disk drive Floppy disk system that contains two disk drives, providing an increased storage capacity.

dual in-line package (DIP) Popular type of integrated circuit package on which a chip is mounted. Provides a protective casing for the integrated circuit and pin connections for plugging the chip into a circuit board.

dual intensity Ability of a terminal or printer to produce characters in regular as well as highlighted or bold formats.

dual processors (1) Two central processing units within a computer system that can function simultaneously. (2) A computer that uses two microprocessors. Dual processors provide faster and more efficient processing. The main objective is to relieve the main processor of the tasks of memory management, graphics displays, and, sometimes, advanced mathematical functions.

dual-sided disk drives Disk drives that use two read/write heads to store and retrieve data on both the top and bottom sides of a disk.

dual y-axis graph In presentation graphics, a graph that uses two y-axes when comparing two data series with different measurement scales. Useful when comparing two different data series that must be measured with two different values axes.

dumb terminal Video display terminal with minimal I/O capabilities and no processing capability.

dummy Pertaining to an artificial argument, instruction, address, or record of data inserted solely to fulfill prescribed conditions.

dummy argument Variables, used as function arguments, that do not have any values.

dummy instruction (1) Artificial instruction or address inserted in a list to serve a purpose other than its execution as an instruction. (2) Instruction in a routine that, in itself, does not perform any functions. Often used to provide a point at which to terminate a program loop.

dummy module Skeleton of module with entry and exit, but no actual processing. Particularly useful in top-down testing when subordinate subfunctions are not ready for integration.

dump Data that results from a dumping process. Duplication of the contents of a storage device to another storage device or to a printer.

dumping Copying all or part of the contents of a storage unit, usually from the computer's internal storage, into an auxiliary storage unit or onto a printer.

duplex Pertaining to a communications system or equipment capable of transmission in both directions.

duplex channel Communications channel that allows simultaneous transmission in both directions.

duplexing Use of duplicate computers, peripheral equipment, or circuitry so that, in the event of a component failure, an alternate component can enable the system to continue.

duplex printing Printing a document on both sides of the sheet, so that the verso (left) and recto (right) pages face each other after the document is bound.

duplicate To copy so that the result remains in the same physical form as the source, such as to make a new diskette with the same information and in the same format as an original diskette. Contrast with copy.

duplication check Check requiring that the results of two independent performances of the same operation be identical. May be made concurrently on duplicate equipment or at different times on the same equipment.

duration   The amount of working time it takes to complete a task.

dust cover   Plastic dust covers used to protect microcomputers, disk units, terminals, printers, and so on from one of their worst enemies.

Dvorak keyboard   Keyboard arrangement designed by August Dvorak. Provides increased speed and comfort and reduces the rate of errors by placing the most frequently used letters in the center for use by the strongest fingers. In this fashion, finger motions and awkward strokes are reduced by over 90 percent in comparison with the familiar QWERTY keyboard. The Dvorak system, although patented in 1936, did not really become popular until its approval by ANSI in 1982. The Dvorak keyboard puts the five vowel keys, AOEUI, together under the left hand in the center row, and the five most frequently used consonants, DHTNS, under the fingers of the right hand.

dyadic   Pertaining to an operation that uses two operands.

dyadic operation   Any operation on two operands.

dye-polymer recording   An optical disc recording process in which dye embedded in a plastic polymer coating on an optical disc is used to create minute bumps on the surface that can be read by a laser. Dye-polymer bumps can be flattened and re-created, thus making an optical disc rewritable.

dynamic   Refers to operations that are performed on the fly, while the program is running.

dynamic RAM (DRAM)   The most common type of computer memory; the computer must refresh DRAM at frequent intervals. Contrast with static RAM, which is usually faster and does not require refresh circuitry.

dynamic address translation (DAT)   In virtual storage systems the change of a virtual storage address to a real storage address during execution of an instruction.

dynamic binding   The implementation consequence of inheritance and polymorphism. As an object-oriented program runs, messages are received by objects. Often the method for handling a message is stored high in a class library. The method is located dynamically when it is needed and binding then occurs at the last possible moment.

dynamic dump   Dump taken during the execution of a program. See snapshot dump.

dynamic relocation   Movement of part or all of an active (currently operating) program from one region of storage to another. All necessary address references are adjusted to enable proper execution of the program to continue in its new location.

dynamic scheduling Job scheduling determined by the computer on a moment-to-moment basis, depending upon the circumstances.

Dynamic Simulation Language (DSL) High-level programming language, suited primarily for simulation of engineering and scientific problems of a continuous nature. Because DSL facilitates the solution of ordinary differential equations that frequently are functions of time, it is particularly useful for transient analysis of dynamic systems.

dynamic storage Any memory device that must constantly be recharged or refreshed at frequent intervals to avoid loss of data. Very volatile storage.

dynamic storage allocation Automatic storage allocation.

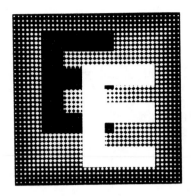

e The symbol used to represent the base of the natural logarithms, 2.71828.

E In floating-point numbers, a symbol that stands for exponent; 17E2 means "17 times 10 to the power 2." See E notation.

early binding In object-oriented programming, static binding. See binding.

EAROM Acronym for Electrically Alterable ROM. ROM memory that can be selectively altered without erasing all stored data, as is done with EPROM devices.

Easy Color Paint An Apple Macintosh graphics program designed for non-professionals. It emphasizes "simplicity, economy and fun." Simply pick a color and pattern, choose a tool, and start painting.

eavesdropping Passive wiretapping, interception of messages, usually without detection.

EBAM Acronym for Electron Beam Addressed Memory, an electronic storage device that uses electrical circuits to control a beam that reads from or writes on a metal oxide semiconductor surface.

EBCDIC Acronym for Extended Binary Coded Decimal Interchange Code, an 8-bit code used to represent data in large IBM mainframes. EBCDIC can represent up to 256 distinct characters and is the principal code used in many of the current computers.

ECAD Acronym for Electronic Computer Aided Design. CAD for electronic design.

echo (1) In data communications, the return of a transmitted signal to its source, with a delay that indicates the signal is a reflection rather than the original. (2) In computer graphics, to provide visual feedback to the designer during graphic input to the system.

echo check   Check on the accuracy of a data transfer operation in which the data received is transmitted back to the source and compared with the original data.

Eckert, J. Presper   Coinventer of ENIAC. Collaborated with John Mauchly at the Moore School of Electrical Engineering, University of Pennsylvania, on developing the Electronic Numerical Integrator And Computer for Army Ordnance between 1943 and 1946. This was the first large-scale, all-electronic digital computer. Its development launched the computer industry as we know it today. See ENIAC and Mauchly, John.

ECL   Acronym for Emitter-Coupled Logic, also called current mode logic. Faster than TTL, but much less popular.

ECOM   Acronym for Electronic Computer Oriented Mail, a process of sending and receiving messages in digital form over telecommunications facilities.

edge   (1) In computer graphics, the straight line segment which is the intersection of two planes' faces of a solid, such as the edges of a cube. (2) Connection between two nodes in a graph. See indegree.

edge card   Circuit board (or card) with contact strips along one edge, designed to mate with an edge connector.

edge connector   A row of etched lines on the edge of a printed circuit board that is inserted into a motherboard or an expansion slot.

edge cutter/trimmer   Device for removing the sprocketed margin from continuous-form printer paper.

edge sharpening   Process of sharpening the edges of a digitized picture.

edit   (1) To check the correctness of data. (2) To change as necessary the form of data by adding or deleting certain characters. Part of a word processing program, page layout program, or graphic program that can edit data for printing, adding special symbols, spacing, deleting nonsignificant zeros, and so on.

editing   Making the corrections or changes in a program or data. See data editing.

editing run   In batch processing, the editing program will check the data for ostensible validity—such as testing to ensure that dates and numbers fall within the expected ranges, comparing totals with separately entered batch or hash totals, and proving check digits—and identify any errors for correction and resubmission.

edit line   "Status report" line displayed on the screen when certain spreadsheet or word processing programs are in use. Tells the user the present location of the cursor, the amount of memory left, and (in some word processing programs) the name of the file in use. In spreadsheets, it will also show the contents or formula of the cell at the cursor location, and one or two more items of information (depending on which spreadsheet is being used).

edit mode An input mode that allows the editing of previously entered information.

editor A program used to write, enter, and edit programs.

EDP Acronym for Electronic Data Processing.

EDS Acronym for Exchangeable Disk Store.

EDSAC Acronym for Electronic Delayed Storage Automatic Computer, the first digital computer to feature the stored-program concept. Developed by Maurice Wilkes at Cambridge University in Great Britain in 1949.

EDVAC Acronym for Electronic Discrete Variable Automatic Computer, the first U.S.-built computer that featured a stored-program unit. Developed at the Moore School of Electrical Engineering, University of Pennsylvania, in 1951, by John von Neumann. See von Neumann, John.

EEROM Storage device that can be erased electrically and reprogrammed.

effective address Address derived by performing any specified address modification operations upon a specified address.

effectiveness Degree to which the output produced achieves the desired purpose.

EFT Acronym for Electronic Funds Transfer. An EFT network transfers funds from one account to another with electronic equipment rather than with paper media, such as checks. Increasingly popular method of paying periodic bills.

EGA Acronym for Enhanced Graphics Adapter, a video display adapter introduced by IBM in 1984. Video display standard for IBM-compatible microcomputers featuring 640 by 350-pixel resolution. EGA can display no more than 16 colors at once. EGA has been superseded by VGA.

egoless programming Concept of arranging the programming tasks so that credit for success or blame for failure must be shared by several programmers rather than just one person. Uses structured walkthroughs and other techniques.

EIA Acronym for Electronics Industries Association; an organization founded in 1924 that is concerned with establishing standards for the electronic industry.

EIA interface Standard interface between peripherals and microcomputers, and modems and terminals. Another name for RS-232C interface.

Eiffel   An object-oriented programming language developed by Bertrand Meyer in 1988.

eight-bit chip   CPU chip that processes data eight bits at a time. Contrast with sixteen-bit chip and thirty-two-bit chip.

elapsed time   The amount of calendar time it takes to complete a computer related task.

elastic banding   In computer graphics, the movement of a line drawn from a specified point on the screen to another point. The second point can be moved around the screen by using a mouse, and the line length will expand or contract as if the line were made of elastic material. This makes alteration of diagrams much easier than it would be if lines had to be rubbed out and redrawn. Elastic banding is much used in computer-aided design programs. Also called rubber banding.

electrical communications   Science and technology by which information is collected from an originating source, transformed into electric currents or fields, transmitted over electrical networks or through space to another point, and reconverted into a form suitable for interpretation by a receiving entity.

electrical schematic   Diagram of the logical arrangement of hardware in an electrical circuit or system, using conventional symbols. Can be constructed interactively by computer-aided design.

electric discharge   A printing method where the paper consists of at least three layers: a substrate, a dark-colored layer that is revealed to form the image and a light-colored surface coating, usually vacuum-coated aluminum. The print head creates the image by emitting sparks that physically remove the surface coating.

electromagnetic delay line   Delay line whose operation is based on the time of propagation of electromagnetic waves through distributed or lumped capacitance and inductance. Used in early computers.

electromechanical   Pertaining to any system or device for processing data that uses both electrical and mechanical principles.

electron beam deflection system   Narrow stream of electrons moving in the same direction under the influence of an electric or magnetic field. See gun and yoke.

electronic   Pertaining to the flow of electricity through semiconductors, valves, and filters, in contrast with the free flow of current through simple conductors. The essence of computer technology is the selective use and combination of electronic apparatus whereby current can be allowed to flow or can be halted by electronic switches working at a very high speed.

electronic accounting machine (EAM)   Data processing equipment that is predominantly electromechanical, such as a keypunch, mechanical sorter, tabulator, or collator.

Electronic Computer Aided Design (ECAD)   CAD for electronic design.

electronically programmable   Pertaining to Programmable ROM or any other digital device in which the data 1s and 0s in binary code can be entered electronically, usually by the user with a piece of equipment called a PROM Programmer.

electronic bulletin board   Computer system that maintains a list of messages so people can call up (with their computer systems) and either post a message or read those already there.

electronic cottage   Concept of permitting workers to remain at home to perform work, using computer terminals connected to a central office.

electronic data processing (EDP)   Data processing performed largely by electronic equipment, especially computers.

electronic data processing system   System for data processing by means of machines using electronic circuitry at electronic speed, as opposed to electromechanical equipment.

electronic disk   A chip that lets the computer regard part of its memory as a third disk drive. Also called a phantom disk or RAM disk.

electronic filing   How computer systems store information electronically on disks or tapes.

electronic funds transfer (EFT)   Cashless method of paying for goods or services. Electronic signals between computers are used to adjust the accounts of the parties involved in a transaction. Commonly used to make periodic payments, such as insurance premiums. Increasingly available as an option for "depositing paychecks." See EFT.

Electronic Industries Association (EIA)   Association of electronic manufacturers and others who set standards, disseminate information, provide industry liaison, and maintain public relations for the industry. EIA was founded in 1924.

electronic journal   Log file summarizing, in chronological sequence, the processing activities performed by a system.

electronic magazine   Magazine published in a floppy disk, video disk or video tape format. A type of electronic publishing.

electronic mail   Process of sending, receiving, storing, and forwarding messages in digital form over telecommunication facilities. Also called E-mail.

electronic marketplace   The buying and selling of information through information services and videotex services. Examples of services that can be subscribed to include The Source, CompuServe and Prodigy.

electronic music Music in which the sounds are produced by electronic means. See computer music and synthesizer.

electronic office Office that relies on word processing, computer and data communications technologies. See automated office.

electronic pen Pen-like stylus commonly used in conjunction with a cathode ray tube for inputting or changing information under program control. Often called light pen.

electronic publishing (1) Technology encompassing a variety of activities that contain or convey information with a high editorial and value-added content in a form other than print. Includes educational software disks, CD-ROM, online databases, electronic mail videotext, teletext, videotape cassettes, and videodisks. (2) Use of a personal computer, special software, and a laser printer to produce very high-quality documents that combine text and graphics. Also called desktop publishing.

electronics Branch of science and technology relating to the conduction and control of electricity flowing through semiconducting materials or through vacuum or gases.

electronic spreadsheet Computer program that turns a computer terminal into a huge ledger sheet. Allows large columns and rows of numbers to change according to parameters determined by the user. A whole range of numbers can be changed when a single entry is varied, allowing complex projections and numerical forecasts to be performed without tedious manual calculations.

electronic thesaurus A program that lists synonyms for a given word.

electron tube Dominant electronic element found in computers prior to the advent of the transistor. See first generation computers and vacuum tube.

electrophotographic A printing process where light is used to create a latent image on a photoconductive intermediary. The latent image is rendered visible by liquid or powder toner, transferred to a paper and fixed by heat, cold, pressure, chemical vapors or a combination of these. Printers using this process often are referred to by the source of light used to create the image—laser, liquid-crystal shutter (LCS), light-emitting diode (LED), etc.

electrosensitive paper Printer paper with a thin coating of conductive material, such as aluminum. Print becomes visible because it darkens where a matrix-type print head allows electric current to flow onto the conductive surface.

electrosensitive printer Nonimpact printer that uses electricity to form characters on specially treated paper.

electrostatic plotter Output device that draws graphic data on paper by using static electrical energy. Generally faster than a pen plotter.

126

electrostatic printer High-speed nonimpact printer that forms characters on chemically treated paper. See xerographic printer.

electrothermal printer High-speed printer that uses heated elements to create characters as matrices of small dots on heat-sensitive paper.

element Item of data within an array, matrix, set, or collection.

elementary diagram Wiring diagram of an electrical system in which all devices are drawn between vertical lines that represent power sources. Contains logic elements, components, wire nets, and text. Can be constructed interactively on a CAD system.

elements of a microcomputer Components of a microcomputer; include a microprocessor for the central processing unit, program and data storage, input/output circuitry, and clock generators.

elite type Size of type that fits twelve characters into each inch of type. Contrast with pica.

em A unit of measure equal to the width of the capital M in a particular font.

E-mail Abbreviation for electronic mail, a communications service for computer users wherein textual messages are sent to a central computer system, or electronic "mailbox," and later retrieved by the addressee. E-mail usually refers to private messages. Bulletin board usually refers to public messages.

embedded command (1) One or more codes inserted into a document that do not print but direct the application program or printer to control printing and change formats. (2) Low-level assembly level instructions that are inserted within a program written in a high-level language. Embedded code is used to make a program more efficient or to produce a capability not available in the high-level language.

embedded controller A controller that is built either into a peripheral such as a disk drive, or into the circuitry of the main board of the system unit.

embedded systems Preprogrammed microprocessors built into another device, such as an automobile, a camera, or a copy machine.

em dash A dash (—) that is one em wide.

empty string String containing no characters. Also called null string.

EMS An acronym for Expanded Memory Specification, a standard form of extra memory that can be used on IBM-compatible microcomputers.

emulate (1) To imitate one hardware system with another, by means of an electronic attachment, such that the imitating system accepts the same

127

data, executes the same programs, and achieves the same results as the imitated system. (2) To have a program simulate the function of another software or hardware product. Printers often have emulation options so that you can specify a brand name in configuration or setup, even though you don't have that brand.

emulator Type of program or device that allows user programs written for one kind of computer system to be run on another system.

en One half the width of the em.

enable To switch a computer device or facility so it can operate. Opposite of disable.

encapsulated PostScript (EPS) A file format developed to facilitate the exchange of PostScript graphics files between applications. Like all PostScript files, EPS files are resolution independent and can be printed by a PostScript printer.

encapsulation In object-oriented programming, the bundling of methods and instance variables within a class or object so that access to the instance variables is permitted only through the object's own methods. The process of hiding all of the details of an object that do not contribute to its essential characteristics. Encapsulation is one of the fundamental elements of the object model. The terms "encapulation" and "information hiding" are usually interchangeable.

encipher To alter data (scramble) so it is not readily usable unless the changes are first undone. See encryption.

enclosure Housing for any electrical or electronic device.

encode To convert data into a code form acceptable to some piece of computer equipment. Opposite of decode.

encoder Device that produces machine-readable output, such as floppy disk, either from manual keyboard depressions or from data already recorded in some other code.

encryption The process of coding, or encrypting, any data, in which a specific code or key is required to restore the original data. The process of encoding communications data.

end-around carry Carry from the most-significant-digit place to the least-significant-digit place.

end-around shift See circular shift.

en dash A dash (–) that is one en wide. A punctuation mark.

endless loop Endless repetition of a series of instructions with no exit from the loop possible. Same as infinite loop.

end mark Code or signal that indicates termination of a unit of data. See stop bit and group mark.

end-of-block (EOB) Termination of a block.

end-of-file (EOF) Termination or point of completion of a quantity of data. End-of-file marks are used to indicate this point on magnetic files. See end-of-tape marker.

end-of-job Condition that alerts the program that a job is done and starts another action.

end-of-message (EOM) Termination of a message.

end-of-page halt Feature that stops the printer at the end of each completed page of output.

end-of-tape marker Marker on a magnetic tape used to indicate the end of the permissible recording area.

end-of-text Transmission control character used to indicate to receiving hardware that the previous character was the last character of message text.

end-of-transmission Control character used to indicate that a transmission has been completed.

end user Person who buys and uses computer software or who has contact with computers.

Engelberger, Joseph A world-renowned robot inventor and entrepreneur. His science-fiction approach to robotics proved to be the motivation that sent him on a lifelong quest that eventually earned him the title "Father of Robotics."

engine The portion of a program that determines how the program manages and manipulates data. Another name for a processor.

Enhanced Graphics Adapter See EGA.

enhanced keyboard A standard keyboard for newer IBM personal computers. It has become the de facto standard for most IBM-compatible microcomputer keyboards.

enhancements Hardware or software improvements, additions, or updates to a computer or software system.

ENIAC Acronym for Electronic Numerical Integrator And Calculator, the first large-scale, all-electronic digital computer. Built by John Mauchly and J. Presper Eckert at the Moore School of Electrical Engineering, University of Pennsylvania, in 1946. Occupied 1500 sq. ft., weighed about 30 tons, contained approximately 18,000 vacuum tubes, and required 130 kw of power. The computing elements consisted of many components with about one million hand-soldered connections. The input/output system was modified IBM card readers and punches. ENIAC could perform 5000 additions per second, relatively slow by today's standards. But in 1946, the only machine that could even compete with it was the ASCC relay calculator, which performed only 10 additions per second. ENIAC made all relay calculators obsolete. It could perform several additions, a multiplication, and a square root in parallel, as well as solve several independent problems at the same time. ENIAC was so successful that it marked the end of the pioneer stage of automatic computer development. After nine years of operation, ENIAC was retired from service in 1955. See Eckert, J. Presper and Mauchly, John.

E notation System of notation used to express very large and very small numbers. Consists of two parts: a mantissa and an exponent. Also called scientific notation.

ENTER key Special key on some keyboards that means "execute a command." Same as RETURN key on some keyboards. Often used interchangeably with carriage return. See immediate-mode commands.

entity Any object that has meaning for a particular application. A computer system may be an entity; a job position, a company, or even a technique or concept could be an entity as well.

entrepreneur One who organizes, manages, and assumes the risk of a business or enterprise.

entry In an electronic spreadsheet, the value or information contained within a specific cell.

entry point The point in a module where control is transferred. Each module has only one entry point.

environment In a computing context, this is more likely to refer to the mode of operation, such as a network environment, than to physical conditions of temperature, humidity, and so forth. With respect to personal computers, everything surrounding the PC, including peripherals and software.

environment division Second of four main parts of a COBOL program.

EOB Acronym for End-Of-Block.

EOF Acronym for End-Of-File. When all the records in a file have been processed, the computer is said to have encountered an end-of-file condition.

EOJ Acronym for End-Of-Job.

EOLN Acronym for End-Of-Line, a flag indicating the end of a line of data. Sometimes abbreviated EOL.

EOM   Acronym for End-Of-Message.

EOT   Acronym for End-Of-Transmission.

EP   Acronym for Electronic Presentations. A process where a user creates a presentation using a desktop computer system. The diskette (containing the presentation) is then inserted into an EP player, which can produce an animated video presentation.

EPO   Acronym for Emergency Power Off; the circuit, and the buttons activating it, that can turn an entire computer off in an emergency. There may be as many as twenty EPO buttons in a large installation.

EPROM   Acronym for Erasable Programmable Read-Only Memory, a special PROM that can be erased under high-intensity ultraviolet light and reprogrammed repeatedly. Compare EAROM. Contrast with ROM.

EPROM programmer   Special machine used to program EPROM chips. Compare PROM programmer.

EPS   Acronym for Encapsulated PostScript. A directly printable PostScript file; the output of a PostScript compatible printer driver captured in a file instead of being sent to a printer. The typical filename extension for encapsulated PostScript files is .EPS.

epsilon   Small quantity of something.

Epson   A well-established make of dot-matrix printers which can print graphics as well as text.

equality   Idea expressed by the equal sign, written = . In many programming languages and program designs the = sign is also used as a "replacement symbol." Contrast with inequality.

equalization   A process by which the range of gray shades in an image is expanded to make the image more attractive.

equation   Mathematical sentence with an = sign between two arithmetic expressions that name the same number. A + 10 = 6 is an equation from which A is calculated to be -4.

equipment   Part of a computer system. See computer, hardware, and peripheral equipment.

equipment bay   Cabinet or case in which electronic equipment is installed.

erasable optical disc   An optical disc on which data can be stored, moved, changed, and erased, just as on magnetic media. Erasable drives perform much like large, interchangeable hard disks. Erasable drives use two lasers rather than one; one laser melts the surface of the media to an amorphous state, effectively erasing any information stored there—the other laser writes or reads information.

erasable programmable read only memory See EPROM.

erasable storage Storage medium that can be erased and reused. Hard disks, floppy disks and magnetic tapes are examples of media that can be erased and reused.

erase To remove data from storage without replacing it.

ERCIM Acronym for European Research Consortium for Informatics and Mathematics. A research consortium with members from Germany, France, Great Britain and the Netherlands.

ergonomics Study of the physical relationships between people and their work environment. Adapting machines to the convenience of operators, with the general aim of maximum efficiency and physical well being. Numeric keypads on standard keyboards, detachable keyboards, and tilting display screens are tangible results. The word comes from ergo (work) and nomics (law or management).

EPROM Acronym for Erasable ROM. See EPROM and EAROM.

error Any deviation of a computed or a measured quantity from the theoretically correct or true value. Contrast with fault, malfunction, and mistake. See intermittent error and round-off error.

error analysis Branch of numerical analysis concerned with studying the error aspects of numerical analysis procedures. Includes the study of errors that arise in a computation because of the peculiarities of computer arithmetic.

error checking (1) Various techniques that test for the valid condition of data. (2) Process by which two telecommunicating computers can verify that the data received was error-free.

error control Any plan, implemented by software, hardware, or procedures, to detect and/or correct errors introduced into a data communications system.

error-correcting code (1) Code in which each acceptable expression conforms to specific rules of construction. Nonacceptable expressions are also defined. If certain types of errors occur in an acceptable expression, an equivalent will result and the error can be corrected. (2) Code in which the forbidden pulse combination produced by the gain or loss of a bit will indicate which bit is wrong. Same as self-correcting code.

error correction System that detects and inherently provides correction for errors caused by transmission equipment or facilities.

error-detecting code (1) Code in which each expression conforms to specific rules of construction. When expressions occur that do not conform to the rules of these constructions, an error is indicated. (2) Code in which errors produce forbidden combinations. A single error-detecting code produces a forbidden combination if a digit gains or loses a single bit. A double error-detecting code produces a forbidden combination if a digit gains or loses either one or two bits, and so on. Also called self-checking code.

error file   File generated during information processing to retain erroneous information sensed by the computer, often printed as an error report.

error guessing   Test data selection technique. The selection criterion is to pick values that seem likely to cause errors.

error handling   Program feature that minimizes the possibility of an error occurring if a keyboard operator pushes the wrong key.

error message   Printed or displayed statement indicating the computer has detected a mistake or malfunction. See warning message.

error rate   In data communications, a measure of quality of circuit or equipment, the number of erroneous bits or characters in a sample.

error ratio   Ratio of the number of erroneous data units to the total number of data units.

error transmission   Change in data resulting from the transmission process. Often a drop in or a drop out.

ESCAPE key   Standard control key available on most computer keyboards. Used to take control of the computer away from a program, to escape from a specific program, or to stop a program. Abbreviated ESC.

ESPRIT   Acronym for European Strategic Program for Research and Development in Information Technology.

EDSI   Short for Enhanced Small Disk Interface, a version of an industry standard interface that connects hard disks to their controllers. ESDI allows the disks to run faster and more reliably.

Ethernet   A form of Local Area Network (LAN) widely used for interconnecting computers. A relatively fast system, Ethernet is popular in DEC and Unix environments. Operational speeds are around one million characters per second. Ethernet was developed by the Xerox Corporation in 1976 and was originally used for linking minicomputers at the Xerox Palo Alto Research Center.

E-time   The portion of the machine cycle when an instruction is actually executed.

ETX   Acronym for End-Of-Text.

European Computer Manufacturer's Association (ECMA)   European organization for business equipment manufacturers, computer vendors and, suppliers. ECMA is based in Geneva, Switzerland.

evaluation   Process of determining if a newly created computer system is actually doing what it was designed to do. See system follow-up.

event   Any occurrence or happening. Also called milestone node, has no time frame associated with it, but typically serves to mark the start or end of activities and to relate activities to each other.

event driven   Refers to multiprogramming; programs share resources based on events that take place in the programs.

evocative typeface   A display type design intended to evoke an era or place.

Excel   A spreadsheet from Microsoft Corporation for the Apple Macintosh and IBM-compatible microcomputer systems. The program provides a wide variety of business graphics and charts and takes full advantage of using laser printers for making presentation materials. It provides a worksheet area of 16,384 rows by 256 columns. Presentation tools, such as multiple fonts, type sizes, object-oriented graphics, variable row heights, shading, custom number formats, and built-in charts. Excel incorporates some of the features of page layout programs.

exception reporting   Technique for screening large amounts of computerized data to display or print reports containing only specific information, especially items outside normal ranges. Plays a key role in management by exception. An exception report shows only data reflecting unusual circumstances.

exception statement   A control structure that catches errors or unusual occurrences.

exchangeable disk   See disk pack.

exchangeable disk store   Type of disk storage, used as a backing storage, in which the disks come in capsules. Each capsule contains several disks; capsules can be replaced during operation of the computer and stored until needed. The exchangeable capsule is often called a disk pack.

exchange buffering   Technique using data chaining for eliminating the need to move data in internal storage.

exclusive OR (XOR)   Boolean operator that gives a truth table value of true if only one of the two variables it connects is true. If both variables it connects are true, then this value is false. Contrast with inclusive OR.

executable statement   Program statement that gives an instruction or some computational operation to be performed right then, such as an assignment statement. Contrast with nonexecutable statement.

execute (1) To run a program on a computer. (2) To carry out the instructions in an algorithm or program.

execute cycle Period of time during which a machine instruction is interpreted and the indicated operation is performed on the specified operand.

execution Operating cycle during which a program is actually being processed, or run.

execution time Time it takes for a program to run from start to finish.

executive Master program that controls the execution of other programs.

exerciser Device that enables users to create and debug programs and hardware interfaces by manual means.

exit That point in an algorithm or program from which control is transferred elsewhere.

expand To return compressed data to its original condition.

expandability Ability to increase the capability of a computer system by adding modules or devices.

expanded memory Memory added to a computer system.

expanded type Type that has been increased laterally so that fewer characters are contained per linear inch.

expansion A means of increasing the capabilities of a computer by adding hardware designed to perform a task that is not built into the basic system.

expansion card A circuit board that plugs into a computer and gives it additional specialized functions (e.g., enhanced graphics, expanded memory, modem).

expansion interface Circuit board that allows one to add disk drives, additional memory, and other peripherals to a basic computer.

expansion slots The sockets on the main board of a computer where accessory cards or expansion cards are inserted.

expansion unit Device, connected to a computer, that contains extra sockets into which additional printed circuit boards can be plugged.

expert system Interactive computer programs that help users with problems that would otherwise require the assistance of human experts. Expert systems capture knowledge in rules that can be communicated to others as advise or solutions. Program that presents the computer as an expert on some topic. The programs often simulate the reasoning process used by human experts in certain well-defined fields.

expert system shell An expert system building program. The program has the basic structure required to find answers to questions; the questions themselves can be added by the user.

explicit address Storage address explicitly stated in a source language program.

exploded pie graph A pie graph in which one or more of the slices has been offset slightly from the others.

exploded view Illustration of a solid construction showing its parts separately, but in positions that indicate their relationships to the whole.

exponent (1) Symbol or number written above and to the right of another symbol or number that denotes the number of times the latter is used as a factor. A short way of writing 10 x 10 is 10^2; 2 is the exponent; 10 is the base. The exponent tells how many times the base is used as a factor. (2) In floating-point notation, exponents are introduced by E; 77E2 means 77 times 10 to the exponent 2." See E notation.

exponential smoothing Weighted, moving-average method of forecasting in which past observations are geometrically discounted according to their age, the heaviest weight being assigned to the most recent data. The smoothing is called exponential because data points are weighted in accordance with an exponential function of their age.

exponentiation Process or function that enables the user to calculate the power of a number. For example, the result of nine to the fifth power may be calculated in a single step without multiplying 9 x 9 x 9 x 9 x 9.

export To transfer information from one system or program to another. Opposite of import.

expression (1) General term for numerals, numerals with signs of operation, variables, and combinations of these. See arithmetic expression. (2) Any arithmetic formula coded in a programming language.

extended addressing Addressing mode that can reach any place in memory and requires more than one byte to locate the data in memory.

Extended Binary Coded Decimal Interchange Code See EBCDIC.

extender board Debugging aid that allows one to monitor circuit boards more conveniently.

extensible language Concept whereby the user adds new features to a programming language by modifying existing ones.

extension (1) Additional feature added to a programming language or computer system. Feature beyond what is regularly available in the standard. (2) In reference to a filename that serves to extend or clarify its meaning.

extent   Collection of physical records contiguous in auxiliary storage.

external CD-ROM   An optical disc equipped with its own case, cables, and power supply.

external data file   Data stored separately from the program that processes it.

external drive   A disk drive that sits in its own case, rather than being mounted in the chassis of the main computer. Often, external drives include their own power supply.

external hard disk   A hard disk equipped with its own case, cables, and power supply.

external label   Identification label attached to the outside of a file medium holder identifying the file, such as a paper label or sticker attached to the cover containing a magnetic disk or tape.

external reference   Reference to a symbol defined in another routine.

external report   Report produced by an organization for use outside the company, often on preprinted forms required by government or for distribution to customers.

external sort   Second phase of a multipass sort program, wherein strings of data are continually merged until one string of sequenced data is formed.

external storage   Same as auxiliary storage.

external symbol   (1) Control section name, entry point name, or external reference. (2) Symbol contained in the external symbol dictionary.

external symbol dictionary   Control information associated with an object program that identifies the external symbols in the program.

extract   To remove specific information from a computer word as determined by a mask or filter.

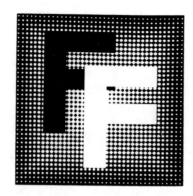

f   Abbreviation for frequency.

fabricated language   Same as symbolic language.

fabrication   Processing of manufacturing materials to desired specifications. See computer-aided manufacturing.

face   (1) In computer graphics or geometry, one side of a solid object, such as a cube. A cube has six faces. (2) In printing and typography, a shortened form of typeface.

FACE   Acronym for Field Alterable Control Element.

facilities   General term that applies to physical equipment, electrical power, communication lines, and other items used in computer and data communications centers.

facilities management   Use of an independent service organization to operate and manage a data processing installation.

facility   (1) Measure of the ease of use of a computer system, a major factor in determining a system's productivity. (2) Channel for electrical transmission between two points.

facing pages   The two pages of a bound document that face each other when the document is open. The even-numbered page (verso) is on the left, and the odd-numbered page (recto) is on the right.

facsimile   The use of computer technology to send digitized text, graphics, and charts from one facsimile machine to another. Abbreviated FAX.

factor analysis   Mathematical technique for studying the interaction of many factors to determine the most significant factors and the degree of significance.

factorial   Product of factors, computed by multiplying all integers from 1 to a specified number. The exclamation point (!) is used to represent factorial. For example, $4! = 1 \times 2 \times 3 \times 4$; $n! = 1 \times 2 \times 3 \times 4...(n-1) \times n$.

fail-safe system System designed to avoid catastrophe, possibly at the expense of convenience. For example, when a fault is detected in a computer-controlled traffic light system, a fail-safe arrangement might be to set all the traffic lights to red rather than turn them off. Similarly, in a power plant operation, overheating might simply disconnect the power supply.

fail-soft system System that continues to process data despite the failure of parts of the system. Usually accompanied by a deterioration in performance. Using the two examples described under fail-safe system, the traffic lights might turn to flashing amber rather than red, and the overheat system might maintain battery power for emergency equipment while the main source of power was turned off.

failure prediction Technique that attempts to determine the failure schedule of specific parts of equipment so they may be discarded and replaced before failure occurs.

fairness Condition that holds when every action requested in a system is guaranteed to execute after a finite amount of time.

fair use A situation in which limited copying of copyright material is legal.

fall-back Backup system brought into use in an emergency situation, especially the reserve database and programs that would be switched in quickly, or even automatically, in the event of a detected fault in a real-time system.

fallout Failure of electronic components sometimes experienced during the burn-in of a new piece of equipment.

FAMOS Acronym for Floating gate Avalanche injection MOS, a fabrication technology for charge storage devices such as PROMs.

fan (1) The cooling mechanism built into computer cabinets, laser printers and other devices to prevent malfunction due to heat buildup. (2) To flip through a stack of laser printer paper to ensure that the pages are loose and will not stick together or jam the printer.

fanfold paper One long continuous sheet of paper perforated at regular intervals to mark page boundaries and folded fan-style into a stack. Fanfold paper is available with vertical perforations, so the sprocket hole strip can be removed. The paper can be divided on the perforations thus enabling the paper to be separated into sheets.

fan-in Number of signal inputs to a digital component.

fan-out (1) Number of TTL unit loads a given TTL device output can supply or drive under the worst-case conditions. (2) Number of programming modules below any given module in a structured program.

farad Unit of measure of capacitance. A capacitor has a capacitance of 1 farad if it will store a charge of 1 coulomb when a 1-volt potential is applied across it.

fatal error Unexpected failure or other problem that occurs while the program is executing. Prevents the computer from continuing to execute the program. If the error is nonfatal, the program will proceed, but not correctly. An operator's mistake that causes the program to crash, destroying the data stored in RAM, would be a fatal error.

fat bits Selection on a painting and drawing program that enlarges a portion of the screen to allow precise manipulation of individual screen elements. Useful for precision work or font designing.

father file System of updating records that retains a copy of the original record as well as provides an amended version. When a file-update program is run, the old master file is termed the father file. The updated file is is termed the son file. The file that was used to create the father file is termed the grandfather file. The technique is particularly applicable to files held on magnetic media, such as disk or tape.

fault Condition, such as a broken wire or a short circuit, that causes a component, a computer, or a peripheral device not to perform to its design specifications.

fault tolerant Continuous operation in the event of failure. Fault tolerant computer systems contain redundant processors.

fax (1) Facsimile. (2) Equipment configuration that facilitates the transmission of images over a common carrier network. (3) A fax machine sends an image to another fax machine, over standard telephone networks. Imagine the process as similar to making a photocopy; reproduction quality of fax is typically lower, though.

FCC Acronym for Federal Communications Commission, an organization of the U.S. Government responsible for regulating interstate communications, communications common carriers, and the broadcast media.

F connector A coaxial connector that uses a screw-on attachment.

FDDI Acronym for Fiber Distributed Data Interface. An evolving standard for 10-Mbps, fiber-optic cable networks.

FE Acronym for Field Engineer.

feasibility study Study concerned with a definition of a data processing problem, together with alternative solutions, a recommended course of action, and a working plan for designing and installing the system.

feathering Adding an even amount of space between each line on a page or column to force vertical justification.

feature Something special accomplished in a program or hardware device, such as the ability of a paint program to create animation cells, or a word processing program to check the spelling of words.

feature extraction Selection of dominant characteristics for pattern recognition. Enables a computer-controlled video camera to recognize objects by such features as shapes and edges.

Federal Privacy Act Federal legislation prohibiting secret personnel files from being kept on individuals by government agencies or contractors. Allows individuals to know what information about them is on file and how it is used within all government agencies and their contractors. Also known as Privacy Act of 1974

feed (1) To supply data or materials to any device. (2) Mechanical process whereby lengthy materials—such as magnetic tape, line printer paper, and printer ribbon—are moved along the required operating position. (3) To insert disks into a disk drive.

feedback (1) Means of automatic control in which the actual state of a process is measured and used to obtain a quantity that modifies the input to initiate the activity of the control system. (2) In data processing, information arising from a particular stage of processing could provide a feedback to affect the processing of subsequent data; for example, the fact that an area of storage was nearly full might either delay the acceptance of more data or divert it to some other storage area. (3) Any process whereby output from a sequential task serves to modify subsequent tasks.

feedback circuit Circuit that returns a portion of the output signal of an electronic circuit or control system to the input of the circuit or the system.

Felt, Dorr (1862-1930) In 1885, designed an experimental multiple-order key-driven calculating machine. Two years later he produced the Comptometer, a practical adding/listing machine.

female connector Recessed portion of a connecting device into which another part fits. Contrast with male connector.

femto Prefix indicating one quadrillionth, or a millionth of a billionth, 10^{-15}.

femtosecond One quadrillionth of a second. There are as many of them (the number one followed by 15 zeros) in one second as there are seconds in 30 million years. In two seconds, light travels from Earth past the moon. In 12 femtoseconds, it moves only five microns, roughly one-tenth the width of a human hair. Abbreviated fs.

ferrous oxide Substance that coats recording disks and tapes. Can be magnetized, thereby permitting information to be recorded on it magnetically.

FET Acronym for Field Effect Transistor. See MOSFET.

fetch To locate and load a quantity of instructions or data from storage.

fetch phase Portion of a computer cycle in which an instruction is fetched from memory.

FF Acronym for Form Feed.

fiber optic cable An advanced form of cabling that uses light to transmit data. This allows for very long distances between nodes.

Fibonacci numbers The Fibonacci numbers are such that, after the first two, every number in the sequence equals the sum of the two previous numbers. The first few numbers are 1, 1, 2, 3, 5, 8, 13, 21, 34, 55, 89, 144, 233, 377, 610, and 987. They have interesting properties and appear frequently in nature.

fiche Microfiche. Sheet of photographic film containing multiple microimages. See COM.

field Single piece of information, the smallest unit normally manipulated by a database management system. In a personnel file, the person's name and age would be separate fields. A record is made up of one or more fields.

field alterable control element (FACE) Chip used in some systems to allow the user to write microprograms.

fieldata code U.S. military code used in data processing as a compromise between conflicting manufacturer's codes.

field effect transistor (FET) Three-terminal semiconductor device that acts as a variable charge storage element. The most commonly used type in microcomputers is the Metallic Oxide Semiconductor (MOS) transistor. See MOSFET.

field emission Emission of electrons from a metal or semiconductor into a vacuum under the influence of a strong electric field.

field engineer (FE) Individual responsible for field maintenance of computer hardware and software.

fielding The arranging for text or numbers to occupy the correct positions on the display screen or on paper.

field of view In computer graphics, the limits of what a simulated camera can see, usually expressed as a horizontal angle centered at the camera. For simplicity of computation, computer graphicists assume that what a camera sees lies within a pyramid—rather than a cone—with the apex at the camera.

field upgradable Hardware capable of being enhanced in the field (in one's office or at a local repair center or computer store).

FIFO Acronym for First In-First Out, a method of storing and retrieving items from a list, table, or stack, such that the first element stored is the first one retrieved. Same as LILO. Contrast with LIFO.

fifth-generation computer The next generation of computers. A term describing new forms of computer systems involving artificial intelligence, natural language, and expert systems. Fifth generation computer systems are expected to appear in the mid 1990s and will represent the next quantum leap in computer technology.

fifth-generation languages Natural languages. These languages use human languages such as English to give people a more natural connection with computers.

figure shift Keyboard key, or the code generated by the key, signifying that the following characters are to be read as figures until a letter shift appears in the message.

file Collection of related records treated as a basic unit of storage.

file backup Copies of data files that can be used to reactivate (restore) a database that has been damaged or destroyed.

file conversion Process of changing the file medium or structure.

file gap Space at the end of the file (on magnetic media) that signifies to the system where the file terminates.

file handling routine That part of a computer program that reads data from, and writes data to, a file.

file label External label identifying a file.

file locking Protects shared files by allowing only one user at a time to make changes.

file layout Arrangement and structure of data in a file, including the sequence and size of its components.

file level model Model concerned with defining data structures for optimum performance of database application programs or queries.

file librarian Person responsible for the safekeeping of all computer files, such as programs and data on magnetic disks or tapes.

file maintenance Updating of a file to reflect the effects of nonperiodic changes by adding, altering, or deleting data.

file manager Simple database management program that uses only simple files and indexes. Also called record manager. Little brother to a database management system.

filename Alphanumeric characters used to identify a particular file.

filename extension Code that forms the second part of a filename and that is separated from the filename by a period. Identifies the kind of data in the file.

file organization Manner in which the applications programmer views the data.

file processing Periodic updating of master files to reflect the effects of current data, often transaction data contained in detail files, such as a monthly inventory run updating the master inventory file.

file protection Technique or device used to prevent accidental erasure of data from a file, such as a gummed tab over the write-protect notch of a 5.25-inch floppy disk.

file-protect ring Device used to protect data on magnetic tape. Accidental writing on the tape is prevented by removing the ring from the tape reel.

file server The central repository of shared files and applications in a computer network.

file size Number of records in a file.

file storage Devices that can hold a reservoir of mass data within the computer system, such as magnetic disk and tape, and CD-ROM units.

file structure Format of fields within a data record. For example, PART NAME in the first field of a record, PART NUMBER in the second field, PRICE in the third field, and so on, specify the structure of a file.

file transfer Movement of a file from one place to another, or from one storage medium to another.

filling In computer graphics, a software function that allows the interior of a defined area to be filled with a color, shading, or pattern of the operator's choosing.

film recorder An output device that takes a 35 mm slide picture from a graphics file which has been created using a graphics program. Widely used in producing presentation-quality hardcopy. Film recorders offer both high resolution (up to 2000 dots per inch) and a true color reproduction capability (up to 6 million simultaneous colors.) Lines show perfectly smooth edges, and colors blend imperceptibly in film recorder images.

FILO Acronym for First In-Last Out, a method of storing and retrieving items from a list, table, or stack, such that the first element stored is the last one retrieved. Same as LIFO. Contrast with FIFO.

filter A software function that modifies an image by altering the gray values of certain pixels. See mask.

find and replace See search and replace.

finder A system program that provides the "desktop" metaphor you encounter when a Macintosh microcomputer is booted up. The finder presents icons (little pictures) depicting applications, documents, file folders, and a garbage can that can be used to discard unwanted files. This highly visual interface program keeps the user from having to type commands directly to the operating system.

fine tune To make small adjustments in order to get best results.

finite To have limits, an end, or a last number. Not infinite.

finite element method Approximation technique used to solve field problems in various engineering fields.

firmware Software that has been copied on integrated circuits, usually ROMs. Since it is on ROM, which cannot be altered, it is neither completely soft nor hard and therefore referred to as firm.

first generation computers First commercially available computers, introduced with UNIVAC I in 1951 and terminated with the development of fully transistorized computers in 1959. Characterized by their use of vacuum tubes, they are now museum pieces. Compare second generation computers, third generation computers, fourth generation computers, and fifth generation computers.

first in-first out See FIFO.

first-order predicate logic Form of logic, used in PROLOG, that allows assertions to be made about the variables in a proposition.

fitting In computer graphics, the calculation of a curve, surface, or line that fits most accurately to a set of data points and design criteria. Compare curve fitting.

fixed Pertaining to a field that always exists within a data record.

fixed area Portion of internal storage that has been assigned to specific programs or data areas.

fixed-head disk unit Storage device consisting of one or more magnetically coded disks on the surface of which data is stored in the form of magnetic spots arranged in a manner to represent binary data. The data are arranged in circular tracks around the disks and are accessible for reading and writing by read/write heads assigned one per track. Data from a given track are read or written sequentially as the disk rotates under or over the read/write head.

fixed-length record Record that always contains the same number of characters.

fixed point   Pertaining to a number system in which each number is represented by a single set of digits, and the position of the radix point is implied by the manner in which the numbers are used.

fixed-point arithmetic   (1) Method of calculation in which the operations take place in an invariant manner without considering the location of the radix point. Illustrated by desk calculators that require the operator to keep track of the decimal point. This occurs similarly with many automatic computers, in which the location of the radix point is the computer user's responsibility. Contrast with floating-point arithmetic. (2) Type of arithmetic in which the operands and results of all arithmetic operations must be properly scaled to have a magnitude between certain fixed values.

fixed-size records   File elements, each of which has the same number of words, characters, bytes, bits, fields, and so on.

fixed-spacing   Printing of characters at fixed horizontal intervals on a page.

fixed storage   Storage whose contents are not alterable by computer instructions, such as read-only storage.

fixed word length   Pertaining to a machine word or operand that always has the same number of bits, bytes, or characters.

flag   (1) Indicator used frequently to tell some later part of a program that some condition occurred earlier, such as an overflow or carry. (2) Symbol used to mark a record for special attention. For example, on a listing of a program, all statements that contain errors may be flagged for the attention of the program writer. (3) Indicator of special conditions, such as interrupts.

flashing   The blinking on and off of characters on a display screen; used to call attention to something on the screen.

flatbed plotter   Digital plotter using plotting heads that move over a flat surface in both vertical and horizontal directions. The size of the bed determines the maximum size sheet of paper that can be drawn. A pair of arms attached to a trolley and controlled by a computer can place the trolley at any part of the paper. A pen attached to the trolley can be raised or lowered to contact the paper. Then, under computer control, this device can draw pictures. If several pens of different colors can be controlled, then pictures can be drawn in color.

flatbed scanner   A scanner with a glass surface upon which you place material to be scanned. Because the original never moves during the scanning process, flatbeds produce more precise results than sheetfed scanners. The scanner can transform a full-page (8.5- by 11-inch) graphic or page of text into a digitized file.

flat pack   Small, low-profile (flat), integrated circuit package that can be spot-welded or soldered to a terminal or a printed circuit board. The pins extend outward rather than pointing down, as on a DIP.

flat panel display terminal Thin-screened peripheral device upon which information may be displayed, such as a plasma display panel.

flat screen Thin panel screen, such as those found on flat panel displays.

Flavors An object-oriented extension to LISP. Flavors was developed at the Massachusetts Institute of Technology.

flexible disk See floppy disk.

flicker Undesirable, unsteady lighting of a display due to inadequate refresh rate and/or fast persistence. Occurs whenever the refresh speed is not fast enough to compensate for natural luminance delay on the screen. See refreshing.

flight computer Computer resident in a spacecraft, an airplane, or a missile.

flight simulator (1) Computer-controlled simulator used by airline companies to train pilots on new aircraft. Some are so realistic that they are acceptable to the FAA for use in renewal of pilot licenses. (2) Flight simulator software running on personal computers provides entertainment and practice in instrument reading and navigation.

flip-flop Device or circuit containing active elements capable of assuming either one of two stable states at a given time. Synonymous with toggle.

flippy-floppy A single-sided 5.25-inch floppy disk that is recorded on both sides. A second write protect notch is punched into the disk so that it can be flipped over and inserted upside down.

float Amount of time following the completion of a task or activity and prior to the start of the next task or activity. Also called slack time.

floating point Form of number representation in which quantities are represented by a number called the mantissa multiplied by a power of the number base.

floating-point arithmetic Method of calculation that automatically accounts for the location of the radix point.

floating-point constant Number, usually consisting of two parts, with one part containing the fractional component of the number; the other part is expressed as a power of the radix (base) of the number. Also called real constant.

floating-point operation Operation done with floating-point arithmetic.

floating-point routine Set of subroutines that cause a computer to execute floating-point operations on a computer with no built-in floating-point hardware.

floppy disk Floppy disks are a form of computer storage medium consisting of a thin flexible disk covered with magnetic oxide held inside a protective sleeve within which it can be rotated. They are lightweight, cheap and portable. The first floppy disks were 8-inch disks (which meant that the whole package was 8 inches square), but these earlier disks are now superseded by 5.25- and 3.5-inch versions. The 3.5-inch version is much improved over its predecessors by having a hard, rather than flexible, casing and a protective "door" over its access holes, which mean that its reliability is likely to be much greater. Storage capacities on disks have increased greatly during development. Early disks offered only about 100 Kbyte on an 8-inch disk. Recent drives offer up to 2 Mbyte on a standard 3.5-inch disk. Floppy disks are standard equipment on virtually every personal computer.

floppy disk case Container, usually made of plastic, for storing and protecting floppy disks.

floppy disk controller Circuit board or chip that controls a floppy disk unit.

floppy disk unit Peripheral storage device in which data are recorded on magnetizable floppy disks.

FLOPS Acronym for FLoating-point Operations Per Second, a measure of the speed at which a computer can compute.

floptical A removable optical disc. The discs and drives are of similar dimensions to floppy disks, but they hold 20 to 25 Mbytes.

flowchart Diagram that uses symbols and interconnecting lines to show (1) the logic and sequence of specific program operations (program flowchart), or (2) a system of processing to achieve objectives (system flowchart).

flowcharter Computer program that automatically generates flowcharts with a visual display screen, digital plotter, or printer.

flowcharting symbol Symbol used to represent operations, dataflow, or equipment on a flowchart.

flowchart template Plastic guide that contains cutouts of the flowchart symbols and is used in the preparation of a flowchart.

flowchart text Descriptive information associated with flowchart symbols.

flow diagram See flowchart.

flowline On a flowchart, a line representing a connecting path between flowchart symbols.

flush (1) To empty a portion of storage of its contents. (2) Pertaining to type set in alignment with the left (flush left) or right (flush right) edge of the line measure.

FM Acronym for Frequency Modulation, the process of changing the value represented by a signal by varying the frequency of the signal.

FO Short for Fiber Optic, a connection that uses light pulses traveling in a transparent glass or plastic wire. Fiber optic connections can carry large amounts of data, and they don't pick up electrical noise.

focusing Sharpening a blurred image on a display screen.

folder A collection of files. You can place files into folders. To access a file that has been placed in a folder, double-click on the folder's icon.

folio A page number.

font A complete assortment or set of all the characters (letters, numbers, punctuation and symbols) of a particular typeface, all of one size and style (e.g., 12 pt. Bookman, 18 pt. Helvetica, 36 pt. Cooper Black, 8 pt. Times Roman). Two types of fonts exist: bit-mapped fonts and outline fonts. Each comes in two versions, screen fonts and printer fonts.

font cartridge A set of bit-mapped or outline fonts for one or more typefaces contained in a module that plugs into a slot in a printer. The fonts are stored in a ROM chip within the cartridge.

font family A set of fonts in several sizes and weights that share the same typeface.

font generator A program that converts an outline font into the precise patterns of dots required for a particular size of font.

font groups Fonts are often divided into three groups: Serif, Sans Serif, and Display. Type styles in the Serif group have additional strokes (serifs) at the bottom of each letter. Type styles in the Sans Serif group do not have serifs. Display (or decorative) type styles can be either Serif or Sans Serif. Type styles in this group are used when you want to create a dramatic effect in headings, logos, and product names. They are rarely used in long passages of text since they are typically difficult to read.

font size The size of a character font in points. The size most often used for text is 10-12 points. Point size is a vertical measurement; horizontal measurement is not taken into consideration.

font substitution Substituting an outline font for printing in place of a bit-mapped screen font. In some systems, the laser printer driver substitutes an outline font for a specific bit-mapped screen font.

font weight Weight refers to the heft and/or slant of a font. Most fonts are available in four weights: Medium (or Roman or Book or Normal), Italic, Bold and Bold Italic (or Bold Oblique). Some decorative fonts (e.g., Zapf

Chancery Medium Italic) are only available in one weight. A few fonts (e.g., Helvetica) are available in many more weights than the four listed above.

footer Information printed at the bottom of a page, such as page numbers.

footnote In a page layout or word processing program, a note positioned at the bottom of the page.

footprint The surface area occupied by a computer or peripheral. A small computer is said to have a small footprint. A machine with a large footprint may need a desk to itself.

force To intervene manually in a program and cause the computer to execute a jump instruction.

forced page break A page break inserted by the user.

forecast Extrapolation of the past into the future. Usually an objective computation involving data, as opposed to a prediction, which is a subjective estimate incorporating the manager's anticipation of changes and new influencing factors.

foreground An area in computer memory for programs that have a high priority.

foreground processing Automatic execution of computer programs that have been designed to preempt the use of computing facilities. Contrast with background processing.

foreground program Program that has high priority and therefore takes precedence over concurrently operating programs in a computer system using multiprogramming techniques. Contrast with background program.

forest Collection of trees.

form A template that indicates both items of data and where they are to be placed. Forms assist in the process of collecting and storing data.

formal language A combination of syntax and semantics that completely defines a programming language.

formal logic Study of the structure and form of valid argument without regard to the meaning of the terms of the argument.

format (1) Specific arrangement of data. (2) Programming associated with setting up text arrangements for output.

format code A word processing code that describes how text will be printed or formatted.

format rule A spreadsheet rule that tells the program how to display a cell's value.

formatted display Screen display in which the attributes or contents of one or more display fields have been defined by the user.

formatter Section of a word processing program that formats the text.

formatting Preparing a diskette for use so that the operating system can write information on it. Formatting erases any previous information there.

form feed (FF) (1) Physical transport of continuous paper to the beginning of a new line or page. (2) Standard ASCII character that causes a form feed to occur.

form letter program Program that can be designed to send out "personalized" letters that look like letters produced on a typewriter.

forms control Operational procedure established by an organization to exercise direction in the utilization of documents used to collect and/or report information.

forms design Creation of data input forms and source documents.

formula Rule expressed as an equation; for example, $C = 2\pi r$ is the formula for finding the circumference of a circle. Way of showing the equal relationship between certain quantities; especially useful for calculating one quantity when given others. The items in a formula consist of constants and variables, and the formula can be evaluated only when values have been assigned to all the variables.

Forrester, Jay Leader in the area of system dynamics; developed magnetic core, an internal memory used in most computers between 1951 and 1964. Headed the team of people at M.I.T. who built the Whirlwind computer, perhaps the most influential of the early computers in terms of today's commercial machines. Both magnetic core memory and the parallel synchronous method for handling information inside the machine were first developed by Whirlwind's designers.

FORTH A programming language designed for real-time control tasks, as well as business and graphics applications. Developed primarily for use on microcomputer systems by Charles Moore. Capabilities include structured programming, top-down development, and virtual memory.

FORTRAN Acronym for FORmula TRANslator, widely used high-level programming language used to perform mathematical, scientific, and engineering computations. FORTRAN was developed in 1957 by Jim Backus and was the first high-level programming language. FORTRAN was extremely popular in the 1950s and 1960s. Many of the general principles of FORTRAN have been absorbed into BASIC and other programming languages.

FORTRAN translation process Process used to produce computed results from a program written in FORTRAN. Includes compiling and executing the program on the computer.

forward chaining Event-driven method of reasoning that proceeds from known conditions to the desired goal.

forward pointer Pointer that tells the location of the next item in a data structure.

FOSDIC Acronym for Film Optical Sensing Device for Input to Computers, an input device used by the Census Bureau to read completed census questionnaire data into a computer.

fourth-generation computers A computer that is made up almost entirely of chips with limited amounts of discrete components. Fourth generation computers are currently being manufactured and sold.

fourth-generation language A user-oriented language that makes it possible to develop programs with fewer commands than those needed for older procedural languages. A nonprocedural language. Also called a 4GL language.

FPLA Acronym for Field Programmable Logic Array, a PLA that can be programmed by the user in the field, whereas an ordinary PLA is programmable only by masking at the semiconductor manufacturer's factory.

fractals An object (or set of points, curves, or patterns) which exhibits increasing detail with increasing magnification. Deals with curves and surfaces with nonintegral, or fractional dimension. In computer graphics applications, this relates to a technique for obtaining a degree of complexity analogous to that in nature from a handful of data points; a method of describing real-world surfaces. Fractals can be used for stunning graphic effects, and can approximate the randomness of nature. Fractals allow images to be highly compressed for computer storage and transmission. Instead of turning an image into bit maps (raster graphics) or lines (vector graphics) as is done routinely in computer graphics, fractals turns an image into a set of data and an algorithm for expanding the data into the real object when required. The term fractal was coined by mathematician Benoit Mandelbrot in 1975. Fractals come from the science of chaos, which, contrary to its name, reveals an orderly pattern in the universe.

fragmentation Presence of small increments of unused space spread throughout disk storage. Occurs whenever files on a disk are deleted and new files are added. The uneven distribution of data on a disk.

frame (1) Video image produced by one complete scan of the screen of a raster-scan display unit. (2) In computer animation, a frame is a single picture. (3) Area, one recording position long, extending across the width of magnetic tape perpendicular to its movement. (4) In computer graphics, an outline or a boundary of some type.

frame buffer In computer graphics, a special area of RAM memory that holds the contents of a screen display. Sometimes used interchangeably with the term "bit map."

frame grabber A device used to capture a still video image for storage or processing in a computer.

frames per second In animation, a measurement of the number of individual pictures that are displayed for each second of action.

frame rate The speed at which screen images are transmitted to, and displayed by, a raster-scan monitor. It is measured in hertz and is about 60 times per second (60 Hz) on a monitor in which each pixel on the screen is refreshed.

framework In object-oriented programming, a class library that is tuned especially for a particular category of application.

Framework A suite of programs consisting of a word processor, spreadsheet, database, and graphics generator. The program are designed to run on IBM-compatible microcomputers. Framework was developed by Ashton-Tate.

Frankston, Bob When Daniel Bricklin got the idea for an electronic spreadsheet, he depended on Frankston to create a workable version of the program. Frankston developed a version of the program from Bricklin's prototype design. The two worked together until they completed the first electronic spreadsheet, VisiCalc, in 1979.

Freedom of Information Act Federal legislation that allows ordinary citizens access to data gathered by federal agencies. See Federal Privacy Act.

free form Type of optical scanning in which the scanning operation is controlled by symbols entered by the input device at the time of data entry.

Freehand A professional design/illustration program for the Apple Macintosh computer. Completely integrated, it combines basic shapes and advanced drawing tools, text-handling capability, full color support and special effects. Features include movable on-screen palettes for color, graphic styles and layers; fast "flicker-free" screen redraw and editing; automatic text on an ellipse; vertical text; and ability to convert characters into editable outlines. Included are WYSIWYG text effects (zoom, shadow and outline, for example), the ability to make transparent holes in objects or fill words with fills or TIFF images, and the ability to view, separate and print 32-bit color TIFF images. Time-saving tools include automatic reblending of blended objects and colors, snap-to-point feature and built-in arrowheads. A full Pantone color palette is provided enabling users to perform color separations for process colors CMYK), spot color or a combination of both. Paint, EPS and PICT files can be imported as well as black and white, gray scale and color TIFF images.

free-form windows A method of presenting windows on the screen that allows them to overlap one another.

free subprogram In object-oriented programing, a procedure or function that serves as a nonprimitive operation upon an object or objects of the same or different classes. A free subprogram is any subprogram that is not a method of an object.

freeware Software provided by a vendor at no charge. Freeware developers often retain all rights to their software thus preventing users from copying it or distributing it further.

frequency Number of times that sound, pressure, electrical intensity, or other quantities specifying a wave vary from their equilibrium value through a complete cycle in unit time. The most common unit of frequency is the hertz, Hz); 1 Hz is equal to 1 cycle per second.

frequency counter Electronic device capable of counting the number of cycles in an electrical signal during a preselected time interval.

frequency shift keying (FSK) Method of data transmission in which the state of the bit being transmitted is indicated by an audible tone.

friction-feed Paper-feed system that operates by clamping a sheet of paper between two rollers. As the rollers rotate, the paper is drawn into the printing device. Many printers use this method, which is effective for single-sheet feeding.

friend In object-oriented programming, a method typically involving two or more objects of different classes, whose implementation for any one class may reference the private parts of all the corresponding classes that are also friends.

friendliness How easy to work with a computer or program is. A user-friendly program is one that takes little time to learn and is easy to use.

friendly interface Term applied to a combination of terminal equipment and computer program designed to be easy to operate by casual users of computers.

frob To fiddle with a picking device, such as a joystick or mouse.

front-end computer Dedicated small computer at the front end of a mainframe. May perform communications line assignment, data conversion, error analysis, message handling, and other data communications functions, freeing the mainframe from these tasks.

front panel Collection of switches and indicators by which the computer operator may control a mainframe computer system.

fry To ruin circuitry by subjecting it to excessive heat or current.

fs   Abbreviation for femtosecond.

FSK   Acronym for Frequency Shift Keying.

full adder   Computer circuit capable of adding three binary bits, one of which is a carry from a previous addition.

full-duplex   Pertaining to the simultaneous, independent transmission of data in both directions over a communications link. Contrast with half-duplex and simplex.

full frame   Process by which a display image is scaled to use the entire viewing area of a display device.

full page display   A monitor that allows viewing an entire page (8.5 in. x 11 in. vertical page) at actual size. Makes for greater flexibility and ease in desktop publishing or word processing applications.

full screen   Condition in which the entire face of the video screen is used for display.

full-screen editing   Ability to move the cursor over the entire screen to alter text.

full-text searching   Retrieval of certain information by searching the full text of an article or book stored in a computer's auxiliary storage.

function   (1) A prewritten routine that can be called into a program to provide the commands to do a particular task. (2) Process that generates a value.

functional description   Phrase used to identify the requirements of a computer system.

functional design   Specification of the working relationships between the parts of a system in terms of their characteristic actions.

functional programming   Programming that uses function application as the only control structure.

functional specification   Set of input, processing, output, and storage requirements detailing what a new system should be able to do. Output of the systems analysis function, it presents a detailed, logical description of a new system.

function codes   Special codes that help control functions of peripheral devices. "Clear display screen" would be a function code.

function keys   Specially designed keys that, when pressed, initiates some function on a computer keyboard, word processor, or graphics terminal. Most software assign function keys (F1, F2, etc.) for common tasks, but not universally. For example, in one word processor, F4 might mean "save file," while in a different word processor, F4 might mean "increase size of character." These special keys are programmed to execute commonly used commands.

function subprogram Subprogram that returns a single-value result.

fuse Safety protective device that opens an electric circuit if overloaded. A current above the rating of the fuse will melt a fusible link and open the circuit. Most computer devices use fuses to protect the equipment from current overloads.

fusible link Widely used PROM programming technique. An excessive current is used to destroy a metalized connection in a storage device, creating a 0, for instance, if a conducting element is interpreted as a 1.

fuzzy Anything in computing that is indeterminate. Fuzzy action deals in similarities and probabilities and is difficult to program, but it is an essential part of artificial intelligence, since humans make considerable use of this type of logic.

fuzzy computer A specially designed computer that uses fuzzy logic. Fuzzy computers are designed for artificial intelligence applications.

fuzzy logic Method of handling imprecision or uncertainty that attaches various measures of credibility to propositions. A form of logic used in some expert systems and other artificial intelligence applications.

G Abbreviation for giga, prefix for 1 billion.

gain Increase in signal power or voltage produced by an amplifier in transmitting a signal from one point to another. Amount of gain is usually expressed in decibels above a reference level. Opposite of attenuation.

gallium arsenide Crystalline material used as a substitute for silicon in chip making. Superior to silicon but far more costly. It is several times faster than silicon.

game paddle A hand-held input device used to move the cursor on the screen through the use of a dial. Game paddles are commonly used in video games.

game theory Branch of mathematics concerned with probability, among other things. Term was first used by John von Neumann in 1928 to describe the strategy of winning at poker. Mathematical process of selecting an optimum strategy in the face of an opponent who also has a strategy.

gamut Total range of colors that can be displayed on a computer display.

Gantt chart A horizontal bar chart that summarizes a project over time. It can show the critical path of a project, progress, milestones, start and end dates, and other information.

gap Space between two records (interrecord gap) or two blocks of data (interblock gap) on a magnetic tape.

garbage (1) Term often used to describe incorrect answers from a computer program, usually resulting from inaccuracies in data entry or a mistake in a computer program but sometimes from equipment malfunction. (2) Unwanted and meaningless data carried in storage. (3) Incorrect input to a computer.

garbage collection A memory management routine that searches memory for program segments, data, or objects that are no longer active and reclaims the unused space. Loosely, a term for cleaning dead storage locations out of a file.

gas plasma display   An output device that works on a principle similar to that of neon signs: a narrow gap filled with neon and argon gas separates two glass plates. An alternating-current voltage applied between closely spaced row-and-column electrodes ionizes the gases between the electrodes, causing them to glow. Once initiated, the glow continues at a reduced voltage.

gate   (1) Logic circuit with two or more inputs that control one output. (2) Controlling element of field effect transistors, governing current flow from source to drain.

Gates, William H.   Bill Gates and his school friend, Paul Allen, created Microsoft BASIC for the microcomputer. Gates and Allen founded Microsoft Corporation in 1975. Microsoft Corporation, under the guidance of Gates has become the largest software development company in the world. A few of the products are MS-DOS, Microsoft Windows, Microsoft Word, Microsoft Works, GW-BASIC, as well as many other software systems. Bill Gates has built Microsoft Corporation into a software powerhouse.

gateway   A hardware/software combination that links systems with different protocols. Used so that one local area network computer system can communicate and share its data with another local area network computer system.

gating circuit   Circuit that operates as a selective switch, allowing conduction only during selected time intervals or when the signal magnitude is within certain limits.

GB   Abbreviation for gigabyte; one billion bytes.

G-base   An object-oriented LISP-based database.

geek   Unsophisticated computer user.

GEM   Acronym for Graphics Environment Manager. A graphics-based operating environment designed by Digital Research. Used primarily on IBM-compatible microcomputers and Atari microcomputers. A program used with the operating system which creates and manages all the icons and graphics features of the computer.

GEM file format   An object file format commonly used by programs that were designed to run under GEM. Ventura Publisher is the most notable example.

Gemstone   An object-oriented database.

gender   The type of connector being used. Male connectors have pins, and female connectors have receptacles for those pins.

gender changer A connector or cable that has two male or two female connectors wired pin to pin, which, in effect, changes a male connector to which it is connected to female or a female connector to male.

generality Pertaining to a computer program whose solution of a problem will serve a variety of users with the same general need. A simple example is a payroll program that writes a warning message if calculated net pay is more than a certain amount. A program with less generality would have fixed limit; a program with more generality would allow each individual user to specify his/her own limit value, or to turn off the warning feature altogether.

generalized routine Routine designed to process a large range of specific jobs within a given type of application.

general-purpose (GP) Being applicable to a wide variety of uses without essential modification. Contrast with special-purpose and dedicated.

general-purpose computer Computer designed to solve a wide class of problems. Majority of digital computers are of this type. Contrast with special-purpose computer.

general-purpose register CPU register used for indexing, addressing, and arithmetic and logical operations.

general register Storage device that holds inputs and outputs of the various functional units of a computing system. Also used for temporary storage of intermediate results.

generate To produce a program by selection of subsets from a set of skeletal coding under the control of parameters; to produce a program by use of a generator.

generation A level of mainframe computer development. The first generation of computers used vacuum tubes, the second generation used transistors, the third generation used early types of integrated circuits, the fourth generation uses large scale integrated circuits. The next generation of computers, the fifth generation, are expected to appear in the mid-1990s and will represent the next quantum leap in computer technology.

generator Software package that contains a number of routines to accomplish specific functions. These routines are capable of accepting input parameters and modifying themselves as the parameters indicate. Used to make the implementation of specific, limited tasks very convenient, such as generating a report. Typically, the user fills out a set of parameter forms defining the task.

generic Pertaining to an item or device without specific reference to trade names.

generic class In object-oriented programming, a class that serves as a template for other classes, in which the template may be parameterized by other classes, objects, and/or operations. A generic class must be initialized before objects can be created. The terms "generic class" and "parameterized class" are interchangeable.

generic function   In object-oriented programming, an operation upon an object.

geocoding   Method of providing a graphic display of data in relation to a geographic area.

geometric model   See model, geometric.

geometry   Branch of mathematics that deals with the relationships, properties, and measurements of solids, surfaces, lines, and angles. Considers spatial relationships, the theory of space, and figures in space. In computer graphics, refers to the specific physical arrangement of lines that make up the shape of a specific entity. Geometry is an essential part of computer graphics programs.

geosynchronous satellite   A satellite which is positioned at the proper distance from earth and at the proper relational speed to appear stationary to an observer on earth. Geosynchronous satellites are necessary for telecommunications over vast distances.

germanium   Chemical element (atomic number 32) used in the manufacture of chips. In its pure state, germanium is an insulator. When small amounts of certain impurities, called dopants, are added, it becomes a semiconductor.

GERT   Acronym for Graphical Evaluation and Review Technique, a procedure for the formulation and evaluation of systems, using a network approach. Compare PERT.

get   To obtain a record from an input file. Another name for load. Compare fetch.

G flops   One billion floating-point operations per second.

ghost   A faint second image that appears close to the primary image on a display or printout.

ghost icon   An outline of an icon or window used to show the current position of the icon or window as it is being dragged to a new location on the desktop.

gibberish   Unnecessary data.

GIF   A graphics format often used for pictures that are transmitted by modem. Especially popular with computer bulletin boards and information services such as CompuServe.

giga · Prefix indicating 1 billion or 10^9. Abbreviated G. Contrast with nano, one billionth.

gigabyte Specifically, 1,073,741,824, or 2^{30}, bytes. More loosely, one billion bytes, one million kilobytes, or one thousand megabytes. Abbreviated GB. Compare terabyte.

gigaflops One billion floating-point operations per second.

gigahertz Frequency of a billion times a second. Abbreviated GHz.

gigascale integration Process of placing over 1 billion integrated circuits on one chip.

GIGO Acronym for Garbage In-Garbage Out, a term used to describe the data into and out of a computer system. If the input data is bad (Garbage In), then the output data will also be bad (Garbage Out).

GKS See Graphical Kernel System.

glare Reflection from the surface of a display screen.

glare filter A fine mesh screen that is placed over a CRT screen to reduce glare from overhead and ambient light.

glitch Popular term for a temporary or random error, problem or malfunction in hardware, such as a malfunction caused by a power surge.

global (1) General term implying a great breadth of scope, as contrasted with local. (2) Pertaining to a variable whose name is accessible by a main program and all its subroutines. (3) Any computer operation applied to a broad set of data.

global character Character used in a searching routine to stand for any character. Allows the operator to search for a character string of a specified length by specifying only some of its characters and using global characters to stand for the others. Also called wild card.

global operation In word processing, an operation performed throughout an entire file.

global search and replace In word processing, the ability to find a string anywhere it appears in a document and to substitute another string for it.

global variable Variable that has the same value regardless of where or in what program it is used.

GMD Abbreviation for German National Research Center for Computer Science. Its research is particularly strong in the fields of software engineering, parallel computing, communications systems and expert systems.

gnomon Object representing direction and dimension that facilitates interpretation of a two-dimensional image of a three-dimensional solid.

go down To crash. See down.

good enough color A phrase used for color printing that does not require an exact color match. Relatively easy to produce with desktop color systems.

GP Acronym for General-Purpose.

GPS Acronym for General Problem Solver, the first program for solving general problems that separated solving methods from knowledge.

GPSS Acronym for General Purpose Systems Simulation, a problem-oriented language used to develop simulation systems.

grabber (1) A device for capturing data, i.e., a video digitizer. (2) A computer program that takes a "snapshot" of the currently displayed screen image by transferring a portion of video memory to a file on disk. (3) Fixture on the end of a test equipment lead wire with a spring-actuated hook and claw designed to connect the measuring instrument to a pin of an integrated circuit, socket, transistor, and so forth.

grabber hand In graphics programs, an on-screen image of a hand that you can position with the mouse to move selected units of graphics or text from place to place on-screen.

graceful degradation Process of undergoing failure in such a way that limited operation can continue. See fail-soft system.

grade Pertaining to the range, or width, of the frequencies available for transmission on a given channel, such as voice-grade.

grammar Rules prescribing how various elements of a language may be combined. See syntax.

grammatical error Error that results when the rules or syntax of a programming language are not followed. Also called a syntax error.

grandfather file The oldest backup file copy. See father file.

granularity The level of modularity of a system. Finer granularity indicates smaller modules and provides greater flexibility.

graph (1) Diagram showing the relationship of two or more variable quantities. A mathematical graph is usually in the form of a curve drawn in a frame of reference formed by the two axes of coordinate geometry. (2) A method of displaying number relationships visually.

Graphical Kernel system (GKS) An internationally accepted standard for computer graphics. GKS is an interface that provides computer users with standardized methods of describing, manipulating, storing, and transferring graphical images.

graphical terminal Visual display terminal that has a screen to display a drawing as well as textual information.

graphical user interface (GUI) A type of display format that enables the user to choose commands, start programs, and see lists of files and other options by pointing to pictorial representations (icons) and lists of menu items on the screen. Graphical user interfaces are used on the Apple Macintosh microcomputer, by the Microsoft Windows program for IBM-compatible microcomputers, and other systems.

graphic character Any ASCII character that is represented by a visible symbol and can be printed; includes letters and digits.

graphic data structure Logical arrangement of digital data representing graphic data for graphic display.

graphic digitizer Input device that converts graphic and pictorial data into binary inputs for use in a computer. See digitizer.

graphic display mode Mode of operation that allows the computer to print graphics on a display screen.

graphic display resolution (1) Number of lines and characters per line able to be shown on a video screen. (2) Measure of the detail in which graphics can be drawn.

graphic display terminal Computer terminal that displays information on a screen, usually a cathode ray tube, TV terminal, or video monitor.

graphic input device Any device, such as a digitizer, that gives the computer the points that make up an image in such a way that the image can be stored, reconstructed, displayed, or manipulated.

graphic limits (1) The boundary of a graphical display screen image in a graphics software program. (2) Plotting area of a graphics device, such as a digital plotter, as defined by its mechanical limits, such as the size of the drum or platen.

graphic output Computer-generated output in the form of visual displays, printouts, or plots.

graphic output device Device used to display or record an image. A display screen is an output device for soft copy, hard-copy output devices produce paper, film, or transparencies of the image.

graphics Any computer-generated picture produced on a screen, paper, or film. Graphics range from simple line or bar graphs to colorful and detailed images. All computers have some amount of graphics capability, but nowadays most feature high-resolution graphics, in which the detail of the diagrams can be considerably finer than was possible in early systems. Modern microcomputers feature high-resolution graphics in color, and printed pictures can also be produced in color.

graphics adapters CGA-EGA-VGA adapters that must be matched with compatible monitors. Note the alphabetical order—it happens to match their order of age and sophistication. CGA was first. EGA was the new standard for a long while. VGA is now the popular standard for color presentations. VGA has higher resolution modes, and sharper text and image quality.

graphics based The display of text and pictures as graphics images, for example, a bit-mapped image.

graphics character A character that can be combined to create simple graphics.

graphics coprocessor A special microprocessor chip, mounted on some video adapters, that can generate graphical images, thereby freeing the computer for other work.

graphics device interface (GDI) A collection of Microsoft Windows routines that allows you to display information without concern for the specific hardware used.

graphics display Any output device that can present an image of graphic data derived from a computer system.

graphics editor A program for editing pictures. Typical operations include drawing, moving, rotating, and enlarging items on the screen.

graphics engine Specialized hardware that performs graphics processing independently of the main central processing unit. Graphics engines are programmed in a graphics language.

graphics file format In a graphics program, the way in which information needed to display the graphic is arranged and stored on disk.

graphics input hardware Peripherals used to put graphics information in the computer, such as a graphics tablet, mouse, and light pen.

graphics language A set of instructions that let a programmer express a graphics image in a high-level language. The language is translated into graphics images by software or specialized hardware.

graphics mode Resolution of the image together with the number of colors a particular video system can display. For example EGA and VGA are considered different graphic modes.

graphics output hardware Peripherals on which the computer displays graphics, such as a display screen, a film recorder, or a laser printer.

graphics package A program that helps depict ideas through graphs and other types of drawings.

graphics primitive In computer graphics, a graphical building block, such as a triangle, circle, line, or arc. A graphics primitive is drawn and manipulated as a single unit.

graphics printer Output device that can produce text, charts, graphics, and artwork.

graphics program (1) A computer program that aids computer users in producing computer generated images. Pictures can be entered into the computer using input devices such as mice, graphics tablets or light pens, and existing pictures on paper can be scanned into the computer using digitized scanners. Once stored in the computers memory, pictures can be manipulated in a variety of ways and printed on paper, display screen or film. Popular graphics programs are Adobe Illustrator, Deluxe Paint, MacDraw, MacPaint, Paintbrush IV Plus, Studio 1, Studio 8, Studio 32, SuperPaint and UltraPaint. (2) Program that causes the computer to generate graphic images.

graphics resolution Measure of the detail in which graphics can be drawn by output hardware. High-resolution pictures have greater detail than low-resolution pictures. See resolution.

graphic scanner A graphics input device that transforms a picture into an image displayed on-screen.

graphics screen Screen that displays graphics information.

graphics spreadsheet A spreadsheet program that displays the worksheet on-screen, using bit-mapped graphics instead of relying on the computer's built-in character set.

graphics tablet Input device that converts graphic and pictorial data into binary inputs for use in a computer. Provides an efficient method of converting object shapes into computer-storable information. Utilizes a flat tablet and a stylus for graphic input. See digitizer.

graphics terminal A "smart" terminal capable of displaying graphics; usually interpret graphics control codes to render images on the display screen.

Graphics Workshop A color paint program for the Commodore Amiga computer. Features include 10-brush library, true antialiasing, true polygons, rays, 4-point curves, color replacement, pattern draw, automatic shadows, animation option and the ability to convert cell animation into page animation.

graph theory Branch of mathematics that belongs partly to combinatorial analysis and partly to topology. Applications occur in electrical network theory, operations research, statistical mechanics, and sociological and behavioral research.

gray-map editor A function found in many imaging programs that allows the user to change the way gray shades are displayed.

gray scale A strip of standard gray tones, ranging from white to black. (1) When used with scanners, it refers to the device's ability to capture more than simply black and white. (2) When used with monochromatic displays, variations in brightness level (gray scale) are used to enhance the contrast among various design elements. The larger the gray scale, the better the picture quality. (3) It refers to the many levels of gray supported by a scanner or a monitor. 8 and 16 levels were early standards; now the standard is 256 levels.

gray value A number that determines the level of gray in a particular pixel. A pixel that is 80 percent gray is darker than a pixel that is 20 percent gray.

greater than Relationship of inequality between two values. The symbol is >, with the point toward the smaller number. 9 > 5 means 9 is greater than 5. Commonly used in comparison to determine alternative processing. Contrast with less than.

greeked text In desktop publishing, unreadable letters or characters that simulate a typeset line.

green-bar paper Computer paper with green bands.

grid (1) Network of uniformly spaced points or crosshatched lines displayed on a visual display screen or digitizer and used for exactly locating a position, inputting components to assist in the creation of a design layout, or constructing precise diagrams. For example, coordinate data supplied by digitizers is automatically calculated by the computer from the closest grid point. The grid determines the minimum accuracy with which design entities are described or connected. (2) Display of an electronic spreadsheet model composed of columns and rows. (3) Horizontal and vertical lines on a chart to aid the viewer in determining the value of a point. (4) On a pie chart, the grid is an implied set of lines radiating out from the center, representing the degrees of a circle.

grid chart Table that relates input data to its applicable applications program.

gridding Graphic image construction constraint that requires all line endpoints to fall on grid points.

gridsheet Same as grid, spreadsheet, or worksheet.

grounding Process of rendering electrical current harmless to humans and computers.

ground station A station for sending and receiving information via satellite.

group In an object-oriented drawing program, to transfer a collection of objects into one object so that the group can be operated on as a whole.

group work Any indicator signaling the beginning or end of a word or other unit of data.

groupware Software that is designed for use in a network and serve a group of users that work on a related project.

guest computer Computer operating under the control of another (host) computer.

GUI Acronym for Graphical User Interface.

gulp Small group of bytes.

gun Group of electrodes constituting the electron beam emitter in a cathode ray tube.

gutter (1) The margin at the binding edge of a page. (2) White space between a multiple-column page layout.

GW-BASIC A version of the BASIC programing language for MS-DOS computers; developed by Microsoft Corporation. GW-BASIC is nearly identical to the BASIC interpreter distributed with IBM microcomputers and is commonly bundled with IBM-compatible microcomputers.

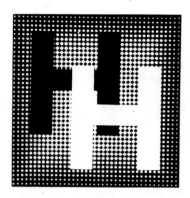

H A suffix indicating that a number is in hexadecimal form. For example, F2A3h indicates that the number is hexadecimal.

hacker (1) A skilled computer enthusiast who works alone and is obsessed with learning about programming and exploring the capabilities of computer systems. (2) A person who gains access to a computer system without authorization.

half adder Computer circuit capable of adding two binary bits.

half-duplex Pertaining to a communications path that can carry a message in either direction but only one way at a time.

half-height drive A disk drive that occupies only half the vertical space of earlier disk drives.

halftone A continuous-tone image, e.g., a photograph, shot through a screen and reproduced as an array of tiny dots. A halftone is a printed reproduction of these tiny dots which the naked eye sees as various tones of gray shading into one another.

halftone cell A halftone dot created on a laser printer or imagesetter. The cell is created by grouping printer dots into a grid. The more dots present in the grid, the larger the cell appears.

halfword Contiguous sequence of bits, bytes, or characters that comprises half a computer word and is capable of being addressed as a unit.

halting problem Problem for which there is no algorithm.

halt instruction Machine instruction that stops the execution of the program.

hand calculator Hand-held calculator suitable for performing arithmetic operations, including complicated calculations.

hand-held computer Portable, battery-operated computer that can be programmed to perform a wide variety of tasks.

hand-held scanner An optical scanner that is operated by manually running a scanning head over an image. Small rollers on the bottom of the scanning head serve to guide the hand movement.

handle (1) In computer graphics, a small square associated with a graphical object that can be used to move or reshape the image. (2) A number that can be used to uniquely identify an object. (3) In programming, a pointer to a pointer. In other words, a variable that contains the address of another variable, which in turn contains the address of yet another variable.

handler (1) Program with the sole function of controlling a particular input, output, or storage device, a file, or the interrupt facility. (2) In object oriented programming, the program instructions (called a script) embedded within an object. The instructions are designed to trap messages that begin within the object.

handshaking Procedures and standards (protocol) used by two computers or a computer and a peripheral device to establish communication.

hands-on Pertaining to the process of physically using a computer system.

handwriting recognition Scanning handwritten material with a computer-controlled visual scanning device to determine information content or to verify a signature.

hanging indent A paragraphing style with a full-measure first line and indented succeeding lines (called turnover lines).

hang-up Nonprogrammed stop in a routine. Usually an unforeseen or unwanted halt in a machine run caused by improper coding of a problem, by equipment malfunction, or by the attempted use of a nonexistent or illegal operation code.

hard clip area Limits beyond which lines cannot be drawn on a digital plotter.

hard contact printing Contact printing in which the mask is pressed against the substrate with appreciable force.

hard copy Printed copy of machine output in readable form, such as reports, listings, graphic images, documents, or summaries. Contrast with soft copy.

hard disk Fast auxiliary storage device either mounted in its own case or permanently mounted inside a computer. A single hard disk has storage capacity of several million characters or bytes of information. This storage media makes computers usable in the real world. Contrast with floppy disk.

hard error Error caused by a malfunction in the hardware.

hard failure Failure of a piece of equipment. Generally requires repair before the unit can be used again.

hard hyphen Hyphen required by spelling and always printed, such as in double-click. Contrast with soft hyphen.

hard sector Wedge-shaped storage division on a floppy disk from time of manufacture. Physically marked by holes punched through the disk to indicate the various sectors. Contrast with soft sector.

hardware Physical equipment, such as electronic, magnetic, and mechanical devices. Contrast with software.

hardware configuration Relationships and arrangement of the various pieces of equipment that make up a computer system, including the cables and communications paths that connect them.

hardware-dependent See machine-dependent.

hardware description languages (HDL) Languages and notations that facilitate the documentation, design, simulation, and manufacturing of digital computer systems.

hardware key Means to secure software from illegal copying. Plugs into a port or expansion slot on a computer and interacts with a program's antipiracy software to allow the program to run only on that machine.

hardware resources CPU time, internal storage space, direct access storage space, and input/output devices, all of which are required to do the work of processing data automatically and efficiently.

hardware specialist Person who diagnoses, repairs, and maintains the equipment of a computer system.

hardwired Pertaining to the physical connection of two pieces of electronic equipment by means of a cable.

harness Group of separate cables bound together.

Harvard Graphics A business graphics program for IBM-compatible microcomputer systems from Software Publishing Corporation. It is a versatile and easy-to-use program for producing business related presentation graphics. The program requires little knowledge of graphics presentation principles because it guides the user through each step of the process and produces output that meets high standards of aesthetics and professional graphics.

Harvard Mark I An electromechanical calculating machine developed by IBM Corporation under the direction of Howard Aiken at Harvard University. It was installed at Harvard in 1944. The Mark I, also called the Automatic Sequence Controlled Calculator (ASCC), could perform three calculations per second.

hash Visual static on the screen.

hashing (1) Key-to-address transformation in which the keys determine the location of the data. (2) The process of applying a formula to a record key to yield a number that represents a disk address.

hash totals Totals of the numbers of identifying fields. Used in error checking.

hatching Shading some portion of a drawing with parallel lines in a single direction. Shading in overlapping directions is crosshatching.

HDBMS Acronym for Hierarchical DataBase Management System.

head (1) Device that reads, records, or erases data on a storage medium, such as a small electromagnet used to read, write, and erase data on a magnetic disk. (2) Special data item that points to the beginning of a list.

head cleaning device Material containing a dirt solvent used to clean the read/write head of a floppy disk drive or a tape drive.

head crash Collision of the read/write head with the recording surface of a hard disk, resulting in loss of data. Usually caused by contamination of the disk, such as from a tiny particle of smoke or dust or from a fingerprint.

header (1) First part of a message, containing all the necessary information for directing the message to its destination(s). (2) Top margin of a page, usually the title of the book, the name of the chapter, the page number, and so on.

header record Record containing constant, common, or identifying information for a group of records that follows.

head positioning Placing a read/write head when data is being read or written by a direct-access storage device. Done by moving an access arm.

head slot Opening in a diskette jacket that exposes the disk surface to read/write heads.

head switching Activating the read/write head that is to read or write data when data are being read or written by a direct-access storage device.

heap (1) Collection of storage locations that a program can borrow for computations and then return. Free memory currently available to load and run programs. (2) A complete binary tree whose nodes contain search keys arranged in descending order.

heap sort See tree sort.

helical wave guide Metal tube containing thin glass fibers and wires capable of transmitting thousands of messages over communications lines. See fiber optics.

help (1) Handy function available on many systems. Supplies the user with additional information on how the system or program works. (2) On screen reference material providing assistance with the program.

help balloon An operating system and application program user help aid that tags a desired object on screen with a comic book style "balloon" full of information on how to use that object.

help screen A display screenful of information displayed by a program that has a help facility.

Helvetica A popular sans serif typeface developed in the 1950s. It is one of the most widely used fonts in the world and is included as a built-in font with many laser printers.

henry Unit of measure of inductance. One henry is the inductance of a circuit in which an electromotive force of 1 volt is produced by a current in the circuit that varies at the rate of 1 ampere per second.

Hercules Graphics Card (HGC) A monochrome video adapter introduced by Hercules Computer Technology in 1982. HGC provides a monochrome graphics mode for IBM PC graphics with a screen size of 720 x 348 pixels.

hermaphroditic Referring to connectors, ones in which each piece has protruding and receptacle parts, rather than one configured as male and one as female.

Hertz Cycles per second. Abbreviated Hz. See frequency.

heuristic Descriptive of an exploratory method of attacking a problem, in which the solution is obtained by successive evaluations of progress toward the final results. In other words, rule of thumb or other non-specific procedures for solving a problem. Pertaining to the use of empirical knowledge to aid in discovery. Contrast with algorithm.

heuristic learning Discovery method of learning from experience. A way computers can learn from their mistakes by eliminating unsuccessful or unproductive options from their operations. See artificial intelligence and machine learning.

Hewlett-Packard Company (HP) A major manufacturer of computer equipment; founded in 1939 by William Hewlett and David Packard in a garage behind Packard's California home. HP has introduced several computer series, workstations, laser printers, and many other electronic products.

Hewlett-Packard Graphics Language (HPGL) A language devised by Hewlett-Packard for storing graphical images.

hex See hexadecimal.

hexadecimal Pertaining to a number system with a radix of 16. Digits greater than 9 are represented by letters of the alphabet. For example, the binary numeral 1110001011010011 can be represented as hexadecimal E2D3.

hexadecimal number A numeral, usually of more than one digit, representing a sum in which the quantity represented by each digit is based on a radix of 16. The digits used are 0, 1, 2, 3, 4, 5, 6, 7, 8, 9, A, B, C, D, E, and F.

hexadecimal point Radix point in a mixed hexadecimal numeral, separating the integer part from the fractional part. In the hexadecimal numeral 3F.6A7, the hexadecimal point is between the digits F and 6.

hidden codes The hidden text formatting codes embedded in a document by an on-screen formatting program.

hidden file Hidden files occupy disk space but do not appear in directory listings. Files are hidden to prevent their display or change. Sometimes called invisible files. You cannot display, erase, or copy hidden files.

hidden line (1) When displaying a three-dimensional object, any line that would normally be obscured from the viewer's sight by the mass of the object itself, visible as a result of the projection. (2) Lines that have been drawn on the screen in background color and will not become visible until the colors are switched. (3) Lines of a diagram that are invisible.

hidden line removal Process of deleting line segments from a drawing when they would be obscured were the object displayed as a solid three-dimensional figure. Many types of computer graphics software and hardware can remove such hidden lines automatically.

hidden objects Distinct graphic entities that would be obscured from view by other entities if they were displayed as solids.

hidden surface Entire surface or plane that would be obscured from view if the graphics figure were displayed as a three-dimensional solid.

hierarchical database management system (HDBMS) Collection of related programs for loading, accessing, and controlling a database in which the data are organized like an inverted tree with a series of nodes connected by branches.

hierarchical directories A term used to refer to the organizational method of arranging files either in a DOS tree structure or in the file-and-folder method of Apple Macintosh computers.

hierarchical model Database model in which each object is of a particular hierarchy in a tree structure.

hierarchical network Computer network in which processing and control functions are performed at several levels by computers specially designed for the functions performed.

hierarchical structure In database management systems, the simplest form of file organization, in which records of various levels are related by owning or belonging to each other.

hierarchy (1) Order in which arithmetic operations within a formula or statement will be executed. See order of operations (2) Arrangement into any graded series.

hierarchy plus input-process-output (HIPO) Design and program documentation method that represents functional structure and data flow in a series of three types of diagrams: visual tables of contents that name the program modules and specify their hierarchical relationships; overview diagrams that describe the input, processing, and output for members of the hierarchy; and detailed diagrams that extend the overview diagrams to include more specific input, processing, and output detail with narrative.

high-density disk A floppy disk that holds more information than a double-density disk. 5.25-inch high-density disks hold 1.2 megabytes and 3.5-inch high-density disks hold 1.44 megabytes.

high-level language Any programming language that allows users to write instructions in a familiar notation rather than in a machine code. Each statement in a high-level language corresponds to several machine-code instructions. Contrast with low-level language.

highlighting (1) Process of making a display segment stand out by causing blinking, brightening, underlining, by reversing the background and the character images, such as dark characters on a light background, or creating a color combination that draws attention to it. (2) Highlighting is often used in word processing and page design programs as a means of selecting characters that are to be deleted, copied, or otherwise acted upon.

high-order Pertaining to the digit or digits of a number that have the greatest weight or significance. In the number 7643215, the high-order digit is 7. Contrast with low-order.

high-persistence phosphor Phosphor coating used on some display monitor screens that holds an image much longer than the coating used on standard display screens.

high-resolution (1) Pertaining to the quality and accuracy of detail that can be represented by a graphics display. Resolution quality depends upon the number of basic image-forming units (pixels) within a picture image—the greater the number, the higher the resolution. High-resolution pictures, produced by a large number of pixels, are sharper than low-resolution pictures. In computer graphics displays, an IBM VGA can produce a higher-resolution display (640 x 480 pixels) than can an IBM CGA

(640 x 200 pixels). (2) In printing, resolution is defined as the number of dots per inch (dpi) that are printed. In general, laser printing is about 300 dpi; typesetters and imagesetters can produce output at 1000 dpi, 2000 dpi, or more.

high-resolution graphics (HRG)   A high-quality image on a display screen or printed form.

high-speed printer (HSP)   Any printer capable of printing from 300 to 3000 lines per minute. See line printer.

high volatility   High frequency of changes to a file during a given time period. See volatile file.

high storage   Upper address range of a computer. In most machines, it is occupied by the operating system.

high-tech   A general term for sophisticated technical innovation; "cutting edge" technology, often involving computers and electronics.

hinting   In desktop publishing, the reduction of the weight of a typeface so that small-size fonts print without blurring or losing detail on 300-dpi laser printers.

HIPO   Acronym for Hierarchy plus Input-Process-Output.

hi-res graphics   Abbreviation of high-resolution graphics, a smooth and realistic picture on a display screen produced by a large number of pixels. Contrast with low-res graphics.

histogram   Vertical bar chart often used to graph statistical information. Column widths represent interval ranges; lengths indicate frequencies.

hit   Successful comparison of two items of data. Compare match.

Hoff, Ted   In 1971, as an engineer with Intel Corporation, Hoff designed the 4004 microprocessor. The single chip contained 2250 transistors, and all of the components of a full-sized central processing unit. This micro-chip caused the computer industry and its suppliers to rethink the future role of the computer.

holding time   In data communications, the length of time a communications channel is in use for each transmission. Includes both message time and operating time.

Hollerith card   Punched card consisting of 80 columns, each of which is divided from top to bottom into 12 punching positions. Can hold 80 characters of alphanumeric data.

Hollerith code   Particular code used to represent alphanumeric data on punched cards. Named after Herman Hollerith, originator of punched card tabulating. Each card column holds one character, and each decimal digit, letter, and special character is represented by one, two, or three holes punched into designated row positions of the column.

Hollerith, Herman (1860-1929) As a statistician and employee of the Census Bureau, he proposed using punched cards in conjunction with electromechanical relays to accomplish simple additions and sortings needed in the 1890 census. The company he set up to manufacture his punched card tabulator became one of the parents of IBM Corporation.

Hollerith Tabulating Machine The first statistical machine that operated on the punched card principle. The functions of the Hollerith Tabulating Machine were to record, compile, and tabulate census data. The machine was completed in time for the 1890 census for which it was first employed. The census data were punched into cards which were then manually fed into an electromagnetic counter and a sorting box. This electric tabulating system permitted the completion of the 1890 census in two and one-half years, one third the time required in the census ten years earlier.

hologram A three-dimensional "photograph" created by holography.

holographic store Storage in the form of a hologram.

holography Method of storing data by making a multidimensional photograph on a storage medium.

home Starting position for the cursor on a display screen. Usually in the top left-hand corner.

homebrew Refers to early microcomputer systems, made by hobbyists, that gave rise to the popularity of the personal computer.

home computer A personal computer designed and priced for use in the home.

homegrown software Software developed at home rather than in software development businesses. Many public-domain software, freeware and shareware are created in the home.

home key Keyboard function that directs the cursor to its home position, usually in the top left portion of the display screen.

home management software Programs designed for home use to help manage and organize the household, such as check balancing, menu file, and stock portfolio accounting programs.

home record First record in a chain of records in the chaining method of file organization.

home row Row of keys on the keyboard where users rest their fingers between keystrokes.

homunculus Infinitely recursive model of the brain. Used in studies of artificial intelligence.

176

Hopper, Grace Mathematician and programmer who developed programs for the MARK 1 and early UNIVAC computers. Later became a pioneer in the field of computer languages, writing the first practical compiler program and playing an important role in the development of COBOL.

horizontal scrolling Moving of horizontal blocks of data or text, allowing users to view more data than can fit on the screen at one time.

horizontal software Programs designed to serve a wide range of users, who must tailor the programs to their own needs. Examples include database management systems, spreadsheets and word processors.

host adapter A board or circuit that connects a specific computer model to a more general controller.

host computer (1) Central processing unit that provides the computing power for remote terminals and peripheral devices connected to it. (2) Computer that is in charge during a telecommunications or local area network session. (3) Central controlling computer in a network of computers.

host language Programming language in which another language is included or embedded.

hot site Fully equipped computer center, ready for use in case of emergency.

hot spot The position in a mouse pointer that marks the exact display screen location that will be affected by a mouse action such as a button press. The mouse pointer's hot spot is a single pixel in size.

hot zone On some word processors, a user-defined region beginning at the right margin of a page and extending about seven spaces to the left. If a word ends in the hot zone, the system automatically places the next character entered at the beginning of the next line.

housekeeping Computer operations that do not directly contribute toward the desired results, but are a necessary part of a program, such as initialization, set-up, and clean-up operations. Sometimes called bookkeeping.

housing Cabinet or other enclosure.

HPC A Hewlett-Packard LaserJet graphics file format.

HPGL Acronym for Hewlett-Packard Graphics Language. An object file format originally developed to drive plotters. Now used to store graphical images.

HSB (Hue, Saturation, Brightness) A type of color system. Hue refers to pure color, that is, light of a distinct wave length—red, green, violet, etc. Saturation refers to the degree that a color is pure or the degree of white it contains. Brightness refers to the color's percentage of black. HSB is used in computer graphics for describing color.

HSP   Acronym for High-Speed Printer.

hue   In the HSB color model, one of the three characteristics used to describe a color. Hue refers to pure color, that is, light of a distinct wave length—red, green, etc.

Huffman tree   Tree with minimum values. See minimal tree and optimal merge tree.

human engineering   Study concerned with designing products that are easier and more comfortable for humans to use. Also called ergonomics.

human/machine interface   Any boundary at which people interact with machines.

hybrid computer system   System that uses both analog and digital equipment. It is used in process control and robotic systems.

hybrids   Circuits fabricated by interconnecting smaller circuits of different technologies, mounted on a single substrate.

HyperCard   An implementation of a hypertext system for the Apple Macintosh family of computers. A HyperCard document consists of a series of cards collected together in a stack; each card can contain text, graphics and sound. Items on the cards can be linked together in a variety of different ways.

hypermedia   A term describing hypertext-based systems that combine text, graphics, sound, and video with traditional data. In a hypertext system, you select a word or phrase and give a command to see related text. In a hypermedia system, such a command reveals related graphics images, sounds, and even snippets of animation or video. Hypercard is an example of a hypermedia application.

HyperTalk   The programming language used in the HyperCard program to manipulate HyperCard stacks. HyperTalk implements object-oriented programming principles.

hypertape   Magnetic tape unit that uses a cartridge rather than a reel of tape. The cartridge consists of a reel of tape and the take-up reel.

hypertext   A document retrieval network having full-text files and dynamic indexes for links among documents. The term hypertext was coined in 1965 by Ted Nelson to describe documents, as presented by a computer, that express the nonlinear structure of ideas, as opposed to the linear format of books, film, and speech.

hyphenation   In page layout and word processing programs, an automatic operation that hyphenates words on certain lines to improve word spacing.

hysteresis A tendency for a display element to stay in either the on or off condition once it has been switched. With, hysteresis, for example, a sustaining voltage can be applied to a display to keep all lighted pixels glowing without lighting any that are supposed to be off.

Hz Abbreviation for Hertz; cycles per second. See frequency.

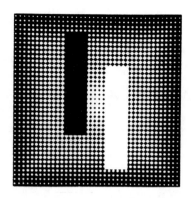

IBG Acronym for InterBlock Gap.

I-beam pointer In a graphical user interface, a special pointer shaped like a capital "I" that indicates the insertion point for text editing.

IBI Abbreviation for Intergovernmental Bureau of Informatics. An organization consisting of members of the United Nations, UNESCO, or U.N. Agencies. The goal is to promote scientific research, computer education and training, and the exchange of information between developed and developing countries. The main focus of IBI is to promote informatics, particularly in developing countries.

IBM-compatible microcomputer A personal computer that is compatible with the IBM Personal Computer and the PS/2 computer.

IBM Corporation The International Business Machines Corporation is the world's largest computer company. It started in New York City in 1911 when the Computing-Tabulating-Recording (CTR) Company was formed by a merger of four companies. Thomas J. Watson, Sr. became the general manager in 1914. Over the next decade, Watson turned CTR into an international enterprise. In 1924 the company was renamed IBM. IBM started making computers in 1953 and has since introduced computers of all sizes—from personal computers to supercomputers. A few models produced by IBM include the 650, 701, 702, 703, 704, 705, 709, 1401, 1410, 1620, 1790 and 1794. In April 1964, IBM introduced the third generation of computers with the introduction of the System/360 family of computers. Throughout the 1970s, IBM introduced several minicomputer systems: System/3, System/34, System/38, Series 1 and 8100. In 1981, IBM introduced the IBM Personal Computer. In 1987, IBM introduced the PS/2 series of personal computers. Today, product lines of the IBM Corporation span personal computers to large mainframes.

IBM draw/paint programs See Art & Letters, Graphics Editor, Artline, ColoRIX, Corel Draw, Deluxe Paint, Designer, DGS Paint, Dr. Halo, Lumena, Painting Effects, PC Paintbrush, Portfolio, Rio-Sable, Tempra, TIPS, Water Color.

IBM ES/9000 The Enterprise System/9000 is a family of mainframes announced by the IBM Corporation in 1990.

IBM PC clone A popular term for personal computers that adhere closely to the appearance and functionality of personal computers in the IBM PC family. Often manufactured abroad, these computers are generally reliable and inexpensive.

IBM PC compatible A term for personal computers that adhere closely to the functionality of personal computers in the IBM PC family. PC compatibles, as opposed to "clones", have never necessarily had to look like standard IBM PC designs, and some manufacturers have insisted in incorporating proprietary, non-standard features in their "compatibles" even while maintaining general compatibility with the MS-DOS, Intel-based features of the IBM PC family.

IBM Personal Computer August 12, 1981, came and went, but nothing would ever be the same again. That day, the IBM Corporation introduced a Personal Computer based on the Intel 8088 microprocessor. The machine went on to become the most significant technology to hit the world since the telephone. Although the IBM PC was not the first, it legitimized the machines in the computer market. It has transformed the way millions of people work, spawned new industries and made computer technology less mysterious. The PC created the home computer movement, allowing people to work out of their living room and "commute" by sending reports to the office over the phone. IBM set the stage for clones when it announced the PC by deciding not to block other companies from providing software or accessories for its PC. It reasoned that if the technology was "open," or non-proprietary, the market for the machines would grow faster. But that decision soon led to the creation of clones of the entire computer. Today, every nation from Hong Kong to Hungary has a local industry cranking out inexpensive PC clones. There are three machines in the PC line: IBM PC, IBM PC-XT and IBM PC-AT.

IBM Personal Computer AT A personal computer, based on the Intel 80286 microprocessor, that was introduced by the IBM Corporation in 1984. The 80286 chip was "upwardly compatible" with the Intel 8088 in the sense that it could run all the PC software written for the 8088-based PCs which preceded it. It also came standard with a hard disk drive, a feature many users were still not accustomed to having at their disposal.

IBM Personal Computer XT A personal computer, based on the Intel 8088 microprocessor and including a hard disk, that was introduced by the IBM Corporation in 1983. The XT type computer occupies a prominent and useful place on desktops throughout the business world.

IBM Personal System/1 (PS/1) A home computer from IBM Corporation introduced in 1990. The PS/1 computer uses an Intel 80286 microprocessor and comes in a small, attractive case, with a color VGA display and a 2400 baud modem built in. The computer contains about everything an ordinary computer user is likely to need.

IBM Personal System/2 (PS/2) A series of personal computers from IBM Corporation introduced in 1987. These computers were designed to replace the IBM Personal Computer line: IBM PC, IBM PC-XT, IBM PC-AT. The PS/2 machines are based on the Intel 8086, 80286 and 80386 microprocessors. The IBM PS/2 runs all or almost all the software developed for the IBM Personal Computer.

IBM System/360 The family of mainframe computers that marked the beginning of the third generation of computers. Along with hardware advances, the 360 introduced comprehensive operating systems to users.

IBM 3080 A series of large-scale mainframes introduced by IBM Corporation in 1980.

IBM 3090 A series of large-scale mainframes introduced by IBM Corporation in 1986.

IC Acronym for Integrated Circuit, a complex electronic circuit fabricated on a simple piece of material, usually a silicon chip.

ICCP Acronym for Institute for Certification of Computer Professionals.

ICES Acronym for Integrated Civil Engineering System, a system developed to aid civil engineers in solving engineering problems. Consists of several engineering systems and programming languages.

icon A pictorial representation of a software function. A symbol used on the display screen to represent some feature of the program. For example, in one program, an icon representing a waste-paper basket is selected if you want to erase information. Non-technical people find symbols easier to understand than technical words.

iconic interface A user interface that displays objects on the screen as tiny pictures that the user can point to and select via a mouse.

ICPEM Acronym for Independent Computer Peripheral Equipment Manufacturers.

identification division First of four main parts of a COBOL program.

identifier Symbol whose purpose is to identify, indicate, or name a body of data.

identity In object-oriented programming, the nature of an object that distinguishes it from all other objects.

identity-based database A database in which entities can be referenced by their unique identities.

idle characters Characters used in data communications to synchronize the transmission. See synchronous transmission.

idle time Time that a computer system is available for use, but is not in actual operation.

IDP   Acronym for Integrated Data Processing.

IEEE   See Institute of Electrical and Electronics Engineers.

IEEE-488   Interface standard mainly used to connect laboratory instruments and other scientific equipment to computers, either for control purposes or to allow the computer to collect data. Type of parallel interface.

IEEE 696/S-100   Identification of a standard, developed by the Institute of Electrical and Electronic Engineers. Ensures the compatibility of all computing products designed to this standard.

IEEE 802   A set of standards developed by the IEEE to define methods of access and control on local area networks.

IFAC   Acronym for International Federation of Automatic Control, a multinational organization concerned with advancing the science and technology of control.

IFF   A graphics format designed for the Commodore Amiga and common to almost all Amiga paint, draw and animation programs.

IFIP   Acronym for International Federation for Information Processing. A multinational federation of organizations, each of whom represent their individual country in information technology. IFIP was founded in 1960 with assistance from UNEXCO. Throughout its history, IFIP has striven (1) to promote international cooperation in the field of information processing, (2) to stimulate research, development and the application of information processing in science and human activity, (3) to further the dissemination and exchange of information relating to its selected field, and (4) to encourage education in information processing.

if-then-else   One of the three basic building blocks of structured programming.

illegal character   Character or combination of bits not accepted by the computer as a valid or known representation.

illuminance   The amount of light falling on a surface area.

illuminate   To increase the brightness or luminosity of graphical output at a display screen.

Illustrator   A PostScript-based, Apple Macintosh drawing program with powerful capabilities. A complete set of tools for drawing, blending, grouping and transforming objects enables users to create very sophisticated graphics. Text can be created and modified in any fashion desired with every aspect of typographic formatting controllable, including outline fonts. A graph module enables users to create publication quality graphs. Any color and percentage of tint can be applied to both text and objects. Color models supported are CMYK and Pantone Color Matching System. Designs can be previewed on-screen in 8- and 24-bit color and black and white. Color separations can be printed using Adobe Separator. In effect, this professional level program is an illustration, page layout, type manipulation and graphing application all rolled into one. Adobe Illustrator was introduced in 1987 by Adobe Systems Incorporated.

image (1) Exact logical duplicate stored in a different medium. If the computer user displays the contents of memory on a display screen, he or she will see an image of memory. (2) In computer graphics, the output form of graphics data, such as a drawn representation of a graphics file.

image enhancement Any accentuation of all or part of a graphics image through such techniques as coloring, shading, highlighting, zooming, reverse video, or blinking.

image-oriented backup Any backup system that creates a mirror image of the disk, without regard to the files themselves. With such a system, the entire disk must be restored from the backup medium to allow access to the files.

image processing Method for processing pictorial information by a computer system. Involves inputting graphics information into a computer system, storing it, working with it, and outputting it to an output device. Once a photograph has been digitized into binary data, the computer can process the data in any way the user wishes in order to enhance the contrast of an image, blend images, change shapes, change colors, and so on.

imagesetter A typesetting device that can transfer output of a desktop publishing system directly to paper or film. Imagesetters commonly print at high resolution (from 1200 dpi to over 3000 dpi). Imagesetters are professional typesetting machines that use chemical photo-reproduction techniques to produce high resolution output.

imagesetter service bureau A company that specializes in the sale of PostScript output, usually at the per page or per color charge. Some bureaus specialize in type-only output, others in film.

Image Studio A powerful gray scale painting program for Apple Macintosh computers. The program includes a selection of brush and paint tools.

Imagewriter A dot matrix printer used with Apple Macintosh and Apple II microcomputers.

imaging The process involved in the capture, storage, display, and printing of graphical two- or three-dimensional images.

imaging model The method of representing output on a display screen. In a graphical user interface, the goal is to use a unified imaging model, so that the text displayed on-screen closely resembles the text printed.

IMG Commonly, though not always, a bitmapped GEM file. Used by GEM Paint, Ventura Publisher, and other programs written to run under GEM.

immediate access Ability of a computer to put data in, or remove it from, storage without delay.

immediate access storage See internal storage.

immediate address Pertaining to an instruction whose address part contains the value of an operand rather than its address. It is not an address at all but rather an operand supplied as part of an instruction.

immediate-mode commands System and editing commands executed as soon as the carriage control key (ENTER, RETURN) is pressed.

impact printer Data printout device that imprints by momentary pressure of raised type against paper, using ink or ribbon as a color medium. See daisy wheel printer, line printer, thimble printer. Contrast with nonimpact printer.

impedance Total opposition (resistance plus reactance) a circuit offers to the flow of alternating current at a given frequency. Measured in ohms.

implementation (1) Process of installing a computer system. Involves choosing the equipment, installing the equipment, training the personnel, and establishing the computing center operating policies. (2) Representation of a programming language on a specific computer system. (3) Act of installing a program. (4) In object-oriented programming, the inside view of a class, object, or module, including the secrets of its behavior.

import To bring information from one system or program into another. PageMaker, for example, can import MacPaint files created by Super-Paint.

IMS Acronym for Information Management System, a database management system software package that provides the facilities for storing and retrieving information from hierarchically structured files and databases.

inactive Pertaining to a transaction that has been loaded into the computer's memory but has not yet been executed.

inactive window Any window not in use.

incidence matrix Two-dimensional array that describes the edges in a graph. Also called connection matrix.

incident light Light falling on an object. The color of an object is perceived as a function of the wavelengths of incident light reflected or absorbed by it.

inclusive OR (OR) Boolean operator that gives a truth table value of true if either or both of the two variables it connects are true. If neither is true, the value is false. Contrast with exclusive OR. Compare NOR, NAND, AND, and logical sum.

increment   (1) Amount added to a value or variable. Contrast with decrement. (2) Distance between any two adjacent addressable points on a graphics input/output device.

incremental backup   Making a copy of files that have changed since the last backup operation, rather than copying all the files on a hard disk. Incremental backups take less time than complete ones, but they require more sophisticated software to manage the backup and restoration processes.

incremental plotter   Digital plotter that outputs graphic data in discrete movements of the plotting head.

indegree   Number of directed edges that point to a node. Contrast with outdegree.

indent   To begin, or move, text a specified number of positions from the left edge or right edge of a page.

indentation   White space found at the beginning of a line of text; often denotes the beginning of a paragraph.

Independent Computer Consultants Association (ICCA)   National network of independent computer consultants, founded in 1976. Through the national organization and local chapters, members exchange ideas and become part of a collective voice in the computer consulting industry.

Independent Computer Peripheral Equipment Manufacturers (ICPEM) Organization composed of companies that specialize in manufacturing one or more lines of computer equipment.

independent consultant   Person trained in the information processing field, who works with businesses and organizations on a temporary basis helping them solve problems. See consultant.

independent variable   Input to a model, so called because it can change.

index   (1) Symbol or number used to identify a particular quantity in an array of similar quantities; for example, X(5) is the fifth item in an array of Xs. (2) Table of reference, held in storage in some sequence, that may be accessed to obtain the addresses of other items of data, such as items in a graphics or data file. See index register.

indexed address   Address modified by the content of an index register prior to or during the execution of a computer instruction.

indexed sequential access method (ISAM)   Means of organizing data on a direct-access device. A directory or index is created to show where the data records are stored. Any desired data record can be retrieved from the device by consulting the index. The index reveals the approximate location of the record or piece of data on the direct-access device, and the computer searches the area indicated by the index until it locates the desired record or piece of data.

indexer Program that generates an index for a document.

index hole Hole punched through a floppy disk that can be read by the electro-optical system in the disk drive to locate accurately the beginning of sector zero on the disk.

indexing Programming technique whereby an instruction can be modified by a factor called an index.

index register Register whose contents can be added to or subtracted from an address prior to or during the execution of an instruction.

indicator Any device that registers a condition in the computer.

indirect addressing Using an address that specifies a storage location that contains either a direct address or another indirect address. Also called multilevel addressing.

induce To produce an electrical charge, current, or voltage by induction. A charge on the gate of a field effect transistor induces an equal charge in the channel.

inductance In a circuit, the property that opposes any change in the existing current. Unit of measure is the henry.

induction Process by which a body having electric and magnetic properties produces an electrical charge, a voltage, or a magnetic field in an adjacent body, without physical contact.

industrial data collection device Input device that can record the time an employee spends on the job. Can be used to determine wages, costs for jobs being done, and so forth.

industrial robot Reprogrammable, multifunctional manipulator designed to move material, parts, tools, or specialized devices through variable programmed motions for the performance of a variety of tasks. Unlike other forms of automation, robots can be programmed to do a variety of tasks, making them the most versatile of manufacturing tools. Many advantages result from the robot's reprogrammability. Since robots can switch tasks with a minimum of startup and debugging costs, a company is able to maximize its use of a proven design and reduce overall manufacturing costs. Major industries using industrial robots include auto industry, aerospace, electronics, home appliances, consumer goods, and off-road vehicles. Recent developments that give robots added intelligence—such as machine vision, tactile sensing, and mobility—make robots suitable for a wider range of industries. The near future will find robots used increasingly in industries such as textiles, food processing, pharmaceuticals, furniture, construction, and health care.

Industry Standard Architecture (ISA)   The industry name and acronym for the architecture and "bus specification" used by most personal computers today. It is based on the 16-bit design specifications of the original IBM PC AT, although the individual implementation by different manufacturers may deviate in some details to allow for improvements in the original design, features and performance.

inequality   Expression of two values not being equal. $A > B$ and $B < A$ are two ways of expressing the same inequality. $A \neq B$ expresses an inequality without identifying its order.

infection   The presence within a computer system of a virus or Trojan Horse.

inference engine   The part of an expert system that takes the information from the user, fits it into the rules in the knowledge base and generates results, which will lead to advice.

inference program   In expert systems, a program that derives conclusions by making inferences based upon available data.

infinite loop   Set of instructions that continuously repeat in a program. Loop with no exit condition. Also called endless loop.

infix notation   Common arithmetic notation in which operators are embedded within operands. Addition of 5 and 3 would be expressed as $5 + 3$. Contrast with prefix notation and post-fix notation.

informal design review   Evaluation of system-designed documentation by selected management, systems analysts, and programmers, prior to the actual coding of program modules, to determine necessary additions, deletions, and modifications to the system design.

informatics   Word used more or less synonymously with information technology.

information   Meaningful and useful facts that are extracted from data fed to a computer. Processed data; data that is organized, meaningful, and useful.

information banks   Large databases that store information pertaining to specific applications.

information bits   In telecommunications, those bits that are generated by the data source and do not include error-control bits.

information center   A department within a business that offers employees computer and software training, help in getting data from other computer systems, and technical assistance. The department is also responsible for computer purchasing decisions.

information explosion   Exponential increase in the growth and diversification of all forms of information. Compare information revolution.

information hiding In object-oriented programming, a design strategy that aims at maximizing modularity by concealing as much information as possible within the components of a design. The terms "information hiding" and "encapsulation" are usually interchangeable.

information networks Interconnection, through telecommunications, of a geographically dispersed group of libraries and information centers for the purpose of sharing their total information resources among more people.

information processing Totality of operations performed by a computer. Involves evaluating, analyzing, and processing data to produce usable information.

information processing center Same as data processing center.

information processing curriculum Same as data processing curriculum.

information providers Large businesses that supply information to a computer network for a fee, such as CompuServe, Prodigy, and Source (The).

information resource management System to manage information as a resource like labor, capital, and raw material.

information retrieval (1) That branch of computer technology concerned with techniques for storing and searching large quantities of data and making selected data available. (2) Methods used to recover specific information from stored data.

information revolution Name given to the present era because of the impact of computer technology on society. Sometimes called the computer revolution.

information science Study of how people create, use, and communicate information in all forms.

information services Broad-based databases that offer a variety of services, ranging from airline reservation information to stock market quotations. See CompuServe, Prodigy, and Source (The).

information storage and retrieval (ISR) See information retrieval.

information system Collection of people, procedures, and equipment designed, built, operated, and maintained to collect, record, process, store, retrieve, and display information.

information technology Merging of computing and high-speed communications links carrying data, sound, and video.

information theory Branch of learning concerned with the likelihood of accurate transmission or communication of messages subject to transmission failure, noise, and distortion. See operations research.

information utility A company from which you can access information via computer.

inherent error Computer error that has incorrect initial values caused by uncertainty in measurements, by outright blunders, or by approximating a value by an insufficient number of digits.

inherit In object-oriented programming, for one class to acquire the characteristics of another.

inheritance In object-oriented programming, a mechanism for automatically sharing methods and data types among classes, subclasses, and objects. Inheritance allows programmers to program only what is different from previously defined classes.

inhouse An activity that takes place on the user's premises.

initial In desktop publishing, an enlarged letter at the beginning of a paragraph or chapter. Initials set down within the copy are drop caps. Initials raised above the top of the text are stickup caps.

Initial Graphics Exchange Specification (IGES) A standard file format for computer graphics that is particularly suitable for describing models created with computer-aided design programs. IGES offers methods for describing and annotating drawings and engineering diagrams.

initialization Process of formatting a diskette so that it is ready for use. Initialization erases any previous information that happens to be on the diskette.

initialize (1) To preset a variable or counter to proper starting values before commencing a calculation. (2) To format a disk.

ink jet printer A printer that sprays ink from jet nozzles onto the paper. A nozzle emits a continuous stream of ink droplets that are selectively guided either to the paper or to a gutter where they may be recycles for reuse or sent into a discard container. Ink jet printers produce high-quality printouts.

in-line coding Coding located in the main part of a routine.

in-line processing Processing of data in random order, not subject to preliminary editing or sorting.

in-line subroutine Subroutine inserted into the main routine as many times as needed.

inner loop A loop contained within another loop. When nesting loops, the inner loop is the one that must run completely before the outer loop can make another run.

input Introduction of data from an external storage medium into a computer's internal storage unit. Contrast with output.

input area Area of internal storage reserved for input data. Contrast with output area.

input data Data to be processed. Often called input. Contrast with output data.

input device Unit used to get data from the human user into the central processing unit, such as a disk drive or keyboard. Contrast with output device.

input job stream See input stream or job stream.

input media Physical substance upon which input data are recorded, such as diskettes and magnetic tape. Compare output media and source media.

input/output (I/O) Pertaining to the techniques, media, and devices used to achieve human/machine communication.

input/output bound Pertaining to a situation in which the central processing unit is slowed down because of I/O operations, which are usually extremely slow in comparison to the internal processing operations of the CPU. Contrast with processor bound.

input/output channel Channel that transmits input data to, or output data from, a computer. See multiplexer channel, RS-232C, and selector channel.

input/output device Unit used to get data from the human user into the central processing unit, and to transfer data from the computer's internal storage to some storage or output device. See input device, output device, and peripheral equipment.

input/output instructions Directions for the transfer of data between peripheral devices and main storage that enable the central processing unit to control the peripheral devices connected to it.

input/output ports Sockets on a computer where the peripherals interface. See peripheral equipment.

input/output processor Auxiliary processor, dedicated to controlling input/output transfers, that frees the central processing unit for non-I/O tasks. Compare front-end processor.

input/output symbol Parallelogram-shaped flowcharting symbols used to indicate an input operation to a procedure or an output operation from a procedure.

input stream Sequence of control statements and data submitted to the operating system on an input unit especially activated for that purpose by the operator. Same as job stream.

inputting Process of entering data into a computer system.

inquiry A request for information.

inquiry processing Process of selecting a record from a file and immediately displaying its contents.

inquiry station Device from which any inquiry is made. Can be geographically remote from the computer or at the computer console.

insert To place data between other previously existing pieces of data.

insertion method See sifting.

insertion point Position at which text is entered into a document.

insert mode In word processing, a text input mode in which text is inserted at the current cursor position without overwriting any text already in the document.

install program A program that prepares a software program to run in the computer. It customizes elements of the new program so a specific computer system can use it.

installation (1) A program provided with an application program that assists you in installing the program on a hard disk and configuring the program for use. (2) General term for a particular computer system.

installation time Time spent installing, testing, and accepting equipment.

installer A program that adds software to a computer system and prepares it for subsequent execution.

instance In object-oriented programming, an object that is a member of a class. Something you can do things to. An instance has state, behavior, and identity. The structure and behavior of similar instances are defined in their common class. The terms "instance" and "object" are interchangeable.

instance variable In object-oriented programming, data contained within an object that describe properties that the object possesses. The terms "field", "instance variable", "member object" and "slot" are interchangeable.

instant feedback Immediate response—to questions, tests, drills, etc.

instantrate In object-oriented programming, to create an object of a specific class.

instantiation In object-oriented programming, the process of filling in the template of a generic or parameterized class to produce a class from which one can create instances.

instant print Feature of some word processing programs that lets one use the system as a typewriter.

Institute for Certification of Computer Professionals (ICCP) Nonprofit organization established in 1973 to test and certify knowledge and skills of computing personnel. A primary objective is to pool the resources of constituent societies so the full attention of the information processing industry can be focused on the vital tasks of development and recognition of qualified personnel. Administers the Certificate in Computer Programming (CCP) and Certificate in Data Processing (CDP).

Institute of Electrical and Electronic Engineers (IEEE) A professional engineering organization founded in 1963 for the furthering of education, research, and standards in the electronics and electrical fields. IEEE has a strong interest in computer technology. It sponsors many educational opportunities and publications for members.

Institute of Electrical and Electronics Engineers Computer Society (IEEECS) Computer speciality group within the IEEE. One of the leading professional associations in advancing the theory and practice of computer and information processing technology.

instruction Group of characters, bytes, or bits that defines an operation to be performed by the computer. Usually made up of an operation code and one or more operands. See machine instruction.

instructional computing Educational process of teaching individuals the various phases of computer science and data processing.

instruction code Same as operation code.

instruction counter Counter that indicates the location of the next computer instruction to be interpreted. Same as program counter.

instruction cycle Time required to process an instruction. This includes fetching the instruction from internal storage, interpreting or decoding the instruction, and executing the instruction. Compare instruction time.

instruction format Makeup and arrangement of computer instruction.

instruction register Hardware register that stores an instruction for execution.

instruction set Set of vendor-supplied codes for a particular computer or family of computers. Synonymous with repertoire.

instruction time Time it takes for an instruction to be retrieved from internal storage by the control unit and interpreted. Often called I-time. Compare instruction cycle.

instruction word Computer word that contains an instruction.

instrument Document designed as a form, report, questionnaire, or guide to be used in a planned systematic data-gathering procedure for the purpose of providing information to the individual, group, or organization initiating the request.

instrumental input Data captured by machines and placed directly into the computer.

instrumentation Application of devices for the measuring, recording, and/or controlling of physical properties and movements.

integer Any member of the set consisting of the whole numbers and their negatives. Examples: -24, -1, 0, 1, 2, 13, 128.

integer BASIC Type of BASIC language that can process whole numbers (integers) only.

integer variable Quantity that can be equal to any integer and can take on different values.

integrate Process of putting various components together to form a harmonious computer system.

integrated circuit (IC) An electronic circuit etched on a tiny germanium or silicon chip. Integrated circuits are categorized by the number of elements (transistors, resistors, etc.) they hold. The categories of IC's are small-scale integration (SSI), medium-scale integration (MSI), large-scale integration (LSI), very large-scale integration (VLSI), super large-scale integration (SLSI), and ultra large-scale integration (ULSI). Integrated circuits were invented in the late 1950s by Jack Kilby (an engineer at Texas Instruments) and Robert Noyce (an engineer at Fairchild Semiconductor).

integrated data processing (IDP) Data processing in which the coordination of data acquisition with all other stages of data processing is achieved in a coherent system, such as a business data processing system in which data for sales orders and purchasing are combined to accomplish the functions of scheduling, invoicing, and accounting.

integrated injection logic (IIL) See I^2L.

integrated software An applications software package containing programs to perform more than one function. The package typically includes related word processing, spreadsheet, database, and graphics programs. Since the information from the electronic spreadsheet may be shared with the database manager and the word processor (and vice versa), this software is called integrated. Some integrated programs, for instance, split the screen into windows and allow the operator to work with a word processing document and a spreadsheet simultaneously. Programs such as Microsoft Works for the Apple Macintosh microcomputer, Framework for the IBM PS/2 microcomputer, and AppleWorks for the Apple II microcomputer are examples.

integration   Combining diverse elements of hardware and software, often acquired from different vendors, into a unified system.

integrity   (1) Preservation of programs or data for their intended purpose. (2) Adherence to a code of behavior or ethics. (3) The integrity of data concerns its accuracy, completeness, and safety.

Intel Corporation   A leading manufacturer of semiconductor devices that was founded in 1968 by Robert Noyce and Gordon Moore in Mountain View, California. In 1971, Intel engineer Marcian E. "Ted" Hoff, designed the 4-bit 4004 microprocessor chip. Throughout the years, Intel has developed a wide variety of chips and board-level products.

intelligence   See artificial intelligence.

intelligent database   A database with the ability to accept queries written in a language close to that used by humans.

intelligent language   Programming language that can learn from or be changed by the programmer or user.

intelligent terminal   Input/output device in which a number of computer processing characteristics are physically built into, or attached to, the terminal unit. See point-of-sale terminal and local intelligence. Compare with smart terminal. Contrast with dumb terminal.

intensity   Amount of light in a graphics display device. Level of brightness emitted by a cathode ray tube. On most visual display devices, intensity can be controlled by manipulating a switch.

Intensity Red Green Blue   A type of color encoding used in IBM's color graphics adapters: CGA, EGA and VGA.

interactive   Yielding an immediate response to input. The user is in direct and continual communication with the computer system. Denotes two-way communications between a computer system and its operators. An operator can modify or terminate a program and receive feedback from the system for guidance and verification.

interactive graphics   Any graphics system in which the user and the computer are in active communication.

interactive graphics system   Computer graphics system in which workstations are used interactively for computer-aided design, all under full operator control, and possibly also for text-processing, generation of charts and graphs, computer-aided engineering, and generation of 35 mm slides or animation pictures.

interactive language   A computer language that permits the programmer to converse with the computer, entering instructions, testing them, changing them, etc. Many languages have both interactive and noninteractive versions.

interactive processing Type of real-time processing involving a continuing dialogue between user and computer; the user is allowed to modify data and/or instructions. See conversational mode and transaction-oriented processing.

interactive program Computer program that permits data to be entered or the flow of the program to be modified during its execution.

interactive query Operation that allows the immediate retrieval of a specific record or records. Essentially a dialogue in which each user input can elicit a response from the system.

interactive system System in which the human user of a device serviced by the computer can communicate directly with the operating program. For human users, this is termed a conversational system.

interactive videodisc A computer-assisted instruction technology that uses a computer to provide access to at least two hours of video information stored on a videodisc.

interblock gap (IBG) Distance on a magnetic tape, or disk, between the end of one block of records and the beginning of the next block of records. Contrast with file gap and interrecord gap.

interconnection Physical and electrical connection of equipment furnished by different vendors.

interface (1) Point of meeting between a computer and an external entity, whether an operator, a peripheral device, or a communications medium. May be physical, involving a connector, or logical, involving software. (2) In object-oriented programming, the outside view of a class, object, or module, which emphasizes its abstraction while hiding its structure and the secrets of its behavior.

interface card Type of expansion board that permits connection of external devices to computers, such as disk interface cards, serial interface cards, and parallel interface cards.

interference Unwanted signals that degrade the quality of wanted signals.

interlace To assign successive addresses to physically separated storage locations on a magnetic disk in such a way as to reduce the access time.

interleaved memory A method of speeding access to dynamic random access memory (DRAM) chips by dividing RAM into two large banks and storing bit pairs in alternate banks; the microprocessor accesses one bank while the other is being refreshed.

interleaving Multiprogramming technique in which parts of one program are inserted into another program so that if there are processing delays in one of the programs, parts of the other program can be processed.

interlock Protective facility that prevents one device or operation from interfering with another, such as the locking of the switches on the control console to prevent their manual movement while the computer is executing a program.

interlude Preliminary housekeeping.

intermittent error Error that occurs intermittently, but persistently, and is extremely difficult to reproduce or to debug.

internal clock Electronic circuit within the computer system that keeps the time of day.

internal data representation Data representation in registers, storage, and other devices inside the computer.

internal documentation (1) Insertion of explanatory comments and remarks into source-language programs. Causes no processing by the computer but acquaints present and future programmers with the functions performed by various parts of the program. (2) Documentation used within a business organization.

internal DOS commands Commands that access DOS programs that are loaded into the computer when the system is booted.

internal font A series of typefaces contained within ROM chips built into a printer.

internal hard disk A hard disk designed to fit within a computer's case and to use the computer's power supply.

internal memory Same as internal storage.

internal modem Modem that plugs directly into computer expansion slots inside the computer. Contrast with acoustic coupler and direct-connect modem.

internal report Report produced by an organization for people inside the organization, usually concerning inventory, quality control, payroll, and so on. Contrast with external report.

internal sort Sequencing of two or more records within the central processing unit. First phase of a multipass sort program. See external sort.

internal storage Addressable storage directly controlled by the central processing unit. Used to store programs while they are being executed and data while they are being processed. Also called immediate access storage, internal memory, main storage, and primary storage. Contrast with auxiliary storage.

International Business Machines Corporation See IBM Corporation.

International Federation for Information Processing (IFIP) Multinational organization representing professional and educational societies actively engaged in the field of information processing. Holds a meeting, at a different location in the world, every three years.

interoperability The ability of devices from a variety of vendors to share data and communicate effectively.

interpolation (1) Method of finding values between any two known values. (2) In computer graphics, this process is often applied to creating curves by joining a series of straight line segments or to defining smoothing curves between specified points. (3) The averaging of a number of points to create a new point.

interpretation One-by-one translation of high-level-language program statements into machine-language instructions. When a program is interpreted, each statement is translated and executed before the next statement is processed. Contrast with compilation.

interpreted language A language implemented by an interpreter.

interpreter Language translator that converts each source-language statement into machine code and executes it immediately, statement by statement. Program that performs interpretation. Contrast with compiler.

interrecord gap Space between records on magnetic disk and tape. Used to signal that the end of a record has been reached. Contrast with file gap and interblock gap.

interrupt Signal that, when activated, causes the hardware to transfer program control to some specific location in internal storage, thus breaking the normal flow of the program being executed. After the interrupt has been processed, program control is again returned to the interrupted program. Can be generated as the result of a program action, by an operator activating switches on the computer console or by a peripheral device causing the interrupting signal. Essential capability for multiprogramming. Often called trapping.

interrupt driven Pertaining to a computer system that makes extensive use of interrupts.

interruption Any break in the normal sequence of executing instructions.

interval timer Mechanism whereby elapsed time can be monitored by a computer system.

interview (1) Fact-gathering method in systems analysis and design. (2) Personal conversation between a job applicant and the person who may offer a job. During an interview, a person has the chance to give the details about his or her skills, education, and past job experience, as well as to find out more about the job and what will be expected of him or her on the job.

intrinsic font A font for which a bit image (an exact pattern) exists that can be used without modification.

inventory control Use of a computer system to monitor an inventory.

inventory management Daily and periodic bookkeeping commonly associated with inventory control and with forecasting needs for items or groups of items.

inverse video Process that shows dark text on a light background display screen. Normally, light background display screen. Normally, light text is shown on a dark background. Same as reverse video.

invert To turn over; reverse. To highlight text or objects by reversing the on-screen display or printout. For example, to invert the colors on a monochrome display means to change light to dark and dark to light.

inverted file File organized so it can be accessed by character rather than by record key.

inverted structure File structure that permits fast, spontaneous searching for previously unspecified information. Independent lists are maintained in record keys that are accessible according to the values of specified fields.

inverter Circuit in which a binary 1 input produces a binary 0 output, and vice versa.

inverting circuit Circuit for changing direct current to alternating current. Contrast with adapter.

invisible refresh Scheme that refreshes dynamic memories without disturbing the rest of the system.

invocation The calling up of a subroutine or procedure.

I/O Acronym for input/output.

I/O board Circuit board that controls the input and output of data between the computer and peripheral devices.

I/O bound Term applied to programs that require a large number of input/output operations, resulting in much CPU wait time. Contrast with compute-bound.

I/O channel Part of the input/output system of a computer. Under the control of I/O commands, the channel transfers blocks of data between internal storage and peripheral equipment.

IOCS Acronym for Input/Output Control System. An early, rudimentary operating system for IBM computers in the 1950s.

ion deposition A printing technology that is used in high-speed page printers.

ionographic printer A printer that uses ion deposition. The image is formed on a dielectric surface and then transferred to plain paper.

I/O port Connection to a central processing unit that provides for data paths between the CPU and peripheral devices, such as display terminals, printers, and disk units.

I/O processor Circuit board or chip used only to handle input/output operations between the computer and peripherals.

IPL-V Acronym for Information Processing Language Five, a list processing language primarily used for working with heuristic-type problems.

IRG Acronym for InterRecord Gap.

IRGB See Intensity Red Green Blue.

IRM Acronym for Information Resources Manager, the person responsible for operating a company's main computer and for monitoring the numerous employees using it.

ISA See Industry Standard Architecture.

ISAM Acronym for Indexed Sequential Accessed Method.

ISO Acronym for International Standards Organization, an international agency responsible for developing standards for information exchange. Has a function similar to that of ANSI in the United States.

ISO 9660 An international format standard for CD-ROM.

isolation (1) In a computer security system, the compartmentalization of information so access to it is on a "need to know" basis. (2) State of being separated or set apart from others.

isometric view In computer graphics, a display method that shows 3-D objects with height and width but without the change in perspective that would be added by depth. In other words, a picture of a three-dimensional object that shows all three dimensions in equal proportions.

ISR Acronym for Information Storage and Retrieval. See information retrieval.

italic A typeface that slants to the right and commonly is used for emphasis.

ITC Avant Garde A modern sans serif typeface designed by the International Typeface Corporation (ITC) and included as a built-in font with many PostScript laser printers.

ITC Bookman   A serif typeface design owned by the International Typeface Corporation (ITC) and included as a built-in font with many PostScript laser printers.

ITC Zapf Chancery   An italic typeface owned by the International Typeface Corporation (ITC) and included as a built-in font with many PostScript laser printers. The typeface was developed by Herman Zapf, a German typeface designer.

item   (1) Group of related characters treated as a unit. A record is a group of related items, and a file is a group of related records. (2) Selection within a menu.

iterate   To repeat automatically, under program control, the same series of processing steps until a predetermined stop or branch condition is reached. See loop and Newton-Raphson.

interation control structure   A looping mechanism.

iterative   Repetitive. Often used when each succeeding iteration, or repetition, of a procedure comes closer to a desired result.

I-time   The portion of a machine cycle where an instruction is interpreted.

jack Connecting device to which a wire or wires of a circuit may be attached and that is arranged for the insertion of a plug. Also called socket.

jacket The plastic cover for a disk. It has holes and slots cut into it to expose the hub and afford the head-of-disk drive access to the disk. 5.25-inch disks use a stiff plastic jacket, with glued or crimped seams. 3.5-inch disks use rigid plastic envelopes, with spring-loaded sliding metal shutters to protect the disk surface from being touched accidentally.

Jacquard, Joseph Marie (1752-1834) Built a weaving machine (Jacquard loom) that used a line of punched cards to control automatically the patterns woven. Some people feel that Jacquard's machine was the beginning of factory automation.

jaggles In a computer graphics display, the stairstepped or saw-toothed effect of diagonals, circles, and curves.

jargon The vocabulary peculiar to a group or profession.

JCL Acronym for Job Control Language. The language used to provide control instructions to the computer for IBM mainframe operating systems.

JES Acronym for Job Entry System, a portion of the operating system that accepts and schedules jobs for execution.

jitter Brief instability of a signal, applied particularly to signals on a video display.

job Collection of specified tasks constituting a unit of work for a computer, such as a program or related group of programs used as a unit.

job abort The cancellation of a job because of problems with software, hardware, or data.

job control language (JCL) Language that defines a job and the resources it requires from the computer system, including constraints on the job, such as time limits. The language is more often interpreted than compiled.

job control statement   One statement, written in a job control language, that defines one aspect of a job.

job number   Identification number assigned to a job.

job queue   Set of programs and data currently making its way through the computer. In most operating systems, each job is brought into the queue and is processed (given control of the computer) when it is the "oldest" job within its own priority. An exception to this is a job of higher priority that has not yet obtained sufficient resources to be processed.

job scheduler   Person who aids computer operators in the running of a large computer installation.

Jobs, Steven   Co-founder (with Stephen Wozniak) of Apple Computer, Inc., developer of several microcomputer systems. In 1977, Jobs and Wozniak introduced the Apple II microcomputer. This popular computer became known as the Volkswagon of computers. In 1984, Apple Computer announced the Macintosh computer. This was Steve Job's electronic baby. He shaped it, nourished it, and pampered it into life. The Macintosh has become one of the most exciting and easy-to-use computers of all time. In 1985, after a management disagreement with Apple president John Sculley, Jobs left Apple Computer and established a new firm, called NeXT, Inc. In 1988, Jobs unveiled the NeXT computer system.

job stream   Input to the operating system. May consist of one or more jobs.

job-to-job transition   Process of locating a program and the files associated with the program and of preparing the computer for the execution of a particular job.

job turnaround   Elapsed time from when a job is given to the computer system until its printed output reaches the person who submitted the job.

Josephson junction   An ultra-fast microelectronic circuit technology that uses superconductor materials, named after Brian Josephson, who discovered the original theory. Josephson junction circuits are immersed in liquid helium to obtain near-absolute zero temperatures required for operation.

journal   A chronological record of operations performed in a computer system.

JOVIAL   Acronym for Jules' Own Version of the International Algorithmetic Language. A high-level programming language used in the 1960s and 1970s. It was developed by Jules Schwartz and patterned after the ALGOL language. JOVIAL was used primarily for working with scientific and command/control problems for the U.S. Air Force.

joystick A lever, pivoted to move in any direction, that controls the movement of a cursor on a display screen. Similar to a mouse, but used mostly when playing video games.

jukebox A robotically serviced device for storing and retrieving multiple optical discs and servicing on demand one or more optical disc drives.

Julian number Form of calendar representation within a computer system. The Julian date indicates the year and the number of elapsed days in the year; for example, 92-029 was January 29, 1992, the 29th day of 1992. 92-043 is February 12, 1992, the 43rd day of 1992 and 93-156 is June 5, 1993, the 156th day of 1993.

jump Departure from the normal sequence of executing instructions in a computer. Synonymous with branch and transfer.

junction That part of a diode or transistor where two opposite types of semiconductor material meet.

junk Garbled data received over a communications line. If proper communication is not established with a remote system, random, meaningless characters (junk) may appear on the screen.

justification (1) Act of adjusting, arranging, or shifting digits to the left or right to make them fit a prescribed pattern. (2) Alignment of text margins on both right and left sides. Justified text is both flush left and flush right. Contrast with ragged left and ragged right.

justify To align the characters in a field. For example, to right justify, the last character (the least significant digit) is written in the last, or rightmost, character position in the field. Alphabetical lists are commonly left justified.

K (1) Abbreviation for kilo, or 1000 in decimal notation. For example, "100K cps means a reading speed of 100,000 characters per second." (2) Loosely, when referring to storage capacity, 2^{10}; in decimal notation, 1024. The expression 8K represents 8192 (8 x 1024).

Kahn, Philippe A former student of Niklaus Wirth, developed a Turbo Pascal compiler for micorcomputers. Turbo Pascal is the most popular version of the Pascal language for microcomputers. Kahn's company, Borland International, Inc., continues to develop software systems for microcomputers.

kb Abbreviation for kilobyte.

kc One thousand characters per second. Used to express the rate of data transfer operations.

Kemeny, John In 1964, with Thomas Kurtz, at Dartmouth College, designed the computer language BASIC, an easy-to-learn, easy-to-use algebraic programming language. Also developed the Dartmouth Time-Sharing System and True BASIC. See Kurtz, Thomas.

kernel Set of programs in an operating system that implement the most primitive of that system's functions. The core of an operating system.

kerning Adjusting the space between characters to create wider or tighter spacing. Reduction of excess white space between specific letter pairs. For example, the pair To can be placed more closely together than the pair Tk because the arm of the T fits over the top of the o. Kerning is especially important with large type sizes.

key (1) Control field or fields that identify a record. See primary key. (2) Field that determines the position of a record in a sorted sequence. See major sort key and minor sort key. (3) Lever on a manually operated machine, such as a typewriter or visual display keyboard. (4) To enter data into a system by means of a keyboard.

key abstraction In object-oriented programming, a class or object that forms part of the vocabulary of the problem domain.

keyboard Input device used to key programs and data into the computer's storage. Since the keyboard is the most frequently used part of the computer, a good keyboard is an essential part of any computer system intended for business purposes.

keyboarding Process of entering programs and data onto input media or directly into the computer by typing on a keyboard, such as using the keyboard of a word processor or computer terminal.

keyboard template A plastic or cardboard card with adhesive that can be pressed onto the keyboard to explain the way a program configures the keyboard.

keyboard-to-disk system Data entry system in which data can be entered directly onto a disk by typing the data at a keyboard.

keyboard-to-tape system Data entry system in which data can be entered directly onto a magnetic tape by typing the data at a keyboard.

key bounce Characteristic of some poorly designed keyboards where a character registers twice for each time the user presses the key.

key disk A method of software protection that requires the presence of a specific disk in a disk drive before the software will function properly.

keypad Input device that uses a set of decimal digit keys (0-9) and two special function keys. Used as a separate device or sometimes located to the right of a standard QWERTY keyboard—one result of ergonomics.

keypunch Keyboard-operated device used to punch holes in punch cards to represent data to be input to a computer by a card reader.

key stations Terminals used for data input on a multiuser system.

keystroke Action of pressing a single key or a combination of keys on a keyboard. Speed in many data entry jobs is measured in keystrokes per minute.

key-to-address See hashing.

keyword (1) One of the significant and informative words in a title or document that describe the content of that document. (2) Primary element in a programming-language statement, such as LET, PRINT, and INPUT in the BASIC programming language. A keyword is followed by a series of arguments used by the keyword to complete a task. (3) Set of words that have special meaning to a computer program. For example, DIR is a command that directs the operating system to produce a DIRECTORY of a disk.

key-word-in-context See KWIC.

kHz Abbreviation for kilohertz.

Kilby, Jack Inventor with Texas Instruments who introduced the integrated circuit in 1958. He also developed an early hand-held electronic calculator. See Noyce, Robert.

Kildall, Gary In 1977, he developed CP/M, an operating system for microcomputers. CP/M becme a standard operating system for microcomputers before the IBM PC (and the PC-DOS) was introduced in 1981. CPM was the first operating system designed to control floppy disk drives.

kill (1) To terminate a process before it reaches its natural conclusion. (2) Method of erasing information. (3) To stop, frequently to abort.

kill file To delete a file.

kilobaud One thousand bits per second. Used to measure data communications speeds.

kilobit One thousand bits.

kilobyte Specifically, 2^{10}, or 1024 bytes. Commonly thought of as 1000. Abbreviated K and used as a suffix when describing memory size. Thus, 24K really means a 24 x 1024 = 24,576-byte memory system. Sometimes abbreviated kb.

kilocycle One thousand cycles. Formerly, one thousand cycles per second, now termed kilohertz.

kilohertz One thousand cycles per second. Used to measure data transmission frequencies.

kilomegacycle One billion cycles per second.

kinematics Computer-aided engineering process for plotting or animating the motion of parts in a machine or a structure under design on the system.

kludge Makeshift. Pertaining to a collection of mismatched components that have been assembled into a system.

knowledge In artificial intelligence, symbolic information used by a domain expert to solve problems. Facts and relationships used to solve problems.

knowledge acquisition In expert system programming, the process of acquiring and systematizing knowledge from experts.

knowledge base Database of knowledge about a particular subject. Contains facts, data, beliefs, assumptions, and procedures needed for problem solution. One of the two critical parts of an expert system. The other part is the inference engine.

knowledge crafting The process of building expert systems.

knowledge domain   In artificial intelligence, an area of problem-solving expertise.

knowledge encoding   The process of entering facts, rules, objects, and other knowledge into an expert system.

knowledge engineer   The individual who develops an expert system. He or she acquires knowledge from human experts and encodes it into an expert system.

knowledge engineering   Engineering discipline whereby knowledge is integrated into computer systems to solve complex problems normally requiring a high level of human expertise.

knowledge industries   Industries that perform data processing and provide information products and services.

knowledge information processor   Name used by the Japanese for their proposed fifth-generation computers which are expected to be totally different from previous generations.

knowledge modeling   The procedure by which knowledge engineers organize the data they gain from domain experts.

KnowledgePro   An expert system with hypertext capabilities for personal computers.

knowledge representation   A means of organizing human knowledge into a data structure that can include facts, rules and common sense.

knowledge system   A large body of knowledge in the form of rules and facts along with an inference mechanism that can be used to solve problems. An expert system.

knowledge work   Occupations where the primary activities involve receiving, processing, and transmitting information.

Koala Pad   An inexpensive digitizing tablet for microcomputers.

Kurtz, Thomas   In 1964, with John Kemeny, at Dartmouth College, designed the computer language BASIC, an easy-to-learn, easy-to-use algebraic programming language. See Kemeny, John.

KWIC   Acronym for Key-Word-In-Context, a method of indexing information by preselected words or phases that takes into consideration the context in which the words are used.

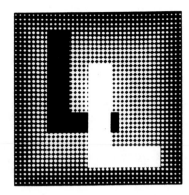

label Identifier or name used in a computer program to identify or describe an instruction, statement, message, data value, record, item, or file.

lag Relative difference between two events, mechanisms, or states.

LAN An acronym for Local Area Network, a connection between computers or computerized systems within a building or immediate neighborhood. Employing a LAN enables users to share files and expensive peripherals such as a laser printer. A group of personal computers networked together.

land Area of a printed circuit board available.

landscape An orientation in which the data is printed across the wider side of the form.

landscape mode A video display screen whose width is greater than its height, like a pastoral landscape painting. Contrast with portrait mode.

landscape monitor A monitor with a screen shape wider than it is high.

language Set or rules, representations, and conventions used to convey information. A way of passing instructions to the computer other than through direct input of number codes. Programming languages are characterized as low-level or high-level.

language processing The use of computer programs to analyze and understand language.

language processor Program that translates human-written source language programs into a form that can be executed on a computer. There are three general types of language processors: assembler, compiler, and interpreter.

language statement Statement coded by a user of a computing system that conveys information to a processing program, such as a language translator program, service program, or control program. May signify that an operation be performed or may simply contain data to be passed to the processing program.

language subset Part of a language that can be used independently of the rest of the language.

language translator program Program that transforms statements from one language to another without significantly changing their meaning, such as a compiler or assembler.

LAN Manager A local area network technology developed by Microsoft Corporation. LAN Manager connects computers and allows users to share files and system resources.

laptop computer A personal computer, small and portable enough to be used comfortably in the lap of a person seated in an automobile or an airplane. Laptop computers today feature full-sized keyboards, flat-screen monitors that fold up and down, hard disks, floppy disks, and powerful microprocessors. Also called a lap computer.

large-scale integrated circuit Process of placing a large number of integrated circuits on one chip. Today's technology produces chips with 100,000 to 10 million components, known as very large-scale integration. Further refinements should produce ultralarge-scale integration (10 million to 1 billion components) and gigascale integration (over 1 billion components).

laser Acronym for Light Amplification by Simulated Emission of Radiation, the technology that uses the principle of amplification of electromagnetic waves by simulated emission of radiation and operates in the infrared, visible, or ultraviolet region. A device emitting coherent photon or electromagnetic energy. In 1957, the laser was conceived and named by Gordon Gould, a graduate student in physics at Columbia University. However, it took him almost 30 years of court battles to obtain the legal rights to the laser. A laser forces light waves to be emitted in phase and of a single wavelength, so the light behaves in a way that accords with wave theory.

LaserJet A series of desktop laser printers from Hewlett-Packard Company. Introduced in 1984, it set the standard for the desktop laser printer market.

laser printer A printer that uses a light beam to transfer images to paper. Laser printers print a full page at a time. A laser is used to "paint" the dots of light onto a photographic drum or belt. The toner is applied to the drum or belt and then transferred onto the paper. In 1975, the IBM Corporation introduced the first laser printer, called the IBM 3800, which was designed for high-speed printing. In 1978, the Xerox Corporation introduced the Xerox 9700 high-speed printer. In 1984, the Hewlett-Packard Company introduced the first desktop laser printer, which has revolutionized personal computer printing and has spawned desktop publishing. Desktop laser printers are technically more like an office copier than a conventional printer. They are very fast in operation and relatively silent.

laser storage Auxiliary storage device using laser technology to encode data onto a metallic surface.

LaserWriter A series of desktop laser printers from Apple Computer, Inc.

last in-first out See LIFO.

last in-last out See LILO.

late binding In object-oriented programming, dynamic binding. See binding.

latency Rotational delay in reading or writing a record to a direct access auxiliary storage device, such as a disk.

layer (1) In computer graphics drawing programs, an overlay on which text or images can be stored. In SuperPaint, for example, you can create illustrations on two layers: a paint layer for bit-mapped graphics and a draw layer for object-oriented graphics. In some graphics programs you can draw and paint on many different layers. (2) Third dimension in a 3-D array.

layering Logical concept that associates subgroups of graphic data within a single drawing. Allows a user to view only those parts of a drawing being worked on and reduces the confusion that might result from viewing all parts of a very complex file.

layout (1) In desktop publishing, the design or process of arranging text and graphics on a page. (2) The arrangement of data items on a data record. (3) Overall design or plan, such as system flowcharts, schematics, diagrams, format for printer output, and makeup of a document (book).

layout sheet Grid paper designed to map the display screen for purposes of program planning. Text and graphics can be sketched in terms of rows and columns or the graphics X-Y coordinates.

LCD Acronym for Liquid Crystal Display, a way to make letters and numbers appear by reflecting light on a special crystalline substance. Features high visibility in high illumination levels but no visibility in low illumination levels. Because of its thin profile, LCD technology is often used in pocket calculators, hand-held computers, briefcase computers, keyboards, watches, and other devices.

LCD printer Short for Liquid Crystal Display printer, an electrophotographic printer that uses an electrostatically charged drum to transfer toner to a piece of paper. Similar to laser printers and LED printers.

LCS Short for liquid crystal shutter, a type of optical technology based on using LCD (liquid crystal display) panels to block or pass light through for display or reaction. LCS technology competes with laser beam methods in the design of high quality page printers.

lead A connection to a circuit element.

leader (1) In page layout and word processing programs, a row of dots and dashes that provide a path for the eye to follow across the page. Leaders are sometimes used in table of contents to lead the readers' eye from the entry to the page number. (2) Blank section of tape at the beginning of a reel of magnetic tape.

leading The vertical spacing between lines of type, measured from baseline to baseline. Font styles which have long ascenders and descenders need more leading than fonts that don't. In publishing, the font size and leading is described as a fraction. For example, 10/12 (which is read "10 on 12") indicates 10 point type with 2 points leading.

leading edge (1) In optical scanning, the edge of the document or page that enters the read position first. (2) Buzz word implying technological leadership: "on the leading edge of technology."

leaf Terminal node of a tree diagram. See root.

learning A procedure in artificial intelligence by which an artificial intelligence program improves its performance by gaining knowledge.

learning machine A machine that can monitor its own behavior and employ feedback to modify that behavior.

lease Method of acquiring the use of a computer system. A lease contract requires no financing and is less expensive than renting the system.

leased line A communications line dedicated to one customer. Also called a private line.

leasing companies Companies that specialize in leasing computer equipment, which they purchase from a computer manufacturer.

least significant digit (LSD) That digit of a number that has the least weight or significance. In the number 58371, the lease significant digit is 1.

LED Acronym for Light-Emitting Diode, a commonly used alphanumeric display unit that glows when supplied with a specified voltage.

LED printer Short for Light Emitting Diode printer, an electrophotographic printer that uses an electrostatically charged drum to transfer toner to a piece of paper. Similar to laser printers and LCS printers.

left justify See justify.

legend (1) Text beneath a graph; it explains the colors, shading, or symbols used to label the data points. (2) Text that describes or explains a graphic.

Leibniz, Gottfried von (1646-1716) German mathematician who in 1672 invented a calculating machine superior to Pascal's calculator, in 1673 introduced a system of the calculus, and in 1693 he recognized the energy of motion and of position.

Leibniz's calculator Calculating machine designed by Gottfried von Leibniz. Performed addition and subtraction in the same manner as Pascal's calculator; however, additional gears were included in the machine that enabled it to multiply directly.

length Number of characters, bytes, or bits in a computer word. A variable word is made up of several characters, ending with a special end character. A fixed word is composed of the same number of bits, bytes, or characters in each word.

less than Relationship of an inequality between two values. The symbol is <, with the point toward the smaller number. 3<8 means 3 is less than 8. Commonly used in comparison to determine alternative processing. Contrast with greater than.

LetraStudio A graphics program from Letraset USA that has the ability to condense, stretch, slant, scale, rotate, flip-flop, or distort a design in real time.

letter quality printing High-quality output produced by some printers. Laser printers, daisy-wheel printers and ink-jet printers are letter quality printers. High-end, 24-pin dot matrix printers provide near letter quality printing.

level Degree of subordination in a hierarchy. Measure of the distance from a node to the root of a tree.

lexicon Any language with definitions for all terms.

LF Acronym for Line Feed.

librarian (1) Person responsible for an organization's library of technical documentation, including manuals used by programmers, operators, and other employees. (2) Person responsible for the safekeeping of all computer files, such as diskettes, disk packs, and magnetic tapes.

library (1) Published collection of programs, routines, and subroutines available to every user of the computer. (2) A storage area, usually on hard disk or a diskette, used to store programs. (3) A collection of items, such as clip-art, intended for inclusion in other programs.

library automation Application of computers and other technology to library operations and services.

library manager Program that maintains the programs stored in an operating system.

library routine Tested routine maintained in a program library.

license contract Piece of paper that authorizes the purchaser of a software product to run the product on his or her computer.

life cycle Course of a program or system from the inception of the original idea through development, implementation, and maintenance, until it is either replaced or no longer useful.

LIFO Acronym for Last In-First Out, the way most microprocessor program stacks operate. The last data or instruction word placed on the stack is the first to be retrieved. Same as FILO. See push down stack. Contrast with FIFO.

ligature In typography, two or more characters designed and cast as a distinct unit for aesthetic reasons. Letter combinations such as ae, fi, ff, fl, ffi, ffl, and oe commonly are printed as ligatures. Some outline fonts available for PostScript laser printers and imagesetters include ligatures for desktop publishing applications.

light-emitting diode See LED.

lightface In desktop publishing, an extra light version of a typeface.

light guide Channel designed for the transmission of light, such as a cable of optical fibers. See fiber optics.

lightness Amount of light or dark present in a particular color.

light pen Electronic device that resembles a pen and can be used to write or sketch on the screen of a cathode ray tube to provide input to the computer. Tool for display terminal operators, connected to the computer by a cable.

lightwave system An optical system that transmits light pulses over optical fibers. This system is capable of transmitting over a billion bits per second. That means 16,000 digitized voice conversations can be transmitted simultaneously over one hair-thin optical fiber.

LILO Acronym for Last In-Last Out, a method of storing and retrieving items from a list, table, or stack, such that the last item placed on the stack is the last to be retrieved. Same as FIFO. Contrast with FILO.

limit check Input control technique that tests the value of a data field to determine whether values fall within set limits or a given range.

limiting operation That operation in a system that has the smallest capacity or slowest speed. Since the capacity of a total system with no alternative routing can be no greater than the operation with the least capacity, the total system can be effectively scheduled by simply scheduling the limiting operation. See bound.

line (1) In computer graphics, a particular set of points. Lines in geometry extend in two directions without end. In mathematics, unless otherwise stated, lines are always thought to be straight. (2) In most programming languages, a line begins with an identifying number and contains one or more statements. Sometimes a statement requires more than one line. (3) In data communications, any type of channel, but especially telephone lines.

linear IC   Analog integrated circuit, as opposed to a digital integrated circuit.

linear list   See sequential list.

linear programming (LP)   Technique for finding an optimum combination when there may be no single best one. Could be used to solve the problem: What combination of foods would give the most calories and best nutrition for the least money? A computer is often used because such problems would take too long to solve by hand. See operations research. Contrast with nonlinear programming.

linear search   Search that begins with the first element and compares until a matching key is found or the end of the list is reached.

linear structure   (1) In database management systems, a mode of file organization in which each primary record can own only one secondary record. The latter functions as an overflow record for the primary record. (2) Sequential arrangement of data records.

line art   Artwork containing only blacks and whites with no shading. Line art can be reproduced accurately by low to medium resolution printers.

line-at-a-time printer   Same as line printer.

line balancing   Management technique used in production environments wherein tasks are assigned to computer graphics workstations in equal proportions, thus raising efficiency.

line chart   Method of charting business data.

line circuit   Physical circuit path, such as a data communications line.

line drawing   Drawing where an object's image is represented by a solid-line outline of the surface.

line feed (LF)   Operation that advances printer paper by one line. See form feed.

line filter   Device used to correct electromagnetic interference that comes in over the power line.

line graph   Graph made by connecting data points with a line. Shows the variations of data over time or the relationships between two numeric variables.

line height Height of one line of type. Measured by the number of lines per vertical inch.

line join The way in which two line segments meet.

line number In programming languages such as BASIC, a number that begins a line of the source program for purposes of identification; a numerical label.

line of code Statement in a programming language usually occupying one line of code.

line plot Graph with displayed data points, and straight lines connecting the points.

line printer A printer that assembles all characters on a line at one time and prints them out practically simultaneously. Line printers are high-speed printing devices that are usually connected to mainframes and minicomputers.

line printer controller Device that provides character print buffers and automatic control and timing for a specific printer.

line screen frequency When a continuous tone image is screened, this is the number of halftone dots per inch making up the screen. Typical line screens are 33, 65, 85, 100, 120, 133, and 150 lines per inch; 200-500 lines per inch for high-quality products.

line segment Portion of a longer line defined by its two end points.

line speed Maximum rate at which signals may be transmitted over a given channel, usually in baud, or bits per second.

lines per inch Abbreviated lpi, lines per inch is the yardstick used to measure halftone resolution.

lines per minute (LPM) Usually used to describe the speed of a line printer.

line style In computer graphics, the method of representing a line in a graphics system, such as with dashes, solid lines, or dots.

line surge Sudden, high-voltage condition. Short surges of high voltage can cause misregistration, false logic, lost data, and even destruction of delicate circuits in computers, data entry terminals, and data communications equipment. These spikes can be a result of inductive load switching of transformers and other types of equipment—even from lightning and static. Equipment can be protected from voltage surges by using surge protectors.

line voltage AC voltage that comes out of a standard wall socket.

line width Actual, physical thickness of a line in a graphics system.

line work Any non-continuous tone image, i.e., without shades of gray or other colors. Usually black-and-white line art or diagram, but can also include EPS art created on a computer that incorporates flat color tints (comic-book coloring).

linguistics The study of language. Syntax determines what makes a sentence of a natural language, or a program of a programming language, grammatical. Semantics specifies how the words of a sentence of the statements of a program, work together to give it its overall meaning. Parsing is the process of breaking a string of words into the pieces—such as noun phrase and verb phrase—specified by the syntax.

link (1) In data communications, a physical connection between one location and another whose function is to transmit data, including satellite links. (2) In hypertext systems, connections between one document and another.

linkage Coding that connects two separately coded routines, such as coding that links a subroutine to the program with which it is to be used.

linker Program that links other programs or sections of programs. Combines separate program modules into one executable program.

linking loader Executive program that connects different program segments so that they may be run in the computer as one unit. Useful piece of software that makes subtasks easily available to a main task.

link/load phase The phase during which prewritten programs may be added to the object module by means of a link/loader.

link register Register of one bit that acts as an extension of the accumulator during rotation or carry operations.

links Data communications channels in a computer network.

Linotronic A series of high-quality typesetting machines known as Linotronic laser imagesetters, which can print at resolutions over 1200 dots per inch (dpi). Imagesetters are commonly used with PostScript desktop publishing systems.

LIPS Acronym for Logical Inferences Per Second, a measure of the speed of expert systems and the PROLOG language.

liquid crystal display (LCD) A flat display used in many portable computers because it is small, and requires little power. The display is made of two sheets of polarizing material sandwiched together with a nematic liquid crystal solution between them. Images are produced when electric currents cause the liquid crystals to align so light cannot shine through.

Lisa A microcomputer introduced in the early 1980s by Apple Computer,

Inc. It featured a graphical user interface and a mouse. The Lisa had its own Apple-generated operating system, called the Lisa Operating System. This was designed to perform file management, memory management, event handling and exception handling. The Lisa was built around the Motorola, Inc. 68000 microprocessor. The Lisa was the forerunner of the Apple Macintosh microcomputer.

LISP Acronym for LISt Processing, a high-level programming language primarily designed to process data consisting of lists. Especially suited for text manipulation and analysis. LISP was developed in the early 1960s by John McCarthy at the Massachusetts Institute of Technology. Typical applications for LISP include expert systems and artificial intelligence software. LISP is the major language of artificial intelligence in the United States.

list (1) Organization of data, using indexes and pointers to allow for nonsequential retrieval. (2) Ordered set of items. (3) To print every relevant item of input data. (4) Command to print program statements; for example, the LIST command in the BASIC language will cause the system to print a listing of the program. (5) Ordered collection of atoms. (6) In artificial intelligence, a type of knowledge representation. An object that consists of a sequence of elements.

listing Generally, any printout produced on a printing device. A source listing is a printout of the source program processed by the compiler; an error listing is a report showing all input data found to be invalid by the processing program.

list price The manufacturer's suggested retail price of a product. See street price.

list processing Method of processing data in the form of lists. The procedure of going through a list and examining the objects in the list for a purpose. Example: the purpose may be to find or delete a given element, or reorder the elements.

list processing language A programming language used for processing non-numeric data, such as LISP and PROLOG. It provides special commands that work with lists of data.

literal Another name for constant, a symbol that defines itself. Contrast with variable.

live data Actual data to be processed by the computer program.

load (1) To read information into the storage of a computer. See get. (2) To put a diskette into a disk drive.

load-and-go Operating technique in which the loading and execution phases of a program are performed in one continuous run. See compile-and-go.

loader Service routine designed to read programs into internal storage in preparation for their execution.

load module Computer program in a form suitable to be immediately executed by the circuitry of the computer.

load point Spot at the beginning of the recording area of a magnetic tape.

load sharing Technique of using two or more computers to handle excess volume during peak periods. It is desirable to have one computer handle less than peak loads and the other act as the fallback equipment.

local (1) Pertaining to computer equipment at one's own location. (2) Pertaining to items used only in one defined part of a program. Contrast with global.

local area network (LAN) Communications network connecting various hardware devices together within a building by means of a continuous cable or an in-house voice-data telephone system.

local echo In telecommunications, a process that sends characters typed on the keyboard directly to the screen without waiting for the remote computer to echo the characters.

local intelligence Processing power and storage capacity built into a terminal so it does not need to be connected to a computer to perform certain tasks. A dumb terminal has no local intelligence.

LocalTalk The physical connectors and cables manufactured by Apple Computer, Inc. for use in AppleTalk networks.

location Place in the computer's memory where information is to be stored.

lock (1) To permit exclusive use of a computer resource. (2) To protect a disk or tape file from being changed or erased.

lock code Sequence of letters and/or numbers provided by the operators of a time-sharing system to prevent unauthorized tampering with a user's program. Serves as a secret password in that the computer will refuse any changes to the program unless the user supplies the correct lock code.

locked-up keyboard Situation in which the computer does not respond to key presses.

locking a disk A disk is locked when it has been write protected. This measure ensures that the contents of a disk are preserved from being written over by other data from a computer.

lockout (1) Suppression of an interrupt. (2) Programming technique used in a multiprocessing environment to prevent access to critical data by both CPUs at the same time.

lock-up   Situation in which no further action may occur.

log   (1) Record of the operations of data processing equipment, listing each job or run, the time it required, operator actions, and other pertinent data. (2) Abbreviation for logarithm, often denoting the base 10 logarithm. Several programming languages use LOG to mean the natural logarithm.

logarithm   Exponent of the power to which a fixed number is to be raised to produce a given number. The fixed number is called the base and is usually 10 or e. In the example $2^3 = 8$, 3 is the logarithm of 8 to the base 2; this means that 2 must be raised to the third power to produce 8.

logarithmic graph   In presentation graphics, a graph displayed with a y-axis incremented exponentially in powers of 10. On an ordinary y-axis, the 10 is followed by 20, 30, 40, 50, and so on. On a logarithmic scale, however, 10 is followed by 100, 1000, 10,000, 100,000, and so on.

logged drive   The disk drive to which the operating system goes when looking for files to retrieve or save. Also called current drive and default drive.

logging-in   Process of establishing communication with, and verifying authority to use, the computer during conversational programming.

logging-off   Process of terminating communication between the computer and the user.

logic   (1) Science dealing with the formal principles of reasoning and thought. (2) Basic principles and application of truth tables and the interconnection among logical elements required for arithmetic computation in an automatic data processing system.

logical data design   Design showing relationships among data; how the data is viewed by applications programs or individual users.

logical decision   Decision as to which of two possible courses of action is to be followed, based upon some comparison of values.

logical design   Specification of the working relationships among the parts of a system in terms of symbolic logic and without primary regard for hardware implementation.

logical error   Programming mistake that causes the wrong processing to take place even though the program is syntactically correct.

logical file   Collection of one or more logical records.

logical format   The way that files are arranged on a disk and the way a directory or other pointers show what goes where. Sometimes two computers use the same physical format but different logical ones. In such a case, although the units won't be able to deal with other disks directly, they will be able to do so with a special transfer program.

logical instruction Instruction that executes an operation defined in symbolic logic, such as AND, OR, or NOR.

logical multiply AND operator. Compare logical product.

logical operations Computer operations that are logical in nature, such as logical decisions. Contrast with arithmetic operations and data transfer operations, which involve no decision.

logical product AND function of several terms. The product is 1 only when all of the terms are 1; otherwise it is 0.

logical record Complete unit of information that contains all fields describing something. In an inventory file containing 2000 different product items, there are 2000 logical records, one for each item. Contrast with physical record.

logical representation Knowledge representation consisting of a collection of logical formulas.

logical schema A standard way of organizing information into accessible parts.

logical sum Inclusive OR function of several terms. The sum is 1 when any or all of the terms are 1; it is 0 only when all are 0.

logical symbol See logic symbol.

logical unit number Number assigned to a physical peripheral device.

logical value Value that may be either true or false, depending on the result of a particular logical decision.

logic bomb A program modification which causes damage when triggered by some condition such as a date, or the presence or absence of data such as a name.

logic card Circuit board that contains components and wiring that perform one of more logic functions or operations.

logic circuits Series of flip-flops and gates that directs electrical impulses to and from the appropriate portions of a computer system.

logic diagram Diagram that represents a logical design and sometimes the hardware implementation.

logic element Device that performs a logic function.

logic error Omissions, incorrect statements, or statements in the wrong location of a program.

logic gates Components in electrical digital circuitry. See gate.

logic operator   Any of the Boolean operations, such as AND, OR, NAND, exclusive OR, and NOR.

logic programming   Approach to knowledge representation, usually associated with PROLOG, which uses logic and inference to express and solve problems. A type of programming based on logic that is relatively independent of the underlying structure of the machine on which it is operating.

logic seeking   Ability of a printer that works bidirectionally to seek out the shortest printing path.

logic structure   Structure that controls the sequence in which computer program instructions are executed. The three structures are sequence, selection, and loop.

logic symbol   Symbol used to represent a logic element graphically.

logic theorist   Early information processing program able to prove theorems.

logic theory   Science that deals with logical operations, which are the basis of computer operations.

log in   To sign in on a computer. Same as log on.

log-in name   Name by which the computer system knows a user. Not generally synonymous with password.

LOGO   High-level programming language that assumes the user has access to some type of graphics terminal. Designed for students and easily employed by those in the younger age groups, it has wide-ranging application in graphic reports of business and industry. Highly interactive, permitting users to learn quickly how to draw geometric patterns and pictures on the screen. One important feature of LOGO is turtle graphics. Turtle graphics enable the programmer to make simple drawings by telling the "turtle" on the screen to move forward, right, left, and so on. Once he or she masters the simple drawing environment, the programmer starts to discover the more sophisticated features of the language. Developed in 1968 at the Massachusetts Institute of Technology by Seymour Papert.

log on   Action by which a user begins a terminal session. Same as log in.

log off   To terminate connection with the computer. Same as log out.

log out   To stop using the computer. Process of signing off the system. Same as log off.

long card   In a microcomputer, a full-length printed circuit card that plugs into an expansion slot.

look-alike   (1) Program that imitates another program so closely that users of the original program can use the look-alike program without learning any new operating instructions. (2) Any product that copies another. Often when a vendor produces a successful product, its competitors offer look-alike products.

look-up See table look-up.

loop Sequence of instructions in a program that can be executed repetitively until certain specified conditions are satisfied.

loop code Repetition of a sequence of instructions by using a program loop. Loop coding requires more execution time than would straight-line coding but will result in a savings of storage. Contrast with straight-line code.

loophole Mistake or omission in software or hardware that allows the system's access controls to be circumvented.

looping Executing the same instruction or series of instructions over and over again.

looping program A program whose main action is a loop. Most programs are of this variety.

loop structure One of three primary structures of a structured program. Provides for repetitive execution of a function until a condition is reached. See sequence structure and selection structure.

loop technology Method of connecting communicating machines together in a computer network.

Lotus 1-2-3 A spreadsheet developed by Lotus Development Corporation. Introduced in 1982, it was the first integrated program developed for the IBM Personal Computer. Lotus 1-2-3 was the first program to include graphics, database management along with spreadsheet capabilities.

Lovelace, Ada Augusta(1815-1852) Ada Augusta, Countess of Lovelace, developed the essential ideas of programming. A skilled mathematician and close friend of Charles Babbage, she wrote about his machine: "The Analytical Engine weaves algebraical patterns just as the Jacquard loom weaves flowers and leaves." The U.S. Pentagon has honored Ada Augusta by naming a computer language ADA.

low activity Condition when a small proportion of the total records are processed during an updating run. See activity ratio.

lower case Noncapitalized alphabetic letters. Contrast with upper case.

low level formatting The most basic formatting done on the hard disk to prepare it for partitioning and high level formatting. This is often done by the manufacturer, which locks out bad sectors at this time.

lower-level management   First-time supervisors who make the operating decisions to ensure that specific jobs are done.

low-level language   Machine-dependent programming language translated by an assembler into instructions and data formats for a given machine. Same as assembly language. Contrast with high-level language.

low-order   Pertaining to the digit or digits of a number that have the least weight or significance. In the number 7643215, the low-order digit is 5. Contrast with high-order.

low-res graphics   Abbreviation of low-resolution graphics, a blocky and jagged picture on a display screen produced by a small number of pixels. Contrast with hi-res graphics.

low-resolution   Pertaining to the quality and accuracy of detail that can be represented by a graphics display. Resolution quality depends upon the number of basic image-forming units (pixels) within a picture image— the greater the number, the higher the resolution. Low-resolution pictures, produced by a small number of pixels, are not as sharp and clear as high-resolution pictures.

LP   Acronym for Linear Programming and Line Printer.

LPM   Acronym for Lines Per Minute.

LSC   Acronym for Least Significant Character. See least significant digit.

LSD   Acronym for Least Significant Digit.

LSI   Acronym for Large Scale Integration.

luggable   A term describing a computer that weighs less than 30 pounds and can be carried in one unit.

Lukasiewicz notation   See Polish notation.

Lumena   A professional draw/paint graphics program designed for use by visual communications professionals who design sophisticated images for output to print, film, and video. It runs on IBM-compatible microcomputer systems. Features include 250 draw/paint tools, color mixing, color separations, and several bit-mapped and vector fonts.

luminance   (1) A measure of the amount of light radiated by a given source, such as a computer display screen. (2) Portions of composite video signal controlling brightness.

luminance decay   Reduction in screen brightness on a visual display terminal that inevitably occurs over time.

luminosity   Same as luminance.

M Abbreviation for mega, meaning one million. Also used to represent 1,048,576. Often used to label the capabililty of storage devices, such as hard disks, diskettes and RAM.

Mac A nickname for the Apple Macintosh computer.

MAC Acronym for Message Authentication Code. A cryptographic checksum for a message. Unlike a digital signature, a MAC requires knowledge of a secret key for verification.

MacDraw A fast, flexible and precise drawing program for the Apple Macintosh computer. Nine drawing tools are provided which have become drawing program standards: line, text, selection, rectangle, rounded rectangle, oval, arc, polygon, and freehand drawing. Up to 16,000 black-and-white or color patterns and 255 customizable pen widths can be used in a document. Font sizes and line spacings can vary from 1 to 127 points; and objects and text can be rotated from 0 to 360 degrees. Multiple, overlapping, transparent layers can be hidden, shown and rearranged in any order. Drawing features include an enhanced polygen, a bezigon tool, a freehand tool and zoom while drawing, duplicate while dragging and edit points while drawing polygon and bezigon objects. Users can interchange with standard file formats such as MacDraw, PICT, CGM, and EPSF.

MacDraw file format The object file format used by the MacDraw drawing program and other programs.

MacDraw Pro An advanced version of the MacDraw drawing program with features to aid specific needs, such as desktop publishing.

machine address Same as absolute address.

machine-aided graphics for illustration and composition (MAGIC) An interactive program for preparation, editing and storage of graphic designs and technical documentation for computers using the UNIX operating system.

machine code Operation code that a machine is designed to recognize.

machine cycle Time period it takes for a computer to perform a given number of internal operations.

machine-dependent Pertaining to a language or program that works on only one particular type of computer. Synonymous with hardware-dependent. Contrast with machine-independent.

machine error Deviation from correctness in data resulting from an equipment failure.

machine-independent (1) Pertaining to a language or program developed in terms of the problem rather than in terms of the characteristics of the computer system. (2) Pertaining to the ability to run a program on computers made by different manufacturers or on various machines made by the same manufacturer. Contrast with machine-dependent.

machine instruction Instruction that a computer can directly recognize and execute.

machine intelligence See artificial intelligence.

machine language Basic language of a computer. Programs written in machine language require no further interpretation by a computer. Contrast with source language.

machine learning (1) Heuristic process whereby a device improves its performance based on past actions. (2) A field of artificial intelligence that attempts to build programs which learn from experience.

machine operator See computer operator.

machine-oriented language Programming language that is more like a machine language than a human language.

machine-readable information Information recorded on any medium in such a way that it can be sensed or read by a machine. Also called machine-sensible.

machine run See run.

machine-sensible See machine-readable information.

machine vision The process by which a computer perceives or recognizes objects in the external world.

Macintosh A series of popular microcomputers from Apple Computer, Inc., introduced in 1984. It uses the Motorola 68000 family of microprocessors and a proprietary operating system that simulates a user's desktop on screen. This standard user interface, combined with its built-in QuickDraw graphics language, has provided a visual, easy-to-use microcomputer. The Macintosh uses a mouse as a primary input device, in addition to a keyboard. Since the introduction of the Macintosh, Apple Computer, Inc.

continues to offer progressively faster and more powerful models of the Macintosh.

Macintosh 128K   The original Macintosh introduced in 1984. It had a 68000 microprocessor running at 8MHz, and it had 128K of memory and a built-in 400K disk drive. It was a revolutionary system due to its ease of use.

Macintosh 512K   An upgrade to the Macintosh 128; a system with 512K of main memory.

Macintosh 512Ke   A 1986 upgrade to the Macintosh 128K and 512K systems. The upgrade included new ROMs and a 800K double-sided disk drive.

Macintosh Classic   The Macintosh Classic, introduced in 1990, replaces the Macintosh Plus and the SE. The Classic runs up to 25 percent faster than the Macintosh Plus. The classic uses a Motorola 68000 processor, a 1.4 MB floppy disk unit and has an optional 40 MB internal hard disk unit. It is the lowest-priced Macintosh system offered to date.

Macintosh Classic II   A 1991 upgrade to the Macintosh Classic. The Classic II uses a Motorola 68030 microprocessor running at 16 MHz which doubles the performance of the Classic.

Macintosh draw programs   See Canvas, ColorStudio, DeskPaint/DeskDraw, Freehand, Illustrator, MacDraw, and Photoshop.

Macintosh LC   A low priced color-capable modular Macintosh system. The LC is powered by the Motorola 68020 microprocessor running at 16 MHz. It is up to 100 percent faster than the SE and Classic systems. The LC includes a 2 megabyte ROM memory, a 1.4 MB floppy disk unit, and an internal 40 megabyte hard disk unit. The Macintosh LC was introduced in 1990.

Macintosh paint programs   See DeskPaint/Deskdraw, Easy Color Paint, MacPaint, Oasis, PixelPaint, Studio 1, Studio 8, Studio 32, SuperPaint, UltraPaint, and VideoPaint.

Macintosh Performa 200/400/600   Three Performa Macintoshes were introduced in late 1992. The Performa 200 is physically identical to a Macintosh Classic II. The Performa 400 is basically a Macintosh LC II. The Performa 600 is similar to a Macintosh IIci, however, it uses a faster 68030 microprocessor and has an optional built-in CD-ROM drive.

Macintosh Plus   This computer had 128K ROMs, an internal 800K disk drive, and 1 megabyte of memory. This machine quickly became the standard for a minimum configuration. Many programs for the Macintosh require a minimum 1 megabyte memory. This computer also introduced the now standard SCSI (Small Computer System Interface) port, which allows the easy addition of one or more hard disks and other peripherals. Apple Computer, Inc. introduced the Macintosh Plus in 1986.

Macintosh Portable   When the original Macintosh was introduced, many people liked it because it was "portable." In reality, it was luggable if you did not have to carry it very far. Since then, the Macintosh has been evolving into larger, heavier, harder-to-move systems. In 1989, Apple Computer, Inc. released a portable Macintosh. The portable is powered by a Motorola 68000 microprocessor running at 16 MHz. This battery operated computer used a liquid crystal display of 640 by 400 pixels and a standard 4 MB RAM memory.

Macintosh PowerBooks   Several notebook Macintoshes, called PowerBooks were introduced in 1991 and late 1992. These portable machines are very popular.

Macintosh Quadra 700/900/950   High performance Macintoshes, introduced in 1991 and 1992, that use Motorola 68040 microprocessors.

Macintosh SE   SE stands for System Expansion. It indicates that this system offers a single expansion slot for adding a card to attach a peripheral. The SE was very similar to the Macintosh Plus in performance. The SE was introduced in 1987.

Macintosh SE/30   This is a high performance Macintosh that uses the more powerful Motorola 68030 microprocessor, has a disk drive that is capable of storing 1.4 megabytes, and a math coprocessor. The SE/30 was introduced in 1989.

Macintosh II   First serious Macintosh for professional production; introduced in 1987. The Macintosh II was the first of the "modular" Macintoshes. The system unit does not contain a monitor, allowing each user to choose a monitor that will perform best in the user's environment. The Macintosh II was the first macintosh to support color and multiple video screens. It has stereo sound and six expansion slots. It was powered by the Motorola 68020 microprocessor running at 16 MHz and had a math coprocessor. The Macintosh II had a 1 megabyte RAM and a built-in hard disk drive.

Macintosh IIci   The IIci is a faster version of the Macintosh IIcx, with a processor that operates about 1.5 times faster (a Motorola 68030 running at 25 MHz). The Macintosh IIci has a standard 5MB RAM memory. The IIci was introduced in 1989. The IIci contains fewer parts than earlier Macintoshes due to its use of 13 special Apple-designed VLSI chips.

Macintosh IIcx   Introduced in 1989, this Macintosh II upgrade used a Motorola 68030 microprocessor running at 16 MHz. The IIcx is a compact version of the Macintosh IIx.

Macintosh IIfx   A Macintosh computer designed for intensive graphics, CAD, and numeric calculations. The IIfx uses a Motorola 68030 microprocessor running at 40 MHz or 1.6 times faster than the IIci's 25 MHz speed. The IIfx has two additional processors (each with the power of an Apple II microcomputer) to handle the flow of information inside the computer. The IIfx uses a standard 4MB RAM memory and available as an option is a 160 MB internal hard disk unit. The Macintosh IIfx was introduced in 1990.

Macintosh IIsi The Macintosh IIsi, introduced in 1990, uses a Motorola 68030 microprocessor running at 20 MHz and runs about five times faster than the Macintosh Classic. The IIsi uses a standard 3 MB RAM memory, a 1.4 MB floppy disk unit and a 40 MB internal hard disk unit.

Macintosh IIx This Macintosh II update used a Motorola 68030 microprocessor, a 68882 math coprocessor and a standard 4 MB RAM memory. The Macintosh IIx was introduced in 1988.

Macintosh IIvx The Macintosh IIvx, introduced in late 1992, uses a Motorola 68030 microprocessor running at 33 MHz.

Macintosh user interface The method of operating an Apple Macintosh microcomputer, originally developed by Xerox Corporation and introduced in 1981 on the Xerox Star workstation. It uses a graphics screen that places objects on a two-dimensional desktop. Programs, files, folders and disks are represented by small pictures (icons) that look like the objects they represent. A mouse is used to select, activate or delete an object represented on the desktop. The Macintosh user interface style has been adapted to many non-Macintosh products, including Windows, GEM and Presentation Manager.

MacPaint A full-featured paint program for the Apple Macintosh microcomputer from Claris Corporation. Originally developed by Bill Atkinson at Apple Computer, Inc. and bundled with every Macintosh microcomputer until Claris Corp. was formed in 1987. Claris produces a more advanced version of the program. MacPaint provides a versatile set of tools for graphic expression. It is an excellent program that uses a mouse to draw lines and shapes on the screen, select patterns, edit drawings, erase lines, shade drawings, manipulate images, stretch shapes and a variety of other graphics functions.

MacPaint file format Bitmap graphics format used by MacPaint and some other Apple Macintosh paint programs. MacPaint files are limited to a resolution of 72 dpi, the same as the screen on the original Macintosh computers.

macro Single, symbolic programming language statement that, when translated, results in a series of machine-language statements.

macro assembler Assembler that allows the user to create and define new computer instructions (called macro instructions).

macro instruction (1) Source-language instruction equivalent to a specified number of machine-language instructions. (2) Machine-language instruction composed of several micro instructions.

MacWrite A full-featured word processing program for the Apple Macintosh microcomputer from Claris Corporation. Originally developed by Apple Computer, Inc. and bundled with every Apple Macintosh microcomputer until Claris Corporation was formed in 1987.

mag Abbreviation for magnetic.

MAGIC See machine-aided graphics for illustration and composition.

magnetic Of, producing, caused by, or operated by magnetism.

magazette A magazine recorded on a diskette.

magnetic bubble memory Memory that uses magnetic "bubbles" that move. The bubbles are locally magnetized areas that can move about in a magnetic material, such as a plate of orthoferrite. It is possible to control the reading in and out of this bubble within the magnetic material. Andrew Bobeck, Richard Sherwood, Umberto Gianola, and William Shockley, of Bell Laboratories, invented magnetic bubble memory. High costs and relatively long access times relegated magnetic bubbles to specialized applications.

magnetic characters Set of characters—used for checks, insurance billings, utility bills, invoices, and so forth—that permit special character-reading devices (MICR readers) to be employed to read the characters automatically. See magnetic ink character recognition.

magnetic core storage System of storage in which data is represented in binary form by means of the directional flow of magnetic fields in tiny, doughnut-shaped arrays of magnetic cores. Retains stored data in the event of a power loss. Used in older computers.

magnetic disk Magnetic device for storing information accessible by a computer. Can be either a rigid platter (hard disk) or a sheet of flexible plastic (floppy disk). See floppy disk and hard disk.

magnetic disk unit Peripheral storage device in which data are recorded on a magnetizable disk surface.

magnetic drum Peripheral storage device consisting of a cylinder with a magnetizable surface on which data are recorded. Used in older computer systems.

magnetic head Device used for reading and writing information on devices such as magnetic tapes or disks.

magnetic ink Ink that contains particles of a magnetic substance whose presence can be detected by magnetic sensors.

magnetic ink character recognition (MICR) Recognition, by machines of characters printed with a special magnetic ink. Used primarily in the banking, credit card, and public utilities industries.

magnetic media Generic name for floppy disks, tapes, and any other devices that store data in the form of magnetic impulses.

magnetic printing A process where a magnetic write head is used to

create a latent image on a drum or a belt, which is then toned, usually with a dry toner. The toned image is transferred to the paper and fixed with either heat or pressure.

magnetic resonance Phenomenon in which a movement of a particle or system of particles is coupled resonantly to an external magnetic field.

magnetic storage Any system that utilizes the magnetic properties of materials to store data on such devices and media as disks and tapes.

magnetic tape Plastic tape having a magnetic surface for storing data in a code of magnetized spots. Information may be represented on tape using an 8-bit coding structure. Information is written on the tape and retrieved from the tape by a tape drive. Tapes are available in reels of 600, 1200, 2400 and 3600 feet, which allows up to 270 MB to be stored.

magnetic tape cartridge Magnetic tape contained in a cartridge. The cartridge consists of a reel of tape and the take-up reel. Similar to a cassette but of slightly different design.

magnetic tape cassette Magnetic tape storage device consisting of .25-inch magnetic tape housed in a plastic container.

magnetic tape code System of coding used to record magnetized patterns on magnetic tape. The magnetized patterns represent alphanumeric data.

magnetic tape density Number of characters that can be recorded on 1 inch (2.54 cm) of magnetic tape.

magnetic tape drive Device that moves tape past a head. Synonymous with magnetic tape transport.

magnetic tape reel Reel used to preserve the physical characteristics of magnetic tape.

magnetic tape transport Same as magnetic tape drive.

magnetic tape unit Device containing a magnetic tape drive together with reading and writing heads and associated controls.

magneto-optic disc An erasable storage disc, similar to a CD-ROM disc. Uses a recording method that combines laser and magnetic technologies to create high-density erasable storage discs. Magneto-optic (MO) drives are immune from disc head crash damage since nothing physically touches the media, provide greater storage capacity than magnetic media, and provide more flexibility of use since the media is removable from the drive.

magnitude (1) Absolute value of a number. (2) Size of anything.

magstripe Small stripe of magnetic material found on the back of most major cards and computerized transit fare cards. Contains information such as account number and card holder's name or points of entry and exit and amount of paid fare remaining.

magtape Magnetic tape.

Mahon, Charles (1753-1816) Third Earl of Stanhope, who invented the Stanhope Demonstrator in 1777, the first arithmetical machine that used geared wheels.

mailbox A disk storage area assigned to a network user for receipt of electronic mail messages.

mailing list program Program that maintains names, addresses, and related data, and produces mailing labels.

mail-merging Process of automatically printing form letters with names and addresses from a mailing list file. A mail-merge program merges address information from one file with textual information from another file.

mainframe Large, expensive computer generally used for information processing in large businesses, colleges, and organizations. Originally, the phrase referred to the extensive array of large rack and panel cabinets that held thousands of vacuum tubes in early computers. Mainframes can occupy an entire room and have very large data-handling capacities. Far more costly than microcomputers or minicomputers, mainframes are the largest, fastest, and most expensive class of computers. Supercomputers are the largest, fastest, and most expensive of the mainframes. Before minicomputers became popular in 1965, all computers were mainframes.

main-line program Section of a program that controls the order of execution of other modules in the program.

main memory Same as internal storage.

main storage Addressable storage directly controlled by the central processing unit. Used to store programs while they are being executed and data while they are being processed. Same as internal storage and primary storage. Contrast with auxiliary storage.

maintainability Characteristic associated with the isolation and repair of a failure.

maintenance Any activity intended to eliminate faults or to keep hardware or programs in satisfactory working condition, including tests, measurements, replacements, adjustments, and repairs.

maintenance programmer Individual who works with programs that have already been implemented into an information system, making changes as needed from time to time. See software maintenance.

maintenance routine Routine designed to help a customer engineer carry out routine preventive maintenance on a computer system.

major sort key Field containing data (such as a last name) by which most data items can be distinguished and sorted. When duplications occur in this field, a minor sort key (such as a first name) may supply the necessary distinction.

male connectors Referring to connectors, ones that have pins or protruding parts rather than sockets or receptacles. Contrast with female connectors.

malfunction Failure in the operation of the central processing unit or peripheral device. The effect of a fault. Contrast with error and mistake. See crash.

Maltron keyboard Keyboard layout that allows potentially much faster speeds, and is easier to learn than the traditional QWERTY keyboard layout. The keyboard is designed so that the keys used most frequently are positioned beneath the strongest digits. Thus, the home keys for the right hand are: 't', 'h', 'o', and 'r'; and for the left hand 'a', 'n', 'i', and 's'. Up to eight keys are assigned to each thumb. Each key is positioned at the correct height for the finger that uses it, thus minimizing unnaturally long finger stretches and making the keyboard less tiring to use than traditional keyboards. Numbers can be typed in sequence.

MAN See metropolitan area network.

management graphics Charts, graphs, and other visual representations of the operational or strategic aspects of a business, intended to aid management in assimilating and presenting business data.

management information system (MIS) Any information system designed to supply organizational managers with the necessary information needed to plan, organize, staff, direct, and control the operations of the organization.

management report Report designed to help manages and decision makers perform their jobs.

management science Mathematical or quantitative study of the management of a business's resources, usually with the aid of a computer.

manager Person responsible for guiding the operations of a computer center, programming group, software development group, service organization, and so on.

manipulating Act of working on data to put it into a form that has greater meaning to the user.

mantissa That part of a floating-point number that specifies the significant digits of the number. In 0.64321×10^3, .64321 is the mantissa. See characteristic.

manual input Data entered manually by the computer user to modify, continue, or resume processing of a computer program.

manual operation Processing of data in a system by direct manual techniques.

manufacturer's software Operating system or set of programming aids that the computer manufacturer supplies or makes available with a computer. See systems programs.

map List that indicates the area of storage occupied by various elements of a program and its data. Also called storage map.

MAP Acronym for Manufacturing Automation Protocol, a communications protocol introduced by General Motors Corporation in 1982. The goal of MAP is to provide common standards for the interconnection of computers and programmable machine tools used in factory automation.

MAPPER Acronym for MAintaining, Preparing and Processing Executive Reports, a fourth-generation language from Unisys Corporation that runs on Unisys mainframes.

mapping Transformation from one set to another set; a correspondence. For example, the process by which a graphic system translates graphic data from one coordinate system into a form useful on another coordinate system. See symbolic table.

margin Number of spaces between the right or left edge of a page (or window) and the beginning of text.

marginal checking Preventive maintenance procedure in which the unit under test is varied from its normal value in an effort to detect and locate components that are operating in a marginal condition.

mark Sign or symbol used to signify or indicate an event in time or space.

mark sensing Ability to mark cards or pages with a pencil to be read directly into the computer via a mark sense reader. Very useful technique for acquiring data by hand and for avoiding the time lag and potential inaccuracy of keypunching. See optical mark reader.

marquee A rectangular area surrounded by dotted lines, used to select objects or selected portions of an image in a drawing/painting program.

maser Acronym for Microwave Amplification by the Stimulated Emission of Radiation, a device capable of amplifying or generating radio frequency radiation. Maser amplifiers are used in satellite communication ground stations to amplify the extremely weak signals received form communications satellites.

mask (1) A patterned plate used to shield sections of the silicon chip surface during the manufacture of integrated circuits. (2) Machine word containing a pattern of bits, bytes, or characters used to extract or select parts of other machine words by controlling an instruction that retains or eliminates selected bits, bytes, or characters.

mask design   Final phase of integrated circuit design by which the circuit design is realized through multiple masks corresponding to multiple layers on the integrated circuit. The mask layout must observe all process-related constraints, and minimize the area the circuit will occupy.

masked diffusion   A process that uses a mask to selectively impregnate a semiconductor material with impurities.

massage   To process data.

mass storage device   Any device used to supply relatively inexpensive storage for large amounts of data. A sort of jukebox for optical discs or tape cartridges. A mass storage unit can automatically load any disc or tape in its library to provide quick access to vast quantities of information.

master clear   Switch on some computer consoles that will clear certain operational registers and prepare for a new mode of operation.

master clock   Device that controls the basic timing pulses of a computer.

master data   Set of data that is altered infrequently and supplies basic data for processing operations.

master file   File containing relatively permanent information used as a source of reference and generally updated periodically. Contrast with detail file.

master file maintenance   Process of updating, changing, or modifying master files.

master/slave computer system   Computer system consisting of a master computer connected to one or more slave computers. The master computer provides the scheduling function and jobs to the slave computer(s).

match   To check for identity between two or more items of data. Compare hit.

matching   Data processing operation in which two files are checked to determine whether there is a corresponding item or group of items in each file.

math coprocessor   A special chip added to a computer to handle advanced mathematic functions, thereby freeing up the processing power of the main CPU.

mathematical functions   Set of mathematical routines available in most programming languages. Usually supplied as part of the language.

mathematical logic   Use of mathematical symbols to represent language and its processes. These symbols are manipulated in accord with mathematical rules to determine whether or not a statement or a series of statements is true or false. See logic.

mathematical model Group of mathematical expressions that represents a process, a system, or the operation of a device. See simulation.

mathematical symbols Symbols used in formulas, equations, and flowcharts.

mathematics Study of the relationships among objects or quantities, organized so that certain facts can be proved or derived from others by using logic.

matrix Orderly array of symbols by rows and columns. The symbols comprising the matrix are called elements or entries of the matrix. Subscripts, are customarily used to indicate the row and column positions of an element in any matrix. Matrices provide a way in which complicated mathematical statements can be expressed simply. Computers are often used in work with matrices.

matrix notation Introduced by English mathematician Arthur Cayley in 1858. He used an abbreviated notation, such as ax = b, for expressing systems of linear equations.

matrix printer Character printer that uses a matrix of dots to form an image of the character being printed. See dot matrix printer.

mature system System that is fully operational and performing all the functions it was designed to accomplish.

Mauchly, John (1907-1980) Coinventor of ENIAC, the first large-scale all-electronic computer. In the 1930s, while head of the Physics Department at Ursinus College in Pennsylvania, Mauchly began experimenting with computers and electronics. During his eight years at the school, he worked on a weather analysis project that led him to the conviction that a high-speed electronic device was necessary to perform complex environmental calculations. In 1941, he joined the Moore School of Electrical Engineering at the University of Pennsylvania, where he met J. Presper Eckert. In early 1943, the two men submitted a proposal to the U.S. Army describing an electronic computer; the Army's Ordnance Department later issued a contract to them to build the machine. The Army needed calculated tables that would indicate to its artillerymen how to aim new guns being developed for World War II. The Moore School had been calculating these tables, but with methods that were proving too slow. Between 1943 and 1946, Eckert and Mauchly developed the Electronic Numerical Integrator And Computer, a landmark leading to the development of many future computer designs. ENIAC was literally a giant. It contained more than 18,000 vacuum tubes, weighed 30 tons, and occupied a room the size of an average three-bedroom house. Following the development of ENIAC, Eckert and Mauchly established their own company. They developed a second computer in 1949 called BINAC (BINary Automatic Computer), which served as a test of the plans they had formulated for UNIVAC I, the world's first general-purpose commercial computer. In 1951, UNIVAC I was installed at the U.S. Census Bureau. The corporation formed by Eckert and Mauchly is now part of Unisys Corporation, a large manufacturer of computing equipment. See Eckert, J. Presper.

mb Abbreviation for megabyte, one million bytes.

MCAD Acronym for Mechanical Computer Aided Design. CAD for mechanical design.

McCarthy, John In 1958, created the programming language LISP. Also developed the concept of interactive computing (while at M.I.T.) and coined the term artificial intelligence. Best known for his work associated with artificial intelligence.

MCGA Acronym for Multi-Color Graphics Array; a type of display adapter for IBM PS/2 compatible computers.

MDA Acronym for Monochrome Display Adapter. A video adapter that provided text on IBM Personal Computers. MDA cards were often replaced with adapter cards which provided both text and graphics. MDA was superseded by VGA.

means/ends analysis Method of reasoning that looks backward and forward from the initial point to the goal in an attempt to reduce differences.

Mechanical Computer Aided Design (MCAD) CAD for mechanical design.

mechanical mouse A mouse that uses a rubber ball that makes contact with several wheels inside the unit. Contrast with optical mouse.

mechanism In object-oriented programming, a structure whereby objects work together to provide some behavior that satisfies a requirement of the problem.

mechanization Use of machines to simplify or replace work previously accomplished by human workers. Compare automation.

media Plural form of "medium." See source media, input media, and output media.

media compatibility The ability of two or more different style units to use the same type of disks as blank disks, whether or not each can read data recorded by the other.

media eraser Device designed to demagnetize magnetic tapes and diskettes. See degausser.

media interchangeability The extent to which disks recorded on one machine can play back on another with the same type of drive. Media interchangeability is excellent for floppy disks, but some removable cartridge hard disks have problems with it.

media specialist Person responsible for cataloging and maintaining storage media such as diskettes, disk packs, magnetic tapes, and other related materials.

medium Any physical substance upon which data are recorded, such as floppy disk, magnetic disk, magnetic tape, and paper.

medium scale integration (MSI) Class of integrated circuits having a density between those of large scale integration and small scale integration.

mega Prefix indicating one million, or 10^6. Abbreviated M. Contrast with micro, one millionth.

MEGA A personal computer series from Atari Corporation that is compatible with the Atari ST series of microcomputers.

megabit Loosely, 1 million bits or 1 thousand kilobits. Actually, 1,048,576 bits, or 1024 kilobits.

megabyte (MB) Specifically, 2^{20}, or 1,048,576 bytes; 1024 kilobytes. Roughly, 1 million bytes or 1 thousand kilobytes.

megacycle One million cycles per second.

megaflop One million floating-point operations per second. Also called Mflops.

megahertz (MHz) Unit of electrical frequency equal to one million cycles per second, a measure of transmission frequency. Megahertz is used to measure a CPU's clock rate.

megapel display In computer graphics, a display system that handles a million or more pixels. A resolution of 1000 lines by 1000 dots per line requires a million pixels for a full screen image.

member object In object-oriented programming, a repository for part of the state of an object; collectively, the member objects of an object constitutes its structure. The terms "field", "instance variable", "member object", and "slot" are interchangeable.

membrane keyboard A keyboard constructed of two thin plastic sheets (called membranes) that are coated with a circuit made of electrically conductive ink. The keyboard is sensitive to touch. It is an economical, flat keyboard used in several early microcomputers. Today, such keyboards are used primarily on printers and special keyboards.

memory Storage facilities of the computer, capable of storing vast amounts of data.

memory allocation See storage allocation.

memory board Expansion board that adds RAM to the computer system, making it possible to store and use additional information.

memory cartridge A plug-in module containing RAM chips that can be used to store programs or data.

memory chip A semiconductor device used to store information in the form of electrical charges. There are two types of memory chips: ROM holds information permanently while RAM holds it temporarily.

memory cycle Amount of time required to move one byte or word of information into or out of memory.

memory dump Printout showing the contents of memory.

memory management Technique of efficiently controlling and allocating memory resources.

memory map A diagram that shows how memory is used. For example, in a display unit there is a memory map of the screen display, with one memory location corresponding to each pixel on the display.

memory protection The process of keeping a program from straying into other programs and vice versa.

memory sniffing Continuous testing of storage during processing.

menu A list of command options available to the user of a computer software program. An on-screen list of command choices.

menu-driven software Computer programs that make extensive use of menus. Software of this type is designed so it may be used easily by people with minimal computer experience. Menus are used to select tasks to be performed.

menu item Any choice in a menu.

merge To combine items into one sequenced file without changing the order of the items. Same as collate.

merge-print program Program that lets the user produce personalized form letters.

MESFET Acronym for MEtal Semiconductor Field Effect Transistor, the main active device used in gallium arsenide integrated circuits to provide current gain and inversion.

mesh Set of branches forming a closed path in a network.

mesh network Network in which nodes are connected to several other nodes (possibly each node is connected to every other) allowing a variety of paths for transmission of messages. Contrast with ring network. See network topologies.

message (1) Group of characters having meaning as a whole and always handled as a group. (2) In object-oriented programming, a request sent to an object to change its state or return a value. An operation that one object performs upon another.

message format   Rules for the placement of such portions of a message as message heading, address text, and end of message.

message header   Leading part of a message that contains information concerning the message, such as the source or destination code, priority, and type of message.

message-passing   In object-oriented programming, a mechanism that allows objects to send messages among themselves.

message queuing   In a data communications system, a technique for controlling the handling of messages, allowing them to be accepted by a computer and stored until they have been processed or routed to another destination.

message retrieval   Capability to retrieve a message sometime after it has entered an information system.

message switching   Switching technique of receiving a message, storing it until the proper outgoing circuit and station are available, and then retransmitting it toward its destination. Computers are often used to perform the switching function.

message switching center   Center in which messages are routed according to information contained within the messages themselves.

metacharacter   In programming language systems, these characters have some controlling role in respect to the other characters with which they are associated.

metaclass   In object-oriented programming, the class of a class; a class whose instances are themselves classes.

metacompiler   Compiler for a language used primarily for written compilers, usually syntax-oriented compilers. A special-purpose metacompiler language is not very useful for writing general programs.

metalanguage   Language used to describe a language.

metallic oxide semiconductor (MOS)   (1) Field effect transistor in which the gate electrode is isolated from the channel by an oxide film. See MOSFET. (2) Capacitor in which semiconductor material forms one plate, aluminum forms the other plate, and an oxide forms the dielectric. See complementary MOS.

meta-metalanguage   Language used to describe a metalanguage.

metaphor   In software development, the use of words or pictures to suggest a resemblance. For example the Apple Macintosh computer uses a desktop metaphor with its icons for paper, files, folders, wastebaskets, and so on.

method In object-oriented programming, the function or procedure that implements the response when a message is sent to an object. Methods determine how an object will respond to a message that it receives. The terms message, method, and operation are usually interchangeable.

methodology Procedure or collection of techniques used to analyze information in an orderly manner. Set of standardized procedures, including technical methods, management techniques and documentation that provide the framework to accomplish a particular function.

metric system Systeme International d'Unites, or SI, the modern version of the metric system currently in use worldwide. It is based on seven base units: meter, kilogram, second, ampere, Kelvin (degrees Celsius), candela, and mole.

metropolitan area network (MAN) A computer network that serves customers in the same city or region and can be accessed by mobile (cellular) telephone.

MFLOP One million floating-point operations per second. Used as a rough measure of a computer's processing speed.

MFT Acronym for Multiprogramming with a Fixed number of Tasks, the tasks being programs.

MHz Abbreviation for megahertz, a million cycles per second.

MICR Acronym for Magnetic Ink Character Recognition.

MICR inscriber A device that adds magnetic characters to a document.

micro (1) One millionth, used as a prefix, for example, a microsecond is a millionth of a second. (2) Computerese for "quite small," as in microcomputer. From the Greek letter mu, meaning "very small." Contrast with mega, one million.

MicroChannelBus The bus design used in the high-end IBM PS/2 computers. This design allows for more than one processor in a single computer, and better handshaking between expansion cards.

microchart Chart showing the ultimate details of the program's or system's design.

microchip A popular nickname for the integrated circuit chip.

microcircuit A miniaturized electronic circuit like those etched on the silicon and germanium wafers characteristic of processors and other products of the semiconductor industry. A microcircuit is made up interconnected transistors, resistors, and other components.

241

microcode Permanent basic subcommands, built into the computer, that are executed directly by the machine's electronic circuits. Generally, in a special read-only storage unit, these commands define the instruction set of a microprogrammable computer.

microcomputer The smallest and least expensive class of computer. Any small computer based on a microprocessor. Also called a personal computer.

microcomputer chip Microcomputer on a chip. Differs from a microprocessor in that it not only contains the CPU but also includes, on the same piece of silicon, a RAM, a ROM, and input/output circuitry.

microcomputer system System that includes a microcomputer, peripherals, operating system, and applications programs.

microdisk A 3.5-inch diskette.

microelectronics Field that deals with techniques for producing miniature circuits, such as integrated circuits, thin film techniques, and solid logic modules.

microfiche Sheet of microfilm about 4 in. by 6 in. (10 cm by 15 cm) upon which the images of computer output may be recorded. Up to 270 pages of output may be recorded on one sheet of fiche.

microfilm Photographic film used for recording graphic information in a reduced size.

microfloppy disk A 3.5-inch floppy disk, which in recent years has become the disk of choice. A 3.5-inch disk holds more data and are much easier to store, transport and handle than their 5.25-inch counterparts. The microfloppy disk was developed by Sony.

microform Medium that contains miniaturized images, such as microfiche and microfilm.

Micrografx Designer A graphic arts and technical illustration program for IBM-compatible microcomputers. Designer mixes, edits, and manipulates different font types. Using advanced spline technology, Designer provides curves, parabolas, and a variety of freehand drawing capabilities.

micrographics A generic name for the microfilm, microfiche, computer output to microfilm processing industry.

micro instructions Low-level instructions used to obtain a macro instruction in machine language or in a source language available to the computer user. See microprogramming.

microjustification In some word processing programs, the ability to add small slivers of blank space between words and between letters within words. The result is easier to read than ordinary justified copy, in which the computer merely adjusts space between words. See microspacing.

micrologic Use of a permanent stored program to interpret instructions in a microprogram.

micro manager The person responsible for managing the acquisition, modification, and maintenance of an organization's microcomputer systems.

microminiature chip An LSI or VLSI chip used for computer storage (memory chip) or control (microprocessor chip).

microminiaturization Term implying very small size, one step smaller than miniaturization.

micron One millionth of a meter, or approximately 1/25,000 of an inch. The tiny elements that make up a transistor on a chip are measured in microns. See angstrom.

microprocessor The complex chip that is the central processing unit (CPU) of the computer. The job of the microprocessor is to control what goes on inside the computer. All processing that a computer does takes place in the microprocessor.

microprogrammable computer Any computer whose instruction set is not fixed but can be tailored to individual needs by the programming of ROMs or other memory devices. Consequently, whether the computer is a mainframe, minicomputer, or microcomputer, theoretically it can be microprogrammed.

microprogramming Method of operating the control part of a computer in which each instruction is broken into several small steps (microsteps) that form part of a microprogram. Some systems allow users to microprogram, and hence determine the instruction set of, their own machine.

MicroPROLOG A reduced version of the PROLOG programming language, designed for use on microcomputer systems.

MicroRIM Database software developed for microcomputers. MicroRIM can be used to create files, update files, select data from the files, sort records, and print reports.

microsecond One millionth of a second, abbreviated µs or µsec.

Microsoft Corporation A leading software company founded in 1975 by William H. Gates and Paul G. Allen. The companies first product was Microsoft BASIC for the Altair 8800 microcomputer. Following products include MS-DOS, Microsoft Windows, Microsoft Word, Microsoft Works, GW-BASIC, as well as many other software systems. Microsoft's position as the supplier of the major software to the world's largest computer base (IBM-compatible microcomputers) gives it considerable influence over the future of the computer industry.

Microsoft BASIC One of the most popular versions of the BASIC programming language, developed by Microsoft Corporation. Also called MBASIC. A version for the IBM PC is called PC BASIC.

Microsoft Excel   See Excel.

Microsoft Windows   A graphics-based operating environment for IBM-compatible microcomputers from Microsoft Corporation. It runs in conjunction with DOS. Some of the graphical user interface features include pull-down menus, multiple typefaces, desk accessories, and the capability of moving text and graphics from one program to another via a clipboard.

Microsoft Word   A full-featured word processing program for IBM-compatible microcomputers and Apple Macintosh computers from Microsoft Corporation. It has a spelling checker, hypenation, style sheets, a glossary, mail merge, automatic text wrap, and a column design feature.

Microsoft Works   An integrated application program that includes a spreadsheet, a database, and a word processor. It provides desktop publishing with drawing and word processing documents. The drawing tools and linked columns of the desktop publishing section let you create professional style layouts.

microspacing   Feature of some printers that allows them to move extremely small distances. Used to do microjustification and shadow printing.

micro-to-mainframe   Refers to connecting a microcomputer to a mainframe network.

microwave   Electromagnetic wave that has a wavelength in the centimeter range. Microwaves occupy a region in the electromagnetic spectrum bounded by radio waves on the side of longer wavelengths and by infrared waves on the side of shorter wavelengths. Used in data communications.

microwave hop   Microwave radio channel between two dish antennas aimed at each other.

microwave transmission   LIne-of-sight transmission of data signals through the atmosphere from relay station to relay station.

MICR reader   Input device that reads documents imprinted with magnetic ink characters.

MIDI   Acronym for Musical Instrument Digital Interface, a standard protocol for the interchange of musical information between musical instruments, synthesizers, and computers.

milestone   An essential activity or step in a project that helps measure the progress of the project.

milk disk   A disk used to gather data from a small computer with a view to processing the data in a larger computer later.

milli   One thousandth, used as a prefix; a millisecond is a thousandth of a second. Contrast with kilo, thousand.

millimicrosecond   Same as nanosecond, one billionth of a second.

millisecond   One thousandth of a second; abbreviated ms or msec.

mini   Short for minicomputer.

miniaturization   Process of making an object smaller in physical size without decreasing its efficiency.

minicomputer   A class of computers with capabilities and a price between microcomputers and mainframes. In 1959, Digital Equipment Corporation (DEC) launched the minicomputer industry with its PDP-1. In 1965, DEC introduced the PDP-8, the first popular, low cost minicomputer. In 1970, DEC introduced the PDP-11,which became the most widely used minicomputer in the world. Data General Corporation, Hewlett-Packard Company, Prime Computer, Inc. IBM Corporation, Wang Laboratories, Inc., and other companies have produced a variety of minicomputers.

minifloppy   A 5.25-inch diskette, introduced by Shugart in 1978.

minimal tree   Tree whose terminal nodes are ordered to make the tree operate at optimum.

minimax   Technique for minimizing the maximal error of a process.

minor sort key   Data field that provides a secondary source of distinctions by which to sort records. Used only when duplications occur in the major sort key.

MIPS   One Million Instructions Per Second. A measure of the processing speed of a computer. Used to describe the average number of machine-language instructions a large computer performs in one second. A computer capable of 2.0 MIPS can execute 2,000,000 instructions per second. A mainframe can typically perform 10 to 50 MIPS; a microcomputer might be in the 0.05 MIPS range.

mirroring   Display or creation of graphic data that portrays an image in exactly the reverse orientation it originally had. Many computer graphics systems will automatically create a mirror image of a graphic entity on the display screen by flipping the entity or drawing on its X or Y axis.

MIS   Acronym for Management Information System.

mistake   Human failing that produces an unintended result, such as faulty arithmetic, use of incorrect computer instructions, incorrect data entry, or use of incorrect formulas in a computer program.

MITS Altair   The first microcomputer kit, offered to computer hobbyists in 1975.

mixed number   Number having both a fractional part and an integer part, such as 63.71, -18.006, and 2948.413.

ML   Acronym for Manipulator Language, an IBM Corporation programming language for controlling robots.

MMU   Short for Memory Management Unit, a specialized coprocessor that takes care of the mapping of logical memory (as seen by programs) to physical memory (the actual memory provided on the system). That procedure lets software act as if it had more memory to work with than the system actually provides (the missing part is simulated by a hard disk) and lets multiple programs running simultaneously share memory more easily.

mnemonic   (1) Pertaining to any technique used to aid human memory. (2) Word or name that is easy to remember and identify.

mnemonic code   Easy-to-remember assembly-language code; for example, a code that uses an abbreviation such as MPY for "multiply."

mnemonic language   Programming language based on easily remembered symbols that can be assembled into machine language by the computer.

mode   (1) An operational state that a system has been switched to. (2) Form of a number, name, or expression. (3) Most common or frequent value in a group of values.

model   (1) Representation of certain key features of an object or system to be studied. Scientific models often make use of complex formulas and involve substantial use of mathematics. If a computer is used to solve the equations and carry out the necessary calculations, the process is called a computer simulation. Modeling and simulation are essential tools in every area of science, business, economics and a number of other fields. (2) A type of database, each type representing a particular way of organizing data. The three database models are hierarchical, network, and relational.

model-based expert system   A system that uses a model-based representation of the underlying structure or behavior of the entity involved. A model-based system is based on deep knowledge rather than surface knowledge. Model-based expert systems are more capable of handling unexpected situations than a heuristic-based system, which is based more on surface knowledge.

model, geometric   Complete, geometrically accurate 3-D or 2-D representation of a shape, a part, or a geographic area, designed on a computer graphics system and stored in the database.

modeling   Process of accurately describing or representing certain parts of a system. Using mathematics to describe a situation or a physical object. The simulation of a condition or activity by performing a set of equations on a set of data.

modem Acronym for MOdulator/DEModulator, a device that translates digital pulses from a computer into analog signals for telephone transmission, and analog signals from the telephone into digital pulses the computer can understand. Provides communication capabilities between computer equipment over common telephone facilities.

modifier In object-oriented programming, an operation that alters the state of an object.

modify (1) To alter a portion of an instruction so its interpretation and execution will be other than normal. The modification may permanently change the instruction or leave it unchanged and affect only the current execution. (2) To alter a program according to a defined parameter.

Modula-2 A high-level, programming language developed in 1979 by Nicklaus Wirth as a replacement for Pascal. The language is similar to Pascal. Modula-2 supports separate compilation of modules, whereas Pascal does not. Modula-2 is very popular as a teaching language at colleges and universities.

Modula-3 A Digital Equipment Corporation/Olivetti collaboration to extend Modula-2 programming language.

modular coding Technique of programming in which the logical parts of a program are divided into a series of individual modules or routines so that each routine may be programmed independently. See top-down programming.

modular constraint In computer graphics, a limitation on the placement of images such that some or all points of an image are forced to lie on the intersections of an invisible grid.

modularity Concept of designing computers in a building-block format to promote efficient and economical upgrading of equipment.

modular programming Programming that produces relatively small, easily interchanged, computer routines that meet standardized interface requirements. Modularity is accomplished by breaking the program into limited segments that perform complete functions and are therefor understandable in themselves. Greatly facilitates development and verification of complex programs and systems. See module and structured programming.

modulation In data communications, the process by which some characteristic of a high-frequency carrier signal is varied in accordance with another, lower-frequency "information" signal. Used in data sets to make computer terminal signals compatible with communications facilities.

modulation depth The difference in brightness between black and white in a CRT display.

modulator Device that receives electrical pulses, or bits, from a data processing machine and converts them into signals suitable for transmission over a communications link. Contrast with demodulator.

module (1) One logical part of a program. A major program may be broken down into a number of logically self-contained modules. These modules may be written (and possibly tested separately) by a number of programmers. The modules can then be put together to form the complete program. This is called modular programming. (2) Interchangeable plug-in item containing components. (3) A set of logically related statements that perform a specific function.

module diagram Part of the notation of object-oriented design, used to show the allocation of classes and objects to modules in the physical design of a system.

modulo Mathematical function that yields the remainder of division. For example, 25 modulo 4 equals 1. This is derived by dividing 25 by 4, which leaves a remainder of 1. This is the modulo value of the operation.

moire pattern (1) An interference pattern created when two regular dot patterns are asymmetrically superimposed. (2) An undesirable grid pattern that may occur when a bit-mapped graphic with gray fill patterns is reduced or enlarged. (3) In scanning, an objectionable pattern caused by the interference of halftone screens. Often produced when you rescan a halftone and a second screen is applied on top of the first.

monadic Pertaining to an operation that uses only one operand. Contrast with niladic.

monadic Boolean operator Boolean operator with only one operand, such as the NOT operator.

monitor (1) A device on which images generated by the computer's video adapter are displayed. (2) Control program or supervisor.

monochrome A term applied to a monitor that displays a single color (white, amber or green) image on a contrasting (black) background, producing a sharp, clear display that is easy to read.

monochrome adapter A video adapter capable of producing one foreground color.

monochrome display A video display capable of displaying only one color.

monolithic (1) Pertaining to a single silicon substrate upon which an integrated circuit is constructed. (2) Complete and all in one piece. For example, a linkage editor combines several fragmentary program modules into a single monolithic program.

monolithic integrated circuit Circuit formed in a single piece of the substrate material, as opposed to a hybrid circuit, in which individual (physically separate) circuit components are electrically interconnected to form the final circuit.

monospace A typeface in which the width of all characters is the same, producing output that looks like typed characters. Courier is an example of a monospace typeface.

Monroe, Jay R. In 1911, using earlier designs of Frank Baldwin, developed the first keyboard rotary machine to attain commercial success.

Monte Carlo method Trial-and-error method of repeated calculations to discover the best solution to a problem. Often used when a great number of variables are present with interrelationships so extremely complex as to eliminate straightforward analytical handling.

more than See greater than.

Morland, Samuel (1625-1695) Improved on Napier's bones to invent a multiplier, and in 1666 invented an arithmetical machine that could calculate the four processes of arithmetic.

morphemics Rules describing how words are changed to form variations such as plurals or verb conjugations.

MOS Acronym for Metallic Oxide Semiconductor.

MOSFET Acronym for Metallic Oxide Semiconductor Field Effect Transistor, a semiconductor characterized by an extremely high input impedance, a fairly high active impedance, and low switching speeds. When a voltage (negative with respect to the substrate) is applied to the gate, the MOSFET is a conductor; if a potential difference is applied between source and drain, there will be current flow.

MOS/LSI See metallic oxide semiconductor and large scale integration.

most significant digit (MSD) That digit of a number that has the greatest weight or significance. In the number 58371, the most significant digit is 5. See high-order and justify.

motherboard Interconnecting assembly into which printed circuit cards, boards, or modules are connected. Main circuit board of a microcomputer. Also called system board and backplane.

Motorola, Inc. A leading manufacturer of semiconductor devices that was founded in 1928 by Paul V. Galvin in Chicago. Although the company produces many consumer electronics products, they are best known in the computer business as the manufacturer of the 68000 family of microprocessors.

Motorola 68000 family A family of microprocessors developed by Motorola, Inc: MC 68000 (a 16-bit processor) developed in 1979, MC 68010 (a 16-bit processor) developed in 1983, MC 68020 (a 32-bit processor) developed in 1984, MC 68030 (a 32-bit processor) developed in 1987, MC 68040 (a 32-bit processor) announced in 1987. The MC 68000 family of microprocessors is used in several popular microcomputers including the Apple Macintosh, Commodore Amiga, and Atari ST.

Motorola 88000 A family of 32-bit RISC microprocessors introduced by Motorola, Inc. in 1988.

mouse A hand-operated pointing device that senses movements as it is moved across a flat surface and conveys this information to the computer. The mouse also has one or more buttons that can be pressed to signal the computer. The mouse's main advantage is that it can move a cursor around on the display screen, including, diagonally, with great precision.

mouse button Switch on top of the mouse that transmits commands to the computer. See click and double-click.

mouse pad A surface to be used with a mouse. As you move the mouse across the mouse pad, the cursor moves across the screen in the same direction.

mouse pointer The on-screen icon or cursor, the movement of which is controlled by the mouse.

movable-head disk unit Storage device or system consisting of magnetically coated disks, on the surface of which data are stored in the form of magnetic spots arranged in a manner to represent binary data. The data are arranged in circular tracks around the disks and is accessible to reading and writing heads on arms that can be moved mechanically to the desired tracks on the disks. Date from a given track are read or written sequentially as the disk rotates. Contrast with fixed-head disk unit.

move (1) To transfer (copy) data from one location of storage to another location. (2) In computer graphics, to change the current position on a graphics coordinate system.

moving average Method of averaging out the roughness of random variation in a data series. Uses only the most recent historical data in the series. The method gets its name from the way it slides along the data series, averaging each data point with its immediate predecessors. The average may disclose trends that would otherwise be obscured by the minor fluctuations along a line.

MPU Acronym for MicroProcessing Unit. See microprocessor.

MPX Acronym for MultiPleXer.

ms Abbreviation of millisecond. Also msec.

MSD Acronym for Most Significant Digit.

MS-DOS Acronym for Microsoft-Disk Operating System, the standard operating system for IBM-compatible microcomputers. MS-DOS was created by Microsoft Corporation and released in 1981. MS-DOS oversees such operations as disk input and output, video support, keyboard control, and many internal functions related to program execution and file maintenance.

MSI Acronym for Medium Scale Integration.

MSSG Abbreviation of message.

MS-Windows See Windows.

MTBF Acronym for Mean Time Between Failures, the average length of time a system or component is expected to work without failure.

MTTF Acronym for Mean Time To Failure, the average length of time in which the system, or a component of the system, works without fault.

MTTR Acronym for Mean Time To Repair, the average time expected to be required to detect and correct a fault in a computer system.

mu Name of the Greek letter μ, the symbol used to denote the prefix micro. For example, μs means microsecond.

μC Abbreviation for microcomputer (μ is the Greek letter mu).

MUG Acronym for MUMPS Users Group.

multiaccess computer Computer system in which computational and data resources are made available simultaneously to a number of users, who access the system through terminal devices, normally on an interactive or conversational basis. May consist of only a single central processor connected directly to a number of terminals (star network), or it may consist of a number of processing systems that are distributed and interconnected with one another (ring network) as well as with other terminals.

multiaddress Pertaining to an instruction format containing more than one address part.

multi-bit Any scan that uses more than one bit to store information about a pixel.

multicomputer system Computer system consisting of two or more central processing units.

Multics An operating system developed in the 1960s by Bell Laboratories and the Massachusetts Institute of Technology. It was first used commercially on General Electric Company mainframes and later on Honeywell computers. Multics was the predecessor of the UNIX operating system.

multidrop line Communications system configuration that uses a single channel or line to service several terminals.

multifile sorting Automatic sequencing of more than one file, based upon separate parameters for each file, without operator intervention.

multifunction board Device that plugs into computers, giving the system more than one new capability, such as a clock/calendar, memory expansion board, or parallel/serial interface.

multifunction optical drive An optical drive that has both WORM and Erasable capabilities and can read or write. A multifunction drive in conjunction with a CD-ROM drive, will provide enormous capabilities and storage facilities.

multijob operation Concurrent execution of job steps from two or more jobs. Compare multiprogramming.

multilayer Type of printed circuit board that has several circuit layers connected by electroplated holes.

multilevel addressing See indirect addressing.

multilinked list List with each atom having at least two pointers.

multimedia Multiple types of media, such as film, videotape, computer disks, sound recordings, photographs, paper, slides, etc.

multipass Process of running through the same data more than once to accomplish a task too complicated to be accomplished in one pass.

multipass sort Sort program designed to sort more data than can be contained within the internal memory of a central computer. Intermediate storage, such as disk, or tape, is required.

Multiplan A spreadsheet program with data-management features, produced by Microsoft Corporation.

multiple-access network Flexible system by which every station can have access to the network at all times; provisions are made for times when two computers decide to transmit at the same time.

multiple-address instruction Instruction consisting of an operation code and two or more addresses.

multiple-address message Message to be delivered to more than one destination.

multiple connector Connector to indicate the merging of several lines of flow into one line, or the dispersal of one line of flow into several lines.

multiple inheritance In object-oriented programming, the ability of subclasses to inherit instance variables and methods from more than one class.

multiple-job processing Controlling the performance of more than one data processing job at a time.

multiple-pass printing Technique used on some dot matrix printers to obtain higher-quality characters. The print head makes one pass, the paper is moved slightly, and another pass is made. The end product is a printed character that is easier to read.

multiple regression Statistical technique for predicting the value of a "dependent variable" that is assumed to be dependent upon one or more explanatory or "independent variables."

multiple user system Computer system designed to allow more than one user on the system at a time. See network.

multiplex To interleave or simultaneously transmit two or more messages over a single channel or other communications facility.

multiplexer(MPX) Device that allows several communications lines to share one computer data channel. Also abbreviated MUX.

multiplexer channel Special type of input/output channel that can transmit data between a computer and a number of simultaneously operating peripheral devices.

multiplexor Alternate spelling of multiplexer.

multiplication time Time required to perform a multiplication. For a binary number, it will equal the total of all the addition times and all the shift time involved in the multiplication.

multipoint line A line configuration in which several terminals are connected on the same line to one computer.

multiprecision arithmetic Form of arithmetic in which two or more computer words are used to represent each number.

multiprocessing Simultaneous execution of two or more sequences of instructions by multiple central processing units under common control.

multiprocessor Computer network consisting of two or more central processors under a common control.

multiprogramming Running two or more programs concurrently in the same computer. Each program is allotted its own place in memory and its own peripherals, but all share the central processing unit. It is made economical by the fact that peripherals are slower than the CPU so most programs spend most of their time waiting for input or output to finish. While one program is waiting, another can use the CPU.

multireel sorting Automatic sequencing of a file having more than one input tape, without operator intervention.

multistar network Data communications network in which several host computers are connected, and each host computer has its own star network of smaller computers.

multitasking The ability to execute more than one program at the same time on the same computer. The computer performs this task by rapidly switching its attention between the various tasks or programs.

multiuser Pertaining to computer systems that allow several users to share a computer's processor, memory, and mass storage simultaneously.

multiviewports Screen display that shows two or more viewing screens that are adjacent but independent.

multivolume file File so large that it requires more than one diskette, replaceable hard-disk cartridge, disk pack, or magnetic tape to hold it.

μP Abbreviation for microprocessor (μ is the Greek letter mu).

μs Abbreviation for microsecond, one millionth of a second (μ is the Greek letter mu). Same as μsec.

Musical Instrument Digital Interface (MIDI) A standard communications protocol for the exchange of information between computers and sound producing equipment, such as synthesizers.

musical language Method by which musical notation may be represented in code suitable for computer input. See computer music.

musicomp Compositional programming language that provides techniques for generating original musical scores as well as for synthesizing music.

music synthesizer Device that can be linked to a computer for recording music, playing music, and so on.

MUX Acronym for MUtipleXer.

MUMPS Acronym for Massachusetts General Hospital Utility Multi-Programming System, a high-level programming language designed specifically for handling medical records. The language is strong in data management and text manipulation features.

MVT Acronym for Multiprogramming with a Variable number of Tasks, the tasks being programs. (Also jokingly called Multiprogramming with a Vast amount of Trouble.)

mylar DuPont trademark for polyester film, often used as a base for magnetically coated or perforated information media, such as magnetic tape.

naive user Person who wants to do something with a computer but does not have the experience needed to program the computer.

NAK International transmission control code returned by a receiving terminal to signify that a frame of information has been received but is incorrect. Contrast with ACK.

name Alphanumeric term that identifies a program, a control statement, data areas, or a cataloged procedure.

name clashing In object-oriented programming, a conflict that can occur in multiple inheritance, when the same method or instance variable is inherited from multiple classes.

NAND Logical operator having the property that, if P is a statement, Q is a statement,... then the NAND of P, Q,... is true if at least one statement is false and false if all statements are true. Combination of NOT-AND. Compare AND, OR, NOR, and XOR.

nano Prefix meaning one billionth. Contrast with giga, one billion.

nanoacre One billionth of an acre, used figuratively to describe the area of an integrated circuit.

nanocomputer Computer capable of processing data in billionths of a second.

nanosecond One billionth of a second; one thousand-millionth of a second; abbreviated ns. Same as millimicrosecond. Light travels approximately one foot per nanosecond, electricity slightly less. The most powerful computers now being manufactured can carry out an instruction in less than a nanosecond. That is, such a machine can execute more than one billion instructions in one second!

Napier, John (1550-1617) Scottish aristocrat who made many contributions to mathematics and computing. Invented logarithms and a calculating device known as Napier's bones.

Napier's bones Set of numbering rods used to multiply, divide, and extract roots. The calculating rods were developed by John Napier in 1614 and used by William Oughtred in 1630 in the invention of the slide rule.

narrowband Pertains to a data communications system that handles low volumes of data at a low range of frequencies.

NASA Acronym for National Aeronautics and Space Administration.

National Computer Graphics Association (NCGA) Nonprofit organization dedicated to developing, promoting, and improving computer graphics applications in business, government, science, and the arts. NCGA brings together users and producers of computer graphics technology in a common, independent forum to share experience and knowledge. This exchange of ideas and viewpoints between the computer graphics industry and the creative people it serves identifies potential applications and spurs development of new technology. Holds an annual meeting that includes presentations, equipment exhibits, and art show.

National Crime Information Center (NCIC) An FBI computerized network of data related to crimes that have occurred throughout the United States. The network is used by law enforcement agencies throughout the U.S. and Canada.

National Educational Computing Conference (NECC) Annual meeting of educators interested in the use of computers in education.

National Software Testing Laboratory (NSTL) A software testing group, created to assist personal computer product manufacturers with real-world testing of software to aid in comparisons with other, similar products and to discover areas where improvements in product performance may be made.

native compiler Compiler that produces code usable only for a particular computer.

native language Computer language peculiar to the machines of one manufacturer. See machine language.

native mode (1) A computer that is running a program in its native machine language. (2) A computer that is running in its highest-performance state, such as the Intel 80386 microprocessor running in 32k-bit protected mode.

natural intelligence Intelligence derived from neural networks. The term was coined to emphasize the difference between artificial intelligence and the intelligence derived from neural networks.

natural language (1) The fifth generation of programming languages. These languages use human languages such as English, German or French to give people a more natural connection with computers. (2) Ordinary human language; unlike precisely defined computer languages, it is often ambiguous and is thus interpreted differently by different hearers.

natural language processing The study of strategies for computer programs to recognize and understand language in spoken and written form. A branch of artificial intelligence programming whose goal is to facilitate communications between humans and computers using written human language. Software that effects two-way translation between ordinary human language and a structure that computers understand.

NBS Acronym for National Bureau of Standards. Now called the National Institute of Standards and Technology. See NIST.

NCGA Acronym for National Computer Graphics Association.

N-channel MOS (NMOS) Circuit that uses current made up of negative changes. Has at least twice the speed but lower density than PMOS.

NCIC Acronym for the FBI's computerized National Crime Information Center, the heart of a large law enforcement network.

NCR Corporation A major manufacturer of computer equipment. In 1884, John Patterson purchased the National Manufacturing Company of Dayton, Ohio, and renamed it National Cash Register Corporation. In 1957, NCR Corporation introduced their first transistorized computer, the NCR 304. Throughout the years, NCR has continued to develop integrated point-of-sale and financial computer systems.

NCR paper Multiple-copy computer paper that produces copies without using carbon paper.

NCSN Acronym for National Computer Services Network, an organization formed to provide a voice for large and small third-party maintenance companies.

NDBMS Acronym for Network DataBase Management System.

NDRO Acronym for NonDestructive ReadOut. See nondestructive read.

near letter quality Printing produced by dot-matrix printers with 24-pin printheads.

NECC Acronym for the National Educational Computing Conference.

negate To perform the logical operator NOT.

negative true logic System of logic in which a high voltage represents the bit value 0 and a low voltage represents the bit value 1.

NEO Neochrome bitmap graphics format used by many programs for the Atari ST computer.

nerd Computer amateur. See geek.

nest A nest occurs when one program structure is placed inside another structure of the same type. For example, a loop can be contained in another loop.

nested block Program block inside another program block.

nested loop Loop that is contained within another loop.

nested subroutine Subroutine reached by a subroutine calling statement (such as GOSUB in the BASIC language) in another subroutine.

nesting Embedding program segments of blocks of data within other program segments or blocks of data. Algebraic nesting involves grouping expressions within parentheses, such as (W*X*(A-B)).

network (1) When two or more computers are connected to allow them to share the same software and information. Used primarily in businesses and schools. (2) System of interconnected computer systems and terminals. (3) Structure of relationships among a project's activities, tasks, and events. (4) A means of organizing data in artificial intelligence systems. A type of knowledge representation in artificial intelligence.

network analysis Listing of the components of a project network, with their start/end dates and float and dependency parameters.

network chart Chart that depicts time estimates and activity relationships.

network database Database that is similar to a hierarchical database, except that each child node may have more than one parent node.

network database management system (NDBMS) Collection of related programs for loading, accessing, and controlling a database. Data records are linked by a complex system of pointers that frequently must be updated.

network gateway Connection by which a local area network (LAN) may be linked to other LANs or to larger networks.

networking (1) Technique for distributing data processing functions through communications facilities. (2) Design of networks.

network interface card An adapter that enables you to hook a network cable directly to a microcomputer.

network management Software that controls Local Area Network access and network resources.

network operating system A control program that resides in a file server within a local area network. It handles the requests for data from all the users on the network.

network theory Systematizing and generalizing of the relationships among the elements of an electrical network.

network topologies Physical arrangements of nodes and interconnecting communication links in networks based on application requirements and geographical distribution of users. Patterns include star network, ring network, multidrop network, tree network, and mesh network. In practice, most networks are made up of some combination of these topologies.

neural-net computing Hardware or software systems that organize computer memory as in human brain cells.

neural network (1) A computer simulation of the brain. (2) Self-organizing systems of simple interconnected processing units which possess a learning rule and are capable of learning.

New Century Schoolbook An easily read typeface developed for textbooks and magazines. New Century Schoolbook often is offered as a built-in font in PostScript laser printers.

Newell, Alan and Herbert Simon Scientists who demonstrated that the computer could be used to study the mind. These pioneers in artificial intelligence initiated symbolic processing with computers.

new media Information delivery systems that combine media, such as text, graphics, voice, and video, using a microcomputer as the controlling framework.

newspaper columns A page format in which two or more columns of text are printed vertically on the page so that the text flows down one column and continues at the top of the next column.

Newton-Raphson Interactive procedure used for solving equations. See iterate.

NewWave An operating environment that provides an object-management shell facility allowing data from various different applications to be merged together to create a compound document.

NeXT Computer A UNIX-based computer system introduced in 1988 by NeXT, Inc. It includes a 68030 microprocessor, high-resolution (1120 x 832) graphics and a 256 MB erasable optical disc. NeXT, Inc. was founded in 1985 by Steven Jobs, co-founder and former chairman of Apple Computer, Inc.

NFS Acronym for Network File System. A portable (able to be moved from system to system) file-server system used mostly in UNIX workstation environments.

nibble Half of a byte, namely, four adjacent bits. Sometimes spelled nybble.

niladic Pertaining to an operation for which no operands are specified. Contrast with monadic.

nil pointer Pointer used to denote the end of a linked list.

nine's complement Numeral used to represent the negative of a given value. Obtained by subtracting each digit from a numeral containing all nines; for example, 567 is the nine's complement of 432 and is obtained by subtracting 432 from 999.

ninety-six column card Punched card used with card-handling equipment. Physically contains 18 rows and 36 columns, and three characters can be punched in each column.

NIST Acronym for National Institute of Standards and Technology. Formerly known as the National Institute of Standards. Its primary function is to promote maximum use of science and technology in the U. S. industry. Another function of NIST is to help define and promote standards for computer equipment and techniques.

nixie tube Vacuum tube used to display legible numbers.

NLP Acronym for Natural Language Processing, a discipline of study that attempts to develop systems that can communicate with humans using the natural language of the user.

NMOS Acronym for N-channel MOS.

node (1) Any terminal, computer or peripheral in a computer network. (2) Point in a tree structure where two or more branches come together. (3) Connecting point on a component, printed circuit board, or logic element where electrical connections can be made. (4) In computer graphics, an endpoint of a graphical element.

noise (1) Loosely, any disturbance tending to interfere with the normal operation of a device or system, including those attributable to equipment components, natural disturbance, or manual interference. (2) Spurious signals that can introduce errors. (3) Any unwanted signal.

noise immunity Device's ability to accept valid signals while rejecting unwanted signals.

noise pollution Noise, especially office noise, that distracts and cuts into productive work time, such as noise from printers, and copy machines.

nonconductor Substance through which electricity cannot pass. Contrast with semiconductor.

nondestructive read Read operation that does not alter the information content of the storage media.

nonerasable storage Storage device whose information cannot be erased during the course of computation, such as punched cards, and certain nondestructible readout magnetic memories.

nonexecutable statement Program statement that sets up a program but does not call for any specific action on the part of the program in which it appears. Contrast with executable statement.

nongraphic character Character that, when set for a printer or display unit, does not produce a printable character image, such as carriage control and upper case.

nonimpact printer Printer that uses electricity, heat, laser technology, or photographic techniques to print output. A printer that prints without striking the paper.

nonlinear programming Area of applied mathematics concerned with finding the values of the variables that give the smallest or largest value of a specified function in the class of all variables satisfying prescribed conditions. Contrast with linear programming.

nonnumeric programming Programming that deals with symbols rather than numbers. Usually refers to the manipulation of symbolic objects, such as words, rather than the performance of numerical calculations.

nonoverlap processing Technique whereby reading, writing, and internal processing occur only in a serial manner. Contrast with overlap processing.

nonprint Pertaining to an impulse that inhibits line printing under machine control.

nonprocedural language Language that states what task is to be accomplished but does not state the steps needed to accomplish it. For example, the computer language for interacting with a database. It specifies what the user wants to know rather than the steps needed to produce the information, which are worked out by the computer. See query language.

nonreflective ink Any color of ink recognizable to an optical character reader. Also called read ink.

nonsequential computer Computer that must be directed to the location of each instruction.

nonswitched line Communications link permanently installed between two points.

nonvolatile storage Storage medium that retains its data in the absence of power. Contrast with volatile storage.

no-op (NOP) Abbreviation of no-operation, as in no-operation instruction.

no-operation instruction Computer instruction whose only effect is to advance the instruction counter. Accomplishes nothing more than to advance itself to the next instruction in normal sequence.

NOP Acronym for No-OPeration. See no-operation instruction.

NOR Boolean operator that gives a truth table value of true only when both of the variables connected by the logical operator are false. Compare AND, OR, and XOR.

normalize (1) To adjust the exponent and fraction of a floating-point quantity so the fraction is within a prescribed range. (2) The breaking down of data into record groups for efficient processing in a relational database system.

Norris, William C. Norris, along with Seymour Cray and seven others founded Control Data Corporation (CDC) in 1957. The first computer produced by CDC was the CDC 1604, a large scientific computer. CDC went on to develop several other scientific computers: CDC 160, CDC 3600, CDC 6600, CDC 7600 and the CYBER line of mainframes. Norris guided the operations of CDC until his retirement in 1986.

Norton Utilities A package of utility programs for IBM-compatible micro-computers, including a benchmark program that measures a computer's throughput, an undelete program that restores files accidently deleted from the disk, management utilities for directories and subdirectories, and data security programs. These programs are designed to make computing easier. Useful for floppy and hard disk users. Developed by Peter Norton Computing, Inc.

NOT Logic operator having the property that, if P is a statement, then the NOT of P is true if P is false and false if P is true.

notation See Polish notation and positional notation.

notebook computer A small, self-contained, portable computer that will fit in an attache case. It usually weighs less than five pounds.

NOT gate Circuit equivalent to the logical operation of negation.

Novell A networking protocol very popular in IBM-oriented corporate environments

Noyce, Robert Developed, with Jean Hoerni, the planar process, in which circuit components are interconnected by photoengraving on a flat, polished wafer, usually silicon, at Fairchild Semiconductor in 1959. See Kilby, Jack.

NRZ Acronym for NonReturn to Zero, one of several methods for coding digital information on magnetic tape.

ns Abbreviation for nanosecond, one billionth of a second.

NSTL See National Software Testing Laboratory.

nucleus That portion of the control program that must always be present in internal storage.

null Pertaining to a negligible value or a lack of information, as contrasted with a zero or a blank that conveys information, such as a numerical value and a space between words. Empty.

null cycle Time required to cycle through an entire program without introducing new data.

null modem A small connection box for hooking up two computers, each of which expects to be linked up through a modem. In addition to crossing the main data wires so that one computer's output is the other's input, it also connects the proper hardware control lines to simulate the signals that a modem would provide when a complete connection had been made.

null string String with no characters. Also called empty string.

number (1) Symbol or symbols representing a value in a specific numeral system. (2) Loosely, a numeral.

number base See radix.

number crunching (1) The rapid processing of large quantities of numbers. Number crunching can be repetitive, mathematically complex, or both, and involves considerable internal processing. Parallel processing and the use of math coprocessors greatly enhance the ability of computers to perform these tasks. (2) A computer-based calculation performed by electronic spreadsheets.

number representation Representation of numbers by agreed sets of symbols according to agreed rules.

number system Agreed set of symbols and rules for number representation. Loosely, a numeral system.

numeral Conventional symbol representing a number; for example, 6, VI, and 110 are different numerals that represent the same number in different numeral systems.

numeralization Representation of alphabetic data through the use of digits.

numeral system Method of representing numbers. In computing, several numeral systems, in addition to the common decimal system, are of particular interest: the binary, hexadecimal, and octal systems. In each system, the value of a numeral is the value of the digits multiplied by the numeral system radix, raised to a power indicated by the position of the digits in the numeral. See positional notation.

numeric Pertaining to numerals or to representation by means of numerals. Compare alphanumeric.

numerical analysis Branch of mathematics concerned with the study and development of effective procedures for computing answers to problems.

numerical control Method of controlling machine tools through servomechanisms and control circuitry so the motions of the tools will respond to digital coded instructions on tape or to direct commands from a computer.

numerical indicator tube Any electron tube capable of visually displaying numerical figures.

numeric character Same as digit.

numeric coding Coding that uses only digits to represent data and instructions.

numeric constant Data using integers or real numbers. See constant.

numeric coprocessor A microprocessor support chip that performs mathematical computations in conjunction with the main microprocessor of a system. It works in tandem with another central processing unit to increase the computing power of a system.

numeric data Data that consists entirely of numbers.

numeric field A field that contains numbers used for calculations.

numeric keypad See keypad.

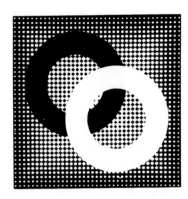

oasis Multiuser operating system used on several microcomputer systems.

Oasis An Apple Macintosh graphics program designed specifically to take advantage of input from a pressure sensitive digitizing tablet. It offers 18 brushes with pressure control, including its ArtistBrush that allows virtually any traditional or fine art medium to be replicated, including oil paint, water color, gouache, chalks, ink, pastels, magic marker, finger paint and charcoal. The brush uses pressure input to produce strokes and to control attributes such as wetness, dry-out speed and gradient. Used with a pressure-sensitive tablet, computer artists can create the look of traditional media.

obey Process whereby a computer carries out an operation as specified by one or more of the instructions forming the program currently being executed.

object (1) In computer graphics, a distinct entity. For example, a star might be an object in a graphics program. (2) A shorthand term for object code. (3) In object-oriented programming, a variable comprising both routines and data that is treated as a discrete entity. The primitive element in object-oriented programming. Something you can do things to. An object has state, behavior, and identity, the structure and behavior of similar object are defined in their common class.

object-based programming A method of programming in which programs are organized as cooperative collections of objects, each of which represents an instance of some type, and whose types are all members of a hierarchy of types united via other than inheritance relationships.

object code Executable machine language commands. The code, generated by a compiler or an assembler, that was translated from the source code of a program.

object computer Computer used for the execution of an object program.

object diagram Part of the notation of object-oriented design, used to show the existence of objects and their relationships in the logical design of a system.

object file   A file containing object code, usually the output of a compiler or an assembler.

object file graphic formats   See CDR, MacDraw, CEM, DFX, EPS, GEM, HPGL, HPC, PIC, PICT, SLD, WMF, and WPG. Contrast with bitmap file formats.

object identity   In object-oriented programming, something about an object that remains invariant across all possible modifications of its state. Can be used to point to the object.

Objective-C   An object-oriented programming language formed by adding Smalltalk inspired constructs to the C language.

object language   Output of a translation process. Usually, object language and machine language are the same. Synonymous with target language. Contrast with source language.

object language programming   Programming in a machine language executable on a particular computer.

object model   In object-oriented programming, the collection of principles that form the foundation of object-oriented design; a software engineering paradigm emphasizing the principles of abstraction, encapsulation, modularity, hierarchy, typing, concurrency, and persistence.

object module   Machine language version of a program.

object orientation   In object-oriented programming, a level of computer abstraction beyond that of procedures and data. Object orientation involves thinking about the world as a set of entities or objects that are related to and communicate with one another.

object-oriented analysis   In object-oriented programming, analysis of a system's requirements in terms of real-world objects.

object-oriented database   In object-oriented programming, a database that allows data to be stored as objects.

object-oriented decomposition   In object-oriented programming, the process of breaking a system into parts, each of which represents some class or object from the problem domain.

object-oriented design   In object-oriented programming, translating the logical structure of a system into a physical structure composed of software objects. A type of software design that adds greater emphasis to the design and abstraction of data structures than does top-down design.

object-oriented graphics   Computer graphics that are based on the use of "construction elements" such as curves, lines, and squares. Object-oriented graphics describe an image mathematically as a set of instructions for creating the objects in the image. Object-oriented graphics enable the user to manipulate objects as entire units. Because objects are described mathematically, object-oriented graphics can also be rotated, magnified and layered relatively easily. Object-oriented graphics can usually be displayed or printed at the full resolution of the monitor or output device, offering more precision than bit-mapped images.

object-oriented interface   A graphical interface that uses icons and a mouse, such as the Apple Macintosh Finder, Microsoft Windows on IBM-compatible microcomputers, or GEM environment on Atari ST and IBM-compatible microcomputers.

object-oriented language   A computer language that supports objects, classes, subclasses, methods, messages, and inheritance. Secondary features may include multiple inheritance, dynamic binding, and polymorphism.

object-oriented programming (OOP)   A programming technology that is generally more flexible and adaptable than standard programming. Object-oriented programming lets you create procedures about objects whose exact type is not known until run time. Xerox's Smalltalk was the first object-oriented language and was used to create the graphical user interface whose derivations and imitations are so popular today. C++ is an object-oriented programming language that combines traditional C programming with object-oriented features.

object program   Instructions that come out of the compiler or assembler, ready to run on the computer. Also called object code and target program. Contrast with source program.

object structure   In object-oriented programming, a set of graphs whose vertices represent objects and whose arcs represent relationships among those objects. An object diagram may represent all or part of the object structure of a system.

object table   A helpful tool for organizing objects in an object oriented program. It consists of a listing of the objects, their methods, and the use to which the objects will be put.

oblique   A style of text created by slanting a roman font to simulate italics when a true italic font doesn't exist on the computer or printer.

oblique axis   An axis that is placed at an angle to the margins of a page.

OCR   Acronym for Optical Character Recognition.

OCR-A   Standard typeface for optical characters.

octal   Pertaining to a number system with a radix of 8. Octal numerals are frequently used to represent binary numerals, with each octal digit representing a group of three binary digits (bits); for example, the binary numeral 111000010001101 can be represented as octal 70215.

octal numeral Numeral of one or more digits, expressing a sum in which the quantity represented by each figure is based on a radix of 8. The digits used in octal numerals are 0, 1, 2, 3, 4, 5, 6, and 7.

octet Byte composed of eight bits.

Odhner, W.T. A Swedish engineer, who in 1878 invented a calculating machine that was based on the "pinwheel" principle. Since then, many calculating machines have used the same principle.

OEM Acronym for Original Equipment Manufacturer, a company or organization that purchases computers and peripheral equipment for use as components in products and equipment that they subsequently sell to their customers.

office automation Application of computers and communications technology to improve the productivity of clerical and managerial office workers. Involves the integration of all information functions in the office, which include word processing, electronic mail, graphics, desktop publishing and data processing. The backbone of office automation is a local area network, which serves as a pathway between all users and computers.

office computer Usually, a microcomputer system for use in an office environment. Likely to include disk units, a printer, and software developed for specific office functions. A local area network is often used to connect users and computers.

office information system System that can include a variety of data entry terminals, word processors, graphics terminals, printers, and computer systems.

office of the future Office that makes extensive use of computers, data communications, and other electronic technologies. In such an office, numerous clerical, secretarial, and communications tasks are done automatically.

offline Pertaining to equipment, devices, or persons not in direct communication with the central processing unit of a computer. Equipment not connected to the computer. Contrast with online.

offline storage Storage not under control of the central processing unit.

offload (1) To transfer jobs from one computer system to another that is more lightly loaded. (2) To output data to a peripheral device.

offpage connector Pentagonal symbol used on a flowchart to link a line of flow on one page with its continuation on a different page.

offset Difference between the value or condition desired and that actually attained.

offset printing A widely used printing process in which a page is reproduced photographically on a metal or paper plate attached to a revolving cylinder. Ink is transferred from the plate to a rubber blanket from which it is transferred to paper.

off-the-shelf Pertaining to any standard, mass-produced hardware or software product readily available from the vendor.

omnifont The ability of an OCR program to recognize most fonts without the need to learn that font.

OMR Acronym for Optical Mark Recognition. A direct-entry method that senses the presence or absence of a mark, such as a pencil mark.

on-board computer Computer resident in another device. For example, a computer aboard a spacecraft.

on-board regulation Arrangement in which each board in a system contains its own voltage regulator.

on-demand report Report providing information in response to an unscheduled demand from a user.

one-address computer Computer that employs only one address in its instruction format.

one-address instruction Instruction consisting of an operation and exactly one address. In special cases, the instruction code of a single-address computer may include both zero and multiaddress instructions. Most present-day computers are of the one-address-instruction type.

one-chip computer Complete microcomputer that is implemented on a single chip.

one-dimensional array Array consisting of a single row or column of elements.

one-for-one (1) Phrase often associated with an assembler in which one source-language statement is converted to one machine-language instruction . (2) Most commonly used type of correspondence.

one-level memory Memory in which all stored items are accessed by a uniform mechanism.

one-pass compiler Language processor that passes through a source language program one time and produces an object module.

one's complement Numeral used to represent the negative of a given value. A one's complement of a binary numeral is obtained by alternating the bit configuration of each bit in the numeral. For example, 01100101 is the one's complement of the binary numeral 10011010.

onion diagram A graphical representation of a system that is made up of concentric circles. The innermost circle is the core, and all outer layers are dependent on the core.

online Pertaining to equipment, devices, and persons that are in direct communication with the central processing unit of a computer. Equipment physically connected to the computer. Contrast with offline.

online database Database that can be directly accessed by a user from a terminal, usually a visual display device.

online fault-tolerant system Computer system designed to function correctly in the presence of hardware failures.

online problem solving Teleprocessing application in which a number of users at remote terminals can concurrently use a computing system in solving problems online. Often, in this type of application, a dialogue or conversation is carried on between a user at a remote terminal and a program within the central computer system.

online storage Storage under control of the central processing unit.

on-screen help Operating assistance for applications that appear directly on the monitor, saving you the bother of looking them up in a manual.

on-screen pasteup A layout on a computer monitor.

on-the-fly-encryption Means that data is encrypted just before it is written to the disk, and decrypted after it has been read from the disk. Software for on-the-fly-encryption can be simple to use as it is often transparent to the user.

OODB Acronym for Object-Oriented DataBase.

OOP Acronym for Object-Oriented Programming.

OOSD Acronym for Object-Oriented Structural Design.

op Contraction of operation.

opacity Pertaining to the ease with which light passes through a sheet of paper, making it more or less translucent.

OPAL Acronym for Operational Performance Analysis Language. A data definition and manipulation language provided with the object-oriented database Gemstone.

op-code See operation code.

Opel, John In 1981, guided IBM Corporation into the microcomputer business. Under his leadership, IBM developed the IBM Personal Computer.

270

open   Process required to begin work with a file or document.

open architecture   (1) A computer or operating system design for which detailed specifications are published by the manufacturer, allowing others to produce compatible hardware and software. Personal computer design that allows additional circuit boards to be inserted in expansion slots inside the computer to support addons. (2) An architecture that allows integration with other languages, conventional software programs, and graphics user interfaces.

open-ended   Capable of accepting the addition of new programs, instructions, subroutines, modifications, terms, or classifications without disturbing the original system.

open file   File that can be accessed for reading, writing, or possibly both. Contrast with closed file.

open prepress interface   Developed by the Aldus Corporation, a system for automating the placement of color photographs, usually when sending desktop files to a high-end system.

open shop   Operation of a computer facility in which most productive problem programming is performed by each problem originator rather than by a group of programming specialists. Contrast with closed shop.

open subroutine   Subroutine inserted into a routine at each place it is used. Contrast with closed subroutine.

open system   A vendor-independent system that is designed to interconnect with a variety of products that are commonly available.

operand   Data unit or equipment item that is operated upon. Usually identified by an address in an instruction. In "ADD 100 TO 400," 100 and 400 are operands. See operation code.

operating ratio   See availability.

operating system (OS)   The master set of programs that manage the computer. Among other things, an operating system controls input and output to and from the keyboard, screen, disks, and other peripheral devices; loads and begins the execution of other programs; manages the storage of data on disks; and provides scheduling and accounting services.

Operating System/2   See OS/2.

operating system shell   Software that translates instructions entered by a personal computer user into commands to the operating system.

operation   (1) Any defined action. (2) Action specified by a single computer instruction or high-level-language statement. Abbreviated op.

operational management Supervisors or leaders responsible for operating details and the employees who perform them.

operation center Physical area containing the human and equipment resources needed to process data through a computer and produce desired output.

operation code Instruction code used to specify the operations a computer is to perform. In "ADD 100 TO 400," ADD is the operation code. See operand.

operations analysis Same as operations research.

operations personnel People responsible for controlling the equipment in a computer center. Operations personnel power up systems, load programs, run programs, report equipment malfunctions, and so on.

operations research Mathematical science devoted to carrying out complicated operations with the maximum possible efficiency. Includes such scientific techniques as linear programming, probability theory, information theory, game theory, Monte Carlo method, and queuing theory.

operator (1) In the description of a process, that which indicates the action to be performed on operands. See arithmetic operator. (2) Person who operates a machine. See computer operator.

optical character Character from a special set of characters that can be read by an optical character reader.

optical character reader Input device that accepts a printed document as input, identifying characters by their shape. See optical character recognition.

optical character recognition (OCR) Information processing technology that converts human-readable data in a special OCR font into another medium for computer input. Light reflected from characters is recognized by OCR equipment. The process by which text on paper is scanned and converted into text files in a computer.

optical communications Transmission of data, pictures, speech, or other information by light. An information-carrying light wave signal originates in a transmitter, passes through an optical channel, and enters a receiver, which reconstructs the original information. Optical fibers and lasers make up a technology that offers the maximum transmitting capacity using devices that occupy little physical space.

optical computer A type of computer, still largely experimental, that uses laser beams instead of wires to process information and works far faster than traditionally wired computers.

optical disc A large capacity storage device. Several types of optical discs are available: CD-ROM (compact disc, read-only memory), WORM (write once, read many) and erasable optical disc drives that let you write data as well as read it. Erasable optical discs are impervious to magnetic fields and can hold data for many years. This storage technology uses a laser beam to store large amounts of data at relatively low cost.

optical fiber   Thread of highly transparent glass that is pulsed very rapidly to carry a stream of binary signals. As well as carrying a high volume of data, optical fibers are immune to the electrical interference that can plague conventional cables. The use of optical fibers is rapidly becoming standard in computer communications.

optical laser disc   See optical disc.

optical mark reader   Input device that reads graphite marks on cards or pages.

optical mark recognition (OMR)   Information processing technology that converts data into another medium for computer input by the presence of a mark in a given position, each position having a value known to the computer that may or may not be understandable to humans.

optical media   A storage device that functions through principles of light. For example, optical discs, which belong to this category, uses light to store and retrieve information.

optical mouse   A mouse that uses reflected light to determine position and movement. Contrast with mechanical mouse.

optical page reader   Input device that accepts a page of printed matter.

optical printer   See electrostatic printer.

optical reader   See optical character reader and optical mark reader.

optical reader wand   Device that reads bar codes and enters appropriate information into a computer. See bar-code scanner.

optical recognition system   A system that converts optical characters, optical marks, bar codes and handwritten characters into electrical signals to be sent to the computer.

optical scanner   See optical character reader.

optical scanning   Any input method by which information is converted for machine processing by evaluating the relative reflectance of that information to the background on which it appears.

optimal merge tree   Tree representation of the order in which strings are to be merged so that a minimum number of move operations occurs.

optimization   In its most general meaning, the efforts and processes of making a decision, a design, or a system as nearly perfect, effective, or functional as possible. The attempt to seek the best possible solution for a given problem.

optimize To write a program or design a system in such a way as to improve performance.

optimizing compiler Compiler that attempts to correct inefficiencies in a program's logic to improve execution times, main storage requirements, and so forth.

optimum Best and most desirable in view of established criteria.

optimum programming Programming to maximize efficiency with respect to some criterion, such as least storage usage, least usage of peripheral equipment, or least computing time.

optimum tree search Tree search whose object is to find the best of many alternatives.

option key Modifier key on some keyboards. When held down, it gives a different interpretation to characters next typed. Special control key.

optoelectronic integrated circuit (OEIC) A computer chip that uses light instead of electrons and wire to transmit information. Its high-speed optical connections use less power and can be packed on a circuit board more densely than the copper wires and traces that carry signals from chips.

opto electronics Technology concerned with the integration of optics and electronics.

optomechanical mouse A type of mouse in which motion is translated into directional signals through a combination of optical and mechanical means.

ordinal number A number that identifies the sequence of an item, for example, file #21. Compare cardinal number.

OR See inclusive OR.

OR circuit See OR gate.

order (1) Arrangement of items according to any specified set of rules. (2) Command found in most electronic spreadsheet programs that permits the user to determine the order of calculation.

ordinate Y axis of a graph or chart. Contrast with abscissa.

organizational control Personnel administrative procedures implemented to protect an information system from infiltration, tampering, or sabotage.

organization chart Diagram showing the organization of a business (how responsibilities are divided within the business). Pictorial representation of the organizational hierarchy, showing the formal relationships among employees of an organization.

OR gate Computer circuit containing two switches whose output is a binary 1 if either or both of the inputs are binary. Implements the OR operator. Contrast with AND gate.

origin In coding, the absolute memory address of the first location of a program or program segment.

original data Data to be processed. Also called raw data.

original equipment manufacturer (OEM) Manufacturer who buys equipment from other suppliers and integrates it into a single system for resale.

originate/answer Pertaining to a modem that can both originate and answer messages. Most telecomputing services are in answer mode, so the user must be in originate mode.

OROM Short for optical read-only memory, meaning optical discs that have their data permanently embedded in them during manufacturing.

OR operator Logical operator having the property that if P is a statement and Q is a statement, then OR of P + Q is true if and only if at least one is true; false if all are false.

orphan (1) First line of a paragraph sitting alone at the bottom of a page of text. Considered undesirable in all forms of printing. (2) Personal computer that has been discontinued and is no longer supported by its manufacturer.

orthographic Type of layout, drawing, or map in which the projecting lines are perpendicular to the plane of the drawing or map.

OS Acronym for Operating System. A group of programs that control a computer and make it possible for users to enter and run their own programs. Some examples of OS are: MS-DOS, OS/2, System 7 and UNIX.

OS/2 A microcomputer operating system from Microsoft Corporation and IBM Corporation that allows multitasking by a single user. OS/2 was introduced in 1987. Several important OS/2 subsystems include Presentation Manager, which provides a graphical user interface, and LAN Manager, which provides networking facilities. OS/2 is designed for use on microcomputers based on Intel 80x86 processors: 80286, 80386 and 80486.

oscillating sort External tape sort that capitalizes on a tape drive's ability to read forward and backward.

oscilloscope Electronic instrument that produces a luminous plot on a flourescent screen, showing the relationship of two or more variables. Used by computer maintenance technicians.

OSI Acronym for Open Systems Interconnection. A networking standard for interconnecting disparate computer systems strongly supported by DEC.

Oughtred, William (1575-1660) English mathematician who invented the slide rule in 1630. See Napier's bones.

outdegree Number of directed edges leaving a node. Contrast with indegree.

outdent In word processing, a line of text that extends farther to the left than other lines in the same paragraph. Opposite of indentation.

outline font A font that is made up of basic outlines for each character. A printer or screen font in which a mathematical formula generates each character, producing a graceful and undistorted outline of the character, which the printer then fills in at its maximum resolution. You can scale outline fonts up and down without introducing distortions. Outline fonts are available as built-in fonts in many PostScript laser printers and as downloadable fonts provided on disk.

out-of-line Pertaining to statements in a computer program that are not in the main line of the program, such as closed subroutines.

output (1) Data transferred from a computer's internal storage unit to some storage or output device. (2) Final result of data that have been processed by the computer. Contrast with input.

output area Area of main storage reserved for output data. Contrast with input area.

output buffer Buffer used to transfer data to an external device.

output channel Channel that connects peripheral units and the central processing unit, and through which data may be transmitted for output.

output data Data to be delivered from a device or program, usually after some processing. Synonymous with output. Contrast with input data.

output device Unit used for taking out data values from a computer and presenting them in the desired form to the user, such as a printer or display screen.

output media Physical substance upon which output information is recorded, such as paper, magnetic disk, or magnetic tape. Compare input media and source media.

output stream Sequence of data to be transmitted to an output device.

outputting Process of producing useful information output.

overflow In an arithmetic operation, the generation of a quantity beyond the capacity of the register or storage location that is to receive the result.

overhead (1) Collective term for the factors that cause the performance of a program or device to be lower than it would be in the ideal case. (2)

Nonproductive effort that takes place when the operating system and programs are performing administrative tasks rather than productive work.

overlap   To do something at the same time that something else is being done; for example, to perform an input operation while instructions are being executed by the central processing unit. This approach permits the computer to work on several programs at once. See multiprogramming.

overlapping   Condition in which windows on a screen display are on top of one another, or overlap the borders of each other.

overlap processing   Simultaneous execution of input, processing, and output activities by a computer system. Contrast with nonoverlap processing.

overlay   (1) In desktop publishing, a sheet laid on top of another to specify spot colors for printing. (2) In programming, a portion of a program that is called into memory as needed, overlaying the previous redundant section of the program. Overlays allow writing programs that are much bigger than those which could fit into memory all at once.

overprint   Process of printing more than once at the same position in order to emphasize or improve the type. For example, to print an element of one color over one of another color.

override   To force a preexisting value to change in a program by superseding it.

overrun   Condition that occurs when data is transferred to or from a nonbuffered control unit with a synchronous medium and the activity initiated by the program exceeds the channel capacity.

overscan   Loss of text at the end of a line if the computer and monitor are not matched properly.

overstriking   Ability of a hard-copy printer to strike a character more than once to produce special effects: boldface characters, character with a line through it, etc.

overwrite   To place data in a location and destroy or mutilate the data previously contained in that location.

PABX Acronym for Private Automated Branch eXchange.

pack To store several short units of data into a single storage cell in such a way that the individual units can later be recovered; for example, to store two 4-bit BCD digits in one 8-bit storage location. Opposite of unpack.

package Program or collection of programs to be used by more than one business organization.

packaged software Software that is packaged and sold in stores and by mail order. The prepared package consists of the program on diskette(s), operating manual and possibly other documentation.

packaged system A fully integrated computer system that includes both hardware and software.

packet Block of data for data transmission. Contains control information—such as routing, address, and error control—as well as data.

packing Process of storing two numbers in a single storage byte.

packing density Number of useful storage cells per unit of area or length, such as the number of characters per inch.

pad (1) Area of plated copper on a printed circuit board that provides a contact for soldering component leads, means of copper-path transition from one side of the printed circuit board to the other, and contact for test probes. (2) To fill a data field with blanks.

pad character Buffer character used to fill a blank.

padding Technique used to fill out a fixed-length block of information with dummy characters, items, words, or records.

paddle A hand-held input device used to move the cursor on the display screen through the use of a dial. Paddles are commonly used in computer games.

page break (1) In word processing, the location where one page ends and another begins. (2) A special code placed in a document to mark the end of a page.

page composition Adding type to a layout.

page composition program A program for designing and producing professional looking documents. Also called a desktop publishing program.

page description language (PDL) A programming language with specialized instructions for describing how to print a whole page. If an application generates output in a page description language, the output can be printed on any printer that supports it.

page design The process of specifying the boundaries of text or graphics on a page. Includes choosing margins, page length, headings and footings.

page frame Location in the rear storage of the computer that can store one page.

page-in Process of swapping programs or data from disk storage to the computer's main storage.

page layout In publishing, the process of arranging text and graphics on a page.

page layout program In desktop publishing, an application program that assembles text and graphics from a variety of files, with which you can determine the precise placement, scaling, sizing, and cropping of material in accordance with the page design represented on-screen. Popular page layout programs are PageMaker, Quark XPress, and Ventura Publisher.

PageMaker A desktop publishing program for IBM-compatible and Apple Macintosh microcomputers. It was introduced in 1985 by Aldus Corporation. This program set the standard for desktop publishing. Paul Brainerd, president of Aldus, coined the term desktop publishing.

page makeup program A program for designing and producing professional looking documents. Also called desktop publishing program.

page-out Process of swapping programs or data from the computer's main storage to disk storage.

page preview A mode found on many page layout and word processing programs that shows a full-page view of how a page will look when printed out, including added elements such as headers, footers, and margins.

page printer Printer in which an entire page of characters is composed and determined within the device prior to printing. The most common example is a laser printer.

page reader Piece of optical scanning equipment that scans many lines of information, with the scanning pattern being determined by program control and/or control symbols intermixed with input data.

page recognition A program that recognizes the content of a printed page which has been scanned into the computer.

pages (1) Equal-size blocks into which a program is divided for storage. (2) Amount of text or graphic material displayed on a screen at one time.

page skip Control character that causes a printer to skip the rest of the current page and move to the top of the next page.

pagination (1) Electronic manipulation of graphics and blocks of type for the purpose of setting up an entire page. (2) Breakup of a printed report into units that correspond to pages. (3) Process of numbering or ordering pages.

paging (1) The process of keeping program pages on disk and calling them into memory as needed. (2) Technique for moving programs back and forth from real (internal) storage to virtual (auxiliary) storage.

paging rate In virtual storage systems, the average number of page-ins and page-outs per unit of time.

paint In computer graphics, the process of creating a graphic image (painting) on the display screen using a paint program and a mouse or graphics tablet.

paintbrush In computer paint programs, a tool used to sketch or paint brushstrokes of varying width and, in some cases, calligraphic or shadowing effects.

paintbrush software A program that generates drawings or illustrations.

paint file format A bit-mapped graphics file format found in paint programs such as Deluxe Paint, MacPaint, PC Paintbrush and SuperPaint.

painting (1) The process of displaying graphic data on a visual display screen. (2) In a paint program, filling a selected area with a solid color or pattern. (3) Displaying the trail of movements of a graphical input device.

Painting Effects An image editing/paint program for IBM-compatible microcomputer systems operating in MS-DOS. The program imports video or scanned images and can create different variations of the scanned or captured image.

paint program A program for creating and manipulating pixel images, as opposed to creating and manipulating object-oriented graphics. A paint program, because it treats a drawing as a group of dots (pixels), is particularly appropriate for freehand drawing. Paint programs create raster graphics images.

Palatino A serif typeface included as a built-in font with many PostScript laser printers.

palette (1) Set of available colors or patterns in a computer graphics system. (2) In a paint program, a collection of drawing tools, such as patterns, colors, different line widths, brush shapes, from which the user can choose.

palmtop A sublaptop portable computer weighing as little as one pound.

PAM Acronym for Pulse Amplitude Modulation, in which the modulation wave is caused to amplitude-modulate a pulse carrier.

pan (1) In computer graphics, to move (while viewing) to a different part of an image. (2) To move the cursor across a spreadsheet.

pane Term for each of the windows that result from splitting a single window.

panel See control panel and plugboard.

panning Movement of displayed graphic data across a visual display screen. Moving a graphic image inside a frame to see its various sections.

Pantone Matching System (PMS) Specific ink color specifications widely used in printing and color graphics. An extensive catalog of Pantone colors are available which describe about 500 colors; each assigned a unique PMS number. The Pantone color-selection system is supported by a variety of high-end illustration programs. A color system standardized by the Pantone Corporation.

paper feed Method by which paper is pulled through a printer. See friction-feed and tractor-feed mechanism.

Papert, Seymour Created the computer language LOGO with the collaboration of other computer scientists, teachers and students. Papert created LOGO in hopes that eventually children will become as comfortable with computers as they are with pencils. To carry out LOGO commands, he invented the turtle, "an object to think with."

paper tape Continuous strip of paper in which holes are punched to record numerical and alphanumerical information for computer processing. Paper tape is used in older computer systems, and has been replaced by newer and more efficient storage methods.

paradigm Fundamental conception that underlies a possible complex structure. Central kernel within a concept. New paradigms result in new conceptions. Popular buzzword among computer designers; the original Greek word meant merely an example, or pattern.

Paradox A relational database management system for IBM-compatible microcomputers.

paragraph Set of one or more COBOL sentences making up a logical processing entity and preceded by a paragraph header or name.

paragraph assembly Process in which a document is assembled on a word processor from paragraphs stored on disks.

parallel (1) Handling all the elements of a word or message simultaneously. Contrast with serial. (2) In computer graphics, it describes lines or planes in a graphics file that are an equal distance apart at every corresponding point.

parallel access Process of obtaining information from, or placing information into, storage where the time required for such access is dependent on the simultaneous transfer of all elements of a word from a given storage location. Also called direct access. Contrast with serial access.

parallel adder Adder that performs its operations by bringing in all digits simultaneously from each of the quantities involved. Contrast with serial adder.

parallel circuit Electric circuit in which the elements, branches, or components are connected between two points with one of the two ends of each component connected to each other.

parallel computers Computers that have multiple processors and are able to perform many mathematical operations and decisions at the same time. Unlike conventional supercomputers, which work on problems sequentially, massively parallel processing computers harness the computing power of hundreds or more microprocessors to tackle different parts of a problem at once. Super fast, high-performance parallel computers are being used for such tasks as running simulations of global warming and searching through massive volumes of radio-telescope data for the faint and complex signatures of binary pulsars.

parallel conversion Process of changing to a new data processing system that involves running both the old and new systems simultaneously for a period of time. Also called parallel run. Contrast with direct conversion. Compare phased conversion.

parallel input/output Data transmission in which each bit has its own wire. All of the bits are transmitted simultaneously, as opposed to being sent one at a time (serially). Contrast with serial input/output.

parallel interface Equipment boundary where information is transferred simultaneously over a set of paths. Contrast with serial interface.

parallel operation Performance of several actions, usually of a similar nature, simultaneously through the provision of individual, similar, or identical devices for each such action. Contrast with serial operation.

parallel port Portion of computer through which a parallel device (such as a printer) can communicate with the computer.

parallel printer Printer that receives information from the computer one character (letter, number, etc.) at a time through eight wires. Additional wires are used to exchange control signals. A parallel printer is designed to be connected to the computer's parallel port.

parallel processing (1) The technique by which all levels of a process are carried out simultaneously. Contrast with serial processing. (2) A method of processing that can run only on a type of computer containing two or more processors running simultaneously. (3) A procedure that consists of the breaking down of a problem into separate components so that the computer program and the computer can work on each component of the problem simultaneously.

parallel processor A computer that is capable of performing multiple operations at the same time.

parallel run Process of running a new system or program in parallel with the old system to ensure a smooth transition and error-free conversion. Same as parallel conversion.

parallel transmission In data communications, a method of data transfer in which all bits of a character are set simultaneously. Contrast with serial transmission.

parameter (1) Any arbitrary constant, especially one characteristic or even definitive of a given system. (2) Variable in an algebraic expression that temporarily assumes the properties of a constant. For example, in $y = mx+b$, m and b are parameters if either is treated as a constant in a family of lines.

parameterized class In object-oriented programming, a class that serves as a template for other classes, in which the template may be parameterized by other classes, objects, and/or operations.

parametric Pertaining to the technique by which a line, curve, or surface is defined by equations based on some independent variable. Used often in computer-aided design systems.

parasitic virus A type of computer virus which attaches itself to another program and is activated when that program is executed. A parasitic virus can either append itself to the end of a program (in which case the program functionality is normally preserved) or overwrite a part of the program (in which case the program functionality is destroyed).

PARC Acronym for Palo Alto Research Center. An advanced research and development arm of the Xerox Corporation which developed many of the underlying techniques for Smalltalk and graphical user interfaces.

parent File whose contents are required, and in some cases are the only sources of information available, to create new records. See child.

parent/child relationship Passing of information from one generation to the next. Older information (parent) is necessary to create new information (child).

283

parentheses Grouping symbol ( ). In arithmetic calculations, operations in parentheses are treated as entities with the highest priority. See order of operations.

parent node A node one level above the node being considered in a hierarchical database or network.

parity bit Extra bit added to a byte, character, or word to ensure that there is always either an even number or an odd number of bits, according to the logic of the system. If through a hardware failure, a bit should be lost in transmission, its loss can be detected by checking the parity. The same bit pattern remains as long as the contents of the byte, character, or word remain unchanged.

parity checking Automatic error detection by using checking bits along with the data bits. See parity bit.

park To position a hard drive's read/write head so that the drive is not damaged while being transported.

Parkinson's Law The task expands to meet the time available for its completion.

parse To break input into smaller pieces so that a program can act upon the information.

parser Program or subroutine that analyzes and understands statements. See Intellect.

parsing (1) Process of separating statements into syntactic units. (2) Analyzing a character string and breaking it down into a group of more easily processed components.

partition (1) Area in memory assigned to a program during its execution. (2) Division of a hard disk. The separate partitions can be used as if they are separate hard disks.

partitioning (1) Subdividing a computer storage area into smaller units allocated to specific jobs or tasks. (2) Breaking up a problem into subtasks.

parts explosion Drawing of all the pieces composing an assembly that illustrates the relation of the pieces to one another.

parts list Collection of the quantities, names, and numbers of all parts used to produce a manufactured item. Most CAD/CAM systems maintain and update such lists automatically during the course of a design and manufacturing process.

parts programmer Programmer who translates the physical explanation for machining a part into a series of mathematical steps and then codes computer instructions for those steps. See APT and numerical control.

party-line Used to indicate a large number of devices connected to a single line originating in the central processing unit.

Pascal High-level structured programming language that has gained wide acceptance as a tool for both applications programming and system development. Pascal was developed in the early 1970s by Niklaus Wirth. Pascal was named after the French mathematician Blaise Pascal. The language provides a flexible set of control structures and data types to permit orderly, top-down program design and development. Pascal is used extensively in the educational field for teaching programming principles and practices. See Turbo Pascal.

Pascal, Blaise (1623-1662) French mathematician who built the first desk-calculator-type adding machine in 1642.

Pascal's calculator First desk-calculator-type adding machine, designed by Blaise Pascal in the seventeenth century. Represented the digits from 0 to 9 with teeth on gears and could perform addition and subtraction.

pass (1) Complete input, processing, and output cycle in the execution of a computer program. (2) Scanning of source code by a compiler or assembler.

passive device Device that passes signals without altering them.

passive graphics Computer graphics operation that transpires automatically and without operator intervention.

password Special word, code, or symbol that must be presented to the computer system to gain access to its resources. Used for identification and security purposes on a computer system. Each user is assigned a specific set of alphanumeric characters to gain entrance to the entire computer system or to parts of the system. Also called lock code.

paste To place information previously cut from a document into a new position. With some computer systems, areas of text or graphics may be cut from a document, saved, and later pasted into another document. See cut-and-paste.

pasteboard In desktop publishing, the work area displayed on a screen upon which art and text will be placed.

patch (1) Section of coding inserted into a program to correct a mistake or to alter the program (2) Temporary electrical connection. (3) In computer graphics, a piece of curvilinear surface, typically with three or four sides. These are attached together at their edges with at least first-order continuity to form complex 3-D surfaces. The edges of a patch are frequently described with polynomials or ratios of polynomials. For example, if both dimensions are described with cubic polynomials, then the patch is said to be bicubic. If ratios of cubic polynomials are used, then the patch is a rational bicubic patch. Although difficult to deal with, one patch can take the place of hundreds of flat polygons and thus greatly reduce the size of a database. (4) To modify a computer system by adding post-installation enhancements. Usually done by a customer engineer.

patching (1) Makeshift technique for modifying a program or correcting programming errors by changing the object code of the program, usually to avoid recompiling or reassembling the program. (2) Making temporary patches to hardware.

patent The legal protection granted by the Patent Office for exclusive use of an original idea or invention.

path (1) A route from one point to another. (2) In computer graphics, an accumulation of line segments or curves, to be filled or overwritten with text. (3) Hierarchy of files through which control passes to find a particular file.

pattern matching The search for similarities between symbolic expressions; i.e., matching a pattern with images or templates in a database.

pattern recognition (1) Recognition of forms, shapes, or configurations by automatic means. A subfield of artificial intelligence. (2) Using a computer to identify patterns. (3) The use of statistical techniques and templates to process and classify patterns of data.

Patterson, John Henry Founder of the National Cash Register (NCR) Company, a manufacturer of cash registers and later, computer equipment. Patterson shaped the thinking of Thomas Watson, Sr., who later became the guiding director of the IBM Corporation.

PC Acronym for Personal Computer, Pocket Computer, Printed Circuit, and Program Counter. The most common use of PC is to refer to IBM Corporation's Personal Computer line. Thus, for example, PC-compatible refers to a computer that can run the same programs as IBM PC or IBM PS/2 microcomputers.

PCB Acronym for Printed Circuit Board, the plastic board into which a computer's various electronic components are soldered. These are linked by thin interconnecting wires printed on its surface.

PC compatibility Refers to a microcomputer that is compatible in some way with the popular IBM Personal Computer and IBM PS/2. Many levels of compatibility are possible.

PC-DOS Acronym for Personal Computer—Disk Operating System. IBM Corporation's trade name for its version of MS-DOS, an operating system developed and licensed by Microsoft Corporation for computers that use Intel Corporation microprocessors. There is effectively no difference between PC-DOS and MS-DOS.

P-channel MOS (PMOS) Relatively old metallic oxide semiconductor technology for large scale integration devices. See PMOS. Contrast with N-channel MOS.

PCM Acronym for Plug Compatible Manufacturer, a business that makes computer equipment that can be plugged into existing computer systems without requiring additional hardware or software interfaces.

p-code Method of translating a source code to an intermediate code, called p-code, by means of a compiler, then using a special p-code interpreter on a host machine to obtain an executable object code. Several versions of Pascal use p-code.

PC Paint A popular painting program for microcomputers, developed by Mouse Systems Corporation.

PC Paintbrush A popular paint program for IBM-compatible microcomputers. Virtually every paint program for the IBM-compatible microcomputers is in some way a subset of Paintbrush. The industry standard PCX graphic format is a product of Paintbrush. Paintbrush creates, refines and retouches images. It includes image editing, automatic text effects, and 256 on-screen colors. The program also offers the capability to blend, smudge, and add gradient flood fills. The program can control many black and white gray-scale, or color scanned images. Aside from normal draw/paint tools, other features include image capture software, outline bit-mapped fonts, and built-in scanner and pre-scan controls.

PCX A bitmapped graphics file format, originally developed for the PC Paintbrush paint program and now used by many other programs.

PDL Acronym for Page Description Language. A standardized coding system that presents all the elements on a page—type, images and graphics, using the same descriptive metaphors. Common PDLs are PostScript, Apple Computer's QuickDraw and Hewlett Packard's HPGL. PostScript has become the default standard for most desktop systems and PostScript interpreters are designed to convert the others to PostScript.

PDM Acronym for Pulse Duration Modulation, pulse time modulation in which the duration of a pulse is varied. Contrast with PAM and PPM.

PDP Designation for older minicomputers manufactured by Digital Equipment Corporation, such as PDP-8, PDP-10, and PDP-11. PDP is an acronym for Programmed Data Processor.

PEEK Computer-language instruction that allows the programmer to look at (peek at) any location in a computer's programmable memory. See POKE.

pel Picture element. See pixel.

pen plotter See plotter and drum plotter. Contrast with electrostatic plotter.

perform To execute instructions in a computer.

performance Major factor in determining the total productivity of a system. Largely determined by a combination of availability, throughput, and response time.

performance monitor   Program that keeps track of service levels being delivered by a computer system.

perfory   Detachable perforated strips on the two sides of fanfold computer paper.

perfs   Perforations in paper to facilitate removing pin-feed edges and tearing continuous paper into separate pages.

periodic report   Report that provides information to users on a regular basis, such as weekly, monthly, or yearly.

peripheral equipment   Input/output units and auxiliary storage units of a computer system, attached by cables to the central processing unit. Used to get data in and data out, and to act as a reservoir for large amounts of data that cannot be held in the central processing unit at one time. The laser printer, hard disk and optical scanner are examples of peripherals.

peripheral equipment operator   In a busy computer room, the computer operator is assigned to the console and rarely leaves it. Additional people assist by mounting a demounting disk packs and tapes, labeling outputs, and operating the various input/output devices as directed. These people are usually called peripheral equipment operators.

peripheral slots   Empty slots built into the housing of some computers so printed circuit cards can be added to increase capabilities without hardware modification. Motherboard sockets into which circuit boards can be plugged.

permanent storage   Same as storage.

persistence   (1) In computer graphics, the rate of decay of luminance of a CRT display after the stimulus is removed. In essence, the "staying power" of a lighted phosphor to dim more slowly. (2) In object-oriented programming, the permanence of an object, particularly relevant in the context of object-oriented databases, which maintain a distinction between objects created only for the duration of execution and those intended for permanent storage. Persistence is one of the fundamental elements of the object model. (3) In artificial intelligence, the length of time data are kept during a program run.

personal computer   The smallest and least expensive class of computer. A computer designed for use by one person at a time. Abbreviated PC. Also called a microcomputer.

personal computing   Use of a personal computer by individuals for applications such as entertainment, home management, education, word processing, and family business.

personal identification number (PIN) Security number that computer systems sometimes require before a user can access the system or before a point-of-sale terminal user can enter or receive information. Commonly used with automatic teller machines.

personalized form letter Computer-generated form letter produced by a word processing system or a merge-print program.

perspective view In computer graphics, a display method by which an illusion of depth is achieved on a two-dimensional surface and by which the space depicted is organized from one point of view.

PERT Acronym for Program Evaluation and Review Technique, a management technique for control of large-scale, long-term projects, involving analysis of the time frame required for each step in a process and the relationships of the completion of each step to activity in succeeding steps. See critical path method. Compare GERT.

PERT chart Diagram representing the interdependencies of work elements against time, typically shown graphically as circles and connecting lines.

Pet computer A low-cost, versatile computer from Commodore Business Machines, Inc. introduced in 1977. The Pet 4032 was designed for personal, educational, and scientific applications. It was one of the earliest personal computers, weighed 46 pounds, and featured 32K bytes of RAM and 18K bytes of ROM.

petri nets Popular and useful model for the representation of systems with concurrency or parallelism.

PFS: First Choice A program that combines five powerful business productivity tools. It is an integrated software program that includes word processing, a database manager, a spreadsheet program, a business graphics program, and an electronics communications program.

PFS: First Publisher An entry-level desktop publishing program for people who want to create newsletters, memos, fliers, and reports. PFS: First Publisher directly reads files from most popular word processing programs and supports a wide variety of printers.

PGA Acronym for Professional Graphics Adapter, a type of display adapter for IBM-compatible microcomputers.

phantom disk A chip that lets the computer regard part of its memory as another disk drive.

phased conversion Method of system implementation in which the old information system is gradually replaced by the new one. Compare parallel conversion. Contrast with direct conversion.

phonemes Distinct sounds that make up human speech (speech utterances such as lk, ch, and sh). Smallest components of speech. The basic sounds of human speech.

phonemics Rules describing variations in pronunciation that occur when spoken words are run together.

phonetic system System that uses data based on voice information (phonemes) to produce sounds that emulate speech.

phonology The analysis of sounds that are synthesized to produce speech.

phosphor Rare earth material used to coat the inside face of cathode ray tubes. Holds the light generated by a monitor's electron guns. Each dot on the screen is actually a phosphor that glows for a given length of time. The dots are used to create an image.

phosphor burn-in What occurs when the same image is left on the screen for extended periods of time, burning itself in so the image can be seen even when the monitor is turned off.

photocomposition Application of electronic processing to the preparation of print. Involves the specification and setting of type, and its production by a photographic process. In desktop publishing, the use of laser printers and imagesetters to accomplish the same ends.

photoelectric devices Devices that give an electrical signal in response to visible, infrared, or ultraviolet radiation.

photolithographic process The procedure used to print the mask pattern of integrated circuits on a silicon wafer.

PhotoMac A Macintosh graphics program from Avalon Development that is designed for manipulating and color separating scanned images. The program features many powerful separation controls. Like all color separation programs, PhotoMac produces four separate versions of a page.

photonic integrated circuit A system that uses light as well as electrons to process information.

photonics The science of building machine circuits that use light instead of electricity.

Photon Paint A paint program intended for Macintosh II computer systems equipped with a color card.

photo-optic memory Memory that uses an optical medium for storage. For example, a laser might be used to record on photographic film. See optical disc.

photo-pattern generation Production of an integrated circuit mask by exposing a pattern of overlapping or adjacent rectangular areas.

photo plotter Output device that generates high-precision artwork masters photographically for printed circuit board design and integrated circuit masks.

photorealism The process of creating images that are as close to photographic quality as possible. In computer graphics, photorealism requires powerful computers and highly sophisticated software and is heavily mathematical.

photoresist Process, utilized in etching semiconductor devices, of selectively removing the oxidized surface of a silicon wafer by masking the part that is to be retained.

Photoshop This powerful and versatile 24-bit image processing program, for the Apple Macintosh computer, can be used as a paint, prepress, color correction and darkroom system. Designers can work with scanned photos, slides, electronic artwork or create original graphics using a full range of filters, painting, drawing and selection tools. It includes sophisticated image manipulation tools, anti-aliased text in any size and resolution and EPS graphics support.

phototypesetter Computer-controlled device that converts text into professional-quality type. A printer similar to a laser printer, but capable of resolutions over 2000 dpi. See imagesetter.

physical design Refers to how data is kept on storage devices and how it is accessed.

physical format The general pattern of magnetic pulses and tracks on a disk or other medium, ignoring what those pulses mean when translated into digital 1s and 0s. Two computers using the same physical format can read each other's disks, but if their logical formats are not the same, they may not be able to make sense of the information.

physical record A collection of logical records. Also called a block.

physical schema The description of how data are physically stored on a disk.

physical security Guards, badges, locks, alarm systems, and other measures to control access to the equipment in a computer center.

pi The ratio of the circumfrence of any circle to its diameter, approximately equal to 3.14159265358979... Its expansion is now known to over 1073 million decimal places.

PIC Acronym for PICture File Format, a graphics file format used by some spreadsheet and graphing programs for IBM-compatible microcomputers.

pica (1) A unit of measure used in typography. A pica is one sixth of an inch, or equivalent to 12 points. (2) A character font that has a print density of 10 characters per inch.

picking device Input device, such as a light pen, mouse, or joystick, used to enter data on a display screen.

291

pico Prefix meaning one-trillionth.

picocomputer Computer capable of processing data in trillionths of a second.

picosecond One trillionth of a second; one thousandth of a nanosecond; abbreviated psec.

PICT Acronym for PICTure file format, a black-and-white object/bit mapped format used by many programs for the Apple Macintosh line of microcomputers and by some programs for the IBM-compatible microcomputers.

PICT2 Acronym for PICTure file format 2, a graphics file format used in many programs for the Apple Macintosh line of microcomputers that can support both black-and-white and color images.

picture graph Bar graph that uses symbols instead of bars.

picture processing (1) In computer graphics, method for processing pictorial information by a computer system. Involves inputting graphic information into a computer system, storing it, working with it, and outputting it to an output device. (2) In artificial intelligence, the transformation of an input image into a second image, which has important properties that will help in better understanding the scene.

Picture Publisher A graphics program that allows you to work with scanned images. You can adjust contrast, brightness, gray map, and other parameters and edit the image on a pixel-by-pixel basis. Image processing choices let you sharpen, blur, or posterize the image.

pie chart Graphical representation of information; charting technique used to represent portions of a whole.

piezoelectric Property of some crystals that undergo mechanical stress when subjected to voltages, or that produce a voltage when subjected to mechanical stress.

piggyback board Small printed circuit board mounted on a larger circuit board to add additional features to the larger circuit board.

piggyback file File capable of having records added at the end, without having to recopy the entire file.

PILOT Textually based computer language originally designed as an author language for computer-assisted instruction. Also used for teaching computer programming to beginners. Composed of powerful and nearly syntax-free conversation-processing statements. PILOT was developed in 1968 by John Starkweather at the University of California.

pilot system Act of trying a new computer system in one area rather than on a wider range of activities. For example, the implementation of a new information system into an organization whereby only a small part of the business uses the new system until it has proved to be successful. The objective of a pilot system is to define the operational requirements, benefits, and risks, prior to enlarging the project and making a major investment.

pin Connection point on a component, printed circuit board, or logic element, where electrical connections can be made.

PIN Acronym for Personal Identification Number.

pin compatible Pertaining to chips and devices that perform identical functions and can be substituted for one another. The devices use the same pins for the same input/output signals.

pin-feed Paper-feed system that relies on a pin-studded roller to draw paper, punched with matching sprocket holes, into a printer. See tractor-feed mechanism. Contrast with friction-feed.

pingpong To alternate two or more storage devices so processing can take place on a virtually endless set of files.

pins Small metal connectors on a DIP that fit into sockets on a printed circuit board.

pipeline processing Overlapping operating cycle function used to increase the speed of computers. Involves decomposing a computer instruction in parts so it can be executed simultaneously. The connection of processors so that the output of one processor becomes the input of another processor.

piracy Either theft, as in the appropriation of a computer design or a program, or unauthorized distribution and use of a computer program.

pitch Density of characters on a printed line, usually expressed in terms of characters per inch; for example, 10 pitch means that 10 characters are printed in every inch.

pixel Short for "picture element," a picture cell; a single dot on the computer display screen. The visual display screen is divided into rows and columns of tiny dots, squares, or cells, each of which is a pixel. Smallest unit on the display screen grid that can be stored, displayed, or addressed.

pixel graphics A technique for representing a picture image as a matrix of dots.

pixel image The representation of a color graphic in a computer's memory.

PixelPaint Professional A popular Apple Macintosh paint program. Features and capabilities include the ability to create a masking tool from any brush, tool, or image. A WetPaint feature allows repositioning and editing of any shape or text before merging it with the rest of the bit map. A gradient editor creates precise color ramps with multiple anchor points. A unique feature of PixelPaint that creates surface textures such as charcoal paper, linen, concrete, canvas and slate; other textures can be scanned in. File formals supported include MacPaint, PICT, TIFF and EPSF. Artwork can be printed to PostScript or QuickDraw printers or produced as 4-color or spot color separations.

PLA Acronym for Programmable Logic Array, an alternative to ROM that uses a standard logic network programmed to perform a specific function. Implemented in either MOS or bipolar circuits. See FPLA.

plaintext The opposite of ciphertext. It comprises text or data in normally readable form rather than encrypted.

planar (1) In computer graphics, a term applied to objects lying within a plane. (2) In the fabrication of chips, planar refers to a processing method used to create silicon-based transistors.

PLANIT Acronym for Programming LANguage for Interactive Teaching, a language designed for use with computer-assisted instruction systems.

plansheet Same as spreadsheet, worksheet.

plasma display panel Type of VDT utilizing trapped neon/argon gas. The image is created by turning on points in a matrix (energized grid of wires) comprising the display surface. The high-resolution image is steady, long-lasting, bright, and flicker-free; selective erasing is possible.

plasticity The degree of flexibility available in artificial intelligence programs.

plate A thin, flexible sheet of metal, paper, or plastic used in offset printing. It contains a photographic reproduction of the page being printed.

platen A backing, commonly cylindrical, against which printing mechanisms strike to produce an impression, such as the roller in a printer against which the keys strike.

PLATO Acronym for Programmed Logic for Automatic Teaching Operations, a computer-based instructional system developed by Donald Bitzer and marketed by Control Data Corporation. PLATO typically runs on large computer systems and combines graphics and text with touch-screen display terminals to provide course instruction in many different disciplines. PLATO was the first system to combine graphics and touch-sensitive screens for interactive training. PLATO programs use artificial intelligence methodology. PLATO programs have been used in genetics, rocketry, natural language, lesson planning, and math tutoring.

platter That part of a hard disk drive that actually stores the information. A round, flat, metallic plate covered on both surfaces with a brown magnetic substance. See hard disk.

PL/C Version of the PL/I programing language, designed to be used in an educational environment.

PL/I High-level general-purpose language designed to process both scientific and business applications. Contains many of the best features of FORTRAN, COBOL, ALGOL, and other languages, as well as a number of facilities not available in previous languages. PL/I was introduced in 1964 by the IBM Corporation.

PL/M Programming language used to program microcomputers, developed by Intel Corporation. High-level language that can fully command the microcomputer to produce efficient run-time object code. Derived from PL/I, a general-purpose programming language, and usually implemented as a cross-compiler.

plot To diagram, draw, or map with a plotter. To create an image by drawing a series of lines.

plotter An output device that draws images with ink pens. A plotter draws images as a series of point-to-point lines.

plotting a curve Locating points from coordinates and connecting these points with a curve that approximates or resembles the actual curve that pictures the relationship existing between variables.

PLT Abbreviation for plotter, a peripheral device for providing output of graphs and technical drawings.

plug Connector on a cable that goes to a jack on a part of the system.

plug compatible Peripheral device that requires no interface modification to be linked directly to another manufacturer's computer system.

plug compatible manufacturer (PCM) A business that makes computer equipment that can be plugged into existing computer systems without requiring additional hardware or software interfaces.

PMOS Acronym for P-channel MOS, the oldest type of MOS circuit, in which the electrical current consists of a flow of positive charges. Contrast with N-channel MOS.

PMS See Pantone Matching System.

PN Acronym for Polish Notation.

poaching Accessing files or program listings in search of information to which the user is not entitled.

pocket computer Portable, battery-operated, hand-held computer that can be programmed in BASIC to perform a wide number of applications. Able to process small amounts of data under the control of complex stored programs. Pocket computers can be plugged into a personal computer for data transfer.

point (1) Typographic measurement equaling approximately 1/72 inch. Abbreviated pt. (2) Smallest unit of graphic information, representing a single location on a coordinate system.

point and click To position the cursor over an object displayed on the screen (point) and press the mouse or pointing device to select it (click).

pointer (1) An indicator on a screen that shows where the next user computer interaction will be. Also called cursor. (2) Address or other indication of one storage location as held in another storage location. Used in a network database to point to related records in the same or different files. (3) A device such as a mouse or tablet stylus that moves the cursor on the screen. (4) The additional connections in a network database between parent nodes and child nodes. (5) A variable that holds the address of another memory object.

pointer tool A tool used in layout and drawing programs to select objects or an entire block of text. It is usually represented by an on-screen arrow.

point identification Complete description of a graphics point, including its coordinate location and any special processing functions implied by it.

pointing device An input device, such as a mouse or graphics tablet, that is used to move the cursor on the display screen

point set curve Curve defined by a series of short lines drawn between points.

point size The vertical measurement of type, roughly equivalent to the distance between the highest ascender and lowest descender, plus a small bit of breathing room on top and bottom.

point-to-point line Communications system configuration consisting of a direct line between the host computer and a remote terminal. Either leased lines or switched lines may be used. Contrast with multidrop line.

Poisson theory Mathematical method for estimating the number of lines needed to handle a given amount of data communications traffic.

POKE Computer-language instruction used to place a value (poke) into any location in the computer's programmable memory. See PEEK.

POL Acronym for Procedure-Oriented Language or Problem-Oriented Language.

polar Pertaining to a situation in which binary 1 is represented by current flow in one direction and binary 0 by current flow in the opposite direction. Contrast with positive true logic.

polar coordinates Graphic system for specifying the location of a point by reference to an angle and a distance from a fixed point. Contrast with Cartesian coordinate system.

polarizing filter   Accessory for terminal screens to reduce glare.

Polish notation (PN)   Logical notation for a series of arithmetic operations in which no grouping symbol is used. Form of prefix notation developed by Polish logician Jan Lukasiewicz in 1929. Contrast with reverse Polish notation.

polling   Communications control method used by some computer/terminal systems whereby a host station asks many devices attached to a common transmission medium in turn, whether they have information to send. Contrast with addressing.

polygon   A multi-sided object.

polyline   In computer graphics, a line consisting of multiple connected segments.

polymorphism   (1) In object-oriented programming, the ability of the same message to be interpreted differently when received by different objects. (2) Many shapes. (3) The ability of a variable to be set equal to a variety of structures.

polymorphic tweening   An animation technique that, based on information about its starting and ending shapes, creates the necessary "in-between" steps to change one object into another.

polyphase sort   External tape sort used for six or fewer tapes.

pooler   Device for consolidating and/or converting key entry data into a form acceptable to the main computer.

pop   To pull or retrieve data from the top of a program pushdown stack. The stack pointer is decremented to address the last word pushed on the stack. The contents of this location are moved to one of the accumulators or to another register. Also called pull. Contrast with push.

pop instruction   Computer instruction that executes the pop operation.

populate   To fill the sockets of a circuit board. A fully populated circuit board is one that contains all the devices it can hold.

populated board   Circuit board that contains all of its electronic components. Contrast with unpopulated board.

pop-up menu   A menu that appears on-screen anywhere other than in the standard menu bar location.

port   That portion of a computer through which a peripheral device may communicate. Plug-in/socket on the back of the computer for connecting cables for peripherals.

portability   Ease with which a program can be moved from one computer environment to another. Many programs written in high-level languages may be used on different machines. These programs are, therefore, portable.

portable computer A self-contained computer that can be easily carried and moved. Compared to desktop models, it has limited expansion slots and disk capacity.

portable program Software that can be used on compatible computer systems.

Portfolio A professional illustrative graphics program for IBM-compatible microcomputers. Aside from an enhanced list of usual drawing tools, there's a raster and vector based system, a full featured text editor with scalable fonts and spelling checker, a feature to import files directly from word processors, an autotrace feature and templates of 2-D and 3-D charts and graphs.

port protection device A black box between a computer system and incoming telephone lines that protects the system from unauthorized access.

portrait An orientation in which the data is printed across the narrow side of the form.

portrait mode A video monitor display screen whose height is greater than its width, like a portrait painting. Contrast with landscape mode.

portrait monitor A monitor with a screen shape higher than it is wide. A popular type monitor in desktop publishing systems.

POS Acronym for Point-Of-Sale terminal.

positional notation Method for expressing a quantity by using two or more figures where-in the successive right-to-left figures are to be interpreted as coefficients of ascending integer powers of the radix. In the decimal numeral 634, which has a radix of 10, the value is $4 \times 10^0 + 3 \times 10^1 + 6 \times 10^2$.

position stat A copy of a halftone which can be placed on a mechanical to illustrate positioning and cropping of the image.

positive true logic Logic system in which a lower voltage represents a bit value of 0 and a higher voltage represents a bit value of 1. Contrast with polar.

possibility theory The theory on which fuzzy logic is based.

POS systems Department stores and supermarkets are currently using POS systems, in which the cash register is actually a special-purpose computer terminal that can monitor and record transactions directly in the store's data files for inventory control, checks on credit card validity, and other data handling functions. See point-of-sale terminal.

post To enter a unit of information on a record.

post edit To edit output data from a previous computation.

postfix notation Arithmetic notation system whereby the operator follows the operands. Addition of 5 and 3 would be expressed as 53 + . Reverse Polish notation is a form of postfix notation.

post-implementation review Evaluation of a system after it has been in use for several months. Compare system follow-up.

post mortem Analysis of an operation after its completion.

post mortem dump Storage dump taken at the end of the execution of a program. Contrast with snapshot dump.

PostScript A proprietary language developed by Adobe Corporation to tell a printer what to print on a particular page. PostScript's chief benefit is its device independence, that is to say that the same file can be printed to printers of varying resolutions.

PostScript font A font defined in terms of the PostScript page-description language rules and intended to be printed on a PostScript-compatible printer.

PostScript laser printer A laser printer that includes the processing circuitry needed to decode and interpret printing instructions phrased in PostScript—a page description language widely used in desktop publishing. The printer converts the PostScript instructions (sent by the computer) into the dots that make up the printed image.

posture The slant of the characters in a font.

potentiometer Device used to develop electrical output signals proportional to mechanical movement.

power Symbolic representation of the number of times a number is multiplied by itself. The process is called exponentiation. 4 to the power of 3 means 4 x 4 x 4; and is written 4^3.

power amplifying circuit Electronic circuit that converts an input AC voltage into an output DC voltage. Compare power supply.

power down (1) To turn off a computer or peripheral device. (2) Steps a computer may take to preserve the state of the processor and to prevent damage to it or to connected peripherals when the power fails or is shut off. Contrast with power up.

power fail/restart Facility that enables a computer to return to normal operation after a power failure.

powerful Hardware is considered powerful if it is faster, larger, and can accomplish more work than comparable machines. Software is considered powerful if it is efficient and provides a wide range of options.

power on To turn the power switch to the ON position or otherwise supply electric current to a device. Also called power up.

power supply A device that provides power to electronic equipment such as computers and peripehrals. Power supplies are rated by wattage; the higher the wattage, the stronger the power supply.

power surge A sudden, brief increase in the flow of current that can cause problems in the proper operation of computer equipment.

power up (1) To turn on a computer or peripheral device. (2) Steps taken by a computer processor when the power is turned on, or restored after a power failure. The processor and peripherals are initialized so that program execution may be started. Contrast with power down.

power user A computer user who has gone beyond the beginning and intermediate stages of computer use. Such a person uses the advanced features of application programs.

pph Abbreviation for pages per hour.

PPM (1) Acronym for Pulse Position Modulation, pulse time modulation in which the value of each instantaneous sample of the wave modulates the position in time of a pulse. (2) Acronym for Pages Per Minute, a measure of output for printing devices, i.e., the number of printed pages output per minute.

pragmatics (1) Investigation of the relationship between symbols and the users of those symbols. (2) The field of linguistics that copes with the ambiguities found in language. (3) The part of natural language processing that attempts to ascertain the intent of the dialogue and give a reasonable reply.

precedence Rules that state which operators should be executed first in an expression.

precision Degree of exactness with which a quantity is stated. A calculation may have more precision that accuracy: the true value of π is accurate only to about five places.

precompiler Computer program that processes the source code of another computer program immediately before that program is to be compiled. It may provide the programmer with one or more of the following: (1) Ability to use convenient abbreviations that are not acceptable to the compiler itself: the precompiler expands (transcribes) the shorthand version into source code that is acceptable to the compiler. (2) Ability to use nonstandard programming statements that are not acceptable to the compiler. This may be done to aid structured programming in a language that is not well suited to it. The added statements are translated into standard-language statements by this structured programming precompiler. (3) Ability to enforce standards. Source statements written by a programmer can be edited for usages that violate the standards the programmer is supposed to be following.

predefined function Standard mathematical procedure available to the user for inclusion in a program.

predefined process (1) Process identified only by name and defined elsewhere. (2) Closed subroutine.

predefined process symbol Rectangular flowcharting symbol used to represent a subroutine.

predicate Another name for keyword in certain programming languages, such as PROLOG and Structured Query Language.

prediction expert system A type of expert system whose conclusion is a prediction of a future event.

predictive reports Business reports used for tactical and strategic decision making.

pre-edit See edit.

prefix notation Method of forming mathematical expressions in which each operator precedes its operands. The expression "x plus y multiplied by z" would be represented by + xy x z. Addition of 5 and 3 would be expressed as + 53. Polish notation is a form of prefix notation.

prehistoric calculations In prehistoric times, people drew symbols on the walls of caves using a charred stick or clays of different colors. Some of these symbols apparently stood for numbers. Human's first conscious calculations probably involved only simple counting: the number of spears a cave man owned, the number of hairy mammoths a cave man saw during a hunt, or the number of animals in the herd.

p-register Program-counter register in which the location of the current instruction is kept.

preliminary study The first phase of the systems life cycle. It involves defining the problem, suggesting alternative systems, and preparing a short report.

preprinted forms Forms that can contain computer-produced output but that enter a computer system with headings and identifying information already imprinted. Commonly used in producing external reports.

preprocessor Program that performs some preliminary processing, such as conversion, formatting, condensing, or other functions on input data prior to further processing.

prescriptive language A computer language that relies on the programmer to provide explicit procedures to compute an answer. Pascal and C are prescriptive languages. Prescriptive languages are also called procedural languages.

presentation graphics High quality professional looking business graphics. Used in proposals, business presentations, manuals and other business related documents. An easy-to-understand display of numerical information. Presentation graphics are visually appealing and easily understood by an audience.

presentation graphics program An application program designed to create and enhance charts and graphs so that they are visually appealing and easily understood by an audience.

Presentation Manager The graphical user interface provided in OS/2, jointly developed by Microsoft Corporation and IBM Corporation. Presentation Manager brings to IBM-compatible microcomputers, running the OS-2 operating system, many of the graphical user interface features associated with the Apple Macintosh computer—pull-down menus, multiple on-screen windows, desktop accessories, and multiple on-screen typefaces.

preset To establish an initial condition, such as control values of a loop or initial values in index registers. See initialize.

press Act of pushing down and holding the button on a mouse. See click.

pressure-sensitive keyboard Keyboard constructed of two thin plastic sheets coated with a circuit made of electrically conductive ink. Economical, flat keyboard used in several older, low-priced microcomputers.

pressure-sensitive pen Stylus used with a digitizer. Contains a pressure transducer that detects and transmits writing pressure as Z-axis data.

PRESTEL Commercial videotex service in Great Britain.

preventive maintenance Maintenance done on a scheduled basis to prevent major problems. Involves cleaning and adjusting the equipment as well as testing the equipment, under both normal and marginal conditions. Contrast with corrective maintenance.

primary cluster Buildup of table entries around a single table location.

primary colors Set of colors from which all others can be derived, but which cannot be produced from each other. The additive primaries (light) are blue, green, and red. The subtractive primaries (colorant) are cyan, magenta, and yellow. The physiological primaries are the pairs red/green, yellow/blue, and black/white.

primary key Unique field for a record, used to sort records for processing or to locate a particular record within a file.

primary storage The electronic circuitry that temporarily holds data and program instruction needed by the CPU. Also called memory, primary memory, main storage, internal storage, and main memory.

Prime Computer, Inc. A company founded in 1972 for the purpose of manufacturing minicomputers. In 1973, Prime announced their first mini-computer, the 200 system. Over the next two decades, Prime introduced several minicomputers, many were developed using innovative technology.

primer An elementary instruction manual.

prime shift Working shift that coincides with the normal business hours of an organization, as opposed to swing shift or graveyard shift.

priming read The first read statement in a program.

primitive (1) The basic building blocks of a language. In the English language individual words are primitives. In this vein, keywords in BASIC or Pascal may be considered as primitives. (2) In computer graphics the most basic graphic entities available, such as points, line segments, or characters. Primitives are the elements from which large graphic designs are created. (3) Basic or fundamental unit, often referring to the lowest level of a machine instruction or the lowest unit of language translation.

primitive element Graphics element, such as a line segment or point, that can be readily called up and extrapolated or combined with other primitive elements to form more complex objects or images.

print buffer Extra RAM in the printer or an add-on board which allows you to send a print job to the printer all at once thereby freeing up the computer for other work.

print chart Form used to describe the format of an output report from a printer. Also called printer spacing chart, printer design form, and print layout sheet.

print control character Control character for operations on a line printer, such as carriage return, page ejection or line spacing.

print density Number of printed characters per unit of measurement, such as the number of characters on a page.

printed circuit (PC) Electronic circuit that is printed, vacuum deposited, or electroplated on a flat insulating sheet.

printed circuit board A flat board that holds chips and other electronic components. Each chip contains hundreds of thousands of elementary components. The back side of the board is "printed" with electrically conductive pathways between the chips and components.

print element That part of a printer that actually puts the image on paper.

print engine   Part of a laser printer. The mechanism that uses a laser to create an electrostatic image of a page and fuse that image to a sheet of paper.

printer   Output device that produces hardcopy output.

printer control language   Language used to control printers.

printer driver   A device driver used to control a printer.

printer engine   The part of a page printer, such as a laser printer, that actually performs the printing.

printer font   A font available for printing. There are three types of printer fonts: built-in fonts, cartridge fonts, and downloadable fonts.

printer format   Pertaining to printing paper divided into print zones. Only one value can be printed in each zone.

printer resolution   The number of dots a laser printer can print on a linear inch. For example, most laser printers image at 300 dpi, while high-end imagesetters print at resolutions of 1270, 2250, and higher.

printer server   A device in a local area network that shares a printer among all users connected to the network. Using a technique called print spooling, the printer server receives files to be printed from network computers, stores the files on disk, and places them in a queue based on the order received. The printer server then parcels out the files, one at a time, to the printer.

printer spacing chart   A chart used to determine and show a report format.

printer stand   Wood or metal stand designed to support a printer.

print head   See print element.

printing orientation   See landscape or portrait.

print layout sheet   Chart used for establishing margin and spacing requirements for a printed report. See print chart.

printout   Form of computer system output, printed on a page by a printer. See hard copy.

print quality   Quality of a printout produced on a printer. See draft quality and letter quality.

print server   A microcomputer dedicated to managing one or more printers in a local area network.

Print Shop   A simple graphics package that performs several useful printing services easily and well. It prints standard and customized signs, greeting cards, posters, and letter heads as well as multipage banners on fan-fold paper with a wide selection of fonts, icons, borders, and graphics. Developed by Broderbund Software.

print wheel Single element providing the character set at one printing position of a wheel printer. See daisy wheel.

print zone In BASIC programming, a fixed-length area on an output device within which data are aligned in columns.

priority (1) The level of importance attached to a job in the computer. (2) A measure of the relative importance of goals, which is used to decide which goals will be attempted first.

priority interrupt Any interrupt given preference over other interrupts within the system.

priority processing Processing of a sequence of jobs on the basis of assigned priorities. See job queue.

privacy Those personal aspects a person chooses to shield from public scrutiny. The right of individuals to select the time and circumstances where information about them is to be made public.

Privacy Act of 1974 An act passed by the U.S. Congress to regulate the storage of data in federal-agency databases and to give individuals the right to see their records, correct errors, and remove data that should not be on the file.

private In object-oriented programming, a declaration that forms part of the interface of a class, object, or module; what is declared as private is not visible to any other classes, objects, or modules.

private automatic branch exchange (PABX) Private automatic telephone switching system that provides telephone communications within a business or factory and controls the transmission of calls to and from the public telephone network.

private line A communications line dedicated to one customer. Also called a leased line.

privately leased line Communications line intended for the use of a single customer. See leased lines.

privileged instruction Computer instruction not available for use in ordinary programs written by users; its use is restricted to the routines of the operating system.

probability theory Measure of the likelihood of occurrence of a chance event. Used to predict the behavior of a group. See operations research.

problem analysis Use of a plan to solve a problem. First step in the program development cycle.

problem definition (1) Formulation of the logic used to define a problem. (2) Description of a task to be performed.

problem description In information processing, the statement of a problem. May include a description of the method of solution, the solution itself, the transformation of data, and the relationship of procedures, data, constraints, and environment.

problem-oriented language (POL) Programming language designed for the convenient expression of a given class of problems.

problem program Program executed when the central processing unit is in the "problem state"; any program that does not contain privileged instructions.

problem scenario A problem and a proposed solution.

problem solving A problem that can be solved by a computer need not be described by an exact mathematical equation, but it does need a certain set of rules that the computer can follow. If the solution to a problem depends upon intuition or guessing, or if the problem is badly defined, the computer cannot be used to solve it. A computer cannot perform tasks properly unless problems are specified correctly in every detail. The instructions must also list in complete detail each step of the solution. Here is an overview of problem-solving steps: (1) A computer user studies the problem and prepares a plan of action, perhaps with the aid of an analyst. (2) A programmer, or the analyst, decides which steps the computer must take to obtain the desired results and specifies the form of input and output. (3) This plan of action is then coded into a set of steps in a programming language. (4) These instructions are prepared for input by keying them directly into the computer's memory via a keyboard or by keying them onto a magnetic disk or magnetic tape. (5) Once in the computer's memory, the program is translated into machine language (the only language the computer understands) by a translating program called an interpreter, compiler, or assembler. (6) The program is now ready to be executed by the computer. The steps of the program are carried out on the data used with the program, and the output is generated.

procedural knowledge Knowledge that specifies how to solve a given problem rather than describing or specifying the problem.

procedure (1) Course of action taken for the solution of a problem. (2) Portion of a high-level-language program that performs a specific task necessary for the program. (3) Another name for a computer program.

procedure division Fourth of four main parts of a COBOL program.

procedure-oriented language (POL) Any high-level, machine-independent programming language designed for the convenient expression of procedures used in the solution of a wide class of problems. Contrast with assembly language, machine language, and problem-oriented language.

process (1) Systematic sequence of operations to produce a specified result. (2) To transform raw data into useful information. (3) An element in a data flow diagram that represents actions taken on data: comparing, checking, authorizing, filing, and so forth.

process architecture In object-oriented programming, the hierarchy of processes that form the physical structure of a system.

process bound Situation in which the computer system is limited by the speed of the processor.

process box In flowcharting, a rectangular box that indicates an action to be taken.

process control Use of the computer to control industrial processes, such as oil refining and steel production.

process-control computer Digital computer used in a process-control system. Generally limited in instruction capacity, word length, and accuracy. Designed for continuous operation in non air-conditioned facilities.

process conversion Changing the method of running the computer system.

process diagram Part of the notation of object-oriented design, used to show the allocation of processes to processors in the physical design of a system. A process diagram may represent all or part of the process architecture of a system.

processing Computer manipulation of data in solving a problem.

processing rights The determination of which people have access to what kinds of data in databases.

processing symbol Rectangular flowcharting symbol used to indicate any processing operation, such as calculating, initializing a counter, or moving data.

processor (1) The central processing unit of a computer. (2) A compiler is sometimes referred to as a language processor.

processor bound Pertaining to system performance that is slowed by the time it takes the central processing unit to perform the actual processing or computations. Same as compute-bound. See limiting operation. Contrast with I/O bound.

Prodigy An on-line information service that offers business, shopping, news, and information services. Prodigy is a partnership of IBM Corporation and Sears. Innovative features of Prodigy include the use of a bit-mapped graphical user interface and unlimited use of the system for a flat fee.

ProDOS   An operating system for the Apple II microcomputer designed to support mass storage devices and floppy disk storage devices. ProDOS stands for Professional Disk Operating System.

production run   Execution of a debugged program that routinely accomplishes its purpose. For example, running a payroll program to produce weekly paychecks is a production run.

productivity   Measures of the work performed by a software/hardware system. Largely depends on a combination of the system's facility and performance.

Professional Graphics Adapter (PGA)   A video adapter introduced by the IBM Corporation and used primarily for computer-aided design applications.

Professional Write   A full-featured word processing program designed for executive users.

program   Series of instructions that will cause a computer to process data. It may be in a high-level source form, which requires intermediate processing before the computer can execute it, or it may be in an object form directly executable by the computer.

program chaining   Process of linking programs or program sections together. Allows programs that are larger than internal memory to be executed through sequential loading and execution of successive sections or modules of that program.

program coding   Process of writing instructions in a programming language.

program control   Descriptive of a system in which a computer is used to direct the operation.

program counter   Counter that indicates the location of the next program instruction to be executed by the computer. Same as instruction counter.

program development cycle   Steps involved in the solution of a problem with a computer: problem analysis, algorithm development, coding, program testing, documentation, and delivery. See design cycle.

program file   File containing computer programs.

program flowchart   Diagram composed of symbols, directional lines, and information about how the computer will be used to solve a problem. See flowchart. Contrast with system flowchart.

program generator   See generator.

program ID   Program identification.

program inspection   A formal technique in which software requirements, design, or code are examined by a person or group other than the author, to detect flaws.

program language   See programming language.

program library   Collection of available computer programs and routines, or portions of programs. Contents of the library are stored for reuse. If they are complete programs, they may be simply reused as is. Parts of programs may be copied into other programs to reduce labor and standardize the use of those copied parts in new programs.

program listing   See listing.

programmable automation   The manufacturing uses of robots and numerically controlled tools.

programmable calculator   Calculator-like device with certain computer-like features.

programmable communications interface   Interface board used for communications control.

programmable function key   Keyboard key whose function changes with the programs within the computer.

programmable logic array (PLA)   Device that provides the sum of a partial product with outputs for a given set of inputs. See FPLA and PLA.

programmable memory   Content-changeable memory, where most computer programs and data are stored. Usually RAM or PROM. Contrast with ROM. See storage.

programmable read-only memory (PROM)   Memory that can be programmed by electrical pulses. Once programmed, it is read-only. A special machine (called a PROM programmer) is used to write in the new program on blank PROM chips.

program maintenance   Process of keeping programs up to date by correcting errors, making changes as requirements change, and altering the programs to take advantage of equipment changes.

programmed check   Check consisting of tests inserted into the programmed statement of a problem and performed by the use of computer instructions.

programmed label   To make the identification of disk and tape files more reliable, most programs include a built-in routine that creates a label record at the beginning of the file. Contrast with external label.

programmed learning An early version of CAI, which used feedback to tell the user if he or she was correct; it could to a limited extent individualize instruction.

programmer (1) Person whose job is to design, write, and test software. (2) A device used to write machine code to a PROM chip.

programmer/analyst Person whose major tasks involve combining system analysis and design functions with programming activities.

programmer board Board that allows a user to program PROM or EPROM memories for use in his or her computer system. See PROM programmer.

programming Process of translating a problem from its physical environment to a language that a computer can understand and obey. Planning the procedure for solving a problem. This may involve, among other things, the analysis of the problem, coding of the problem, establishing input/output formats, establishing testing and checkout procedures, allocation of storage, preparation of documentation, and supervision of the running of the program on a computer.

programming aids Computer programs that aid computer users, such as compilers, debugging packages, linkage editors, and mathematical subroutines.

programming environment Facilities that aid in the development of programs. The tools may be libraries of subroutines, editors, debuggers, etc.

programming language A set of statements that control the operations of a computer. A means for computer users to provide a series of instructions for a computer to follow. There are four types of programming languages: machine language, assembly language, high-level language, and fourth-generation language.

programming librarian One of three nucleus members of the chief programmer team. Maintains and operates the development support library. Duties include code creation, submission of computer runs, and filing and logging of all outputs.

programming linguistics Three interconnected concepts of syntax, semantics, and pragmatics that can be used to describe languages for communication between any two systems, whether mechanical, electrical, or human.

programming team Group of individuals assigned to a programming project. See chief programmer.

program overlay A program module that is moved from auxiliary storage into computer memory when it is needed for processing.

program specifications Document that identifies the data requirements of a system, the files required, the input/output specifications, and the processing details.

program stack   Area of computer memory set aside for temporary storage of data and instructions, particularly during an interrupt. See pop, push, pushdown list, pushdown stack, and stack.

program stop   Stop instruction built into the program that will automatically stop the computer under certain conditions, upon reaching the end of the processing, or upon completing the solution of a problem.

program storage   Portion of internal storage reserved for the storage of programs, routines, and subroutines. In many systems, protection devices are used to prevent inadvertent alteration of the contents.

program switch   Point in a programming routine at which two courses of action are possible, the correct one being determined by a condition prevailing elsewhere in the program or by a physical disposition of the system.

program testing   Executing a program with test data to ascertain that it functions as expected. See testing.

progress reporting   Input of actual time, resource utilization and task/activity completions.

project control   Phase of a project management cycle that compares actual performance with the planned schedule and implements corrective measures to avoid project completion delays.

projecting   Producing a two-dimensional graphics display of a three-dimensional scene.

projection   Extension of past trends into the future. Computer-supplied information can be invaluable in this business management technique.

project library   Database of projects, tasks, and activities that can be modified and applied when planning new projects.

project manager   Person responsible for the enforcement of a project's goals. Sometimes called a project team leader.

project plan   Phase of a project management cycle that involves the development and organization of the work plan.

project schedule   Phase of a project management cycle that details the start and completion times for each task and activity.

PROLOG   Acronym for PROgramming in LOGic, a logic-based programming language. Invented in France in 1972 by Alan Colmeraner and Philippe Roussel at the University of Marseilles. PROLOG is widely used in programming applications such as expert systems and artificial intelligence software. PROLOG is similar in structure and syntax to LISP. PROLOG provides tools by which the programmer can state knowledge about the world as well as a set of rules by which conclusions can be drawn from this knowledge.

PROM Acronym for Programmable Read-Only Memory. A permanent memory chip that is programmed by the customer rather than the chip manufacturer. Contrast with ROM, which is programmed at the time of manufacture.

PROM programmer Device used to program PROMs and reprogram EPROMs by electrical pulses. Sometimes called PROM burner. See programmer board.

prompt Character or message provided by the computer to indicate that it is ready to accept keyboard input. Usually an on-screen question or instruction that tells the user which data to enter or what action to take, such as "Enter name:"

proof (1) A trial copy of a page or publication used to check accuracy. (2) Short for proofread, meaning to check for mistakes.

proofing program Same as dictionary program or spelling checker.

proofreader's marks In desktop publishing, a standard set of notations for indicating errors or corrections on a proof.

propagated error Error or mistake occurring in one operation and affecting data required for subsequent operations so the error or mistake is spread through much of the processed data.

propagation delay Time delay in a satellite communications system.

proportional font A set of characters in a particular style and size in which a variable amount of horizontal space is allotted to each letter, number of special character. In a proportional font, the letter I, for example is allowed less space than the letter w.

proportional spacing If the horizontal space allotted to a printed character is proportional to the width of that character, the spacing is said to be proportional. Since this book is typeset in proportional spacing, the "w" in the word "write" consumes more space than the "i." Standard typewriter style, in contrast, allots equal space to all characters.

proposition Statement in logic that can be true or false.

proprietary software Program owned by an individual or business because it is either copyrighted or not yet released to the public. One cannot legally use or copy this software without permission. Contrast with public domain software. See software piracy.

prosodics Rules for interpreting variations in stress and intonation in speech.

protect To prevent unauthorized access to programs or a computer system. To shield against harm. Often means write-protecting a disk.

protected cell A spreadsheet cell that cannot be edited, deleted, or moved.

protected mode In IBM-compatible microcomputers using Intel 80x86 microprocessors, an operating mode in which programs running simultaneously cannot invade each other's memory space or directly access input/output devices, preventing system failures during multitasking operations.

protected storage Storage locations reserved for special purposes, in which data cannot be stored without undergoing a screening procedure to establish suitability for storage therein.

protocol A software method that allows programs on separate machines to communicate. Protocols define signal type, how the signals are received, and the physical arrangement of the network. In object-oriented programming, the set of messages to which an object can respond.

prototype A limited working system or subset of a system (hardware or software) that is developed to test design concepts. An initial version of a system.

proving Testing a machine to demonstrate that it is free from faults, usually after corrective maintenance.

PS/1 A home computer from IBM Corporation introduced in 1990. The PS/1 computer uses an Intel 80286 microprocessor.

PS/2 A series of personal computers from IBM Corporation introduced in 1987. This second generation of IBM personal computers superseded its original personal computer series. The PS/2 introduced three major changes: VGA graphics, Micro Channel bus, and 3.5-inch floppy disks.

psec Abbreviation for picosecond; one trillionth of a second.

pseudocode An intermediate form of writing program instructions—instructions that approach the computer programming language but are written in an English-like language instead of a true programming language so that programming logic can be checked more easily. An example of a pseudocode sequence follows.

```
For every coin in the cup
  Pull out a coin
    If it is a 50 cent piece
      Put it in the half-dollar pile
    Else if it is a 25 cent piece
      Put it in the quarter pile
    Else if it is a 10 cent piece
      Put it in the dime pile
    Else if it is a 5 cent piece
      Put it in the nickel pile
    Else if it is a 1 cent piece
```

```
Put it in the penny pile
Else discard it
Do next coin until cup is empty.
```

pseudocomputer Software interpreter program written in the native machine language of a conventional microprocessor.

pseudolanguage Language, not directly understandable by a computer, used to write computer programs. Before a pseudoprogram can be used, it must be translated into a language that the computer understands (machine language). Same as symbolic language.

pseudo-operation Operation that is not part of the computer's operation repertoire as realized by hardware; hence, an extension of the set of machine operations.

pseudorandom number Number generated by a computer in a deterministic manner. These numbers have been subjected to many statistical tests of randomness and, for most practical purposes, can be used as a random number.

p-system Microcomputer operating system with a principal advantage that programs written for it will work on a wide variety of machines. Translates p-code into the machine language appropriate to a specific computer. See UCSD P-system.

publication language Well-defined form of a programming language suitable for use in publications. A language such as this is necessary because some languages use special characters that are not available in common type fonts.

publication window In desktop publishing, a display screen consisting of a pasteboard, icons, scroll bar, ruler, and toolbox.

public domain software Software not protected by copyright laws and therefore free for all to reproduce and trade without fear of legal prosecution. Any computer program donated to the public by its creator. Public domain software may be duplicated by others at will.

public key A cryptographic key which can be used to encrypt but is not capable of decryption. See secret key.

public network Communications service open to anyone, usually on a fee basis.

publishing cycle In desktop publishing, the movement of a document from creation to final printing.

Publish It! A full-featured desktop publishing program that allows the designing, layout, production, and printing of professional looking documents. Publish It! runs on IBM-compatible microcomputers.

puck Hand-held, manually controlled, graphics input device used to pinpoint coordinates on a digitizing tablet. Has a transparent window containing cross hairs and allows coordinate data to be digitized into the system from a drawing placed on the digitizing tablet surface.

pull See pop.

pull-down menu A second-level menu, or list of commands, that appears from the top of the screen when a command needs to be given and then disappears when the selection has been made. A pull-down menu is usually used as an extension to a menu bar. To select an option on a pull-down menu, one presses and holds down the mouse button while dragging the mouse pointer down the menu until the wanted option is highlighted.

pull instruction Instruction that pulls or retrieves data from the top of the program push-down stack. Same as pop instruction.

pull-out quote In desktop publishing, a quotation extracted from the copy of text and printed in larger type in the column.

pulse Abrupt change in voltage, either positive or negative, that conveys information to a circuit.

pulse modulation Use of a series of pulses that are modulated or characterized to convey information. Types of pulse modulation include amplitude (PAM), position (PPM), and duration (PDM) systems.

punched card Cardboard card used in data processing operations, in which tiny rectangular holes at (possibly) hundreds of individual locations denote numerical values and alphanumeric codes. Punched cards were used extensively in early computer systems, but have been replaced with interactive display terminals and floppy disks.

purchasing The buying of raw materials and services.

pure procedure Procedure that never modifies any part of itself during execution.

purge To erase a file from memory or from a disk; to clean up.

push Putting data into the top location of a program stack. The stack pointer is automatically incremented to point to the next location, which becomes the top of the stack. Also called put. Contrast with pop.

pushdown list List written from the bottom up, with each new entry placed at the top of the list. The item to be processed first is the one on the top of the list. See LIFO.

pushdown stack Set of memory locations or registers in a computer that implements a pushdown list.

push instruction Computer instruction that implements a push operation.

push-pop stack Register that receives information from the program counter and stores the address locations of instructions on a last-in-first-out basis. Two operations are involved in stack processing: pushing describes the filling of the stack from registers; popping involves emptying the stack for transfer to registers.

pushup list List of items in which each item is entered at the end of the list and the other items maintain their same relative position in the list. See FIFO.

put See push.

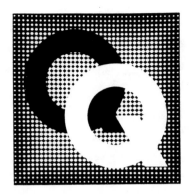

quad-density Term used to specify the data storage density of a computer disk system. Quad-density of a computer disk system. Quad-density systems can store up to four times the data that can be stored on single-density disks. Double-sided double-density disks are quad-density disks.

quadratic quotient search Hashing algorithm that uses a quadratic offset when probing subsequent table locations.

quality control Technique for evaluating the quality of product being processed by checking it against a predetermined standard and taking the proper corrective action if the quality falls below the standard.

quality engineering Establishment and execution of tests to measure product quality and adherence to acceptance criteria.

quantify To assign numeric values to nonnumeric objects.

quantity Any positive or negative real number in the mathematical sense.

quantum Smallest unit of measure employed in a system.

Quark Xpress A page layout program for the Apple Macintosh computer from Quark, Inc. It is noted for its precise typographic control and sophisticated graphics capabilities. Quark Xpress allows unlimited document length and includes many word processing features.

quasi language See pseudolanguage.

Quattro A spreadsheet for IBM-compatible microcomputers from Borland International, Inc. The program provides advanced graphics and presentation capabilities.

query To ask for information. To make a request for information from a database system.

query by example To ask for information from a database system by defining the qualifications for selected records on a sample record, rather than describing a procedure for finding the information.

query language A user's language for retrieving data from a database management system. A query is typically issued in the form of a sentence or near-English command.

query response Message sent to a computer terminal in answer to a specific request from the operator.

question-answer Process of interacting with the computer. The computer asks the user a question, and the user provides the answer.

queued access method Any access method that automatically synchronizes the transfer of data between the program using the access method and the input/output devices, thereby eliminating delays for I/O operations.

queue Group of items waiting to be acted upon by the computer, such as messages to be transmitted in a data communications system. The arrangement of items determines the processing priority. See job queue.

queuing Method of controlling the information processing sequence.

queuing theory Form of probability theory useful in studying delays or lineups at servicing points. Research technique concerned with the correct sequential orders of moving units. May include sequence assignments for bits of information or whole messages. See operations research.

quibinary code Binary coded decimal code used to represent decimal numbers in which each decimal digit is represented by seven binary digits.

QuickBASIC A variation of the BASIC programming language published by Microsoft Corporation. QuickBASIC is a compiler that recognizes modern control structures and enables programmers to omit line numbers. The compiler enables you to create structured programs, complete with indentations. QuickBASIC programs execute much faster than their interpreted counterparts.

QuickC A variation of the C programming language published by Microsoft Corporation.

quick disconnect Type of electrical connector that allows rapid locking and unlocking of the mating connector halves.

QuickDraw A graphics language system built into the ROM of the Apple Macintosh computer. Application programs call on QuickDraw for on-screen displays. QuickDraw consists of a series of primitive shapes, lines, and fill patterns which can be mathematically modified. When printing to PostScript printers, QuickDraw must be translated during the printing process by a program called a PostScript interpreter.

QuickPascal A variation of the Pascal programming language published by Microsoft Corporation.

quit To exit the current program.

QWERTY keyboard Keyboard arrangement that is standard on most keyboards found on typewriters, word processors, and computers. Developed more than a century ago to slow down swift typists and prevent jamming of the old mechanical typewriters. The design is called QWERTY after the first six letters on the top alphabetic line of the keyboard. Now that electronics can accommodate high-speed typing, QWERTY is no longer efficient. Many businesses are replacing QWERTY keyboards with the more efficient Dvorak keyboard. Some computer companies now offer keyboards with a switch that will change from one keyboard to the other.

R Acronym for register, request, and reset.

race condition Indeterminate state that results when two computer instructions are operating concurrently and it is not possible to know which one will finish first.

rack Metal frame or chassis on which panels of electrical, electronic, or other equipment such as amplifiers and power supply units, may be mounted.

radian Central angle subtended in a circle by an arc whose length is equal to the radius of the circle. Thus the radian measure of an angle is the ratio of the arc it subtends to the radius of the circle in which it is the central angle (a constant ratio for all such circles). A straight line (180-degree angle) has an angle of π, or 3.1415927, radians; a 90-degree angle is 1.5707963, or $\pi/2$ radians. Trigonometric functions in many high-level programming languages work on radians rather than degrees.

radio button In a graphical user interface, the round option buttons that appear in dialog boxes. Only one radio button can be selected within a group of radio buttons.

Radio Shack A manufacturer and distributor of electronic equipment, including microcomputer systems sold under the name of TRS-80 or Tandy. A division of the Tandy Corporation. Radio Shack developed one of the first personal computer systems, the TRS-80 Model 1, in 1977.

radix Base number in a number system, such as 2 in the binary system or 10 in the decimal system. Synonymous with base.

radix complement See complement.

radix point In a number system, the character (a dot) or implied character that separates the integral part of a numeral from the fractional part. See binary point, decimal point, hexadecimal point, and octal point.

radix sorting Same as digital sorting.

rag The irregularity along the left or right ends of the lines on a printed page. See ragged left and ragged right.

ragged left margin Refers to text printed with a straight right margin and an uneven left margin. Also called flush right. Contrast with left justify.

ragged right margin Text printed with a straight left margin and an uneven right margin. Also called flush left. Contrast with right justify.

raised flooring Elevated flooring used in computer rooms so connecting cables can be laid directly between equipment units.

RALU Acronym for Register, Arithmetic, and Logic Unit, a major part of a microprocessor where arithmetic and logic operations are performed.

relative cell reference In spreadsheet processing, a reference to a location in the worksheet that is interpreted with respect to the formula's current cell location.

RAM Acronym for Random Access Memory, a memory into which the user can enter information and instructions (write) and from which the user can call up data (read). Working memory of the computer, into which applications programs can be loaded from outside and then executed.

RAM card Printed circuit board containing RAM chips. By plugging such a board into some computers, their internal storage can be expanded.

RAM cache A section of random access memory (RAM) set aside to serve as a buffer between the central processing unit and the disk drives.

RAM chip A semiconductor storage device. RAM chips can be either static or dynamic memory.

RAM disk A chip that lets the computer regard part of its memory as a third disk drive. Also called a phantom disk.

random access Process of obtaining data from, or placing data into, a storage location in which access is independent of the order of storage. Another name for direct access. Contrast with sequential access.

random access memory (RAM) Memory whose contents can be read or written on directly without regard to any other memory location. See RAM.

random files Files not organized in any sequence. Data are retrieved based on the address of the record on the direct access device.

randomizing The process of applying a formula to a key to yield a number that represents a disk address. Also called hashing.

random logic design Designing a system by using discrete logic circuits.

random number Patternless sequence of digits. Unpredictable number, produced by chance, that satisfies one or more of the tests for randomness. See pseudorandom number.

random-number generator Computer program or hardware designed to produce a pseudorandom number or series of pseudorandom numbers according to specified limitations.

random processing Processing of data randomly. Same as direct access processing. Contrast with sequential processing.

range Span of values that an element may assume.

range check Check applied to a numeric element to verify that it falls within a particular range, such as the months being in the range of 01 to 12. See data editing.

rank (1) To arrange in an ascending or descending series according to importance. (2) Measure of the relative position in a group, series, array, or classification.

raster display Video display that sweeps a beam through a fixed pattern, building up an image with a matrix of points. See raster graphics. Contrast with vector display.

raster fill Process used by a graphics camera to fill in the spaces between the raster lines of a video screen to give a screen picture a more finished appearance.

raster graphics Manner of storing and displaying data as horizontal rows of uniform grid or picture cells (pixels). Raster scan devices recreate or refresh a display screen thirty to sixty times a second to provide clear images for viewing. Raster display devices are generally faster and less expensive than vector tubes.

raster image A display image formed by a pattern of pixels in a rectangular array.

raster image file format (RIFF) A file format for paint-style graphics.

raster image processor A device that converts a vector image into a raster image prior to printing on an output device that requires raster technology.

rasterization The conversion of vector graphics to equivalent images composed of pixel patterns (bit-mapped images).

raster scan Generation of an image on a display screen made by refreshing the display area line by line.

rat's nest Feature on printed circuit design systems that allows users to view all the computer-determined interconnections between components.

This makes it easier to determine whether further component placement improvement is necessary to optimize signal routing.

raw data   Data that have not been processed. Such data may or may not be on machine-readable media. Also called original data.

ray tracing   In computer graphics, a method of adding a degree of realism to an image through the use of reflections, refractions, and shadows. A sophisticated and complex approach to producing high-quality computer graphics. Ray tracing is a very process-intensive operation.

RDBMS   Acronym for relational database management system.

read   To get information from any input or file storage media, such as reading a floppy diskette by sensing the patterns of magnetism. Contrast with write.

reader   Any device capable of transcribing data from an input medium.

read head   Magnetic head designed to read data from the media. Contrast with write head. Compare read/write head.

reading wand   Device that senses marks and codes optically, such as a device that reads price tags in a point-of-sale terminal.

read ink   See nonreflective ink.

read-only memory (ROM)   Special type of computer memory, permanently programmed with one group of frequently used instructions. Does not lose its program when the computer's power is turned off, but the program cannot be changed by the user. In many microcomputers, the BASIC language intrepreter and operating systems are contained in ROM. See EPROM, firmware, PROM, and solid state cartridge.

read-only storage   See read-only memory.

readout   Manner in which a computer represents the processed information, such as by visual display, printer, and digital plotter.

read/write head   Small electromagnet used to read, write, or erase data on a magnetic storage device, such as a disk or tape. See read head and write head.

real constant   Number that contains a decimal point, such as 26.4 or -349.0. Also called floating-point constant.

real number   Any rational or irrational number.

real storage   Internal storage in a virtual storage system.

real-time   Descriptive of on-line computer processing systems that receive and process data quickly enough to produce output to control, direct, or affect the outcome of an ongoing activity or process. For example, in an airline reservations system, a customer-booking inquiry is entered into the computer to see whether space is available. If a seat is booked, the file of available seats is updated immediately, thus giving an up-to-date record of seats reserved and seats available. See transaction-oriented processing.

real-time clock   Piece of hardware that interrupts the processor at fixed time intervals to synchronize the operations of the computer with events occurring in the outside world, often involving human/computer interaction.

real-time expert system   An expert system that has its input data from an ongoing, constantly varying process.

real-time image generation   Performance of the computations necessary to update an image being completed within the refresh rate, so the sequence appears correctly to the viewer. An example is flight simulation, in which thousands of computations must be performed to present an animated image, all within the rate of 30-60 cycles per second at which the frames change.

real-time output   Output data removed from a system at a time of need by another system.

real-time systems   Computer systems in which the computer is required to perform its tasks within the time restraints of some process or simultaneously with the system it is assisting. Usually, the computer must operate faster than the system assisted so as to be ready to intervene appropriately.

reasonableness check   Technique whereby tests are made on processed data to indicate whether a gross error exists. Programming instructions would check if the data lies within preset upper and lower limits and initiate some action if the data are not reasonable. See data editing.

reboot   To stop and boot the operating system again. Usually occurs by human intervention as the result of a problem. Similar to "reset" on a home appliance. To restart.

recalculating   The process of recomputing values in electronic spreadsheets automatically.

receive   To capture messages transmitted by a sender.

receive only (RO)   Designation used to indicate the read-only capabilities of terminals and other equipment lacking keyboards. See RO terminal. Contrast with send only.

receiver   Recipient of messages dispatched by a sender.

recompile   To compile a program again, usually after debugging or because the program needs to be run on a different type of computer.

reconstruction Restoring the database system to a previous state after data have been tampered with or destroyed.

record Collection of related items of data treated as a unit. Description of an item in a database. Each item is represented by a record that consists of one or more fields. Everyday examples of a record include an entry in a dictionary or a listing in a phone book.

recording density Number of useful storage cells per unit of length or area; for example, the number of characters per inch on a magnetic tape or the number of bits per inch on a single track of a disk. Also called packing density.

record layout Arrangement and structure of data elements in a record, including the size and sequence of its components.

record length Measure of the size of a record, usually specified in units such as words, bytes, or characters.

record locking Protects shared database records by allowing only one user at a time to make changes. Used in local area networks.

record manager Another term for file manager.

record number Number automatically assigned to each new record as it is created. Serves as a reference number and may be transparent to the user.

records management Custodial care concerned with the creation, retention, and scheduled destruction of an organization's paper and film documents.

recover To continue program execution after a failure. To overcome a problem.

recoverable error Error condition that can be sensed and corrected, thereby allowing continued operation of a program.

rectangular coordinate system System in which every point in a plane is given an address in the form of a pair of numbers, called the coordinates of the point. Same as Cartesian coordinate system.

rectifier Electrical device that changes alternating current into direct current. Compare power supply.

recto The right-hand (odd-numbered) page in a two-sided printing of a book or document.

recurring costs Budgeted items that are not one-time expenditures, such as personnel, supplies, equipment rental, and overhead costs associated with a computer system.

recursion   Set of operations or program statements in which one of the operations or statements is specified in terms of the entire set. Continued repetition of the same operation(s).

recursive   Pertaining to a process that is inherently repetitive. The result of each repetition is usually dependent upon the result of the previous repetition. An object is said to be recursive if it partially consists of or is defined in terms of itself.

recursive procedure   Procedure A that, while being executed, either calls itself or calls another procedure B, which in turn calls procedure A.

recursive subroutine   Subroutine capable of calling itself, or a subroutine that invokes another subroutine, which in turn invokes the original subroutine.

red-green-blue monitor   High-resolution color display unit. See RGB monitor.

reduced instruction set computer (RISC)   A microprocessor that has only a relatively small set of instructions. RISC design is based on the premise that most of the instructions a computer decodes and executes are simple, thus RISC architecture limits the number of instructions that are built into the microprocessor but optimizes each so it can be carried out very rapidly.

reduction   Process of saving computer storage by eliminating empty fields or unnecessary data to reduce the length of records.

redundancy   (1) Duplication of a feature to prevent system failure in the event of the feature's malfunction. (2) Repetition of information among various files, sometimes necessary but often undesirable.

redundancy check   Check based on the transfer of more bits or characters than the minimum number required to express the message itself, the added bits or characters having been inserted systematically for checking purposes. See parity bit and parity checking.

redundant code   Binary coded decimal value with an added check bit.

redundant information   Message expressed in such a way that the essence of the information occurs in several ways.

reentrant   Pertaining to a routine that can be used by two or more independent programs at the same time.

reentrant code   Assembly-generated machine-language programs that may be shared simultaneously by any number of users.

reentrant subroutine   In a multiprogramming system, a subroutine of which only one copy resides in internal storage, shared by several programs.

reference edge See aligning edge.

reflectance In optical scanning, a relative value assigned to a character or color of ink when compared with the background.

reflectance ink In optical scanning, ink that has a reflectance level that very nearly approximates the acceptable paper reflectance level for a particular optical character reader.

reformat To change the representation of data from one format to another.

refresh circuitry Electronic circuitry necessary to restore (1) the information displayed on a visual display screen, and (2) the data stored in dynamic RAM, which steadily lose their charge.

refresh display cycle Time between successive raster scans or passes through the vectors to be displayed on a vector device. The phosphors on the face of a CRT are excited and glow as the result of each pass of the electron beam in each refresh cycle. The refresh rate usually occurs at a level fast enough to eliminate the flicker from the brightening and fading of the phosphors each time they are struck. Typically, the image must be regenerated at a rate of 1/30th or 1/60th of a second.

refreshing Process of constantly reactivating or restoring information that decays or fades away when left idle. Phosphor on a CRT screen needs to be constantly reactivated by an electron beam to remain illuminated. Typically, the image must be regenerated at a rate of 30 to 60 hertz to avoid flicker. Likewise, cells in dynamic memory elements must be repeatedly accessed to avoid losing their contents. See dynamic RAM and raster scan.

refresh memory Area of computer memory that holds values indicating whether a particular dot of a graphics raster is on or off. May also contain information on brightness and color.

refresh rate Rate at which the graphic image on a CRT is redrawn in a refresh display; time needed for one refresh of the displayed image.

regenerate To renew some quantity. Used in storage devices to write back information that has been read in a destructive manner.

region In multiprogramming with a variable number of tasks, a term often used to mean the internal storage space allocated.

region fill In computer graphics, the technique of filling a defined region on the screen with a selected pattern, color, or other attribute.

register (R) High-speed device used in a central processing unit for temporary storage of small amounts of data or intermittent results during processing. See general-purpose register.

registration   Accurate positioning relative to a reference.

regression analysis   (1) Technique in model-building used to define a dependent variable in terms of a set of independent variables. (2) Construction of a "line of best fit" to best illustrate the pattern of a set of data points.

regression testing   Tests performed on a previously verified program whenever it is extended or corrected.

relation   (1) Equality, inequality, or any property that can be said to hold (or not hold) for two objects in a specified order. (2) In a relational database model, a table, the basic form of information storage. (3) In a network/hierarchical database model, a named association among sets of entities.

relational database   A database organization scheme that treats files as tables of data in which the rows represent fixed-length records and columns represent fields. Multiple keys can be used for retrieving the data stored within the database. A database in which some data items in one type of record refer to records of a different type. Relational databases give the user the flexibility to link (join, or create a relationship between) information stored in many disk files. It allows you to interchange and cross reference information between two different types of records, such as comparing the information in a group of invoices to the information in an inventory. Most people do not need relational databases. If you merely want to keep track of a mailing list, you don't require a relational database. If you want to keep a simple inventory of something, you don't need a relational database. However, if you want to print out a mailing list of people who ordered products from your inventory, you will need a relational database. Relational databases are more powerful, more complex, more difficult to use, and more expensive than other database systems.

relational expression   Expression that contains one or more relational operations.

relational model   Database model that organizes data logically in tables.

relational operator   Symbol used to compare two values; specifies a condition that may be either true or false, such as = (equal to), < (less than), and > (greater than).

relational structure   Form of database organization in which all data items are contained in one file and are linked together by a trail of logical pointers. Relationships among these data items can be altered at will, and the information can be obtained by interactive query or batch processing.

relative address   Address to which a base address must be added to form the absolute address of a particular storage location.

relative coding   Coding that uses machine instructions with relative addresses.

relative movement Movement of an object on the screen to a new position in terms of the last position rather than from 0.0. "Move 4, 8" would move a marked point four units to the right and eight units up from the last recorded point. Contrast with absolute movement.

relative vector In computer graphics, a vector with end points designated in relative coordinates.

relay Magnetically operated switch used in pre-electronic computers.

release number The number that identifies a specific version of a program. A program labeled 3.5, for example, is the sixth release of Version 3 of the program (the first was Version 3.0).

release version Version of a program currently available for purchase.

reliability Measure of the ability of a program, system, or individual hardware device to function without failure.

relocatable addresses Addresses used in a program that can be positioned at almost any place in internal storage.

relocatable program Program existing in a form that permits it to be loaded and executed in any available region of a computer's internal storage.

relocate To move a program or part of a program coded so it may be executed anywhere in computer storage.

remarks Verbal messages inserted into a source language program that do not cause any computer processing steps but are helpful notes for future users who may attempt to understand or alter the program. Used as internal documentation. See comments.

remote Physically distant from a local computer, such as a terminal or printer.

remote access Communication with a computer facility by a station (or stations) distant from the computer.

remote batch processing Processing of data in batches at a remote location by using a small computer system. See batch processing.

remote computing services Services offered to customers by computer service centers. Examples are batch processing, interactive problem solving, and consulting.

remote job entry (RJE) Refers to computer programs used to submit processing jobs from remote terminals.

remote processing Processing of computer programs through an input/output device remotely connected to a computer system. See remote batch processing.

remote site Outpost in a distributed computer network.

remote station See remote terminal.

remote terminal Device for communicating with a computer from sites that are physically separated from the computer, often distant enough so that communications facilities, such as telephone lines, are used rather than direct cables. See terminal.

removable media Diskettes, hard disk cartridges, or optical disc cartridges that can be removed from the device that reads data from them or writes data to them.

rendering In computer graphics, a three-dimensional image that incorporates the simulation of lighting effects, such as reflections and shadows.

reorder point Lowest amount of stock that can be on hand before ordering more of an item. Essential parameter in inventory control.

repagination Process in which a page layout or word processing program adjusts a multipage document as it is revised to ensure uniform page length and appearance.

repaint Redrawing of an image on a visual display device to reflect updated graphic or textual data. Feature on many graphics systems that automatically redraws a design displayed on the visual display screen.

repeat counter Program counter that records the number of times an event takes place in a program for later comparison.

repeating decimal number Nonterminating decimal number, such as .3333333... or .31282828....

repeat key Keyboard key that can be held down so it repeatedly makes contact without need for additional pressing.

repertoire Complete set of instructions that belongs to a specific computer or family of computers. Also called instruction set.

repetition instruction Instruction that causes one or more instructions to be executed an indicated number of times.

replace In word processing, command that enables user to search for a word and replace it with another one.

report Usually associated with output data; involves the grouping of related facts so as to be easily understood by the reader. Common means of presenting information to users. Most reports are on-screen display or printed listings showing selected information extracted from a database.

report file File generated during data processing, usually used to print out or display desired output.

report generation Manipulation and organization of data to create an on-screen or hard-copy document from all or part of a database file.

report generator Program that is used to create a report.

reporting by exception See exception reporting.

report writer Utility program that generates standard and custom reports from information stored in data files.

reproduce To copy information on a similar medium, such as to obtain a duplicate diskette from a specific diskette.

reprographics The duplication of printed materials using high-speed duplicators and offset printing presses.

reprogramming Changing a program written for one computer so that it will run on another.

reprographics Technology that includes reproduction and duplication processes for documents, written materials, pictures, drawings, and films, as well as methods of their mass reproduction, such as photocopy, offset printing, microfilming, and offset duplicating.

request for bid (RFB) Specifications regarding hardware or software are developed and made available to vendors. Vendors are asked to submit a bid that describes the hardware or software and tells the price and conditions under which it can be purchases or leased.

request for proposal (RFP) Document sent to hardware/software vendors requesting them to propose equipment and software to meet system specifications.

request for quotation (RFQ) Document sent to hardware/software vendors requesting them to quote prices for equipment and/or software that meets system requirements.

requirements list Formal written statements that specify what the software must do or how it must be structured.

rerun To repeat all or part of a program on a computer, usually because of a correction, a false start, or an interrupt.

reserve accumulator Auxiliary storage register allied to the main accumulator in a central processing unit. See accumulator.

reserved words Certain words that, because they are reserved by operating systems, language translators, and so on for their own use, cannot be used in an applications program—such as READ, FOR, and LET in the BASIC programming language. See keyword.

reset (R) (1) To return computer components to a specified static state. (2) To place a binary cell into the zero state.

reset key Key on a keyboard that normally is used to restart the computer.

reside To be recorded in. For example, a program may reside on a disk or in memory.

resident font Built-in font in a printer.

resident program Program that occupies a dedicated area of a computer's main memory (ROM or RAM) during the operating session. Contrast with transient program.

residual value Value of a piece of equipment at the end of a lease term.

resilient Pertaining to a system capable of continuing execution despite failure.

resistor Component of an electrical circuit that produces heat while offering opposition, or resistance, to the flow of electric current.

resizing Process of scaling a graphics file or entity according to predetermined parameters.

resolution A term used to describe the amount of information that a video display can reproduce. A pixel is the smallest unit on the display screen grid that can be stored, displayed, or addressed. The resolution of a picture is expressed by the number of pixels in the display. A high-resolution picture looks smooth and realistic. It is produced by a large number of pixels. A low-resolution picture is blocky and jagged. It is produced by a small number of pixels. Low-resolution pictures represent surfaces with ragged edges, while high-resolution produces a finely defined image. A picture with 640 x 480 pixels is much sharper than a picture with 512 x 342 pixels.

resolution, plotter Measure of the quality of a plotted image. The number of addressable points on a digital plotter determines the resolution; the more points, the higher the resolution.

resource Any component of a computer configuration. Memory, printers, visual displays, disk storage units, software, materials, and operating personnel are all considered resources.

resource allocation Sharing of computer resources among competing tasks or activities.

resource file Programs or data, stored on disk or tape, for use by applications programs.

resource leveling Scheduling of activities with float time to optimize the use of resources, thereby avoiding large fluctuations in resource requirements.

resource sharing Sharing of one central processor by several users as well as several peripheral devices.

response position In optical scanning, area designated for marking information on an optical mark recognition form.

response time Time it takes the computer system to react to a given input. Interval between an event and the system's response to the event.

restart To resume execution of a program. To reboot.

results Product of computer processing.

reticle Photographic plate used to create an integrated circuit mask.

retrieval Recovery of data stored in a computer system.

retrieving Process of making stored information available when needed.

retrofit To update or add to an existing system to improve it.

return Set of instructions at the end of a subroutine that permits control to return to the proper point in the main program.

RETURN key Key on a computer keyboard used to make the display cursor or a printer carriage move to the beginning of the next line. Used like an ENTER key on other keyboards to execute a command.

reusable Attribute of a routine that permits the same copy of the routine to be used by two or more tasks.

reverse Polish notation Form of postfix notation in which the operands are entered before the operators. The expression $z = a(b+c)$ is represented in reverse Polish notation as bc + a x z =, where this expression is read from left to right. Contrast with Polish notation.

reverse video A term used to indicate, in some video terminals, the ability to display dark characters on a light background. The inverse of the normal foreground and background colors on a video screen. For example, the reverse video of light characters on a dark background would be dark characters on a light screen background. Commonly used to highlight text or special items on the screen.

review Evaluation of a new system's performance.

rewind To return a magnetic tape to its starting position.

rewrite To erase and reset.

RF Acronym for Radio Frequency, the general term for a broad spectrum of electromagnetic radiation ranging in frequency from 10,000 to 40 billion cycles per second. RF radiation has been used primarily for the purpose of communication.

RF modulator   Device that lets a microcomputer use any ordinary television set for output.

RFP   Acronym for Request For Proposal.

RFQ   Acronym for Request for Quotation.

RGB   (Red, Green, Blue) The most common color model. It's the way color is created on computer monitors. Red, green and blue are called the additive primaries, because they create white light when combined, and any two produce the subtractive primaries: cyan, magenta and yellow.

RGB monitor   A display screen that requires separate red, green, and blue video signals from the video source. RGB monitor is synonymous in IBM-compatible microcomputer computing with the Color Graphics Adapter (CGA) standard.

ribbon cable   A type of flat cable made of individual insulated wires joined side by side. It is inexpensive to manufacture, easy to put connectors on with automated equipment, and physically flexible. Commonly used to connect disk drives or printers to a computer.

ribbon cartridge   Plastic holder that contains a printer ribbon.

RIFF   Acronym for Raster Image File Format. A graphics file format used to store gray-scale images. Used most often in Letraset's ImageStudio and Ready, Set, Go software packages.

right justify   See justify.

rigid disk   Same as hard disk.

ring   Cyclic arrangement of data elements. See circular list.

ring network   Computer network in which each computer is connected to other computers, forming a continuous loop, or circle. Usually employed when the computers are geographically close. Contrast with star network.

Rio-Sable   A true color object oriented draw and image processing program. It allows users to compose scenes that combine video capture, TV-quality electronic color images or high resolution scanned images with vector-based text and geometric shapes. The program includes flexible draw and edit features for high resolution and video captured files operating in MSDOS.

RIP   Short for Raster-Image Processor, the part of a printing system that translates from the input data in the form provided by the computer to the actual dots or lines sent to the marking device.

ripple sort   See bubble sort.

RISC   Short for Reduced Instruction Set Computer, a computer system designed to minimize the number of different underlying operations that the microprocessor does in hardware in order to optimize the execution speed. Such systems depend on the software for functions that formerly were handled by the microprocessor.

risk analysis   The analysis of a system's assets and vulnerabilities in an attempt to establish the expected loss when a given disaster occurs.

Ritchie, Dennis   A Bell Laboratories research scientist who, in 1971, with Kenneth Thompson, developed and implemented the UNIX operating system. The UNIX system has led a generation of software designers to new ways of thinking about programming. Ritchie also developed the C programming language.

river   In desktop publishing, the presence of irregular white space between words that accidently line up vertically or diagonally.

RJE   Acronym meaning Remote Job Entry.

RO   Acronym for Receive Only.

Roach, John   In 1977, Tandy Corporation's Radio Shack division released the TRS-80 microcomputer. Roach, then a vice-president at Radio Shack manufacturing, guided the development of this popular microcomputer.

roam   To move a display window around on a visual display screen.

robo stick   An input device used to manipulate the cursor and to create graphics.

robot   A computer-controlled device that can physically manipulate its surroundings. It is equipped with sensing instruments for detecting input, signals, or environmental conditions, with a calculating mechanism for making decisions, and with a guidance mechanism for providing control. Often robots can speak, respond to verbal instructions, move about, and pick up objects.

robotic control language   A computer language specifically designed to control a robot. It differs from other computer languages in that it controls the movements of robots.

robotics   The science of robot design and use. The branch of engineering devoted to the creation and training of robots. Robots are computer-controlled devices capable of performing many of the tasks performed by humans. Roboticists work within a wide range of fields, such as computer science, bionics, mechanical engineering, electrical engineering, artificial intelligence and cybernetics, all toward the end of producing robots with as much sensitivity, independence, and flexability as possible. See artificial intelligence.

robustness   Quality that causes a software program or set of programs to be able to handle, or at least avoid disaster in the face of, unexpected circumstances, such as when given improper data. An example is the deliberate inclusion of program logic to process anticipated errors in the input, such as testing for the presence of alphabetic data that was accidentally keyboarded into a location reserved for numbers; when such an error is detected, the record containing it is shunted aside from further processing, but program execution is not halted.

rollback System that will restart the running program after a system failure. Snapshots of data and programs are stored at periodic intervals, and the system rolls back to restart at the last recorded snapshot.

roll out To record the contents of internal storage in auxiliary storage.

rollover Buffer that can store typed characters and commands when they are entered faster than the computer system can process them.

roll paper Printer paper in continuous form on a spool. Contrast with fanfold paper.

ROM Acronym for Read-Only Memory. Generally, a solid state storage chip programmed at the time of its manufacture and that cannot be reprogrammed by the computer user. Also called firmware, since this implies software that is permanent or firmly in place on a chip. Contrast with PROM and EPROM.

Roman In typography, a medium-weight typeface in which all letters are upright.

ROM BIOS Acronym for Read-Only Memory, Basic Input/Output System. A special chip used to provide instructions to the computer when the computer is turned on.

ROM cartridge Plug-in module that contains software permanently stored in ROM. A method of entering data and/or programs into a computer. The module can contain one or more printer fonts, programs, games or other information.

ROM simulator General-purpose device used to replace ROMs or PROMs in a system during program checkout. Because it offers real-time in-circuit simulation, it can be used in the engineering prototype or reproduction model to find and correct program errors or in the production model to add new features.

root Top element or node in a tree diagram, from which branches extend eventually to leaf nodes.

root directory Under DOS, the first, top-level directory.

rotating memory Magnetic information storage device in the form of a round platter that is spun like a phonograph record. See magnetic disk.

rotation In computer graphics, the turning of a computer-modeled object relative to an origin point on a coordinate system. In three-dimensional graphics, an object can be rotated in space, usually around the axis, to provide different views. See transformation.

rotational delay Time it takes for a record contained on one of the sectors of a disk to rotate under the read/write head.

rote learning A type of learning in which all knowledge is explicitly provided by an external source, as by programmers in conventional computer programming.

rough draft In desktop publishing, the preliminary page layouts done by the designer using pencil sketches to represent page design ideas. A roughly drawn sketch of a finished document.

round See round off.

rounding Process of dropping the least significant digit or digits of a numeral, and adjusting the remaining numeral to be as close as possible to the original number.

round off To truncate the rightmost digit of a number, and to increase by one the remaining rightmost digit if the truncated digit is greater than or equal to half of the number base. The base 10 number 463.1076 could be rounded to 463.108 or 463.11 or 463.1, depending upon the precision desired.

round-off error Error resulting from rounding off a quantity by deleting the less significant digits and applying the appropriate rule of correction to the part retained; for example, 0.2751 can be rounded to 0.275 with a round-off error of 0.0001, or rounded to 0.28 with a round-off error of 0.0049. Contrast with truncation error.

round robin Scheduling method that engages each device and process at its turn in a fixed cycle.

router Device that connects networks of the same type, allowing equipment on one LAN to communicate with devices on another. Also called a bridge.

routine Short set of program code that performs a specific task. Typically used in reference to assembly language programs. Sometimes used as a synonym for program.

routing Assignment of a path for the delivery of a message.

row (1) Horizontal members of one line of an array. (2) Vertical divisions of an electronic spreadsheet. Together with columns, rows serve to form the spreadsheet matrix. Contrast with column.

RPG Acronym for Report Program Generator, a popular business-oriented programming language, highly structured and relatively easy to learn. Allows users to program many business operations as well as to generate reports. Fairly simple RPG programs can perform rather sophisticated business tasks. RPG was introduced by the IBM Corporation in 1964; RPG II was introduced in 1970.

RPROM Acronym for Reprogrammable PROM. See EPROM.

RS Acronym for Recommended Standards, developed by the Electronic Industries Association.

RS-232C The standard for serial interfaces (serial refers to the eight bits of each character successively sent down one wire) used by most computers, modems, and printers. A 25-pin physical interface.

RTF Acronym for Rich-Text Format, a defacto document-formatting standard, developed by Microsoft Corporation, for exchanging information between program applications running within its Windows environment.

rubber banding In computer graphics, changing the shape of an object made up of connected lines by "grabbing" a point on an anchored line and "pulling" it to the new location.

ruggedized computer Computer designed to be used in special environments, such as aboard a space vehicle, on a ship, in a missile, in a submarine, in a tank, or in farm equipment.

rule (1) A statement about the relationships of various facts or data. (2) A thin line printed above, below, or to the side of some element, either to set that item off from the remainder of the page or to improve the look of the page. (3) In expert systems, a statement that can be used to verify premises and to enable a conclusion to be drawn.

rule-based expert system An expert system based on a set of rules that a human expert would follow in diagnosing a problem.

ruler An on-screen ruler, marked off in inches or other units of measure, is used to show line widths, paragraph indents, center of page, tab settings, etc.

rules-based deduction Technique of obtaining conclusions in which knowledge is represented as a set of simple rules that guide the dialogue between the system and the user.

run Single or continuous execution of a program by a computer on a given set of data. See execute.

run manual Manual or book documenting the processing system, program logic, controls, program changes, and operating instructions associated with a computer run.

running foot A line of text at the bottom margin of a page; usually a page number or footnote. Also called footer.

running head A line of text at the top margin of a page; usually the title of the book, the name of the chapter, the page number, and so on. Also called header.

run time Time during which data are fetched by the control unit and actual processing is performed in the arithmetic-logic unit. Also called execution time. Contrast with compilation time.

RWOD Acronym for Rewritable Optical Disc; generally erasable and re-usable like magnetic disk.

S-100 bus A type of computer bus having 100 connections, standardized by the IEEE, and used extensively in early microcomputers built around the Intel 8080, Motorola 6800, Motorola 68000, and Zilog Z-80 microprocessors.

salami technique The theft of small amounts (slices) of assets from a large number of sources. An embezzlement technique that gets its name from taking a "slice" at a time, such as a few cents from many bank accounts.

sales representative A person who sells computers and related equipment and software. Most representatives work for computer manufacturers, service organizations, or computer stores.

SAM Acronym for Sequential Access Method, a method for storing and retrieving data on a disk file.

sample data Set of hypothetical data used to see if a flowchart is logical and if a program works. See test data.

sampling Collecting a subset of data relevant to a system.

sampling rate Frequency at which sampling occurs.

sampling ratio When electronically scanning art or photographs, the number of pixels recorded from the original image vs the final line screen during printing. The scanner may record at 300 dpi but the finished piece is printed at 150 dpi, a ratio of 2:1. The desired ratio of desktop scans is 1.5:1 to 2:1, that is 1.5 or 2 pixels are scanned for every halftone dot printed.

sans serif Letters of typefaces without serifs—the ornate, widened bases and tops seen on some characters of some type fonts. As a matter of fact, sans means "without" in French. Sans serif fonts have very clean lines and are typically considered friendly, casual and familiar.

sapphire Material used as a substrate for some types of integrated circuit chips.

satellite Earth-orbiting device capable of relaying communications signals over long distances. A radio receiving/transmitting station in geosynchronous orbit 25,000 miles (35,965 kilometers) above earth and broadcasting with a geographically focused beam.

satellite computer (1) Additional computer, usually smaller, that supports a larger computer system. An economy of processing can be effected if the satellite computer handles lower-level functions, such as remote terminal coordination, data validity checking, code conversion, and input/output functions. (2) Any offline auxiliary computer.

saturate To reach maximum capacity, beyond which nothing else can be absorbed or retained. For example, a diskette is saturated when all of its tracks are full of data.

saturation In the HSB color model, one of the three characteristics used to describe a color. Saturation refers to the degree that a color is pure or the degree of white it contains. A highly-saturated color is one that contains little white; a less-saturated color looks washed out.

save To store information somewhere other than in the computer's internal memory, such as on a tape or disk, so it can be used again.

SBC Acronym for Small Business Computer and Single-Board Computer.

scalable font Characters which can be scaled to any size via a page description language. By contrast, bitmap fonts must be loaded for every size, using up storage space. Scalable fonts provide more flexibility than bit-mapped fonts by eliminating the need to store a variety of different font sizes in the computer's memory.

scalar value Integer declared as such in a programming language and possessing a value within a fixed range. Contrast with vector.

scale (1) To adjust the magnitude of a quantity so as to fit it into the available storage location. (2) To change the size of a graphics file by a specified quantity to make it fit a specified boundary. (3) Quantity by which graphic data are multiplied or divided to fit size limitations.

scale factor One or more factors used to multiply or divide quantities occurring in a problem and to convert them into a desired range, such as the range from +1 to -1.

scaling (1) Process of changing one bit-map density into a bit-map of another density. Scaling usually involves enlarging or contracting an image. (2) Process of changing the size of an image. Scaling by a factor of three multiplies all dimensions of an image by 3.

scan (1) To examine point by point in logical sequence. (2) Algorithmic procedure for visiting or listing each node of a data structure. (3) Operation required to produce an image on a visual display screen. Involves moving an electron beam across the inner surface of the screen, one line at a time, to light the phosphor that creates a displayed image. (4) In optical technologies, to view a printed form a line at a time in order to convert images into bit-mapped representations.

scan area That area of a form or document that contains information to be scanned by an optical character reader.

scan head An optical sensing device in an optical scanner or facsimile machine that is moved across the image to be scanned.

scan line Horizontal line on a raster display screen.

scanned image A bit-mapped, or TIFF, image generated by an optical scanner.

scanner An optical reading device that can recognize text, drawings and photographs and convert them into electronic representation of the images. Scanners can be differentiated by whether they process color or are limited to shades of gray. Scanner resolution is determined by the amount of information available from the scanning sensor for a given area. Common resolutions in desktop scanners are 200-600 dots per inch. More powerful systems can scan up to 8000 lines per inch or more.

scanner channel Device that polls individual channels to see if they have data ready to be transmitted. See polling.

scan path In optical scanning, a predetermined area within the clear area where data to be read must be located. The position of the scan path and the amount of data that can be read will generally depend upon the machine involved.

scan rate The number of times a CRT screen is refreshed in a given time period.

scatter diagram An analytical graphic in which data items are plotted as points on x-y coordinate axes.

scatter read/gather write "Scatter read" refers to placing information from an input record into nonadjacent storage areas. "Gather write" refers to placing information from non-adjacent storage areas into a single physical record.

SCDP Acronym for Society of Certified Data Processors.

scenario An imagined sequence of events that determine key system inputs and parameters to a decision-making model. For each scenario, one can then run the model on a computer, observing how system variables interact over time.

schedule A list of events in the order they should occur.

scheduled report Report produced at regular intervals to provide routine information to users.

scheduled maintenance Maintenance of a computer system at fixed intervals to maintain its reliability.

scheduler Program that schedules jobs for processing.

scheduling (1) Task of determining what the succession of programs should be in a multiprogramming computer center. (2) Allocating a nonsharable resource, such as CPU time, or an I/O device to a particular task for a period of time.

schema Structure for organizing knowledge relative to context or expectations. The definition of an entire database.

schematic symbols Symbols used in schematic diagrams.

Scheutz, George (1785-1873) In 1834, started construction of a machine similar to Charles Babbage's difference engine. The machine was completed and used for printing mathematical tables. See Babbage, Charles.

Scheckhardt, Wilhelm (1592-1635) German professor of mathematics who invented a calculating machine in 1624.

scientific applications Tasks that are traditionally numerically oriented and often require advanced engineering, mathematical, or scientific capabilities. Seldom require the extensive file-handling capabilities of business applications.

scientific computer A computer that is capable of high-speed mathematical processing or "number crunching." See supercomputer.

scientific notation Notation in which numbers are written as a "significant digits" part, or mantissa, times an appropriate power of 10, or exponent. For example, 0.32619×10^7 or $0.32619E+07$, stands for 3,261,900. See E notation.

scientific programming language A programming language that is designed to handle mathematical formulas and matrices, such as BASIC, FORTRAN, Pascal, C, and Modula-2.

scissoring Automatic erasing of all portions of a design on the visual display device that lie outside user-specified boundaries.

SCM Acronym for Society for Computer Medicine, an organization that brings together physicians and computer scientists, emphasizing the use of automation for medical applications.

scope (1) Range of control of a software program. (2) Oscilloscope.

SCR Acronym for Silicon Controlled Rectifier, a semiconductor device useful in controlling large amounts of DC current or voltage. Basically, it is a diode turned on or off by a signal voltage applied to a control electrode called the gate. Its characteristics are similar to the old vacuum tube thyratron, which is why it is sometimes called a thyristor.

scrambling Similar to encryption, in which data or transmissions are "scrambled" so they can only be retrieved by authorized users.

scrapbook A storage location for frequently used text and pictures. The stored images can be inserted into new documents as required.

scratch To delete data from memory.

scratch file Temporary file created during the processing of substantial files of data by copying all or part of a data set to an auxiliary storage device.

scratchpad Small, fast storage used in some computers in place of registers. Also called cache memory.

screen (1) A television-like output device that can display information. (2) A pattern of tiny dots used as shading in a graphic.

screen angle The angle at which a halftone screen is printed.

screen capture (1) The transfer of the image on the current display screen into a graphics file. (2) A printout of the current screen display.

screen dump Process of transferring the information currently appearing on a display screen to a printer or saved as a file on disk; a "snapshot" of the screen.

screen fonts The bitmapped representations of a printer font that is used to display the font on the screen. A screen font is designed to mimic the appearance of printer fonts when displayed on medium-resolution monitors.

screen generator Special utility program used to create customized screen displays.

screen overlay (1) A clear, fine-mesh screen that reduces the glare on a video screen. (2) A window of data that in part overlays another window of data.

screen position Physical location of graphic data on a visual display screen.

screen resolution A measure of the crispness of images and characters on a screen, usually specified in terms of the number of pixels in a row or column.

screen saver A program that produces moving patterns on the screen after a specified number of minutes without keyboard or mouse activity. Pressing a key on the keyboard or moving the mouse restores the screen. Screen savers are used to prolong the life of a monitor; they prevent one image from being burned into the screen phosphors. See also phosphor burn-in.

screen size Measure of the amount of information that a video display screen can display. Screens can be measured diagonally, as TV sets (usually a diagonal measure in inches), or by the number of vertical and horizontal dot or character positions. See resolution.

screen update Process of changing screen contents to reflect new information.

script font A typeface that looks like fine handwriting or calligraphy.

scripts Framelike structures for representing sequences of events.

scroll To move information (graphics or text) up/down or right/left on a computer display screen.

scroll arrow An arrow displayed at the ends of each scroll bar. Clicking or holding the mouse pointer on the scroll arrow causes the document in the window to move.

scroll bar In some types of graphical user interface, a vertical or horizontal bar at the side or bottom of a window that can be used with a mouse for moving around in a document.

scroll box A box that slides in a scroll bar to indicate the relative position of a displayed document.

scrolling The vertical or horizontal movement of information (text or graphics) on a display screen in order to display additional information.

SCS Acronym for Society for Computer Simulation.

SCSI Stands for Small Computer Systems Interface. The SCSI is a general purpose parallel interface designed for connecting one or more computers and one or more peripherals—a total of 8 devices may be connected to one bus. It is an industry standard interface for high-speed access to peripheral devices. Used extensively on the Apple Macintosh computer. SCSI's great advantage is its ability to chain together multiple devices on a single I/O card, each of which has a unique address.

Sculley, John During the first nine years of its existence, Apple Computer, Inc. became a dynamic leader of the personal computer industry. John Sculley now guides Apple Computer in today's world of educational and business computing. Under Sculley's guidance, new Macintosh computer and laser printer products have been developed that will aid people in using computers.

SEAC Acronym for Standard Eastern Automatic Computer, built by the United States Bureau of Standards.

sealed module A disk drive containing the disks, access arms, and read/write heads sealed together. Also called a Winchester disk.

search (1) To examine a set of items for those that have some desired property or predetermined criterion, such as a particular name or graphic image. (2) A procedure for automated problem solving in which a computer seeks a solution by selecting among various possible alternates.

search and replace Software feature that finds a designated character sequence and replaces it with a new one. Important in word processing applications. See global search and replace.

search key Data to be compared to specified parts of each item for the purpose of conducting a search.

search memory See associative storage.

search tree A hierarchical arrangement of choices used in solving a problem through search.

secondary key Field used to gain access to records in a file; not required to be unique.

secondary storage Memory device that supplements the primary internal memory of a computer. Same as auxiliary storage. Contrast with main storage.

second generation computers Computers belonging to the second era of technological development of computers, when the transistor replaced the vacuum tube. Prominent from 1959 to 1964, when they were displaced by computers using integrated circuitry.

second source Manufacturer who produces a product interchangeable with the product of another manufacturer.

secret key An encryption key that must not be disclosed. If they are revealed, the security offered by an encryption algorithm is compromised. Not all encryption keys have to be kept secret. See public key.

sector An area on a disk. Disks are usually divided into sectors and tracks. The address where data is stored is made up of the sector and track number. On most computers, a sector is the smallest unit of information sent between the disk drive and the CPU.

sector method A method of organizing data on a disk in which each track is divided into pie-shaped sectors that hold a specific number of characters.

secure kernel Protected segment of a systems program.

security State achieved by hardware, software, or data as a result of successful efforts to prevent damage, theft, or corruption.

security controls Methods to ensure that only authorized users have access to a computer system and its resources. See password.

346

security files Back-up files for important and critical data and information.

security program Program that controls access to data in files and permits only authorized use of terminals and other equipment.

security specialist Person responsible for the physical security of the computer center and logical security for data resources.

seed Value used initially by an algorithm. For example, a random number generating program may use a seed number (constant) to begin generating a series of random numbers.

seek To position the access mechanism of a direct access device at a specified location.

seek time Time required for an access arm to position over a particular track on a disk.

segment (1) To divide a program into parts such that some segments may reside in internal storage and other segments may reside in auxiliary storage. Each segment will contain the necessary instructions to jump to another segment or to call another segment into internal storage. (2) Smallest functional unit that can be loaded as one logical entity during execution of an overlay program. (3) As applied to the field of telecommunications, a portion of a message that can be contained in a buffer of specified size.

segmentation Technique for dividing computer programs into logical, variable-length blocks.

segmented bar chart Bar chart made up of two or more segments positioned atop each other to represent elements of a whole. Similar to a pie chart, except that varying sizes of bars can be used to allow comparisons of the whole as well as its constituent parts.

select To pick out a group of records from a database according to a specifications provided by the user. For example, to select all records with the year greater than 1991.

selection Choosing between alternatives.

selection sort Sort that selects the extreme value (smallest or largest) in a list, exchanges it with the lst value in the list, and repeats with a shorter list.

selection structure One of three primary structures of a structured flowchart. Provides a choice between two alternative paths, based upon a certain condition. Also called decision structure and IF-THEN-ELSE. See sequence structure and loop structure.

selector In object-oriented programming, an operation that accesses the state of an object but does not alter that state.

selector channel   In certain computer systems, an input/output channel that can transfer data to or from only one peripheral device at a time. Contrast with multiplexer channel.

self-adapting   Pertaining to the ability of a system to change its performance characteristics in response to its environment.

self-checking code   See error-detecting code.

self-compiling compiler   Compiler written in its own source language and capable of compiling itself.

self-complementing code   Code with the property that the binary one's complement of the weighted binary number is also the number's nine's complement in decimal notation.

self-correcting code   Numerical coding system in which transmission errors are automatically detected and corrected. Same as error-correcting code.

self-validating code   Code that makes an explicit attempt to determine its own correctness and proceed accordingly.

semantic net   A knowledge representation scheme that organizes human knowledge into a weblike structure consisting of nodes—objects, concepts and events—connected by links that specify the nature of the connections.

semantics   Study of the science of meaning in language forms. Pertains to the relationships between symbols and what they represent. See programming linguistics.

semaphores   Synchronization primitives used to coordinate the activities of two or more programs or processes running at the same time and sharing information.

semiconductor   A crystalline substance, usually germanium or silicon, that conducts electricity when it is "doped" with chemical impurities. It is the material from which integrated circuits are made.

semiconductor device   Electronic element fabricated from crystalline materials such as silicon or germanium that, in the pure state, are neither good conductors nor good insulators and are unusable for electronic purposes. When certain impurity atoms, such as phosphorus or arsenic, are diffused into the crystal structure of the pure metal, the electrical neutrality is upset, introducing positive or negative charge carriers. Diodes and transistors can then be implemented.

Semiconductor Industry Association (SIA)   A consortium of semiconductor product producers formed to address the interests of the semiconductor industry and provide a collective voice for lobbying efforts.

semiconductor storage   Memory device whose storage elements are formed as solid state electronic components on an integrated circuit chip.

semirandom access Method of locating data in storage that combines in the search for the desired item some form of direct access, usually followed by a limited sequential search.

sense (1) To examine, particularly relative to a criterion. (2) To determine the present arrangement of some element of hardware. (3) To read holes punched on a card.

sense probe Input mechanism that activates sensitive points on a visual display screen and thereby provides input to a computer.

sense switch Computer console switch that may be interrogated by a program. Very useful when debugging a large, complex program.

sensitivity Degree of response of a control unit to a change in the incoming signal.

sensors Devices to detect and measure physical phenomena, such as temperature, stress, heartbeat, wind direction, and fire. Translate physical stimuli into electronic signals that may, for example, be input into computers.

separated graphics Graphics characters with spaces between them. When a set of characters, with a space at one side and at the top or bottom, is printed in adjacent positions, the spaces will separate the graphics characters.

sequence (1) Arrangement of items according to a specified set of rules. (2) In numeric sequence, normally in ascending order.

sequence check Check used to prove that a set of data is arranged in ascending or descending order.

sequence structure One of three primary structures of a structured flowchart, in which instructions are executed in order. See selection structure and loop structure.

sequential Pertaining to the occurrence of events in time sequence, with little or no simultaneity or overlap of events.

sequential access Process of obtaining data from storage files in the order in which it was stored. Required with magnetic tape, which must be searched serially from the beginning to find any desired record. May be used with magnetic disk storage, which is more commonly accessed randomly. Also called serial access. Contrast with direct access.

sequential computer Computer in which events occur in time sequence with little or no simultaneity or overlap of events.

sequential data set Data set whose records are organized on the basis of their successive physical positions, such as on magnetic tape.

sequential data structure Data structure in which one atom is immediately adjacent to the next atom. Also called contiguous data structure.

sequential device Peripheral device from which data are read or into which data are written in order; nothing can be omitted.

sequential file organization A file whose records can be accessed only sequentially.

sequential list List stored in contiguous locations. Also called dense list and linear list.

sequential logic Circuit arrangement in which the output state is determined by the previous state of the input. Contrast with combination logic.

sequential machine Mathematical model of a certain type of sequential switching circuit.

sequential processing Processing of files ordered numerically or alphabetically by key. Contrast with direct access processing and random processing.

sequential storage Auxiliary storage where data are arranged in ascending or descending order, usually by item number.

serial (1) Pertaining to the sequential occurrence of two or more related activities in a single device. (2) Handling of data in a sequential fashion. Contrast with parallel.

serial access Descriptive of a storage device or medium in which there is a sequential relationship between access time and data location in storage; that is, the access time is dependent upon the location of the data. Also called sequential access. Contrast with direct access. See serial processing.

serial adder Adder that performs its operations by bringing in one digit at a time from each of the quantities involved. Contrast with parallel adder.

serial cable One common term for a cable for connecting devices with serial ports (where each byte is sent, bit by bit, down a single wire).

serial computer Computer in which each digit or data word bit is processed serially by the computer. Contrast with parallel computer.

serial data Data transmitted sequentially, one bit at a time.

serial input/output Data transmission in which the bits are sent one by one over a single wire. Contrast with parallel input/output.

serial interface Interface on which all the data moves over the same wire, one bit after the other. Contrast with parallel interface.

serializability   When several users access data at the same time, the result must be equivalent to that which occurs when they access the data one at a time. This effect is called serializability.

serial mouse   A mouse that connects to a computer's serial port.

serial operation   Computer operation in which all digits of a word are handled sequentially rather than simultaneously. See conversational operation. Contrast with parallel operation.

serial port   Input/output port in a computer through which data are transmitted and received one bit at a time.

serial printer   Printer that receives information from the computer one bit at a time through a single wire. (One character equals eight bits). One or more additional wires may be necessary to exchange control signals. Prints one character at a time. Serial printers are designed to be connected to the computer's serial port.

serial processing   Reading and/or writing records on a file, one by one, in the physical sequence in which they are stored. See serial access. Contrast with parallel processing.

serial transmission   Method of data transfer in which the bits composing a character are sent sequentially. Required for telephone data transfer. Contrast with parallel transmission.

Series/1   A series of minicomputers from IBM Corporation, introduced in 1976.

serif   An ending stroke on the arms, tails and stems of characters in certain typeface designs. Serif type styles are typically considered businesslike, formal, and authoritative.

serif face   A typeface that contains serifs, or finishing strokes.

server   (1) The central computer in a local area network (LAN); it is responsible for managing the LAN. The server is dedicated to serving devices attached to the network. (2) In object-oriented programming, an object that never operates upon other objects, but that is only operated upon by other objects.

service bureau   Organization that provides data processing services for other individuals or organizations. See imagesetter service bureau.

service contract   Contract with a computer dealer, computer store, or service company that ensures immediate repair of a computer system.

service programs   Programs that supplement the control programs of an operating system, such as language translators, utility routines, and programmer aids.

351

service window The hours during the day or night that are covered by a maintenance agreement. Service provided outside of the "window" is. not covered by the contract.

servomechanism Feedback control system.

session Period of time during which a computer system operator works from a a terminal at one sitting.

set (1) To place a binary cell into the 1 state. (2) To place a storage device into a specified state, usually other than denoting zero or blank. (3) Any collection of related things. (4) In a relational database model, a collection of things. (5) In a network/hierarchical database model, a one-to-many relationship, the path by which one record type is connected to another.

SETL High-level language designed to facilitate the programming of algorithms involving sets and related structures.

setup Arrangement of data or devices to solve a particular problem.

setup time Time between computer runs or other machine operations that is devoted to such tasks as changing disk packs and moving forms, and other supplies to and from the equipment.

shade (1) In computer graphics, the quantity of black mixed with a pure color. (2) To give added dimension to an image by including changes in appearance caused by light and shadow.

shading symbols Block graphics characters that are part of some computer graphics built-in character sets. Provide different dot densities, giving the appearance of different levels of shading.

shadow memory In 32-bit computers, a portion of random access memory set aside for the storage of ROM routines during an operating session so that these routines can be executed at the microprocessor's fastest possible speed.

shadow printing A style applied to text in which a duplicate of each character is shifted, often down and to the right, to create a shadow effect.

Shannon, Claude E. Made contributions to Boolean algebra, cryptography, and computing circuits, and to communications with his mathematical theory of information. His ideas were important in the development of the binary system of information storage on which the modern computer is based. His ideas gave impetus to the field of information science.

SHARE Organization of users of medium-and large-scale IBM data processing systems.

shared file Direct access device that may be used by two systems at the same time. May link two computer systems.

shared logic   Concurrent use of a single computer by multiple users.

shared memory   Memory accessed by two or more programs in a multitasking environment.

shared resource   Computer resource shared by more than one user or computer system.

shareware   Software that is passed around. The authors let you copy and share their programs freely, but retain the copyrights. Shareware provides income to its author in the form of "contributions," much like public TV. Payment is strictly voluntary. Even though shareware is given away free, the maker hopes that satisfied users will voluntarily pay for it.

sharpness   Clarity and quality of an image produced on a visual display device, digital plotter, printer, film recorder, and other devices. See resolution.

sheetfed scanner   A scanner into which you feed single pages.

sheet feeder   Device that attaches to the printer, designed to automatically insert and line up single sheets of paper or envelopes in much the same way as an operator would perform the task. Usually sits above the printer platen and is operated either mechanically or electrically by the printer. See friction-feed.

shell   (1) An operating environment layer that separates the operating system from the user. The shell provides a graphical icon-oriented or menu-driven interface to the system in order to make it easier to use. (2) A high-level expert system framework. A shell is an expert system without the domain knowledge.

Shell sort   An algorithm, developed by Donald Shell, used for ordering data; it is faster than the bubble sort and the insertion sort.

shield   A foil or braided wire covering for a cable that prevents excessive noise pickup or radiation.

shielding   Protection against electrical or magnetic noise.

shift   To move the characters of a unit or information columnwise right or left. For a number, this is equivalent to multiplying or dividing by a power of the base of notation.

shift-click   To click the mouse button while depressing the shift key on the keyboard.

shift-key   Key on a computer keyboard that, when pressed, makes letters print as capitals instead of lower-case letters and allows some special characters to be printed. On many keyboards, acts as a shift lock and must be pressed again to return to lower case.

Shockley, William Bradford Bell Labs scientist who, along with Walter Brattain and John Bardeen invented the transistor. Instrumental in inventing magnetic bubble memory.

short card In a microcomputer, a plug-in printed circuit board that is half the length of a full size accessory card or expansion card. Short cards plug into the microcomputer's expansion slots.

shortest operating time Scheduling procedure for scheduling jobs that take the shortest amount of computer time first.

shutdown Termination of electrical power to all or part of the computer system components, whether intentional or inadvertent.

SIA See Semiconductor Industry Association.

sidebar A block of text or a graphic image placed to the side of the main body of text in a document.

side effect Consistent result of a procedure that is in addition to the basic result.

SideKick A desktop accessory program that provides a computerized calculator, notepad, appointment calendar, and automated phone dialer. These features can be used alone or in combination with each other; some features can also be used with other software. Developed by Borland International Inc.

sift To extract certain desired items of information from a large amount of data. Compare select.

sifting Method of internal sorting by which records are moved to permit the insertion of other records. Also called insertion method. Compare bubble sort.

SIG Acronym for Special Interest Group. Often a sub-unit of a professional organization. Made up of members with common interests, e.g., a "Computers in Education" SIG, a "Computer Graphics" SIG, or a "Computers in Medicine" SIG.

SIGGRAPH A special interest group on computer graphics that is part of the Association for Computing Machinery (ACM). Each year SIGGRAPH holds an annual conference. The conference has become a focus for the exchange of information regarding fundamental discoveries and the latest innovations in the field of computer graphics. The conference includes lectures, exhibits, films and a computer art show.

sign Used in the arithmetic sense to describe whether a number is positive or negative.

signal In communications theory, an intentional disturbance in a communications system. Contrast with noise.

signal-to-noise ratio In data communications, the ratio of the (wanted) signal to the (unwanted) noise.

signaling rate Rate at which signals are transmitted over a communications link.

sign digit Digit in the sign position of a word.

sign extension Duplication of the sign bit in the higher-order positions of a register. Usually performed on one's complement or two's complement binary values.

sign flag Flip-flop that goes to position 1 if the most significant bit of the result of an operation has the value of 1.

significant digit Any digit that contributes to the precision of a number. The number of significant digits is counted beginning with the digit contributing the most value, called the most significant digit, and ending with the one contributing the least value, called the least significant digit.

sign-off (1) Process of disconnecting from a time-sharing computer network. (2) Dissolution of any user/computer interface.

sign-on (1) Process of getting connected to a time-sharing computer network. (2) Establishment of any user/computer interface.

sign position Position at which the sign of a number is located.

silicon A nonmetallic chemical element used in the manufacture of integrated circuits, solar cells, and so forth. It is a chemical element (atomic number 14, symbol Si) widely found in sand and clay. Next to oxygen, silicon is the most abundant element in the Earth's crust. It was discovered by Swedish chemist Baron Jons Jakob Berzelius in 1823. Silicon grows with a native oxide on its surface. It is perfect for delivering and protecting an exact wiring pattern of millions of integrated circuits that make up a chip. Also, it is cost-attractive and easy to handle environmentally. The chip manufacturing process starts with common sand, or quartz, that is purified into polycrystalline silicon. In its raw form, the "poly" looks very similar to a lump of coal, only shinier. A complex process and advanced technologies convert this raw material into computer chips. Building a chip of a particular design requires several months in a series of 150 to 200 chemical and physical processes. The various steps of chip fabrication are grouped into nine broad categories—oxidation, photolithography, diffusion, metalization, sputtered quartz, terminal metals, dicing, chip placement and module encapsulation. Adding to the complexity, chips must be fabricated in ultra-clean environments that are about 1,000 times cleaner than a hospital operating room. This is necessary to assure their quality and reliability.

silicon chip Tiny portion of a silicon wafer with thousands of electronic components and circuit patterns etched on its surface.

silicon-controlled rectifier (SCR) Semiconductor device that, in its normal state, blocks a voltage applied in either direction.

silicon disk drive A drive that uses banks of RAM as a storage device.

Silicon Valley Nickname for an area south of San Francisco noted for its large number of electronic, semiconductor, and computer manufacturing firms. Also known as Silicon Gulch.

silicon wafer Silicon slice on which integrated chips are fabricated. After fabrication, the wafer is cut into many individual chips, which are then mounted in dual in-line packages.

SIMM Acronym for Single In-line Memory Module. A module designed to add memory to a computer system. A special type of RAM chip that plugs into a socket on the computer's motherboard.

Simon, Herbert and Alan Newell The two scientists who demonstrated that the computer could be used to study the mind. These pioneers in artificial intelligence initiated symbolic processing with computers.

simplex Pertaining to a communications link capable of transmitting data in only one direction. Contrast with full-duplex and half-duplex.

SIMSCRIPT High-level programming language specifically designed for simulation applications.

Simula A language developed in the late 1960s for programming simulations. Simula included class and inheritance mechanisms and is considered to have influenced today's object-oriented languages. Simula was a forerunner of Smalltalk.

simulation Representation of certain features of the behavior of a physical or abstract system by the behavior of another system, such as the representation of physical phenomena by means of operations performed by a computer, or the representation of operations of a computer by those of another computer.

simulator Device, computer program, or system that represents certain features of the behavior of a physical or abstract system. For example, a computer-controlled aircraft simulator is used by most airline companies to train pilots.

simultaneous input/output Process in which some computer systems allow new information to be input while other information is being output.

simultaneous processing Execution of more than one program at the same time, each program using a separate CPU.

single address See one-address instruction.

single-board computer Computer that contains all its circuitry on one board, including the CPU, ROM, RAM, and peripheral interfaces.

356

single density   Method of storing data on a diskette. See double density.

single entry   Unique point where execution of a program module begins.

single exit   Unique point where termination of a program module occurs.

Single In-line Memory Module (SIMM)   A module designed to ad memory to a computer system. SIMMs are used in the Apple Macintosh line of computers.

single precision   Pertaining to the use of one computer word to represent a number. Contrast with double precision and triple precision.

single-sided disk   Diskette with only one side used for reading and writing information. Contrast with double-sided disk.

single step   Operation of a computer in such a manner that only one instruction is executed each time the computer is started.

single-user computer   A microcomputer designed for use by one person; a personal computer.

site license   License permitting a customer to make multiple copies of a piece of software and distribute them freely within the facility.

sixteen-bit chip   Microprocessor chip that processes information sixteen bits at a time. Contrast with eight-bit chip and thirty-two-bit chip.

sizing   The process of changing the size or shape of a window.

sketching   Computer graphics technique in which a trail of lines is drawn or sketched along the path of the cursor.

sketch pad   Working storage area displayed on a visual display screen that permits the operator to add and delete graphic or textual information easily before it is entered into permanent storage.

skew   In computer graphics and optical scanning, a condition in which a character, line, or reprinted symbol is neither parallel with nor at right angles to the leading edge. See stair stepping.

skip   To ignore one or more instructions in a sequence of instructions.

skip factor   In a computer graphics program, an increment that specifies how many data points the program should skip as it constructs a chart or graph.

slab   Part of a word.

slack time   See float.

slave   Device controlled by another device.

slave tube Cathode ray tube connected to another in such a way that both tubes perform identically.

SLD A slide file format for AutoCAD.

sleeve Protective envelope for storing a diskette.

slew To move paper through a printer.

slewing Pertaining to the speed at which numerically controlled machine tools move from one position to another.

slice (1) The thin substrate resulting when a silicon ingot is cut; the wafer. (2) Special type of chip architecture that permits the cascading of devices to increase word bit size.

slide Photographic representation of a visual screen display.

slide show Computer graphics software that displays graphics images in a timed sequence on the video display screen, similar to a slide show. Some programs can produce interesting effects, such as fading out one screen before displaying another and enabling you to choose a path through the images available for display.

slot (1) Single board position in a backplane. (2) In data communications, a unit of time in a multiplexed channel. (3) In artificial intelligence, an element of a frame that is filled with descriptive information about a particular object or concept. (4) In object-oriented programming, a respository for part of the state of an object; collectively, the slots of an object constitute its structure. The terms "field," "instance variable," "member object" and "slot" are interchangeable.

SLSI Acronym for Super Large Scale Integration.

slug (1) In desktop publishing, a code inserted in headers or footers that generates page numbers when the document is printed. (2) In line printers, a metal casting that carries the image of a printable character. Prints by striking the paper.

small caps A font of capital letters that are smaller than the standard capital letters in that typeface.

Small Computer System Interface (SCSI) A general purpose parallel interface for high-speed access to peripheral devices.

small scale integration (SSI) Class of integrated circuits that has the fewest number of functions per chip.

SmallTalk An object-oriented programming language in which text is entered into the computer by using the keyboard, but all other tasks are performed using a mouse. SmallTalk systems are characterized by a high degree of pictorial interaction. SmallTalk was developed in the late 1970s by Alan Kay at Xerox Corporation's Palo Alto Research Center (PARC). It was used on Xerox's Alto computer, which was designed for it. SmallTalk has served as the forerunner of various computer languages and environments in use today. SmallTalk was the first truly object-oriented programming language and environment.

smart Having some computational ability of its own. Smart devices usually contain their own microprocessors. A synonym for intelligent.

smart card Credit card with a built-in microprocessor and memory that can be used as an identification or financial transaction card.

smart machines Machines that use microprocessors as their control elements.

smart terminal Terminal that contains some capacity to process information being transmitted or received, although not as much as an intelligent terminal. See local intelligence. Contrast with dumb terminal.

smash To destroy an area of storage by overwriting with another program.

SME See Society of Manufacturing Engineers.

SMIS Acronym for Society for Management Information Systems, a professional organization for fostering improved management performance and information exchange.

smooth To apply procedures that decrease or eliminate rapid fluctuations in data.

smooth scrolling Ability to scroll text without it jerking from one line to the next.

SNA Acronym for Systems Network Architecture.

snapshot dump Dynamic dump of the contents of specified storage locations and/or registers performed at specified points or times during the running of a program.

snap, snap to The automatic movement of a selected object or point to the nearest designated grid line, grid intersection, or connection point.

SNOBOL Acronym for StriNg-Oriented symBOlic Language. Unique language that provides complete facilities for the manipulation of strings of characters. SNOBOL was developed in 1962 by Ralph Griswold at Bell Laboratories and was the forerunner of languages such as LISP. Nowadays, the language is little used because the language statements do not provide for structured programming. However, the characteristics of SNOBOL make it suitable for artificial intelligence applications.

SO Acronym for Send Only, a designation used to indicate the send-only capabilities of equipment. Contrast with receive only.

Society for Computer Simulation (SCS)   Only technical society devoted primarily to the advancement of simulation and allied technologies, notably those dealing with management, social, scientific, biological, and environmental problems. Has a worldwide membership.

Society of Certified Data Processors (SCDP)   Organization that represents the interests and wishes of certified computer professionals, formed in 1971. Members control what positions, actions, and directions the organization takes.

Society of Manufacturing Engineers (SME)   A professional society of manufacturing engineers, industrial engineers, computer professionals and others involved in manufacturing disciplines. SME has Special Interest Groups (SIGs) for all areas of manufacturing. The Computer and Automated Systems Association (CASA) and Robotics International (RI) groups are very active in developing and promoting advanced manufacturing techniques and philosophies.

soft clip area   Limits of the area where data can be presented on a plotting device.

soft copy   Data presented as a display screen image, in audio format, or in any other form that is not hard copy.

soft fails   Noise bursts in microelectronic circuits caused by cosmic-ray particles may result in spontaneous changes in the information stored in computer memories. These changes are called soft fails. This sensitivity to cosmic rays is one of the unanticipated results of the ever-decreasing size of the components of integrated microelectronic circuits, and it presents new considerations in the development of very large scale integrated circuits.

soft font   A font that is downloaded from a computer to a printer from files stored on a disk.

soft hyphen   Conditional (nonrequired) hyphen printed only to break a word between syllables at the end of a line. Contrast with hard hyphen.

soft keys   Keys on a keyboard that can have a user-defined meaning. Called soft keys because their meaning can change from user to user or program to program.

soft return   Combination line feed/carriage return command, entered by a program containing the word wrap feature to begin a new line within a paragraph. Unlike a hard return, it is conditional—the computer executes the command only when the current word doesn't fit in the line in progress.

soft sector   Method of marking sectors or sections on a disk by using information written on the disk. Method of determining positioning of data on the disk by software calculations rather than by physical monitoring of the disk. Contrast with hard sector.

software The generic term for any computer program or programs; instructions that cause the hardware to do work. Contrast with the "iron" or hardware of a computer system.

software base Software available for a particular computer system. The broader the software base, the more versatile the compute system.

software broker Individual who specializes in marketing software packages.

software command language A high-level programming language developed to work with an application, such as a database management program.

software company Software house.

software compatibility Ability to use programs written for one system on another system with little or no change.

software development Creation of sets of programs that meet the requirements of a user.

software development tools Programs used to develop, analyze, debug, and perfect software. These tools include compilers, editors, debuggers, linkers, optimizers and libraries.

software documents Written or printed material associated with computer equipment and software systems.

software encryption Encoding or decoding of computerized data by using programming techniques rather than hardware devices, such as scramblers.

software engineering A term coined in 1967 by the Study Group on Computer Science of the NATO Science Committee to imply the need for software manufacture based on the types of theoretical foundations and practical disciplines traditional in established branches of engineering. Software engineering is concerned with the development and implementation of large-scale software systems on production-model computers. Encompasses a broad range of topics related to the controlled design and development of high-quality computer software, including programming methodology (structured programming, egoless programming, software quality assurance, programming productivity aids) and management of software projects (structured walk-throughs, chief programmer teams, program support library, HIPO technique).

software flexibility Property of software that enables it to change easily in response to different user and system requirements.

software house Company that offers both general software packages and specific software packages for sale to computer system owners. See packaged software.

software librarian Person in charge of a large collection of software (usually on disk packs, diskettes, or magnetic tapes) in a company. See custodian.

software license Contract signed by the purchaser of a software product in which he/she is usually made to agree not to make copies of the software for resale.

software maintenance Ongoing process of detecting and removing errors from existing programs. Done by maintenance programmers.

software monitor Program used for performance measurement purposes.

software package A prewritten program that can be purchased for use with a specific computer to perform a specific task. Usually includes the programs, stored on a storage media (floppy disk, CD-ROM and so on), and an operating manual. Examples of software packages for microcomputers include word processing packages such as WordPerfect and Microsoft Word, paint packages such as SuperPaint and Deluxe Paint, educational packages, desktop publishing packages such as PageMaker and Ventura Publisher, game packages, and so on.

software piracy Copying of commercial or proprietary software without permission of the originator.

software portability Ease with which a program can be moved from one computer environment to another. As third-party software becomes more prevalent in the computer industry, portability becomes a more valuable attribute of that software.

software product Vendor package comprising programs, data, documentation, and sometimes vendor assistance. Also called programming product.

software protection Resistance to unauthorized copying of software. See software piracy.

software publisher Business that designs, develops, and distributes software packages.

software resources Program and data resources that represent the software associated with a computing system.

software science Discipline concerned with the measurable properties of computer programs.

software security The protection of software assets such as user application programs, database management software, and the operating system.

software system Entire set of computer programs and their documentation, as used in a computer system.

software tools Programs that help programmers write other programs. Such tools include compilers, editors, debuggers, clip-art libraries, source-code libraries, and so on.

software transportability Ability to take a program written for one computer and run it without modification on another computer. See software portability.

soldered Refers to the way chips are placed on circuit boards. Chips are soldered onto the board with a melted metal that seats them securely in place. Today, some boards have snap-in chips, making it easier for end users to add and replace chips as necessary.

solicitation Request to vendors to submit bids for hardware, software, or services. See request for proposal and request for quotation.

solid A black or one-color area on a printed page that contains no artwork, text or patterns.

solid modeling A mathematical technique for representing three-dimensional images and cross-sections of solids. Unlike wireframe and surface modeling, solid modeling systems ensure that all surfaces meet properly and that the object is geometrically correct.

solid state The generic name given to integrated circuits and other electronic systems containing no moving parts as part of their prime functions.

solid state device Device built primarily from solid state electronic circuit elements.

S-100 bus Standard means of interconnection between some older microcomputers and peripheral equipment. So named because popularity made it standard, and it has 100 electrical contacts.

son file See father file.

sonic pen A pencil-shaped device using sound to select a screen location.

SOP Acronym for Standard Operating Procedure, the status quo.

sort To arrange data into a new sequence according to a logical system.

sort effort Number of steps needed to order an unordered list.

sorter A program that sorts data.

sort generator Program that generates a sort program for production running.

sorting Process of arranging data according to a logical system.

sort/merge program Generalized processing program that can be used to sort or merge records in a prescribed sequence.

SOS Acronym for Silicon On Sapphire, the process of fabricating integrated chips on layers of silicon and sapphire.

sound Any wave motion in air that is detected by the ear. Most computes have commands that enable sounds to be generated, ranging from simple beeps to multichannel music with harmony.

sound chip The integrated circuit that executes sound instructions. Microcomputers use specialized sound chips that are microprocessors in their own right. A distinguishing feature of these chips is their ability to synthesize sound effects.

sound hood Device that fits over a printer during use to dampen noise. Also called acoustical sound enclosure.

source (1) One of three terminals or electrodes of a field effect transistor. Origin of the charge carriers that flow past the gate to the drain. (2) A disk, file, or document from which data is taken or moved.

Source (The) An information utility service available to subscribers. It allows users with microcomputers and modems to play games, access databases, check flight schedules, post messages, receive and send electronic mail, read newspaper wire services, and a host of other things. Personal computer users can use The Source network via a common telephone hookup. It is operated by The Source Telecomputing Corporation.

source code Symbolic coding in its original form before being processed by a computer. The computer automatically translates source code into a code the computer can understand.

source computer Computer used to translate a source program into an object program.

source-data automation Process whereby data created while an event is taking place is entered directly into the system in a machine-processable form. See point of sale terminal and transaction-oriented processing.

source disk Disk from which a file or program is copied. Contrast with target disk.

source document Any original document from which basic data is extracted, such as an invoice, a sales slip, or an inventory tag.

source language Any low-level language, such as assembly language, or any high-level language—such as BASIC, Pascal, or COBOL—in which a source program is written.

source media Checks or other source documents from which raw data is derived. Compare input media and output media.

source program A program as originally coded, before being translated into machine language. It is converted to a machine language program by a compiler, interpreter, or assembler.

source program listing Printed version of a program as the programmer wrote it.

source register Register that contains a data word that is being transferred.

source statement A single statement in the source code of a program.

SPA Acronym for Systems and Procedures Association, a professional organization whose purpose is to promote advanced management systems and procedures through seminars, professional education, and research.

space (1) One or more blank characters. (2) State of a communications channel corresponding to a binary zero.

spacebar At the bottom of a keyboard, the long, narrow key that generates spaces. When pressed once, it causes a space to be placed into text at the insertion point.

spaghetti code A program written with poor structure and very little discernable logic flow. The term was first used by Edsger Dijkstra. It often implies an excessive use of the GOTO statement.

span Difference between the highest and lowest values in a range of values.

spanning tree Subgraph of a graph with two properties: (a) it is a tree, and (b) it contains all the nodes of the original graph.

sparse array Array in which most of the entries have a value of zero.

spatial data management Technique that allows users access to information by pointing at pictures on a display screen, representing databases, document files, or any category of information.

spatial digitizer Device often used in computer graphics to simulate three-dimensional objects; a three-dimensional scanner.

spec Abbreviation for specification. More often specs.

special character Graphics character that is neither a letter, a digit, nor a blank; for example, plus sign, equal sign, asterisk, dollar sign, comma, period, and so on.

special function key Key on a keyboard to control a mechanical function, initiate a specific computer operation, or transmit a signal that would otherwise require multiple key strokes.

Special Interest Group (SIG)   Any special group within an organization that holds meetings, sponsors exhibits, and publishes documents related to some special interest, topic, or subject. The Association for Computing Machinery (ACM) has more than thirty SIGs. These groups elect their own officers, set their own dues, and are self-supporting.

Special Libraries Association (SLA)   This international organization of libraries and information specialists promotes the establishment of resource centers for various interest groups, such as banks, museums, and law firms.

special-purpose   Being applicable to a limited class of uses without essential modification. See dedicated. Contrast with general-purpose.

special-purpose computer   Computer designed for solving only a few selected types of numerical or logical problems. Uses range from automobiles, cameras, and home appliances to monitoring flights of space vehicles. Contrast with general-purpose computer.

special-purpose programming language   Programming language designed to handle one specific type of problem or application.

specification   Detailed description of the required characteristics of a device, process, or product.

specification sheet   Form used for coding RPG statements.

specs   Specifications.

SpectraColor   A color paint program for the Commodore Amiga computer.

speech processing   The field of artificial intelligence whose goal is to recognize and synthesize spoken human speech.

speech recognition   Process of presenting input data to the computer through the spoken word. The discrimination of speech sounds by a computer.

speech recognition device   Device that accepts the spoken word through a microphone and converts it into digital code that can be understood by a computer.

speech synthesis   The computer generation of sound that resembles human speech. The synthesis is accomplished through the use of stored sounds and algorithms.

speech synthesizer   Device that converts numerical code into recognizable speech, which is played over a loudspeaker. Peripheral that converts output signals into an artificial human voice that "speaks." See digital speech.

speed of light Speed at which light travels—186,284 miles per second. Limiting factor in the speed of data transmissions within and between computers and peripherals.

spelling checker Computer program, usually associated with word processing, that compares typed words against a word list and informs the user of possible spelling mistakes. A sophisticated spelling checker can have a base dictionary of well over 100,000 words and can provide the user with the ability to create special-purpose dictionaries of words not included in the base dictionary.

spider configuration Type of distributed system in which a central computer system is used to monitor the activities of several network computer systems.

speech understanding systems Artificial intelligence programs whose goal is to understand human speech.

spike Sharp-peaked, short-duration voltage transient. Brief sudden surge of electricity. A spike that affects the power supply of the computer can wipe out data. Spike suppressors can be inserted between the computer and the 120 volt AC receptacle to reduce this problem.

spindle An axle for mounting a disk or reel of magnetic tape.

Splash! A paint program for IBM-compatible microcomputers. With a palette of over 256,000 colors, 60 patterns and brush sizes, color fills, stamps, and spray cans, the Splash! user is equipped to prepare drawings for publications.

spline In computer graphics, a piecewise polynomial with at least first-order continuity between the pieces. A mathematically simple and elegant way to connect disjoint data points smoothly, hence, it is used not only for generating smooth curves and surfaces between sparse data points, but also for smooth motions between parameters sparsely located in time, such as those used to describe the key-frames in an animation.

split screen Display screen that can be partitioned into two or more areas (windows) so different screen formats can be shown on the screen at the same time. It implies that one set of data can be manipulated independently of the other.

splitting a window Act of dividing a window into two or more panes.

spooler Software that coordinates the movement of data between a file and the printer.

spooling The process of storing information in a special area of memory or a disk in preparation for being sent to the printer. The spooler is typically used to speed up the apparent throughput of a computer system.

spot color The use of one or more extra colors on a page, used to highlight specified page elements. Colors are usually specified as PMS codes.

spreadsheet A program that uses a matrix consisting of rows and columns to perform calculations on numerical data. Spreadsheets are widely used in most businesses to perform both simple and complex financial computations. Popular spreadsheets are Lotus 1-2-3, Excel, SuperCalc and Quattro. The first spreadsheet, VisiCalc, was produced by Dan Bricklin and Bob Frankston in 1978 for the Apple II microcomputer.

sprites Small, high-resolution objects that can be moved independently of other text or graphics on the monitor. They can change color and size and move in front of or behind other objects on the monitor. Used to create animated sequences.

sprocket holes Equally spaced holes on both edges of continuous forms for use by a tractor-feed mechanism to feed paper through a printer.

SQL See Structured Query Language.

squeezer Person who lays out the LSI circuit in its original "large" form.

SRAM Short for Static Random-Access Memory, meaning memory chips that can hold data stored in them without requiring a regular clock signal. SRAM chips are more expensive and hold less data than DRAM chips, but they can work faster.

SSI Acronym for Small Scale Integration.

ST A personal computer series from Atari Corporation. The Atari ST family of personal computers are high-performance personal computers with capabilities for computer graphics in color.

stack Sequential data list stored in internal storage. Rather than addressing the stack elements by their memory locations, the computer retrieves information from the stack by popping elements from the top (LIFO) or from the bottom (FIFO). See program stack and stack pointer.

stack pointer Register used to point to locations in the stack. Incremented by one before each new data item is pulled or popped from the stack, and decremented by one after a word is pushed onto the stack. See stack, pop, and push.

staffing Hiring and training workers.

stairstepping A rough or "stairstep" appearance in a line or curve that should be smooth.

stand-alone Descriptive of a single, self-contained computer system, as opposed to a terminal that is connected to and dependent upon a remote computer system. A stand-alone device will operate by itself, requiring no other equipment.

stand-alone graphics system Graphics system that includes a microcomputer or minicomputer, storage, video display terminal, and other input/output devices.

stand alone program   A program, such as a word processing or spreadsheet program.

stand-alone system   Self-contained computer system that can work independently, not connected to or under the control of another computer system. A stand-alone system contains all the hardware and software a user requires.

standard   (1) Guide used to establish uniform practices and common techniques. (2) Yardstick (meterstick!) used to measure performance of any computer system function. May be laid down by a statutory body or simply created by a major manufacturer's practice. See ANSI.

standard cell   A technique for designing integrated circuits where predefined functions such as processing elements and memories are obtained from libraries and used in the design process.

standard interface   Standard physical means by which all peripheral devices are connected to the central processing unit, such as a standard form of plug and jack. See RS-232C.

standardize   To establish standards or to cause conformity with established standards.

Standard Pascal   A version of the Pascal programming language that is described in the Pascal User Manual and Report by Kathleen Jensen and Niklaus Wirth.

standards enforcer   Computer program used to determine automatically whether prescribed programming standards and practices have been followed.

standby equipment   Duplicate set of equipment to be used as backup if the primary unit becomes unusable because of malfunction.

standby time   (1) Period between placing an inquiry into the equipment and the availability of the reply. (2) Period between the setup of the equipment for use and its actual use. (3) Period during which equipment is available for use but is not being used.

Stanhope, Charles   An English radical politician and experimental scientist who in the late 1770s invented three calculating machines, which were intended primarily for performing multiplication and division by repeated addition and subtraction.

Star   A workstation from Xerox Corporation that introduced the desktop user interface in 1981. Although the Star was not successful, it was the inspiration for Xerox's subsequent machines and for Apple's Macintosh microcomputer.

star network   Network configuration consisting of a central host computer and satellite terminals that connect to the computer to form a star pattern. The remote terminals may be geographically widespread.

start bit (1) Bit or group of bits that identifies the beginning of a data word. See group mark. (2) Bit indicating the beginning of an asynchronous serial transmission. Contrast with stop bit.

start/stop symbol An oval symbol used to indicate the beginning and end of a flowchart.

startup Process of setting computer system devices to proper initial conditions and applying appropriate electrical power.

startup disk Diskette that contains the information to start the computer system.

startup screen A graphics file that, when placed in the System Folder on an Apple Macintosh computer, is displayed when the computer is turned on. Any bit-mapped graphic image can be used as a startup screen. For example, you can display a fish, a tree, or even a picture of a favorite movie star.

state (1) Condition of bistable devices used to represent binary digits. By definition, such devices can have only two states; the state of a switch describes whether it is on or off. (2) In object-oriented programming, one of the possible conditions in which an object may exist.

statement Expression of instruction in a computer language.

statement label Line number or symbol of a statement in a source-language program.

state-of-the-art Phrase that implies being up-to-date in technology. Pertaining to the very latest technology; at the forefront of current hardware or software technology.

static Not moving or progressing; stationary; at rest.

static analysis Analysis of a program performed without executing the program.

static binding In object-oriented programming, binding denotes the association of a name with a class; static binding is a binding in which the name/class association is made when the name is declared (at compile time) but before the creation of the object that the name designates.

static dump Storage dump performed at a particular point in time with respect to a machine run, often at the termination of a run. See post mortem dump. Contrast with dynamic dump.

staticizing Process of transferring an instruction from computer storage to the instruction registers and holding it there, ready to be executed.

static memory Memory that retains its programmed state as long as power is applied. Does not need to be refreshed, and does not require a clock. See nonvolatile storage.

static RAM   Memory that doesn't need to be refreshed many times a second, as is required with dynamic RAM. Does not lose its contents as long as power to the computer is on. Once the computer puts a value into a static memory location, it remains there. Abbreviated SRAM.

static typing   In object-oriented programming, the addition of types to each object at compile time.

station   One of the input or output points on a data communications system. Synonymous with workstation. See terminal.

statistics   Branch of mathematics that collects information and tabulates and analyzes it.

status   Present condition of a system component.

status report   Analysis of actual project costs and time expended against the plan, with variances calculated and displayed.

stem   In typography, the main vertical stroke of a character.

step   (1) To cause a computer to execute one instruction. (2) One instruction in a computer routine.

stepped motor   Mechanical device that rotates by a fixed amount each time it is pulsed. Often used in disk drives and digital plotters.

stepwise refinement   The process of breaking major program modules down into lower-level components.

Stibitz, George   In the design of his analytical engine, Charles Babbage listed four elements a machine had to include to perform the functions of a human computer: an arithmetic unit; a memory; automatic "choice" of computing sequence; and input and output. In 1946, George Stibitz, then a research mathematician with Bell Telephone Laboratories, designed several relay calculators that incorporated the ideas of Babbage. See Babbage, Charles.

stickup initial   In desktop publishing, an enlarged initial letter at the beginning of a paragraph that rises above the top of the first line.

stochastic process   Any process dealing with events that develop in time or space and that cannot be described precisely, except in terms of probability theory.

stop bit   (1) Bit or group of bits that identifies the end of a data word and defines the space between data words. See group mark. (2) Bit indicating the end of an asynchronous serial transmission. Contrast with start bit.

stop code   Specific control character.

storage   Descriptive of a device or medium that can accept data, hold it, and deliver it on demand at a later time. The term is preferred over memory. See auxiliary storage, internal storage, PROM, protected storage, RAM, and ROM.

storage allocation   Assignment of specific programs, program segments, and/or blocks of data to specific portions of a computer's storage. Sometimes called memory allocation. See program storage.

storage block   Contiguous area of internal storage.

storage capacity   Number of items of data that a storage device is capable of containing. Frequently defined in terms of computer bytes (K bytes or M bytes).

storage device   Device used for storing data within a computer system, such as hard disk, floppy disk, magnetic tape, and optical disc.

storage dump   Printout of all or part of the contents of the internal storage of a computer. Often used to diagnose errors. Also called memory dump. See post mortem dump and snapshot dump.

storage key   Indicator associated with a storage block or blocks; it requires that tasks have a matching protection key to use the blocks. See privileged instruction and storage protection.

storage location   Position in storage where a character, byte, or word may be stored. Same as cell.

storage map   Diagram that shows where programs and data are stored in the storage units of the computer systems. Also called map.

storage pool   Group of similar storage devices; disk drives in a computer installation are collectively referred to as the disk pool.

storage protection   Protection against unauthorized writing in and/or reading from all or part of a storage device. Generally implemented automatically by hardware facilities, usually in connection with an operating system. Sometimes called memory protection. See storage key.

storage tube   Electron tube into which information can be introduced and then extracted at a later time. Used in first generation computers.

storage unit   See storage device.

store   (1) British term for storage. (2) To place in storage.

store-and-forward   In data communications, the process-handling messages used in a message-switching system.

stored-program computer   Computer capable of performing sequences of internally stored instructions and usually capable of modifying those instructions as directed by the instructions. Same as digital computer.

stored-program concept Instructions to a computer as well as data values are stored within the internal storage of a computer. The instructions can thus be accessed more quickly and may be more easily modified. This concept, introduced by John von Neumann in 1945, is the most important characteristic of the digital computer. See von Neumann, John.

straight-line code Repetition of a sequence of instructions by explicitly writing the instructions for each repetition. Generally, straight-line coding will require less execution time and more storage space than equivalent loop coding. Feasibility is limited by the space required as well as by the difficulty of coding a variable number of repetitions. Contrast with loop code.

streaming cartridge A type of cartridge tape drive that records whole tracks of a cartridge at one time, rather than stopping and starting for individual blocks. Because the mechanism is simpler, it is less expensive than incremental recorders and can hold more data per cartridge. Used primarily for backup of hard disk drives.

street price The current price of a computer product at a computer store, mail order business, or other retail business. The street price of a product is often considerably lower than the retail price of a product. It is an average price charged by dealers around the country. See list price.

STRESS Acronym for STRuctural Engineering System Solver, a problem-oriented language used for solving structural engineering problems.

stress testing Ensuring through trial operation that the program or system will continue to perform reliably in spite of data inaccuracies and extraordinary data volumes.

strikethrough A line drawn through a selected range of text. Marking text in this manner indicates that the text is to be deleted at some future time.

string Connected sequence of characters or bits treated as a single data item. The word "windsurfer" is a string of ten characters.

string handling Ability of a programming language to operate on strings of characters.

string length Number of characters in a string.

string manipulation Technique for manipulating strings of characters.

string processing languages Programming languages designed to facilitate the processing of strings of characters.

string variable String of alphanumeric strings.

stringy floppy Computer storage device that holds a magnetic tape, called a wafer. The enclosed wafer tape is thinner, narrower, and faster than conventional cassette tapes.

stroke (1) In computer graphics, a line created as a vector. (2) In data entry, a keystroke. (3) In paint programs, a "swipe" of the paintbrush made when creating a graphic image. (4) In printing, the weight, or thickness, of a character.

stroke writer Vector graphics terminal that represents objects on a screen by a series of lines (vectors).

structural description A description of an object based on the components of the object and the relationships among components.

structural design (1) Overall organization and control logic of processing. (2) In artificial intelligence, an approach to expert system design which consists of reducing the problem to a set of subgoals. A module is designed for each subgoal.

structure (1) Organization or arrangement of the parts of an entity. Manner in which a program is organized. The design and composition of a program. A structured program is one in which the purpose of the program can be found easily by reading the listing, and the main part of the program can be used as an index to find the details of how actions are carried out. (2) In object-oriented programming, the concrete representation of the state of an object.

structure chart Design tool for documenting the organization or program modules and the control logic that relates them to one another. Graphic representation of top-down programming.

structured analysis The examination of a complex problem by breaking it down into simple functions.

structured coding Method of writing programs with a high degree of structure.

structured data Data generated in a byte/character format which is stored, as organized information such as textual data.

structured design Methodology for designing programs and systems through top-down, hierarchical partitioning and logical control structures.

structured English Approach to languages that is based on replacing symbols with recognizable English words.

structured flowchart Method of representing problem solutions in terms of three flowcharting structures: the sequence structure, the selection structure, and the loop structure.

structured graphics See object-oriented graphics.

structured programming A programming technique used in the design and coding of computer programs. The approach assumes the disciplined use of a few basic coding structures and the use of top-down concepts to decompose main functions into lower-level components for modular coding purposes. The technique is concerned with improving the programming process through better organization and programs, and with better programming notation to facilitate correct and clear descriptions of data and control structures. The physical structure of a well-organized program corresponds to the sequence of steps in the algorithm being implemented. Good languages for structured programming must have a carefully thought out assortment of control structures and data-structure definition facilities. Good practices lead to reduced cost of program modification and maintenance as well as original development.

Structured Query Language (SQL)   A relational database language developed by the IBM Corporation. SQL allows users to present near-English queries to the database manager in order to view the database in a variety of different ways.

structured walkthrough   A formal review process in which a designer or programmer leads one or more members of the development team through a segment of design or code.

structure knowledge   One of three types of knowledge found in diagnostic expert systems. It is the knowledge of the parts the expert system is to diagnose.

STRUDL   Acronym for STRUctural Design Language, a programming language used for the design and analysis of structures.

stub   A routine that contains no executable code. A dummy-program module.

stub testing   Top-down module testing process that involves using a small dummy-program module inserted and called in a larger program at the location of and in lieu of another routine.

Studio/1   An Apple Macintosh graphics program that combines black and white painting, scanning and animation with a computer slide-show capability. Very advanced black and white graphics can be created; all basic painting tools are included, and some not-so-basic capabilities such as polygon selection, rotating ellipse, Bezier curves and sophisticated distortion, shearing, and bending options. A built-in scanner interface allows images to be input directly from a scanner while in the program. Most unique is the ability to also create full animation incorporating graphics, art, motion and sound. Designers can define complex paths for objects and have the program create the animation, or use a feature which allows automatic painting on consecutive frames. With a built-in HyperCard driver, Studio/1 can also import/export in PICT, MacPaint, PICS, TIFF, EPSF and compressed animation formats.

Studio/8   An Apple Macintosh paint program that supports color. Studio/8 can select any part of an image and turn it into a custom paintbrush. The program remembers up to eight brushes. Images can be tinted, smoothed, smeared, and blended.

Studio/32   A powerful Apple Macintosh paint program that supports 32-bit full color, giving computer artists virtually unlimited colors and tools to work with. Even better than its power is its unintimidating, intuitive interface which lets users easily handle advanced features such as masking, transformation effects and color control. Special features include selection techniques, tear-off menus, 3-D perspectives, custom gradients, variable dithering and slide-show presentation utilities. It has the ability to keep text as a separate layer for editing. Strong Pantone color matching support is provided with an interface allowing users to locate colors by number or color qualities. Other color editing modes supported include CMYK, HSV and RGB. Files can be imported and exported in PICT, MacPaint, TIFF and EPSF formats.

style   Variation in the appearance of a typeface (e.g. italic, bold, shadow, outlined, normal).

style sheet   In word processing and desktop publishing, a file that contains formatting instructions but not text. Style sheets contain such information as margin sizes, column widths, paragraph indention, spacing, fonts, size, and style. Applying a stylesheet to text automatically formats the text according to the stylesheet's specifications.

stylus   In computer graphics, a pointer that you operate by placing it in a display space or a graphics tablet. To draw a point, the user touches the stylus (also called a pen) tip to the surface of the graphics tablet. The stylus and graphics tablet are preferred drawing devices for artists.

subclass   In object-oriented programming, the refinement of a class into a more specialized class.

subdirectory   File that lists the names of other files, and is displayed in a disk directory rather than the name of each file. This system allows files to be classified together to save space in a disk directory. A directory within another directory.

sublaptop   A hand-held or pocket-size portable microcomputer, weighing as little as one pound.

submenu   An additional set of options related to a prior menu selection.

subprogram   Segment of a program that can perform a specific function. Can reduce programming time when a specific function is required at more than one point in a program. If the required function is handled as a subprogram, the statements for that function can be coded once and executed at the various points in the program. Subroutines and functions may be used to provide subprograms.

subroutine   Subsidiary routine within which initial execution never starts. Executed when called by some other program, usually the main program. Also called subprogram. See closed subroutine, open subroutine, and nested subroutine.

subroutine reentry Initiation of a subroutine by one program before it has finished its response to another program that called for it. May happen when a control program is subjected to a priority interrupt.

subschema Logical organization of data required for a particular program. An individual user's partial view of the database.

subscript (1) Integer value, appended to a variable name, that defines the storage elements composing an array or a matrix. (2) In noncomputer typefonts, a letter or digit written below and to the right of a symbol to distinguish it from variations of the same symbol, such as Θ_a and Θ_b. Contrast with superscript.

subscripted variable Symbol whose numeric value can change, denoted by an array name followed by a subscript, such as CHESS(2,4) or A(7). See subscript and variable.

subset Any set contained within another set.

substrate In microelectronics, the physical material on which a circuit is fabricated. Silicon is the most widely used substrate for the manufacturing of chips.

substring Portion of a character string.

subsystem A system under the control of the main system. A microcomputer might serve as a data collection subsystem for the mainframe.

suite Set or group of closely related programs. A set of interacting programs.

summary report A management information system report limited to totals or trends.

Sun Microsystems, Inc. A manufacturer of network-based, high-performance workstations founded in 1982.

SuperCalc A spreadsheet for IBM-compatible microcomputers from Computer Associates. It was one of the first spreadsheets in the early 1980s. Several enhanced versions of the spreadsheet have been released.

superclass In an object-oriented programming inheritance hierarchy, a more general class that stores variables and methods that can be inherited by other classes.

supercomputer Largest, fastest, and most expensive mainframe computer available. Used by businesses and organizations that require extraordinary amounts of computing power. Sometimes called number crunchers because they perform between hundreds of millions to several billions of operations per second. They are very expensive and are typically used for the most complex computational tasks. Some applications of supercomputers include nuclear energy research, petroleum exploration, electronic design, realtime animated graphics, and structural analysis. Supercomputers are typically 50,000 times faster than microcomputers.

superconductor   Ultra-fast electronic circuit.

superconducting computers   High-performance computers whose circuits employ superconductivity and the Josephson effect to reduce cycle time.

super large scale integration   Use of ultra-high-density chips that contain millions of components per chip.

SuperPaint   An Apple Macintosh graphics program that combines drawing and paint capabilities. Drawing features include a freehand drawing tool capable of creating editable Bezier paths, hairline widths and varying vertical and horizontal widths for lines, PostScript halftone gray values available as fill patterns and a capability to align selected objects in relationship to each other. Editing capabilities include mixing of fonts, styles and sizes within a single block of text; the ability to edit text in the Draw layer after performing any transformation command; group/ungroup and lock/unlock commands; the ability to simultaneously open and edit multiple points along a Bezier curve; and snap-to-grid options. SuperPaint was introduced in 1986. The latest version, SuperPaint 3.0 was released in late 1991. This version of SuperPaint supports color.

superscript   Letter or digit written above and to the right of a symbol to denote a power or to identify a particular element of a set, such as the 3 in x^3. Contrast with subscript.

Super 3D   An Apple Macintosh graphic program. It includes built-in animation and its enhanced version uses color blending techniques. Super 3D can set up any number of key frames and automatically creates the in between frames with multiple light sources and a choice of rendering algorithms.

supervisor   The part of the operating system that schedules and coordinates the execution of other programs.

supply company   Company that offers a number of supplies that may not be produced and distributed by computer manufacturers, such as printer paper, printer ribbons, and diskettes.

support   Help and verbal advice that a vendor supplies a customer.

support library   Library that contains complete programs and subroutines that have already been developed, tested, and documented.

suppress   To eliminate leading zeros or other insignificant characters from a computer printout. See zero suppression.

suppression   Elimination of some undesired components of a signal.

surface modeling A display method used by some computer-aided design (CAD) programs that gives on screen constructions the appearance of solidity. Surface modeling creates the appearance of a firm surface either by filling the shape or by removing hidden lines from within it. Surface modeling is a more complex method for representing objects than wireframe modeling, but not as sophisticated as solid modeling.

surface of revolution Figure resulting from the rotation of a curve around a fixed axis set at a specified angle.

surge Sudden sharp increase in voltage. Also called a spike.

surge protector Device that protects electrical equipment from being damaged by short surges of high voltage by filtering them out. A computer or other device is plugged into the surge protector, which itself is plugged into a standard electrical outlet. See line surge and transient suppressors.

surging Sudden and momentary changing of voltage or current in a circuit.

suspend To halt a process in a manner that allows resumption, perhaps by a system interrupt.

swapping (1) In virtual storage, bringing a new page into internal storage from auxiliary storage and replacing an existing page. (2) In a network system, bringing the program into internal storage or storing it on a storage device. (3) Transferring out a copy of what is in internal memory to auxiliary storage while simultaneously transferring into internal memory what is in auxiliary storage. (4) The process of exchanging one item for another, as in swapping floppy disks as needed, in and out of a single drive.

swarm Several program bugs.

swim Situation in which the images displayed on a video display screen move due to some hardware instability or defect, such as a slow refresh rate. Undesirable movement of an image on a video display screen.

switch (1) In programming, a point at which a program may branch to one or more different program statements, depending upon the conditions of specified parameters at that point. (2) Physical or electronic means of changing the state of a component or device, such as an on/off toggle switch.

switched lines Data communication lines that connect through telephone switching centers to a variety of destinations. Contrast with leased lines and dedicated lines.

switching algebra Name given to Boolean algebra when it is applied to switching theory.

switching circuit Constituent electric circuit of switching or digital systems. Well-known examples of such systems are digital computers, dial telephone systems, and automatic inventory systems.

switching theory Theory applied to circuits that have two or more discrete states.

Swivel 3D An Apple Macintosh 3-D graphics program that can be used to create, manipulate and render complex objects. The program also includes image mapping, independent light sources and environment mapping.

symbol (1) A letter or mark representing quantities, relations, or operations. (2) In artificial intelligence, an entity chosen to represent a person, object, concept, operation, relationship, or attribute of an object in the world.

symbolic address Address, expressed in symbols convenient to the program writer, that must be translated into an absolute address (usually by an assembler) before it can be interpreted by a computer. Contrast with explicit address.

symbolic coding Coding in which the instructions are written in nonmachine language. Coding using symbolic notation for operation codes and operands.

symbolic debugger A debugger that allows the programmer to trace the values of variables in a program by requesting a particular symbol or name from the source code.

symbolic device Name used to indicate an input/output file, such as SYSDSK to specify a magnetic disk unit. Compare symbolic I/O assignment.

symbolic editor System program that helps computer users in the preparation and modification of source-language programs by adding, changing, or deleting lines of text.

symbolic I/O assignment Name used to indicate an input/output unit, such as PTR used to specify a printer. Compare symbolic device.

symbolic language Pseudolanguage made up of letters, characters, and numbers that are not the internal language of the computer system. In artificial intelligence, a computer language that excels at symbol manipulation as opposed to numerical processing. LISP and PROLOG excel at symbol manipulation. A language should have facilities for efficient symbol manipulation available if it is to be used in artificial intelligence programming.

symbolic logic Discipline that treats formal logic by means of a formalized artificial language whose purpose is to avoid the ambiguities and logical inadequacies of natural language.

symbolic modeling The technique of representing a body of symbolic knowledge in a computer program so that the program can draw conclusions and answer questions about the body of knowledge.

symbolic name See name.

symbolic processing Processing that distinguishes artificial intelligence programming from other types of programming. Formal reasoning with symbols. The manipulation of symbols using strategies and heuristics, as opposed to the manipulations of numbers or the use of algorithms.

symbolic programming (1) Using a symbolic language to prepare computer programs. (2) An alternate name for artificial intelligence. The advantages of the term symbolic programming are that it avoids the futuristic connotations and the inevitable comparisons with human beings.

symbolic table Table for comparing a set of symbols to another set of symbols or numbers; for example, in an assembler, the symbol table contains the symbolic label address of an assembled object program.

symbol manipulation The recognition, assembling, and modification of symbols. The thrust of artificial intelligence has been to use symbols to make inferences, and this is the core of symbol manipulation.

symbol string String consisting solely of symbols.

symbol structure A data structure made up of symbols.

symbol table List of names used in a program with brief descriptions and storage addresses.

Symphony A software package, produced by Lotus Development Corporation that provides word processing, database management, spreadsheet, data communications, and graphics. Symphony, with its emphasis on the spreadsheet, is a number-dominated program that is designed for financial analysts who are chiefly concerned with manipulating numbers in a variety of ways. Many users consider Symphony's word processing and database management capabilities secondary to its speed, raw power, size, and ability to number-crunch.

sync character Character transmitted to establish character synchronization in synchronous communications.

synchronization Adjustment of the chronological relationships between events, either to cause them to coincide or to maintain a fixed time difference between them.

synchronization check Check that determines whether a particular event or condition occurs at the proper moment.

synchronous communications Method of exchanging data at very high speeds between computers. Involves careful timing and special control codes. Contrast with asynchronous.

synchronous computer Computer in which each operation starts as a result of a signal generated by a clock. Contrast with asynchronous computer.

synchronous network Computer network in which all the communications channels are synchronized to a common clock.

synchronous operation Operation of a system under the control of clocked pulses.

synchronous transmission Data transmission in which the bit are transmitted at a fixed rate. Transmitter and receiver both use the same clock signals for synchronization. Contrast with asynchronous transmission.

synergy The concept that the whole is greater than the sum of its parts.

synonyms (1) Records with duplicate disk addresses. (2) Two or more keys that produce the same table address when hashed.

syntactic ambiguity A program in the field of natural language understanding, which refers to the possible multiple interpretations a sentence can have. Example: "I hit the man with the baseball." Did you use the baseball to hit the man, or did you hit the man who was holding the baseball? This type of ambiguity is very difficult for a computer.

syntactic analysis The study of the structure of the sentence, which is important in natural language processing.

syntax (1) Rules governing the structure of a language and its expressions. All assembly and high-level programming languages possess a formal syntax. (2) The order in which the symbols in an expression are arranged. (3) The rules that specify the use of symbols in an expression.

synthesizer Output device that generates and processes sound automatically. Some synthesizers include microprocessors, which are used as controlling devices. A voice synthesizer produces sounds that closely resemble a person speaking, musical instruments, and so on.

sysgen A contraction for system generation, the process of installing or transferring an operating system.

SYSOP Acronym for SYStem OPerator, the person who operates an electronic bulletin board.

system Composite of equipment, skills, techniques, and information capable of performing and/or supporting an operational role in attaining specified management objectives. Includes related facilities, equipment, material, services personnel, and information required for its operation to the degree that it can be considered a self-sufficient unit in its intended operational and/or support environment.

System/3 and System/7 Minicomputers introduced by IBM Corporation in 1967-70.

System 7 (1) Operating system for the Apple Macintosh computer. System 7 expands the Macintosh capabilities including an upgraded finder, file sharing capability, truetype fonts, inter application communications and virtual memory. (2) An IBM Corporation minicomputer system.

System/32 - System/38 Minicomputer systems introduced by IBM Corporation: System/32 was released in 1975; System/34 was introduced in 1977; System/36 was introduced in 1983; and System/38 was introduced in 1978.

System/360 A series of mainframes introduced by IBM Corporation in 1964. It was the first family of compatible computer systems ever introduced. The introduction of this family of computers brought about the third generation of computers.

System/370 A family of compatible mainframes introduced by IBM Corporation in 1970. This series of computers replaced the older System/360 mainframes.

system analyzer Portable device that can be used as a troubleshooting unit for field service of complex equipment and systems.

system board Main circuit board of a microcomputer. Also called motherboard and backplane.

system chart Type of flowchart. See system flowchart.

system commands Special instructions given to the computer when one operates in the conversational time-sharing mode. Direct the computer to execute programs (RUN), list them (LIST), save them (SAVE), and do other similar operations.

system diagnostics Program used to detect overall system malfunctions.

system disk The disk that contains the operating system and other systems programs that are necessary to start the computer.

system failure A malfunction of the hardware or systems software within a computer system.

system flowchart Graphic representation of an entire system or portion of a system consisting of one or more computer operations. Composed of interconnected flowcharting symbols arranged in the sequence that the various system operations are performed. Essentially an overall planning, control, and operational description of a specific application. Contrast with program flowchart. See dataflow diagram and flowchart.

system folder In an Apple Macintosh environment, the folder that contains the System File and the Finder, the two components of the Macintosh's operating system.

system follow-up Continuing evaluation and review of a newly installed system to see that it is performing according to plan.

system generation (SYSGEN) Process of initiating a basic system at a specific installation. Involves modifying the generalized operating system received from the vendor into a tailored system meeting the unique needs of the individual user.

system implementation Final phase in the creation of a new system. During this phase a system is completely debugged, and it is determined whether it is operational and accepted by the users.

system installation Activities by which a new system is placed into operation.

system interrupt Break in the normal execution of a program or routine that is accomplished in such a way that the usual sequence can be resumed from that point.

system level (1) A description of the interface or connection that runs between computer subsystems such as the main board and disk controller or between parts of a multiprocessor computer. (2) An operation that is performed by the operating system or some other control program.

system loader Supervisory program used to locate programs in the system library and load them into the internal storage of the computer.

system maintenance Activity associated with keeping a computer system constantly in tune with the changing demands placed upon it.

system priorities Priorities established to determine the order in which information system projects will be undertaken.

system programmer (1) Programmer who plans, generates, maintains, and controls the use of an operating system with the aim of improving the overall productivity of an installation. (2) Programmer who designs programming systems. Contrast with applications programmer.

system reset Operation that occurs whenever a computer is fooled into thinking that it was turned off and turned on again.

system testing All programs that make up the system are tested in the sequence in which they will be executed.

systems analysis Examination of an activity, procedure, method, technique, or business to determine what must be accomplished and how the necessary operations may best be accomplished by using data processing equipment. Art or science of analyzing a user's information needs and devising aggregates of machines, people, and procedures to meet those needs.

systems analyst One who studies the activities, methods, procedures, and techniques of organizational systems to determine what actions need

384

to be taken and how these actions can best be accomplished. One who does systems analysis.

systems design Specification of the working relationships between all the parts of a system in terms of their characteristic actions.

systems engineer One who performs systems analysis, systems design, and/or systems programming functions.

systems house Company that develops hardware and/or software systems to meet user requirements.

systems manual Document containing information on the operation of a system. Sufficient detail is provided so management can determine the dataflow, forms used, reports generated, and controls exercised. Job descriptions are generally provided.

systems programmer One who understands the interaction between the application software and the systems software on a specific computer system. See system programmer.

systems programming Development of programs that form operating systems for computers. Such programs include assemblers, compilers, control programs, and input/output handlers. Contrast with applications programming.

systems programs Programs that control the internal operations of the computer system, such as operating systems, compilers, interpreters, assemblers, graphics support programs, and mathematical routines. Contrast with applications programs.

systems resource Any resource of a computer system that is under the control of the operating system.

systems security Technical innovations and managerial procedures applied to the hardware and software (programs and data) to protect the privacy of the records of the organization and its customers.

systems software Programs that run the computer system and aid the applications programmer in doing his/her task. Typically developed by a vendor and sold to a computer user. The vendor who sells systems software may be the same vendor who sold the user the computer (still the most common case) or may be an independent software vendor.

systems study Investigation to determine the feasibility of installing or replacing a business system. See feasibility study.

systems synthesis Planning of the procedures for solving a problem.

systems testing Testing of a series of programs in succession to make sure that all programs, including input and output, are related in the way the systems analyst intended.

tab Carriage control that specifies output columns.

table Collection of data in a form suitable for ready reference. The data are frequently stored in consecutive storage locations or written in the form of an array of rows and columns for easy entry. An intersection of labeled rows and columns serves to locate a specific piece of information. Tables are useful for holding tabular data, like the data found in spreadsheets.

table look-up Procedure for using a known value to locate an unknown value in a table.

table plotter See flatbed plotter.

tablet In computer graphics, a locator device with a flat surface and a mechanism that converts indicated positions on the surface into coordinated data.

tabulate (1) To print totals. (2) To form data into a table.

tagged image file format (TIFF) A common file format used to store bit-mapped graphic images. TIFF simulates gray-scale shading.

tail Special data item that locates the end of a list.

tailor-made Refers to a program specially written for one particular task, business, or set of people. Tailor-made programs are usually commissioned by an individual customer and not sold to anyone else.

talking computer Computer system that uses a speech synthesizer to produce speech.

tandem computers Two computers connected together and working on the same problem at the same time.

Tandy Corporation A leading manufacturer of personal computer and electronics. In 1977, Tandy introduced one of the first personal computers, the Radio Shack TRS-80 Model I. Several other TRS-80 models were developed, and in 1984, Tandy started building IBM-compatible microcomputers. Today, Tandy markets a variety of microcomputer systems through their company-owned Radio Shack stores.

tangible benefit Benefit to which a specific dollar amount can be assigned.

tape Strip of material that may be punched or coated with a magnetically sensitive substance and used for data input, storage, or output. Data are usually stored serially in several channels across the tape, transversely to the reading or writing motion. See magnetic tape and paper tape.

tape backup A mechanism which reads and writes information on magnetic tape to provide a copy of your data in case of an accident. The tape cartridge or cassette is capable of holding at least 20 MB of data.

tape cartridge See magnetic tape cartridge.

tape cassette Sequential access storage medium used in older microcomputer systems for digital recording.

tape deck See magnetic tape unit.

tape drive See magnetic tape drive.

tape handler See magnetic tape unit.

tape label Usually the first record on a magnetic tape reel, containing such information as the date the tape was written, identification name or number, and the number of records on the tape.

tape librarian Person responsible for the safe keeping of all computer files, such as programs and data files on magnetic tapes, floppy disks and microfilm.

tape library Special room that houses a file of magnetic tape under secure, environmentally controlled conditions. See disk library and data protection.

tape mark Special code used to indicate the end of a tape file.

Tape Operating System(TOS) Operating system in which the programs are stored on magnetic tape.

TARGA Acronym for Truevision Advanced Raster Graphics Adapter. A file format created by Truevision for image capture boards; compatible with NTSC standards.

Targa board A video graphics board from Truevision that is used in high-resolution graphics applications.

target disk Disk to which a program or file is copied. Contrast with source disk.

target language Language into which some other language is to be properly translated. Usually has the same meaning as object language.

target printer A specific printer selected for printing a job.

target program Same as object program.

tariff In data communications, the published rate for a specific unit of equipment, facility, or type of service provided by a communications common carrier.

task Element of work that is part of getting the job done, such a loading of programs into computer storage.

taxonomy The classification of objects as to how they are alike and different.

TB Abbreviation for terabyte.

TCP/IP Acronym for Transmission Control Protocol/Internet Protocol. A networking protocol with broad support deriving from its ability to connect disparate hosts.

teacherless learning Learning using intelligent computer-assisted instruction programs.

tear-off menu A screen menu that can be moved off its primary position, relocated to any part of the display screen and kept active.

technical writer Person who prepares proposals, training manuals, reference manuals, programming manuals, books, and reports associated with computer equipment and software or other technical fields.

technology (1) Knowledge and methods used to create a product. (2) Activities that are directed toward the satisfaction of human needs that produce alterations in the material world.

technology transfer Application of existing technology to a current problem or situation.

telecommunications Transfer of data from one place to another over long distances, using telephone lines, microwaves and/or satellites. See data communications and teleprocessing.

telecommunications specialist person responsible for the design of data communications networks.

telecommuting Working at home with telecommunications between office and home.

teleconference A conference among people remote from one another who are linked by telecommunication devices. Considered an alternative to travel and face-to-face meetings, a teleconference is conducted with two-way video, audio, and, as required, data and facsimile transmission.

telecopying Long-distance copying. Same as facsimile.

telematics Convergence of telecommunications and automatic information processing.

telemetry Transmission of data from remote measuring instrument by electrical or radio means; for example, data can be telemetered from a spacecraft in outer space and recorded at a ground station located on Earth.

Telenet Communications network that enables many varieties of user terminals and computers to exchange information.

teleprocessing Use of telephone lines to transmit data and commands between remote locations and a data processing center or between two computer systems. Combined use of data communications and data processing equipment. See telecommunications.

telesoftware Computer programs sent by telephone line or television as part of the teletext signal.

teletext One-way communications medium used in some videotex services. Images, each constituting a single frame of TV data in a special, compressed format, are transmitted in a continuous sequence. Users indicate which frame they would like to see by interaction with the decoding unit in their local TV sets.

television receiver (TV) Display device capable of receiving broadcast video signals (such as commercial television) by means of an antenna. Can be used in combination with a radio-frequency modulator as a display device for several microcomputers. See video monitor.

Telex Telegraph service provided by Western Union.

Telpak Service offered by communications common carriers for the leasing of wideband channels between two or more points.

template (1) Plastic guide used in drawing geometric flowcharting symbols. (2) In computer graphics, the pattern of a standard, commonly used component or part that serves as a design aid. Once created, it can be subsequently traced instead of redrawn whenever needed. (3) In a spreadsheet program, a worksheet that has already been designed for the solution of a specific type of problem. (4) Plastic sheet placed over keyboard keys to help the user remember tasks performed by each key. (5) In page layout and word processing programs, templates are predesigned page formats. You use the template by loading the file, adding the text and/or graphic images, and printing.

template matching A technique in which a computer identifies objects by comparing shapes derived from the digitized image with stored prototype patterns. This technique was first popularized in early artificial intelligence programs, for example, the sentence-processing program ELIZA. A template is "I x all Y." Matches for this template are "I hate all war.", "I love all people.", and "I like all animals."

temporary storage In programming, storage locations reserved for intermediate results. Synonymous with working storage.

Tempra An image editing program for IBM PC-compatible microcomputers operating in MS-DOS. Features include color mapping, video capture, show and print utilities. Virtual paint canvas allows importing, creating, and/or retouching images up to 8192 x 8192 pixels for precision editing and printing.

ten-key pad Separate set of keys numbered 0 through 9 on a keyboard that allow easy entry of numbers. Similar to a calculator keypad.

ten's complement Number used to represent the negative of a given value. Obtained by subtracting each digit from a number containing all 9s and adding 1; for example, 654 is the ten's complement of 346 and is obtained by performing the computation 999-346+1. Synonymous with true complement. Compare one's complement, two's complement, and nine's complement.

tera Prefix meaning one trillion.

terabyte (TB) Specifically, 1,009,511,627,776, or 2^{40} bytes. More loosely, one thousand gigabytes, one million megabytes, one billion kilobytes, or one trillion bytes. Used to measure capacities of high-capacity data storage.

term The data structure of a logic program, for example a constant, variable or compound term. It is the smallest portion of an expression to which a value can be given.

terminal Keyboard/display or keyboard/printer device used to input programs and data to the computer and to receive output from the computer.

terminal emulation (1) The ability of a personal computer to act, generally via modem, as a terminal to a host system. (2) Situation in which special software makes a computer behave as though it were a terminal connected to another computer.

terminal error Error of sufficient consequence that the program cannot continue. See fatal error.

terminal node A node that ends a path.

terminal stand Wood or metal stand designed to support a computer terminal.

terminal symbol   Oval flowcharting symbol used to indicate the starting point and termination point or points in a procedure.

terminator   In a network, a device used to signify the end of the series.

ternary   (1) Pertaining to a characteristic or property involving a selection, choice, or condition in which there are three possibilities. (2) Pertaining to the numeration system with a radix of 3.

test data   Data especially created to test the operation of a given program. Usually, one or more hand-calculated results, or otherwise known results, will be associated with test data so the program under test may be validated. Also data known to be invalid are used as test data. See testing.

test driver   Program that directs the execution of another program against a collection of test data sets.

testing   Examination of a program's behavior by executing the program on sample data sets, including both valid and invalid data, in an effort to explore all possible causes of misbehavior. See debug, program testing, stress testing, and systems testing.

test plan   General description of what testing will involve, including specification of tolerable limits.

test run   Run carried out to check that a program is operating correctly. During the run, test data generate results for comparison with previously prepared results.

Texas Instruments Inc   A manufacturer of semiconductors and computer equipment.

text   Words, letters, and numbers that express the information to be conveyed. Contrasted with graphics, which are shapes, lines and symbols.

text composition   In desktop publishing, evenly spaced lines, usually set in the same type size and style.

text editing   General term that covers any additions, changes, or deletions made to electronically stored material.

text editor   Computer program used to manipulate text; for example, to erase, insert, change, and move words or groups of words. The manipulated text may be another computer program.

text file   File containing information expressed in text form. Same as data file.

text formatting   (1) The process of controlling the appearance of a document so that it will look good on paper. (2) Output generated by computer software that closely resembles galleys set on conventional composing machines.

text generation   The process of constructing meaningful text using a computer.

text letter   A typeface that looks like early brush stroke lettering.

text processing   Manipulation of alphabetic data under program control.

text graphics   Graphic images created by combining ASCII characters.

text system   Collection of hardware and specially written software used together to manipulate textual information. See word processing.

texture   In computer graphics, any 2-D pattern used to add the appearance of complexity to a 3-D surface without actually modeling the complexity. For example, a surface could be made to appear reflective to simulate glass or metal, or a brick texture pattern could be used on an architectural drawing of a brick house.

texture mapping   In computer graphics, the application of graphic representations of surface textures to objects.

text window   Area on some computer graphics systems display screens within which text is displayed and scrolled.

TGA   Bitmap format for images created on high-resolution video boards. Because of their resolution, these files can be very large. Because they can have up to 16 million colors, the palette often has to be compressed before the files can be used. See TARGA.

theorem   A statement that can be proved. The conclusion of a valid argument.

theorem prover   A program that starts with a goal and searches for implications whose conclusions will unify with the goal. A theorem prover has a database consisting of a set of axioms. Its inference mechanism makes inferences that lead to the satisfaction of the goal.

theorem proving   The branch of artificial intelligence involved in using computers to prove mathematical and logic theorems.

thermal printer   A nonimpact printer that uses a paper treated to form a dark image when exposed to heat. Black, blue and purple image papers are common. The print head consists of an array of resistive elements (thin or thick film) that moves across the paper printing serially, or an array of elements in which the paper moves past, printing an entire line at a time. To print, the head normally must be in contact with the paper.

thermal wax-transfer printer   A nonimpact printer that uses heat to melt colored wax onto paper to create an image. It uses pins to apply the heat.

thesaurus program   With a word processing program, this program provides a list of synonyms and antonyms for a word in a document.

thin film Computer storage made by placing thin spots of magnetic materials on an insulated base (usually a flat plate or wire); electric current in wires attached to the base is used to magnetize the spot.

thin window display One-line display used on keyboards, pocket computers, and so on. Usually an LCD or LED display.

third generation computers Computers that use integrated circuitry and miniaturization of components to replace transistors, reduce costs, work faster, and increase reliability. Introduced in 1964 and still the primary technology for digital computers. Compare first generation computers, second generation computers, fourth generation computers, and fifth generation computers.

third-party vendor A company that specializes in obtaining equipment from manufacturers or original owners. The equipment is then leased or sold to another company.

thirty-two-bit chip CPU chip that processes data thirty-two bits at a time. Contrast with eight-bit chip and sixteen-bit chip.

Thomas, Charles Xavier (Colmar, Thomas) Made a calculating machine in 1820 credited with being the first that ever did work practically and usefully.

Thompson, Kenneth A Bell Laboratories research scientist who, in 1971, with Dennis Ritchie, developed and implemented the UNIX operating system. The UNIX system has led a generation of software designers to new ways of thinking about programming.

thrashing Overhead associated with memory swapping in a virtual memory system. Also called churning.

threaded Pertaining to a program consisting of calls to several separate subprograms.

threaded tree Tree containing additional pointers to assist in the scan of the tree.

three-dimensional array Array that provides a threefold classification: row, column, and layer.

three-dimensional graphics (3-D) A graphic image in three dimensions—height, width and depth. A three-dimensional image is rendered on a two-dimensional medium; the third dimension, depth, is usually indicated by shading or by means of perspective.

threshold A predefined level used by a scanner to determine whether a pixel will be represented as black or white.

throughput Measure of the total amount of useful processing carried out by a computer system in a given time period.

thumbnail layout In desktop publishing, a quickly drawn sketch that shows major elements in a document.

thumbwheel Device for positioning an input cursor; consists of a rotatable wheel that controls the movement of that cursor in one axis. Normally, thumbwheels are found in pairs, one controlling vertical cursor movement; the other, horizontal movement.

Thunderscan An inexpensive high-resolution scanner that replaces the ribbon cartridge in an Apple ImageWriter printer, and converts photographs and printed images into data that can be stored on a disk. Developed by Thunderware, Inc.

thyration See SCR.

thyristor Bistable device comprising three or more junctions. See SCR.

tie-breaker Circuitry that resolves the conflict that occurs when two central processing units try to use a peripheral device at the same time. See contention.

tie line Leased communications channel.

tie mark Any marking along a scale to indicate values. Can be used to denote points between identified numerical values.

TIFF Acronym for Tagged Image File Format; which is basically a standardized header (tag) defining the exact data structure of the images to be processed. A common bitmapped file format. The TIFF format will handle gray-scale shading and images with a resolution up to 300 dpi. TIFF was developed by the Aldus Corporation. TIFF files are very large.

tightly coupled Pertaining to computers that are dependent upon one another.

tile A single sheet or portion that can be combined with others to form an oversize page, or to split a page into such sections.

tiled The display of objects side by side.

tiled windows A screen display divided into nonoverlapping windows.

tiling In computer graphics, the filling of an object with a design or pattern instead of a solid cover. Tiling is used to cover defined areas of the screen with particular images.

tilting screen Video display screen that can be angled back and forth from top to bottom for easier viewing—one result of ergonomics.

time-division multiplexing (TDM) Merging of several bit streams of lower bit rates into a composite signal for transmission over a communication channel of higher bit-rate capacity. See concentrator.

time-delay A modem feature that allows a computer to call another computer and transfer a file at a future time.

time log Logging of how the computer system was used during a specified time period, such as 24 hours.

timer Computer's internal clock.

Times Roman An attractive and easy-to-read serif font that is included as a built-in font with many laser printers.

time-sharing Method of operation in which a computer facility is shared by several users for different purposes at (apparently) the same time. Although the computer actually services each user in sequence, the high speed of the computer makes it appear as though the users are all handled simultaneously.

timing diagram In object-oriented programming, part of the notation of an object diagram, used to show the dynamic interactions among various objects in an object diagram.

tint screen A uniform screen pattern used for visual effect in a layout.

TIPS An imaging program for IBM-compatible microcomputers.

time slicing Allotment of a portion of processing time to each program in a multiprogramming system to prevent the monopolization of the central processing unit by any one program.

title bar In a graphics environment, the line of text at the top of a window that indicates the name of the application or file in that window.

toggle (1) A keystroke that turns a function of a program on or off. (2) A device having two stable states. (3) The ability to go back and forth between two distinctly separate functions on a CRT.

token (1) Symbol representing a name or entity in a programming language. (2) Group of bits, such as eight 1s, used in some bus networks to signal network access by a particular station. (3) A physical object, sometimes containing sophisticated electronics, which is used to gain access to a system. Some tokens contain a microprocessor and are called "intelligent tokens."

tone In computer graphics, the degree of tint and shade in color.

toner Very fine black powder which is fused to paper in laser printing. The equivalent of black ink.

toner cartridge In a laser printer, the disposable container that holds the electrically charged dry ink and drum used in creating an image on the paper.

tool (1) An object or icon used to perform operations in a computer program. Tools are often named either by what they do or by the type of object on which they work. (2) In some computer systems, an applications program. (3) In artificial intelligence, an inference engine, a user interface, and procedures for entering knowledge.

toolbox A group of icons that perform such functions as pointing, cropping, drawing, etc.

toolkit A collection of programs designed to aid a programmer in the development of software.

tool palette A collection of on-screen functions that are grouped in a menu structure for interactive selection.

top-down development Architectural discipline for computer program development wherein the high-level functions are coded and tested in an outline form early in the development process. Lower-level detail is added and tested progressively. From specifications and interfaces the complete package is constructed beginning with the highest levels of control, such as job control languages and operating system services, progressing to program control modules, and extending to successively more detailed levels of program modules in a hierarchically descending structure. The effect of this approach is twofold. First, the actual system integration effort occurs simultaneously with the development; and second, an increasingly capable operational system is in use during development.

top-down programming Programming method that begins with the most general statement of a program and divides it into increasingly detailed sets of routines.

topology Physical layout of a computer network. Interconnection of devices and communication channels into a network configuration.

TOPS An inexpensive and easy-to-use local area network which allows up to 32 computers to be connected in a single local network, allowing the sharing of drives, files, and printers.

TOS Operating system for the Atari ST microcomputer. TOS controls how the computer operates the GEM Desktop, the mouse, and any peripheral devices you connect to the computer.

touch-sensitive screen Display screen on which the user can enter commands by pressing designated areas with a finger or other object. This method takes advantage of an individual's natural instinct to point.

touch-sensitive tablet Input device that converts graphics and pictorial data into numerical form for use by a computer. Graphic data can be generated by pressing the tablet with a stylus.

touch-tone telephone Push-button telephone used in teleprocessing systems.

tower configuration A floor-standing cabinet that is taller than it is wide.

trace (1) Scanning path of the beam in a raster display. (2) Electrical pathway on circuit boards that connect electronic components.

tracing routine Routine that provides a time history of the contents of the computer operational registers during the execution of a program. A complete tracing routine would reveal the status of all registers and locations affected by each instruction each time the instruction is executed.

track (1) Path along which data are recorded on a continuous or rotational medium, such as magnetic tape or magnetic disk. (2) To follow or record the moving position of a video display cursor, stylus, mouse, or other input device.

track ball Device used to move the cursor around on a computer display screen. Consists of a mounting, usually a box, in which is set a ball. As the user spins the ball, the cursor moves at the speed and in the direction of the ball's motion. The housing is stationary, as opposed to the mobile mouse unit.

tracking Moving a cursor or predefined symbol across the surface of the visual display screen with a light pen, electronic pen, track ball, or mouse.

tracking symbol Small symbol on a video display screen that represents the position of the cursor.

tractor-fed printer Printer through which paper with holes along its edges is fed by sprocket wheels within the device.

tractor-feed mechanism Pair of pin-studded belts that rotate in unison and pull paper, punched with marginal holes, into a printer. See pin-feed and continuous forms. Contrast with friction-feed.

tradeoff Balancing of factors in a computer system.

traditional programming Programming using procedural languages such as BASIC, C, or Pascal. Such languages support program construction based on determining the sequence of procedures that act on a separate set of data.

traffic intensity Ratio of the insertion rate to the deletion rate of a queue.

trailer record Record that follows a group of records and contains data pertinent to the group.

training manual Manual designed to be used while learning to use a computer system or program.

trajectory The motion of a robot.

Tramiel, Jack Founder of Commodore International Ltd.; introduced the Commodore PET microcomputer in early 1977, which became extremely popular in the United States and Europe. Later, Tramiel and Commodore developed the VIC-20 and Commodore 64 microcomputers. More recently, Tramiel has guided Atari Corporation in the development of several new microcomputers, including the Atari ST.

transaction An exchange of one value for another. In a cash sale, cash is exchanged for merchandise.

transaction code One or more characters that form parts of a record and signify the type of transaction represented by the record.

transaction file A file that contains all changes to be made to the master file: additions, deletions, and revisions.

transaction processing Activities related to the processing of transactions as they occur.

transaction trailing In database management systems, the creation of an auxiliary file that traces all file updates.

transborder Pertaining to data communications between computer systems located across national borders.

transcribe To copy from one external storage medium to another. The process may involve conversion.

transducer Any device or element that converts an input signal into an output signal of a different form.

transfer (1) To copy or read, transmit, and store an item or block of information. (2) To change control. See branch, conditional transfer, jump, and unconditional transfer.

transfer address See entry point.

transfer rate Speed at which accessed data can be moved from one device to another. See access time and seek time.

transform To change the form of data without changing its meaning. See convert.

transformation In computer graphics, one of the modifications that can be made to the placement or size of an on-screen image. The three basic transformations are translation, scaling, and rotation.

transformer AC device used in computer power supplies to reduce 115 volts 60 Hertz to a lower, more suitable voltage usable by computer equipment.

transient (1) Pertaining to a phenomenon caused in a system by a sudden change in conditions that persists for a relatively short time after the change. (2) Pertaining to a momentary surge on a signal or power line that may produce false signals and cause component failures.

transient error   Type of error that occurs only once and cannot be made to repeat itself.

transient program   Program that does not reside in the computer system's main memory. When needed, the computer reads the program from a disk or tape. Contrast with resident program.

transistor   A semiconductor device used for controlling the flow of current between two terminals. Transistors were developed at Bell Laboratories during World War II and used for the first time in second-generation computers. They were developed by William Shockley, Walter Brattain, and John Bardeen.

transistor-transistor logic (TTL)   Family of integrated circuits characterized by relatively high speed and low power consumption. Logic circuits based on bipolar devices, usually low-power Schottky circuits that are fast but expensive because gold-plated Schottky diodes are required on every TTL bus input.

translate   To change data from one form of representation to another without significantly affecting the meaning. See language translation.

translation   (1) In computer graphics, the movement of an image to a new position on the screen. Under translation, every point in the image moves in the same direction with the same speed at any given instant. (2) See language translation.

translator   Computer program that performs translations from one language or code to another. See assembler, compiler, interpreter, and translation.

transmission   Sending of data from one location and receiving of data in another location, usually leaving the source data unchanged. See data transmission.

transmission facility   Communications link between remote terminals and computers, such as communication lines, microwave transmission lines, communications satellites, lasers, telephone lines, fiber optics, and waveguides.

transmit   To send data from one location and to receive the data at another location.

transparency   The clarity of a program. The degree to which an artificial intelligence program is understandable.

transparent   Pertaining to any process that is not visible to the user. For example, the details of how a file is stored on tracks and sectors are transparent to the user.

transponder A device in a communications satellite that receives a transmission from earth, amplifies the signal, changes the frequency, and transmits the data to a receiving earth station.

transpose To interchange two items of data.

transputer A 32-bit RISC chip used for parallel processing.

transversal Execution of each statement of a program for debugging purposes.

trap Programmed conditional jump to a known location, automatically executed when program execution reaches the location where the tap is set. See interrupt.

trapdoor Breach created intentionally in an information processing system for the purpose of later collecting, altering, or destroying information.

trapping Hardware provision for interrupting the normal flow of control of a program while transfer to a known location is made. See interrupt.

tree Connected graph with no cycles. Also called tree diagram. See forest.

tree diagram Pictorial representation of the logical structure of a program or system. See leaf, node, and root.

tree network Network in which a hierarchy of nodes provides control and communication. Can be represented on paper as the inverse of a family tree. The apex of the network, or top of the tree, represents the primary control for the network, but certain levels of control may be delegated down to intermediate branches. See network topologies.

tree sort Sort that exchanges items treated as nodes of a tree. When an item reaches the root node, it is exchanged with the lowest leaf node. Also called heap sort.

tree structure Another term for hierarchical structure, a form of database organization.

trend line Calculated extension of a data series for the purpose of predicting trends beyond known data.

triad (1) Any group of three, such as three bits, bytes, or characters. (2) In a color CRT, one set of red, green, and blue phosphors.

trichromatic Three-colored. In computer graphics, trichromatic generally refers to the three primary colors (red, green, and blue) combined to create all others.

trigger (1) A concept referring to the execution of procedures as a part of an object-oriented database. A trigger is a procedure that is automatically activated whenever a predefined condition arises. Triggers are like methods, but they are not encapsulated along with the local data on which they operate. (2) Button on a joystick.

trigonometry Branch of mathematics dealing with the relations of the sides and angles of triangles, including the various algebraic functions of these relations. In a right triangle, the basic relationships are called trigonometric functions. Trigonometric functions are represented as library routines in many programming languages.

trilogy A language which is a combination of logic, procedural languages, and database languages. It is similar to PROLOG.

triple click To press and release the mouse button three times rapidly in quick succession.

triple precision Retention of three times as many digits of a quantity as the computer normally uses. See precision. Contrast with single precision and double precision.

tristate logic Form of transistor-transistor logic in which output stages or input and output stages can assume three states. Two are normal low-impedance 1 and 0 states; the third is a high-impedance state that allows many tristate devices to time-share bus lines.

tristimulus values Relative amounts of three primary colors combined to create other colors.

Trojan horse Pertaining to a crime in which a computer criminal places instructions in someone else's program that will allow the program to function normally but also to perform illegitimate functions. For example, a program designed to attract your attention on the screen by displaying graphics. While you watch the screen, the Trojan horse secretly erases or damages files on the hard disk. See also virus.

tron Popular high-tech suffix, such as in datatron and cyclotron.

troubleshoot To try to find a malfunction in a hardware unit or a mistake in a computer program. Synonymous with debug. See bug, debugging aids, and test data.

TRS-80 The first family of personal computers from Radio Shack, a division of Tandy Corporation. The TRS-80 Model I was one of the first personal computers.

True BASIC Structured version of the BASIC programming language. Developed in 1983 by the inventors of the original BASIC language, John Kemeny and Thomas Kurtz. True BASIC is a version of BASIC that does not require line numbers and that includes advanced control structures that make structured programming possible. True BASIC is used to teach the principles of structured language. True BASIC is compiled rather than interpreted, so it produces compact, fast-running code (and gives error messages before it begins to execute the program).

true complement   Synonymous with ten's complement and two's complement.

truncate   (1) To reject the final digits in a number, thus lessening precision; for example, 3.14159 truncates the series for π, which could conceivably be extended indefinitely. (2) To cut off any characters that will not fit into an allotted space, such as a ten-character name field on a printed report, in which Rumplestiltskin would appear as Rumplestilt.

truncation error   Error due to truncation. Contrast with round-off error.

trunk   Direct line between two telephone switching centers.

truth table   Systematic tabulation of all the possible input/output combinations produced by a binary circuit.

T-switch   An electrical switch that allows the user to change the connections between computing equipment just by turning the dial on a switch. T-switches are useful for sharing infrequently used or expensive peripheral devices, such as a laser printer.

TTL   An acronym for Transistor-Transistor Logic. A medium/high speed family of logic integrated circuits.

tunnel diode   Electronic device with switching speeds of fractional billionths of seconds. Used in high-speed computer circuitry and memories.

triple   A record, or row, in a relational database model.

turbo   A trade name for hardware and software that implies high speed.

Turbo C   A compiler for the C programming language from Borland International.

Turbo Pascal   A very popular variation of the Pascal programming language. Turbo Pascal provides an integrated package that includes an editor, compiler and linker. Turbo Pascal was designed in 1984 by Philippe Kahn of Borland International, and closely follows the definition of standard Pascal. In addition to the standard, Turbo Pascal includes a number of extensions to the language.

Turbo PROLOG   An implementation of the PROLOG programming language, developed by Borland International Inc., for use on microcomputers.

TURING   Programming language developed in 1982 by R. C. Holt and J. R. Cordy at the University of Toronto, whose primary design goal was to eliminate some of the inadequacies of the Pascal programming language. Runs under the UNIX operating system.

Turing, Alan M.   (1912-1954) English mathematician and logician who, shortly before his death, completed the design of one of the world's first modern high-speed digital computers. Acknowledged by many as the father of artificial intelligence. He argued that a machine could be built which could emulate human thinking.

Turing machine A hypothetical logic machine. Mathematical model of a device that changes its internal state and reads from, writes on, and moves a potentially infinite tape, all in accordance with its present state, thereby constituting a model for computer-like behavior.

Turing's test Developed by British mathematician Alan Turing, this is a game to determine whether a computer might be considered to possess intelligence. Participants in the game include two respondents (a computer and a human) and a human examiner who tries to determine which of the unseen respondents is the human. According to this test, intelligence and the ability to think would be demonstrated by the computer's success in fooling the examiner.

turnaround form Output document that serves as an input medium during a subsequent phase of processing.

turnaround time (1) Time it takes for a job to travel from the user to the computing center, to be run on the computer, and for the program results to be returned to the user. (2) Time spent between transmissions in data transmission using a half-duplex channel.

turnkey system Prepackaged, ready-to-use computer system containing all the hardware, software, training, and maintenance support needed to perform a given application. All the prepared system needs is is the "turn of the key." For example, a turnkey desktop publishing system might consist of a CPU, monitor, hard disk, scanner, laser printer and appropriate software. While easier to set up than off-the-shelf systems, equipment, training, and support choices are sometimes limited.

turn off Act of turning off (powering down) a computer system.

turn on Act of turning on (powering up) a computer system.

turtle A robot that moves about on the floor, or a shape that moves about on the screen. Both types are used to demonstrate programming, and can draw a trail showing where they have been.

turtle graphics Graphics accomplished by a simulated robot that have been incorporated into LOGO and other computer languages. Used to teach geometry and computer graphics concepts.

tutorial Hardware or software training manual. Can be a printed document or recorded in magnetic form on a disk or tape.

tutorial program Computer program that explains new material and then tests the user's retention.

TV terminal Common television set used as a computer output device. See video monitor and television receiver.

tweak To fine tune or adjust a piece of equipment. To enhance. To make final small changes to improve software performance.

twinkle box Input device consisting of optical sensors, lenses, and a rotating disk, and capable of determining the three-dimensional position of a light-emitting object by angular light sensing.

twisted wire Data communications medium that consists of pairs of wires, twisted together, and bound into a cable. Used to transmit information over short distances.

two-dimensional array Arrangement consisting of rows and columns. See matrix. Contrast with one-dimensional array.

two-dimensional graphics (2-D) A graphic image in two dimensions—height and width.

two-pass Pertaining to an operation or program that has to manipulate its data twice. It partially accomplishes its purpose on the first pass through the data. The operation is completed in the second pass through the data.

two's complement Method of representing negative numbers. A positive or negative binary number is changed to the opposite sign by changing all 1s to 0s and all 0s to 1s, then binarily adding 1. Synonymous with true complement. Compare one's complement, nine's complement, and ten's complement.

type ahead In word processing, a feature that prevents the loss of characters when the operator is typing faster than the computer can display characters on the screen.

typeface Collection of letters, numbers, and symbols that share a distinctive appearance (e.g. Helvetica, Times Roman, Bodoni, Schoolbook, Courier, and Palatino).

typeface family A group of typefaces that include the normal, bold, italic and bold-italic variations of the same design; a related group of type fonts.

type font Complete set of characters in a consistent and unique typeface.

typematic Any keyboard character that repeats for as long as it is pressed.

typeover Ability of an impact printer to strike a character more than once to produce a boldface effect on the printed copy. See overstriking and shadow printing.

typeset quality Printer resolution of 1200 to 2540 dots per inch.

typesetting The production of camera-ready copy on a laser printer (low-quality typesetting) or an imagesetter (high-quality typesetting).

type size The size, in points, of a typeface.

type style The weight (such as normal or bold) or posture (such as italic) of a font.

type table A file used by certain OCR programs that contains character shapes for a particular font. The program refers to the type table when recognizing that font.

typing In object-oriented programming, the enforcement of the class of an object, which prevents, objects of different types from being interchanged.

typo In desktop publishing, a typesetting or clerical error in producing typed copy.

typography The science and art of designing typefaces and of composing printed works.

UCSD Pascal   A high-level programming language, developed largely by the Institute for Information Science at the University of California, San Diego, under the direction of Kenneth L. Bowles. It contains a number of extensions to Standard Pascal particularly ones that handle graphics and character strings.

UCSD p-system   Program development system created by Kenneth Bowles at the University of California at San Diego (UCSD). Includes an operating system, a text editor, and compilers for FORTRAN, Microsoft BASIC, and Pascal. The p refers to "pseudocomputer." The system compilers produce a very compact p-code, which runs on a pseudocomputer. An interpreter converts the p-code into acceptable code for the actual computer on which the program is run, making the system very portable. Only a very small interpreter need be written for each computer on which the p-system runs.

ultrafiche   Microfiche holding images reduced a hundredfold or more.

ultralarge-scale integration   Process of placing millions of integrated circuits on a single chip. Abbreviated ULSI.

UltraPaint   An Apple Macintosh graphics program that combines black-and-white painting, color painting, grayscale image editing and object drawing. All basic paint tools are featured plus tools and special effects including blended fills, additive and subtractive lasso, marquee and wand selection masking, three pattern/color airbrush, chalk, quill pen, auto tracing, editable brushes, patterns, 256 color palette and 1 degree rotation. Image manipulation includes contrast and brightness controls, charcoal, water droplet and smear. For drawing, all standard tools are provided plus Beizer curves and smooth polygons with complete editing control. WYSIWYG text and up to eight object-oriented layers per drawing. File formats supported include MacPaint, TIFF, MacDraw, and PICT.

ultraviolet light   Light with rays shorter than those of visible light but longer than X rays. Used to erase data or instructions stored in an Erasable PROM. Once the EPROM has been erased, it can be reprogrammed by using a PROM programmer.

unary See monadic.

unattended operation Data transmission and/or reception without an operator.

unbundled Pertaining to services, programs, training, and so on sold independently of computer hardware by the hardware manufacturer. Contrast with bundled.

unconditional transfer In program control, an instruction that always causes a branch away from the normal sequence of executing instructions. Contrast with conditional transfer.

uncontrolled loop Program loop that does not reach a logical end.

underflow (1) Condition that arises when a computer computation yields a result smaller than the smallest possible quantity the computer is capable of storing. (2) Condition in which the exponent plus the excess become negative in a floating-point arithmetic operation.

underline To format a selection of text so that the text is printed with a line slightly below it.

undo Command that undoes the effect of the previous command and puts the text or graphics back the way it was. Some programs provide multiple undo levels, letting you take back commands you gave in the past.

unfragmented A hard disk that has most of its files stored in consecutive sectors rather than spread out over the disk. Such an arrangement allows more efficient reading of data with less time required to move the read/write head to gather the information.

unibus High-speed data communications bus structure shared by the CPU, internal memory, and peripherals.

uninterruptable power supply Battery-operated device that supplies a computer with electricity in the event of a brownout or blackout.

unipolar Having one pole. Contrast with bipolar.

Unisys A computer company formed in 1986 as a merger of the Burroughs Corporation and the Sperry Corporation, both large mainframe manufacturers. Unisys continues to emphasize the product lines of both companies, and in addition, has introduced several new mainframe, minicomputer, and personal computer products.

unit Any device having a special function, such as the arithmetic-logic unit, central processing unit, or disk unit.

unit position Extreme right position of a field, especially an integer numeric field.

UNIVAC I First commercial electronic digital computer. Completed in 1951, it was used by the Census Bureau for processing some of the data from the 1950 census. Forty-eight of these computers were built. See Mauchly, John.

universal asynchronous receiver/transmitter Integrated circuit device that receives serial data and converts it into parallel form for transmission, and vice versa.

universal identifier Standard multidigit number assigned to an individual to be used in verifying her or his identity.

universal language Any programming language available on many computers, such as Pascal, COBOL, and BASIC. Same as common language.

universal product code (UPC) A bar code developed to identify products and manufacturers of products. The code is to be read by optical code readers.

UNIX An easy-to-use operating system developed by Ken Thompson, Dennis Ritchie and coworkers at Bell Laboratories. Since the UNIX operating system is very easy to use, its design concept had a great influence on operating systems for microcomputers. UNIX is widely used on a great variety of computers, from mainframes to microcomputers. It is a powerful operating system that has many high-level utility programs, and it is capable of running a number of jobs at once. It has many applications including office automation, network control, and control of numerically controlled machinery. Since it also has superior capabilities as a program development system, UNIX should become even more widely used in the future. UNIX exists in various forms and implementations.

unpack To separate short units of data that have previously been packed. Opposite of pack.

unpopulated board Circuit board whose components must be supplied by the purchaser. Contrast with populated board.

unset To change the value of a bit (or a group of bits) to binary 0.

unstructured data Storage of retrievable information that is not organized into bytes or characters and customarily stored as a sequential bit stream representing pixels that must be reconstructed in its entirety to achieve intelligible results.

up State of a computer system that is currently operating.

up-and-running Used to indicate that a computer system or a peripheral device has just been put into operation and is working properly.

UPC Acronym for Universal Product Code.

update (1) A software update usually occurs whenever a minor change has been made to the software. Updates are often free to registered owners of the software. (2) To make data files more current by adding changing, or deleting data.

upgrade (1) A software upgrade usually occurs whenever new features or major enhancements are added to the software. The cost for upgrades (to registered owners of the software) is usually substantially lower than the retail price for the product. (2) To reconfigure a computer system to increase its computing power. For example, to upgrade a microcomputer system with a faster and larger hard disk.

upload To transfer information (files) from a smaller computer to a larger computer.

upper case Capital letters. All VCTs have the capability of using these. Contrast with lower case.

uptime Period of time that equipment is working without failure. Contrast with available time and downtime.

upward compatible Term used to indicate that a computer system or peripheral device can do everything that the previous model could do, plus some additional functions. See compatibility.

usability Worth of a system as evaluated by the person who must use it.

user (1) Anyone who owns or utilizes a computer for problem solving or data manipulation. (2) Anyone who requires the services of a computer system. Also called end user.

user-defined function Any function that has been defined by the user.

user-defined key Computer keyboard key that has a predefined function or whose function can be changed by a program. The function is performed by the computer whenever the key is depressed.

user-friendly Term applied to software and/or hardware that has been designed to be easily used, without the user having to remember complex procedures. Very easy for the inexperienced person to use.

user group Group of computer users who share the knowledge they have gained and the programs they have developed on a computer or class of computers of a specific manufacturer. Usually meet to exchange information, share programs, and trade equipment. Provide a valuable opportunity to get and give advice on computer hardware, software, and applications. Often a member can talk to someone who used a product he or she is considering buying or using. Newsletters also offer useful information.

user involvement Involvement of users in the systems development life cycle process.

user-oriented language See problem-oriented language and procedure-oriented language.

user profile Information used as a part of a security system, such as the user's job function, areas of knowledge, access privileges, and supervisor.

user's manual Document describing how to use a hardware device, a software product, or a system.

user terminal See terminal.

utility Program that helps the user run, enhance, create, or analyze other programs, programming languages, operating systems and equipment.

utility programs Computer programs that provide commonly needed services, such as transferring data from one medium to another (disk to tape) and character conversion. Vendors of large computer systems commonly supply a set of utilities with their systems. Utilities are designed to facilitate or aid the operation and use of the computer for a number of different applications and uses. Examples of utilities are memory-dump programs, program debugging aids, file-handling programs, mathematical routines, sorting programs, and text editors.

utility server A device that allows everyone on a network to use several peripheral devices.

utilization statistics Measure of a computer's performance based on the time log.

V Used as a prefix to indicate virtual, meaning capabilities that substitute for some real device or feature that isn't really there. For example, Vdisks—the emulation of disk drives in memory, VM—the emulation of memory on disks, and Vslots—the emulation of slots through interface ports.

VAB Acronym for Voice Answer Back, an audio response device that can link a computer system to a telephone network, thus providing voice response to inquiries made from telephone-tape terminals.

vaccine A program designed to counter the effects of a virus program.

vacuum tube Device for controlling flow of electrical current. Dominant electronic element found in computers prior to the advent of the transistor. Those computers using vacuum tubes are referred to as first generation computers.

validation Examination of data for correctness against certain criteria, such as format (patterns of numbers, spaces, and letters), ranges (upper and lower value limits), check digits, and equivalent entries on a master file.

value (1) Any constant or quantity stored in a computer's memory. (2) In a spreadsheet, data consisting of a number representing an amount, a formula, or a function.

value-added network System in which a carrier leases communication lines from a common carrier, enhances them by adding improvements, such as error detection and faster response time, and then leases them to a third party.

value rule A spreadsheet formula that tells the program how to calculate a cell's value.

vaporware Slang for announced software that may never materialize. In other words, a program promised by a publisher but never released.

VAR An acronym for Value-Added Reseller, a person or company that buys equipment at a discount from manufacturers, combines it into systems or adds software, and then sells it to end customers.

variable Quantity that can assume any of a given set of values. For example, in a BASIC program that states PRINT A, B, C, the variables A, B, and C represent the actual values that will be printed. See subscripted variable. Contrast with constant.

variable-length record Record in a file in which records are not uniform in length. Contrast with fixed-length record.

variable name Alphanumeric term that identifies a data value in a program. The term can assume any of a set of values.

variable word length Pertaining to a machine word or operand that may consist of a variable number of bits, bytes, or characters. Contrast with fixed word length.

VAX Designation for a family of 32-bit minicomputer systems manufactured by Digital Equipment Corporation. VAX machines were introduced in 1977 and range from desktop personal computers to large-scale mainframes.

Vbase An object-oriented database.

VDL Acronym for Vienna Definition language, a language for defining the syntax and semantics of programming languages.

VDT Acronym for Video Display Terminal, an input/output device consisting of a display screen and an input keyboard. Synonymous with CRT terminal.

VDU Acronym for Visual Display Unit, a peripheral device on which data are displayed on some type of screen.

vector (1) List of numbers, all of which are expressed on the same line, such as a single column or row. (2) Quantity having magnitude and direction, as opposed to scaler value. (3) In computer science, a data structure that permits the location of any item by the use of a single index or subscript. (4) Type of cathode ray tube on which graphic data are represented by lines drawn from point to point rather than by illumination of a series of contiguous positions, as on a raster display device. (5) In plotting, an element of a line connecting two points. (6) In computer graphics, a line drawn in a certain direction from a starting point to an ending point.

vector font A font in which the characters are drawn in arrangements of line segments rather than arrangements of curves or bits.

vector graphics monitor A monitor that generates pictures by drawing numerous straight-line segments (vectors) on the screen.

vector image An image defined as a series of straight line vectors. The beginning and ending points of each line are stored and later adjusted as the image is sized.

vector pair Data points that make up the opposite ends of a vector.

vector processor A processor that performs simultaneous high-speed calculations on numerical elements. Vector processors are used extensively in systems that require intensive graphics operations.

vendee Person or business that purchases a hardware or software system.

vendor (1) Company or business entity that sells computers, peripheral devices, or computer related services. (2) Any supplier from whom a vendee may purchase material.

Venn diagram Diagram that uses circles and ellipses to give a graphic representation of logic relationships.

Ventura Publisher A desktop publishing program for IBM-compatible microcomputers and Apple Macintosh computers from Ventura Software, Inc. The program provides typeset-quality desktop publishing. It formats files created with word processors, graphics programs, scanners or within the program itself. It is an excellent product for creating documents such as brochures, newsletters, or long structured documents like catalogs, technical manuals and books. It imports a wide variety of text and graphics files.

verify (1) To determine whether a data processing operation has been accomplished accurately. (2) To check data validity.

version Specific release of a software product of a specific hardware model. Usually numbered in ascending order. For example, DOS 5.0 is a later version of a disk operating system than is DOS 4.1 or DOS 3.3.

verso The left-side (even-numbered) page in a two-sided printing of a book or document.

vertex (1) Point where two sides of an angle meet. (2) Highest or lowest point on a graphed line.

vertical applications Programs designed for specific professions or to do specialized kinds of work. Dentists can purchase applications, for example, that are designed expressly to manage a dental practice scheduling, billing, ordering supplies, and so forth. There are hundreds of vertical applications available.

vertical justification See leading.

vertical market Market consisting of a group of similar customers.

vertical market software Software for a group of similar customers such as printers, dentists, artists, or doctors.

vertical recording Technology that strives to stand magnetic bits of information on end instead of side by side on a disk as they are today. Using this technology, several billion bytes of information could be stored on one disk.

vertical scrolling Ability of a system to move up and down through a page or more of data displayed on the video screen. See scrolling.

vertical software Specialized applications software that is designed for a particular discipline or activity. Examples include software that controls a spacecraft and simulates the game of blackjack.

very high-level language Fourth generation programming language.

very-high-speed integrated circuit (VHSIC) An integrated circuit that performs operations at a very high rate of speed.

very large scale integration (VLSI) Process of placing a large number (usually between 100,000 and 10,000,000) of components on one chip.

vesicular film A coating for optical disc platters that permits the raising of small bumps on the surface instead of the pits used in standard CD-ROM discs for recording data. Bumps, unlike pits, can be flattened out to make an optical disc erasable and thus rewritable.

VGA Acronym for Video Graphics Array. An IBM high-resolution video display standard for its personal computers. VGA displays images at 640 pixels horizontally by 480 pixels vertically. This color bit-mapped graphics display standard was introduced by IBM Corporation in 1987 with its PS/2 computers.

VHSIC See very-high-speed integrated circuit.

video Visual display, especially on a video display terminal.

video buffer The memory on a video adapter used to store the data waiting to be shown on the video display.

video digitizer Input device that converts the signal from a video camera into digital form and stores it in computer storage, where it can be analyzed or modified by the computer. See digitizer.

videodisc An optical disc used to store video images and associated audio information.

video display page A portion of a computer's video buffer that holds one complete screen image.

video display terminal (VDT) Device for entering information into a computer system and displaying it on a screen. A typewriterlike keyboard is used to enter information. See cathode ray tube, display, and screen.

video game machine Microprocessor-controlled machine designed principally for running commercially produced cartridges and disks that contain games and educational programs.

video graphics Computer-produced animated pictures.

video graphics board A video display board that generates text and graphics and accepts video from a camera or video recorder.

video input camera Video camera that converts images (photographs, real-life situations, drawings) into dot-by-dot images in a computer's memory. The digitized images may be shown on a display screen or printed on paper by a graphics printer.

video monitor The device on which images generated by the computer's video adapter are displayed.

VideoPaint A powerful Apple Macintosh paint program. Its extensive features include over 40 sophisticated special effects—for example, spherization, blur, smudge, contour, Bezier curves, diffuse, dithering, fractals, custom shading, anti-aliasing brush and waterdrop tools, and a multi-layer painting environment. It has a strong 3-D modeling feature and includes wire frame creation and rendering with full control over light sources, shades and texture plus the ability to wrap images around 3-D models.

video RAM (VRAM) A special type of dynamic RAM (DRAM) used in high-speed video applications.

video signal Electronic signal containing information specifying the location and brightness of each point on a CRT screen, along with timing signals to place the image properly on the screen.

videotex Interactive electronic information system that includes news, electronic mail, shopping, banking, weather and stock reports services.

vidicon Tube inside a TV camera that converts the image of a scene into an electrical signal.

view (1) To display information on a computer display screen. (2) The display of a graphical image from a given perspective. (3) In CAD programs, an image of a 3-D graphics model as it would be seen from a particular viewpoint. (4) In database systems, way of presenting the contents of a database to the user, not necessarily the same as the way the fields and records are stored in the database. Different users or programs that call upon the database for information may have unique views of the data.

viewdata Same as videotext.

viewport Process that allows a user to place any selected picture in a chosen location on a video display screen. Compare window.

virtual Appearing to be rather than actually being, as in virtual storage.

virtual address In virtual storage systems, an address that refers to virtual storage and must, therefore, be translated into a real storage address when it is used.

virtual function   In object-oriented programming, a special member function that is invoked through a base class reference or pointer and is bound dynamically at run time.

virtual image   An image that has been copied into a computer's memory but that is too large to be displayed all at one time on the screen. Methods such as scrolling and panning are used to bring unseen portions of a virtual image into view.

virtual machine   Illusion of having many copies of the existing computer running simultaneously.

virtual memory   Storage that is actually provided on a disk drive or other mass storage device but appears to programs to be part of the main memory of the computer. Thus, the programs seem to use more main memory than is actually provided.

Virtual Storage Access Method (VSAM)   A highly efficient mass-storage device (disk) file access system for IBM mainframe systems.

virus   A computer program which can wreak havoc on a system, either by destroying data or simply gumming up the works. It is called a virus because it acts like a biological virus does in a human—the computer virus is not actually a live organism. Viruses usually enter via shareware or public domain programs, though there have been reports of viruses being carried by commercial software. Some viruses are not immediately apparent and so their origins cannot be traced. A virus program "infects" computer files by inserting in those files copies of itself. This is usually done in such a manner that the copies will be executed when the file is loaded into memory, allowing them to infect still other files, and so on. Viruses often have damaging side effects. Virus preventive programs are available. See boot virus, parasitic virus, and Trojan horse.

visible page   The image that is being displayed on the screen.

VisiCalc   The first electronic spreadsheet, introduced in 1978 for the Apple II microcomputer. VisiCalc was conceived by Dan Bricklin and programmed by a friend, Bob Frankston. The name is derived from VISIble CALCulation. VisiCalc displays information on a screen as an electronic sheet or grid. Locations within the grid are treated as variables. To manipulate a variable, the user applies an operation to the variable's location in the grid. VisiCalc was followed by SuperCalc, MultiPlan, Lotus 1-2-3, Microsoft Excel, and many other spreadsheets.

vision recognition   Method for processing pictorial information by computer. For example, an artificial intelligence computer can recognize a TV image of a horse and say (or print out), "It is a horse." Recognizing images is a very complex process for machines. See image processing.

visual display Visual representation of data such as a picture or diagram drawn on a display screen or a diagram produced by a plotter.

visual operating system An operating system that relies on icons, selected by a mouse, for giving commands to the computer.

visual page Visual representation consisting of one or more stored screen display files.

visual programming A way for programmers to interact with software and the programs they construct. The term indicates a new dimension added to programs and software systems, namely the ability to gain different insights and new ways to deal with software through visual and graphical means. Although software can be very complex, visual programming can give one the means to cut through that complexity by providing ways to represent software clearly and concisely in both static and dynamic modes and in two or three dimensions, with color and highlighting.

VLDB Acronym for Very Large Data Base, a database distributed among multiple computers with different database management systems.

VLSI An abbreviation for Very Large Scale Integration. Micro chips that typically have more than 250,000 components each. VLSI methods allow thousands of integrated circuits to be placed on each chip and keep production costs relatively low. As VLSI technology improves, both a CPU and its memory may eventually be located on a single chip.

Virtual Machine (VM) Refers to a functional equivalent of an entire computer and VM is the IBM Corporation's implementation of this concept in their mid-size to large-scale systems.

VM See Virtual Machine.

vocabulary Codes or instructions that can be used to write a program for a particular computer.

voice actuation Control of the computer by spoken commands.

voice communications Transmission of sound in the human hearing range. Voice or audio sound can be transmitted either as analog or digital signals.

voice grade Pertaining to computer-to-computer links that employ the lines used in normal telephone communications.

voice input Input device that permits a human voice to be used as input to a computer. Also called speech recognition.

voice mail Messages spoken into a telephone, converted into digital form, and stored in the computer's memory until recalled, at which time they are reconverted into voice form.

voice output Audio response device that permits the computer to deliver output by the spoken word. Range of uses includes computer-assisted instruction and self-service gas stations. See phonetic system.

voice recognition system System designed to recognize and understand the voice and vocabulary of the user.

voice response Computer output in spoken form.

voice synthesis Ability of a computer to use stored patterns of sounds within its memory to assemble words that can be played through a loudspeaker.

volatile Refers to the loss of data in semiconductor storage when the current is interrupted or turned off.

volatile file Any file in which insertion of new records or deletion of old records occurs at a high rate. Access time is critical.

volatile storage Storage medium whose contents are lost if power is removed from the system. See dynamic RAM. Contrast with nonvolatile storage.

volatility When a file is processed, percentage of records added or deleted. Important parameter in designing a database.

voltage Electrical pressure. High voltage in a computer circuit is represented by 1; low (or zero) voltage is represented by 0.

voltage regulator Circuit that holds an output voltage at a predetermined value or causes it to vary according to a predetermined plan, regardless of normal input-voltage change or changes in the load impedance.

voltage surge protector See surge protector.

volume Physical unit of a storage medium, such as diskette, hard disk, disk pack, or tape reel, capable of having data recorded on it and subsequently read.

von Neumann, John (1903-1957) One of the outstanding mathematicians of this century. He built one of the first electronic computers, contributed much to game theory, and introduced the stored-program concept.

von Neumann architecture Standard computer design based on stored programs and sequential processing.

von Neumann bottleneck The constraints in calculation ability brought about by the von Neumann architecture which dictates one step at a time.

von Neumann machine A machine that consists of a central processing unit (CPU) and memory. The CPU fetches, executes, and returns. It treats data and programs in the same way. Most current computers are based on the von Neumann machine. Contrast with parallel computers.

VRC Acronym for Vertical Redundancy Check.

VS Acronym for Virtual Storage.

VSAM See Virtual Storage Access Method.

vulnerability Weaknesses in a computer system that pose security hazards.

wafer Thin, circular disk on which many integrated circuits are fabricated and subsequently diced up into individual chips. It is a slice, approximately 1/30 inch thick, from 3 to 6 inches in diameter.

wait state Condition in which the central processing unit is idle, not executing instructions.

wait states A condition that occurs when a processor runs faster than its memory chips can retrieve data, thereby forcing the processor to wait periodically. Fast computers have no wait states, slower computers have one or two wait states.

wait time Time during which a program or a computer waits for the completion of other activities.

walkthrough One or more individuals "play computer" and follow the logic of a program through the steps performed by the computer in executing a program.

WAN Acronym for Wide Area Network, a network of geographically distant computers and terminals.

wand Hand-held optical device that can read and identify coded labels, bar codes, and characters.

Wang, An Came from China to the U.S. in 1945 to study applied physics at Harvard University. In 1951 he found Wang Laboratories, a computer manufacturing company he guided for almost 40 years. In 1988, two years before he died, Wang was inducted into the National Inventors' Hall of Fame for his 1948 invention of a pulse transfer device that enabled magnetic core memories to be used in computers.

Wang Laboratories A major manufacturer of computers founded in 1951 by Dr. An Wang. In 1970, Wang introduced its first word processing system. Eight years later it was one of the largest suppliers of small business computers and word processors.

warm boot   Process of fooling the computer into thinking that its power has been turned off although power is still on. Contrast with cold boot.

warm start   Same as warm boot.

warm-up time   Interval between the energizing of a device and the beginning of the application of its output characteristics.

Warnier-Orr   A method of program design that uses top-down methods. Braces or curly brackets are used to indicate how the details of each step are arranged.

warning message   Diagnostic message produced by a compiler to alert the user to a nonfatal error.

warranty   Limited protection for hardware and software products. Similar to warranties for most consumer products.

Water Color   A raster-based paint program designed to emulate the watercolor process operating in MS DOS. The program emulates standard artist tools. Users can mix colors and water and use either nylon or natural bristle brushes as they would on a real canvas. Layering techniques allow objects to be quickly added or deleted.

WATS   Acronym for Wide Area Telephone Service.

Watson, Thomas J., Jr.   Guided IBM Corporation into its leadership position in the computer industry.

Watson, Thomas J., Sr. (1874-1956)   Guiding spirit of IBM Corporation, a superb salesman and president of IBM until 1952. Although his motto was THINK, he did not think there would be much demand for digital computers.

WCCE   Acronym for World Conference on Computers in Education.

weed   To discard currently undesirable or needless items from a file.

weight   The variation in the heaviness of a typeface.

What if?   (1) Premise on which most electronic spreadsheet programs operate. New values may be substituted to determine the resultant effect on other values. (2) In artificial intelligence, a term used in expert systems. The process is as follows: once a set of data have been entered, questions have been answered, and a conclusion has been reached, changing a portion of the data of answering a question differently to see how the conclusion would be altered.

wheel printer   Printer with a printing mechanism that contains the printing characters on metal wheels. Type of line printer.

Whirlwind I   A digital computer developed at the Massachusetts Institute of Technology in 1950. The Whirlwind I computer used magnetic core as a storage device. This use of core storage was so successful that most of the computers designed after 1952 used magnetic cores for memory.

white noise   Continuous noise produced over all audible frequencies to "fill in the gaps" between discontinuous office distractions such as printers, keyboards, and footsteps.

white space   (1) A character that does not result in a printed number, letter, or symbol, e.g. space or tab. (2) The portion of the page not printed. A good page design involves the use of white space to balance the areas that receives text and graphics.

wholeness   The degree of complexity of an expert system.

whole number   Positive number without a fractional part, such as 84 or 22.0 or 0 (the only nonpositive whole number). Positive integer or zero.

wide area network (WAN)   Data communications network designed to serve an area of hundreds or thousands of miles. WAN's are generally implemented by linking together several remote Local Area Networks (LANs) through the use of gateways and bridges over dedicated telephone lines.

wideband   In data communications, a channel wider in bandwidth than a voice-grade channel. Same as broadband. Compare narrowband.

widow   Last line of a paragraph sitting alone at the top of a page of text. Considered undesirable in all forms of printing. Compare with orphan.

Wiener, Norbert (19894-1964)   American scientist who coined the term cybernetics, a new branch of science. Believed that many thought processes in the human brain could be determined mathematically and adapted for computers. Pioneer in the theory of automata. See artificial intelligence.

wild card   Method of file-naming conventions that permits an operating system to perform utility functions on multiple files with related names, without the programmer or user having to specify each file by its full, unique name. For example, if a word processor is directed to search for "Don," it might locate "Donald" as well as "Donna" if both were present in the file. See global character.

Wilkes, Maurice Vincent   Headed the team of people at the University of Cambridge (Great Britain) who built the Electronic Delay Storage Automatic Calculator (EDSAC) in 1949.

Winchester disks   A particular form of hard disk in which several disk platters and their associate heads are sealed inside an enclosure. This enclosure is then kept as airtight as possible to exclude dust. The absence of dust allows for the read/write heads to be kept very close to the disk (closer than the size of an average dust particle) which means that the data can be packed much tighter than would otherwise be possible. The Winchester sealed disk technology was first developed by the IBM Corporation. Although originally a self-contained, removable module, the term is used today to refer to any fixed hard disk.

window   Portion of the video display area dedicated to some specified purpose. Special software allows the screen to be divided into multiple windows that can be moved around and made bigger or smaller. Windows allow the user to treat the computer display screen like a desktop where various files can remain open simultaneously.

windowing   Act of displaying two or more files or disparate portions of the same file on the screen simultaneously.

windowing software   Programs that enable users to work with multiple on-screen windows. The Apple Macintosh Finder, Microsoft Windows and the OS/2 Presentation Manager are all examples of windowing environments..

Windows   A graphics-based operating environment for IBM-compatible microcomputers from Microsoft Corporation. It runs in conjunction with DOS. Some of the graphical user interface features include pull-down menus, multiple typefaces, desk accessories, and the capability of moving text and graphics from one program to another via a clipboard.

windows environment   Any operating system or program that provides multiple windows on screen. Microsoft Windows, Presentation Manager and Finder are examples of windows environments.

windows program   A program written to run under Microsoft Windows.

wire-frame model   In computer graphics, a display of a three-dimensional object composed of separate lines that resemble strands of wire joined to create a model.

wire pairs   Wires twisted together in an insulated cable that is frequently used to transmit information over short distances.

wire wrap   Type of circuit board construction. Electrical connections are made through wires connected to the posts that correspond to the proper component leads.

Wirth, Niklaus In 1968, in Switzerland, he developed the computer language Pascal (named for Blaise Pascal), a popular high-level programming language that facilitates the use of structured programming techniques. In 1979, Wirth created Modula-2, an enhanced version of Pascal that supports the separate compilation of program modules and overcomes many other shortcomings of Pascal.

wizard Experienced hacker.

WMF Acronym for Windows Metafile Format. A common graphics file format for applications that run under Microsoft Windows.

word Logical unit of information. Group of bits, characters, or bytes considered as an entity and capable of being stored in one storage location. Compare keyword.

Word See Microsoft Word.

word length Number of bits in a word, usually 8, 16, 32, or 64.

WordPerfect A full-featured word processing program for IBM-compatible microcomputers, Apple Macintosh, and other computers. It was introduced in 1980 by WordPerfect Corporation. Features include on-screen columns, text boxes, styles, borders, graphics drawing/editing, sort, merge, table of contents/index generation, line numbering, spelling checker and on-line thesaurus. Imports and exports MacWrite documents, as well as WordPerfect documents that were created on many different computers.

word processing (WP) Technique for electronically storing, editing, and manipulating text by using an electronic keyboard, computer, and printer. The text is recorded on a magnetic medium usually floppy disks. The final output is on paper. Words and letters are manipulated electronically, making it easy to copy and edit text. Popular word processing programs are Microsoft Word, WordPerfect, DisplayWrite, Professional Write, WordStar and FullWrite Professional.

word processing center Central facility that contains the word processing equipment and personnel that prepare written communications for an organization.

word processing operator Individual who operates word processing equipment.

word processing program Software that guides the computer system in writing, editing, and formatting text. Same as word processor.

word processing system Information processing system that relies on automated and computerized typing, copying, filing, dictation, and document retrieval. Increasingly used in modern office.

word processor Computer program that provides for manipulation of text. Can be used for writing documents; inserting or changing words, paragraphs, or pages; and printing documents.

Works See Microsoft Works.

WordStar The first full-featured word processing program for IBM-compatible microcomputers. It was introduced in 1978 by WordStar International. WordStar gave sophisticated word processing capabilities to personal computer users at significantly less cost than the dedicated word processing machines of the time. Several different versions of WordStar are available today.

word wrap Feature that automatically moves a word to the beginning of the next line if it will not fit at the end of the original line. Feature found in word processing and page layout programs.

workbench Programming environment in which hardware and software items are shared by several users.

working storage Same as temporary storage.

worksheet window The portion of the worksheet visible on-screen.

workspace Loosely defined term that usually refers to the amount of internal storage available for programs and data and allocated for working storage.

workstation Configuration of computer equipment designed for use by one person at a time. This may have a terminal connected to a computer, or it may be a stand-alone system with local processing capability. Examples of workstations are a stand-alone graphics system, and a word processor.

work year Effort expended by one person for one year. Term used to estimate the personnel resources needed to complete a specific task.

World Conference on Computers in Education (WCCE) International computer education conference sponsored by the International Federation for Information Processing and the American Federation of Information Processing Societies. Held every four years in a different country. See National Conference on Computers in Education.

worm A destructive routine in a program that is designed to corrupt information on a disk. A worm differs from a virus in that it cannot replicate itself or attach itself to other programs. A worm usually exists as a program in its own right.

WORM Stands for WriteOnce/Read Many. It describes storage devices upon which data, once written, cannot be erased. WORM drives write data by burning holes into the surface of a special type of disk. The disks last for decades. This indelible record is highly desirable in fields that require permanent, unalterable storage of important documents.

Wozniak, Stephen Co-founder of Apple Computer, Inc., developer of several microcomputer systems, including the Apple II, Apple IIc, and Apple IIe. See Jobs, Steven.

WPG A WordPerfect graphics file format.

WPM Acronym for Words Per Minute, a measure of data transmission speed.

wraparound (1) Continuation of an operation, such as a change in the storage location from the largest addressable location to the first addressable location. (2) A visual display cursor movement from the last character position to the first position.

wraparound type Type that wraps around a graphic image in a body of text.

write (1) Process of transferring information from the computer to an output medium. (2) To record data in a storage device. Contrast with read.

write-enable ring Plastic ring that must be placed on a tape reel before information can be recorded on the tape. Compare write-protect ring.

write head Magnetic head designed to write data onto the media. Contrast with read head. Compare read/write head.

write-inhibit ring Plastic ring used to prevent data from being written over on magnetic tapes. Same as write-protect ring.

write-protect (1) To mechanically prevent a 3.5 in. diskette from being written to. To write-protect a disk, move the write-protect tab so you can see through the Write-Protect Notch, or so the tab is at the bottom position in the notch. (2) 5.25 in. diskettes may be protected from the possibility of undesired recording of data by application of a gummed tab over the write-protect notch. An uncovered write-protect notch will allow writing to the diskette.

write-protect ring Plastic ring that, when removed from the back of a tape reel, prevents writing on the tape. Also called write-inhibit ring. See file-protect.

WYSIWYG An abbreviation for What You See Is What You Get. Refers to word processors that generate screen images that are identical in position and type appearance to the final document, as opposed to those that show the formatting or special type requested only when the document is printed. The advantages are twofold: planning a visually pleasing final product is easier, and errors in the printed document can be found instantly when the document file is reloaded into the word processor.

WYKIWYL Acronym for What You Know (by using a colleague's hardware/software) Is What You Like (and often end up buying).

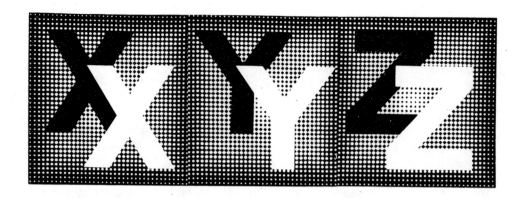

X axis On a coordinate plane, the horizontal axis. Contrast with Y axis and Z axis.

XENIX Variation on the UNIX operating system, created by Microsoft Corporation for use on microcomputers.

xerography A copying system that depends on an image formed from electrostatic charges. Powdered ink is attracted to the charged parts of a surface and then fused onto paper. The method is the basis of most type of office copiers and also of laser printers.

x-height The height of lowercase letters without ascenders and descenders.

Xmodem A method of transmitting data to another computer through modems. Transfers data in packages of 128K.

XOR Acronym for eXclusive OR.

XT The first IBM Personal Computer that included a hard disk; introduced in 1983. XT stands for eXtended Technology.

X-Windows A graphical user interface for Unix, developed at MIT, that many firms have made a standard. Essentially a graphics display server, X-Windows is the opposite of most client server systems where the workstation is the client and the larger machine is the server. X-Windows depends upon the power of the server to support the interface, while the back-end or client system provides data processing and manipulation.

X-Y chart Form that allows plotting of one data series against another, without a time axis. Often used to determine if there is a correlation between two series, with the direction, slope, and curvature of the line showing the relationship.

x-y matrix A group of rows and columns. Used as a reference framework for two-dimensional structures, such as 2-D graphics images, charts, tables, mathematical graphs and plots, digitizer tablets, digital plotters and display screens.

X-Y plotter Output device that draws points, lines, or curves on a sheet of paper based on X and Y coordinates from a computer. See plotter.

x-y-z coordinate system A three-dimensional system of Cartesian coordinates that includes a third (z) axis running perpendicular to the horizontal (x) and vertical (y) axis.

Y axis On a coordinate plane, the vertical axis. Contrast with X axis and Z axis.

YIQ A color model designed for the Macintosh II microcomputer. It stresses luminance as a component of color.

Ymodem A method of transmitting data to another computer through modems. Transfers data in packages of 1024K, which makes it faster than the Xmodem transmission protocol. See also Xmodem.

yoke That part of the electron beam deflection system used for addressing a video display.

zap (1) Command in many electronic spreadsheet programs that irretrievably erases all information on the spreadsheet. (2) To delete a file or clear a screen accidentally.

Zapf Chancery A typeface developed by Hermann Zapf, a German typeface designer and owned by the International Typeface Corporation (ITC). The typeface is included as a built-in font with many PostScript laser printers.

Zaph Dingbats A set of decorative symbols developed by Hermann Zapf, a German typeface designer. Zaph Dingbats are used for decorative purposes in a document. The typeface is included as a built-in font with many PostScript laser printers.

Z axis On a coordinate plane, the axis that represents depth. Contrast with X axis and Y axis.

Z-80 Zilog-80. An 8-bit microprocessor from Zilog Corporation that was widely used in many early microcomputer systems.

zero Numeral normally denoting lack of magnitude. In many computer, there are distinct representations for plus and minus zero.

zero flag Flip-flop that goes to logic 1 if the result of an instruction has the value of zero.

zeroize To initialize a program with zeros. To fill spaces in memory with zeros.

zero suppression Suppression (elimination) of nonsignificant zeros in a numeral, usually before or during a printing operation. For example, the numeral 00004763, with zero suppression, would be printed as 4763.

Commonly used in pagination so early pages of a report will be numbered 1, 2, ... rather than 01, 02, ... or 001, 002, ...

zone bits Special bits used along with numeric bits to represent alphanumeric characters in ASCII and EBCDIC codes.

zoom To view an enlarged (zoom in) or reduced (zoom out) portion of a page on screen.

zoom box A box symbol that appears in the right corner of some program windows. Clicking in the zoom box causes the window to expand to fill the entire screen or to contract to a smaller size. Clicking it again returns the window to its original size.

zooming Changing of a view on a graphics display by either moving in on successively smaller portions of the currently visible picture or moving out until the window encloses the entire scene. Capability that proportionally enlarges or reduces a figure displayed on a visual display screen. See image enhancement.

Zuse, Konrad German pioneer in the development of computing equipment. In 1941, he completed the Zuse Z-3, a machine with some remarkably advanced features. The speed of this machine was about the same as the Automatic Sequence Controlled Calculator (ASCC).

Ø The numeral zero. The slash is used to distinguish it from a capital O.

1.2 M   Refers to 1.2 megabytes of storage on a high-density (HD) 5.25 inch floppy disk.

1-2-3   See Lotus 1-2-3.

1.4 M   Refers to 1.4 megabytes of storage on a high-density (HD) 3.5 inch floppy disk.

2-D graphics   A graphic image in two dimensions—height and width.

3-D graphics   A graphic image in three dimensions—height, width, and depth. A screen picture which has the illusion of being solid. The simplest 3-D picture is called a wire-frame drawing. All the lines which make up the picture are shown, even if they would be hidden if the object really were solid.

3.5-inch disk   A floppy disk, called a microfloppy, encased in a plastic housing.

4GL   Short for fourth-generation language. A user-oriented language that makes it possible to develop programs with fewer commands than those needed for older procedural languages. An example of this type of language is Structured Query Language (SQL).

5.25-inch disk   A flexible piece of mylar encased in a protective covering that records data. Also called a floppy or minifloppy disk.

7-bit track   An older tape recording scheme that places data on seven separate parallel tracks on reels of 1/2 inch magnetic tape.

8-bit color   Refers to systems that allocate 8 bits of information for each pixel (spot) in the image. This provides 256 possible colors or levels of gray.

8-bit microcomputer   A microcomputer that uses a central processing unit with an 8-bit data bus and processes one byte (8-bits) of information at a time.

8-bit color Refers to systems that allocate 8 bits of information for each pixel (spot) in the image. This provides 256 possible colors or levels of gray.

8-bit microcomputer A microcomputer that uses a central processing unit with an 8-bit data bus and processes one byte (8-bits) of information at a time.

9-bit track A tape recording scheme that places data on nine separate parallel tracks on reels of 1/2 inch magnetic tape.

16-bit microcomputer A computer that works with information in groups of two bytes (16-bits) at a time.

24-bit color Refers to systems that allocate 24 bits of data to each pixel (spot) in the image. Usually, the bits are allocated as 8 bits each for the three additive primary colors (red, green, and blue). That arrangement provides over 16 million color possibilities.

30 percent rule A rule for determining the positioning of points and Beizer control handles. The distance from a Bezier control handle to its point should be approximately 30 percent of the length of its segment.

32-bit microcomputer A computer that works with information in groups of 32-bits at a time.

80-20 rule An empirical rule related to data usage in large databases that states that 80% of the accesses to a database will deal with only 20% of the data.

90-10 rule An empirical rule for very large databases that states that in order to find the data relevant to a query, nine times as much data as is needed to answer the query must be brought into main memory for processing.

101 key keyboard A standard keyboard for newer IBM personal computers.

286 See 80286.

287 See 80287.

360 System/360. The first IBM family of mainframe computers.

360 K Refers to 360 kilobytes of storage on a 5.25-inch floppy disk.

370 System/370. A large family of IBM mainframe computers.

386 See 80386.

386DX See 80386DX.

386SX   See 80386SX.

387   See 80387.

486   See 80486.

720K   Refers to 720 kilobytes of storage on a 3.5-inch floppy disk.

303x   A series of mainframes introduced by IBM Corporation in 1977: 3031, 3032 and 3033.

308x   A series of large-scale mainframes introduced by IBM Corporation in 1980: 3081 and 3084.

309x   A series of large-scale mainframes introduced by IBM Corporation in 1986.

3270   A terminal used with IBM mainframes.

3770   A terminal used with IBM mainframes.

4004   The first microprocessor manufactured by Intel Corporation.

43xx   A series of medium-scale mainframes introduced by IBM Corporation in 1979: 4300, 4321, 4331, 4341, 4361 and 4381.

5100   A desktop computer introduced by IBM Corporation in 1974.

6502   An 8-bit microprocessor manufactured by MOS Technology; made popular in many early home computers such as the Apple II, Commodore 64 and Atari 800 series computers.

6800   An 8-bit microprocessor manufactured by Motorola Corporation. It was the precursor of the popular 68000 family of microprocessors.

8048   A single-chip microcomputer.

8080   An 8-bit microprocessor manufactured by Intel Corporation. It was introduced in 1974 and influenced the design of several future microprocessors.

8086   A 16-bit microprocessor manufactured by Intel Corporation; introduced in 1978. This chip was the forerunner of Intel's 80x86 line of microprocessors. The 8088 used in many PC compatibles is a slightly less capable version of this chip. Produced under license by other manufacturers.

8087   A math coprocessor manufactured by Intel Corporation; designed to be used with 8086 and 8088 microprocessors.

8088   A 16-bit microprocessor developed by Intel Corporation. This microprocessor was used in the original IBM PC and IBM PC XT computers, as

433

well as millions of PC compatibles. It is now considered obsolete, although it continues to be used in some portable computers. Produced under license by other manufacturers.

8100   A minicomputer introduced by IBM Corporation in 1978.

8514   A high-resolution display system from the IBM Corporation. Introduced as the high-end offering for IBM PS/2 models to be used for desktop publishing, computer-aided design, and other uses requiring many colors and high resolution.

9370   A series of entry-level mainframes introduced by IBM Corporation in 1986.

21064   A Reduced Instruction Set Computing (RISC) chip from Digital Equipment Corporation. This 150 MHz microprocessor is said to perform up to 300 million instructions per second. Introduced in 1992.

65816   A 16-bit microprocessor manufactured by Western Digital Design; it can emulate the 6502 microprocessor.

680x0   Refers to Motorola Corporation family of microprocessors: 68000, 68010, 68020, 68030, and 68040.

68000   A 16-bit microprocessor manufactured by Motorola Corporation; introduced in 1979. The 68000 family of microprocessors is used in several popular microcomputers, including the Apple Macintosh, Commodore Amiga and Atari ST. Other more powerful versions, including the 68020, 68030 and 68040 have been successfully introduced in more recent versions of these and other computers, and have taken the 68000 line into the 32-bit world.

68020   A 32-bit microprocessor manufactured by Motorola Corporation; introduced in 1984.

68030   A 32-bit microprocessor manufactured by Motorola Corporation; introduced in 1987.

68040   A 32-bit microprocessor manufactured by Motorola Corporation; announced in 1987.

68881   A math coprocessor manufactured by Motorola Corporation; designed to be used with 68000 and 68020 microprocessors.

68882   A math coprocessor manufactured by Motorola Corporation; designed to be used with the 68030 microprocessor.

80x86   Refers to Intel Corporation's family of microprocessors: 80286, 80386, and 80486.

80x87   Refers to Intel Corporation's family of math coprocessors: 80287, 80387, and 80387SX.

80286 A 16-bit microprocessor manufactured by Intel Corporation; introduced in 1982 and used in the IBM Personal Computer AT computer and compatibles. Manufactured by several other companies now as well.

80287 A math coprocessor manufactured by Intel Corporation; designed for use with 80286 and 80386 microprocessors.

80386 A 32-bit microprocessor manufactured by Intel Corporation. There are two versions of this microprocessor: the 80386SX and the 80386DX.

80386DX A 32-bit microprocessor manufactured by Intel Corporation. It was introduced in 1985.

80386SX A microprocessor manufactured by Intel Corporation. It was introduced in 1988 as a low-cost alternative to the 80386DX. The 80386SX is basically an 80386DX microprocessor limited by a 16-bit data bus. The 80386SX is a slower speed version of the 80386 with the same flexibility.

80387 A math coprocessor manufactured by Intel Corporation; designed for use with the 80386DX microprocessor.

80387SX A math coprocessor manufactured by Intel Corporation; designed for use with the 80386SX microprocessor.

80486 A 32-bit super microprocessor manufactured by Intel Corporation. It was introduced in 1989 and has the built-in equivalent of an 80387 math coprocessor. The 80486 is approximately 50% to 30% faster than the 80386, depending on the application.

80860 A 64-bit RISC-based microprocessor from Intel Corporation.

82385 A cache controller chip that governs cache memory in fast personal computers using the Intel 80386 and 80486 microprocessors; developed by Intel Corporation.

88000 A family of 32-bit RISC microprocessors introduced by Motorola, Inc. in 1988.

COMPUTER PIONEERS

All over the world, there have always been people who were interested in finding out why and how things happen. There were also those who wanted to find out how to do things better and more easily. These people were our scientists, inventors and developers. This *Computer Dictionary* contains snapshot views of many important people, each of whom contributed an important building block to the foundations of computer science and information processing.

Perhaps one way to understand anything complex is to examine its historical development. And one way to look at the history is through the lives of men and women who made it. Shown in this section are illustrations of 74 famous computer pioneers. Each of these individuals are briefly discussed in the *Computer Dictionary*.

437

LIST OF COMPUTER PIONEERS

1. Aiken, Howard
2. Allen, Paul
3. Amdahl, Gene
4. Atanasoff, John
5. Babbage, Charles
6. Backus, John
7. Baldwin, Frank
8. Bardeen, John
9. Berry, Clifford
10. Bollee, Leon
11. Boole, George
12. Brattain, Walter
13. Bricklin, Daniel
14. Burroughs, William
15. Bush, Vannevar
16. Bushnell, Nolan
17. Corbato, Fernando J.
18. Cray, Seymour
19. da Vinci, Leonardo
20. Devol, George
21. Dijkstra, Edsger
22. Eckert, J. Presper
23. Engelberger, Joseph
24. Felt, Dorr
25. Forrester, Jay
26. Frankston, Bob
27. Gates, William
28. Hoff, Ted
29. Hollerith, Herman
30. Hopper, Grace
31. Jacquard, Joseph
32. Jobs, Steven
33. Kahn, Philippe
34. Kemeny, John
35. Kilby, Jack
36. Kildall, Gary
37. Kurtz, Thomas
38. Leibniz, Gottfried
39. Lovelace, Augusta Ada
40. Mauchly, John
41. McCarthy, John
42. Monroe, Jay
43. Moreland, Samuel
44. Napier, John
45. Norris, William
46. Noyce, Robert
47. Odhner, W. T.
48. Olsen, Kenneth H.
49. Opel, John
50. Oughtred, William
51. Papert, Seymour
52. Pascal, Blaise
53. Patterson, John
54. Ritchie, Dennis
55. Roach, John
56. Scheutz, George
57. Schiekhardt, Wilhelm
58. Sculley, John
59. Shannon, Claude
60. Shockley, William
61. Stanhope, Charles
62. Stibitz, George
63. Thomas, Charles
64. Thompson, Kenneth
65. Turing, Alan
66. von Neumann, John
67. Wang, An
68. Watson, Thomas, Jr.
69. Watson, Thomas, Sr.
70. Wiener, Norbert
71. Wilkes, Maurice
72. Wirth, Niklaus
73. Wozniak, Stephen
74. Zuse, Konrad

1. Howard Aiken

2. Paul Allen

3. Gene Amdahl

4. John Atanasoff

5. Charles Babbage

6. John Backus

7. Frank Baldwin

8. John Bardeen

440

9. Clifford Berry

10. Leon Bollee

11. George Boole

12. Walter Brattain

13. Daniel Bricklin

14. William Burroughs

15. Vannevar Bush

16. Nolan Bushnell

442

17. Fernando J. Corbato

18. Seymour Cray

19. Leonardo da Vinci

20. George Devol

443

21. Edsger Dijkstra

22. J. Presper Eckert

23. Joseph Engelberger

24. Dorr Felt

25. Jay Forrester

26. Bob Frankston

27. William Gates

28. Ted Hoff

29. Herman Hollerith

30. Grace Hopper

31. Joseph Jacquard

32. Steven Jobs

33. Philippe Kahn

34. John Kemeny

35.Jack Kilby

36. Gary Kidall

37. Thomas Kurtz

38. Gottfried Leibniz

39. Augusta Ada Lovelace

40. John Mauchley

41. John McCarthy

42. Jay Monroe

43. Samuel Moreland

44. John Napier

45. William Norris

46. Robert Noyce

47. W. T. Odhner

48. Kenneth H. Olsen

49. John Opel

50. William Oughtred

51. Seymour Papert

52. Blaise Pascal

53. John Patterson

54. Dennis Ritchie

55. John Roach

56. George Scheutz

57. Wilhelm Schiekhardt

58. John Sculley

59. Claude Shannon

60. William Shockley

61. Charles Stanhope

62. George Stibitz

63. Charles Thomas

64. Kenneth Thompson

65. Alan Turing

66. John von Neuman

67. An Wang

68. Thomas Watson, Jr.

69. Thomas Watson, Sr.

70. Norbert Wiener

71. Maurice Wilkes

72. Niklaus Wirth

73. Stephen Wozniak

74. Konrad Zuse

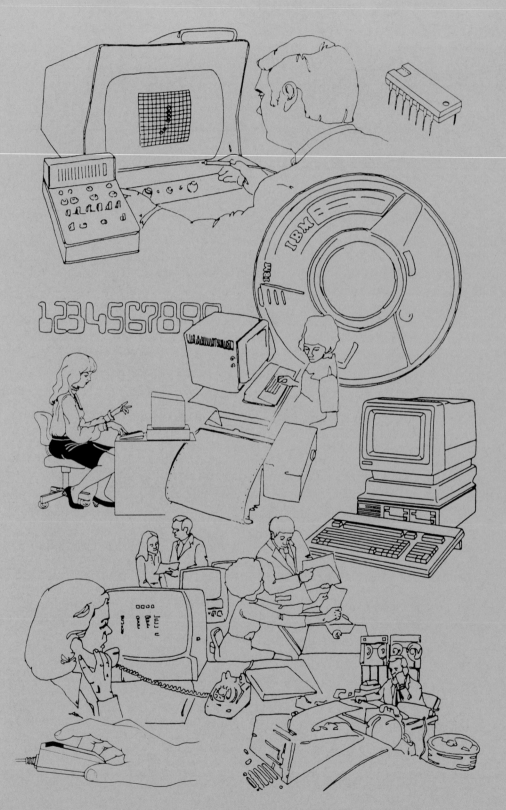

458

ABOUT
THE
AUTHOR

Donald D. Spencer is an internationally known computer science educator and author. He received his Ph.D. degree in computer science and has worked in the computer field since 1959. Dr. Spencer is the author of over 180 computer science books published by 20 different textbook publishers. Several of his books have been translated into German, Hungarian, French, Italian, Spanish, Japanese and other languages. He worked on some 25 different mainframe computers and 20 different microcomputer systems, and has been involved in a number of pioneering projects.

Dr. Spencer has taught computer science in college and industry, and has held computer related positions in several industrial organizations. He has spoken at many conferences and seminars on educational computing. Dr. Spencer has made frequent lectures about computers to students and teachers in elementary schools, secondary schools and colleges. He is a past chairman of the National ACM Committee on Secondary School Programs. Dr. Spencer is currently a member of several school and college committees on computer science education.

He is a member of several educational and professional societies including the Association for Computing Machinery (ACM), the National Council of Teachers of Mathematics (NCTM), the Institute for Electrical and Electronics Engineers (IEEE), the International Society of Technology in Education (ISTE), the Mathematical Association of America (MAA), and the National Service Robot Association (NSRA). Several million copies of his books have been used by students, teachers, professionals, and general audience readers all over the world.